GOOD HOUSEKEEPING'S
RECIPES FOR 1982

HEARST BOOKS
New York

Good Housekeeping Staff

Editor in Chief
John Mack Carter

Food Director
Mildred Ying

Associate Director
Susan Deborah Goldsmith

Associates
Ellen H. Connelly, Joyce A. Kenneally

Assistants
Diane Simone Dixon, Normajean Sarle,
Victoria Scocozza

How-to line illustrations:
Elliot Kreloff

Spot engravings from *Food and Drink,*
Second Revised Edition, copyright 1979,
1980 by Dover Publications, Inc., New
York City

Library of Congress Cataloging in Publication Data

Main entry under title:

Good housekeeping's recipes for 1982.

Includes index.
1. Cookery.
TX715.G6433   1982   641.5   82-15676
ISBN 0-87851-305-1

10   9   8   7   6   5   4   3   2   1

PRINTED IN THE UNITED STATES OF AMERICA

Contents

CONTENTS

Condiments and Sauces — 169
Pickles and Relishes/169
Sauces and Salad Dressings/176
Jelly, Conserves, and Preserves/178
Spreads/181

Cakes — 185

Cookies — 215

Desserts, Pies and Tarts, and Candies — 228
Dessert Sauces and Toppings/228
Frozen Desserts/229
Fruit Desserts/234
Creams, Mousses, and Soufflés/239
Custards and Puddings/243
Pastries/246
Pies and Tarts/249
Candies/263

Beverages — 269

Appendix — 271
How to Follow Our Recipes/271
Measuring Ingredients/271
Equivalent Amounts/272
1982 Recipes, Month by Month/274

Index — 277

iv

Foreword

Creating new recipes for America's cooks is a way of life at *Good Housekeeping*. Every year we develop and test more than 500 recipes in the Good Housekeeping Institute's kitchens for publication in our magazine. Each of these recipes is tried again and again by the home economists on our staff to make certain that it is clear and concise, and that it omits no steps or essential information, and—most important—that any cook who follows it will produce an appetizing, nutritious, and delicious dish. All the ingredients are listed in the order in which they are used, and the time required to complete the recipe and the number of servings produced are given in the first line to save you time and help you plan each meal. In addition, the steps are numbered for easy reference, and you'll find that you never have to turn a page to complete a recipe.

This book is the second volume in an annual series designed to answer the continuing requests that we receive from readers of *Good Housekeeping* magazine for a more permanent record of the recipes that we create each year. You will find here all the prized favorites that first appeared in the magazine in 1982 in each month's specially featured recipe section, as well as the recipes that appeared in "Favorites from Our Dining room," "30-Minute Entrées and Desserts," and "Susan, Our Beginning Cook." For greater convenience in making recipe selections, we have rearranged the recipes into food categories—from appetizers and salads through main dishes and desserts. A new feature for this volume is a month-by-month listing of the year's recipes, which, combined with a detailed, cross-referenced index, will make it easier than ever to track down an already tried favorite, or to choose from among several possibilities using similar ingredients or from a particular category.

I am especially proud that this complete collection of 1982 recipes continues more strongly than ever the *Good Housekeeping* tradition that began in 1885 of developing original recipes. I also want to give special thanks to Debby Goldsmith and Ellen Connelly for their invaluable assistance on this project.

—Mildred Ying
Director, Food Department, Good Housekeeping *Magazine*

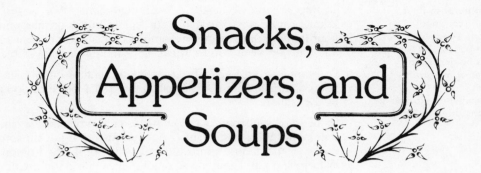

Snacks, Appetizers, and Soups

SNACKS

Cheddar Straws

TIME: start early in day or up to 1 week ahead—**YIELD:** 6 dozen

2 cups all-purpose flour
½ teaspoon salt
ground red pepper
1 cup butter or margarine
8 ounces Cheddar cheese,
   shredded
½ cup iced water

1. In large bowl, with fork, combine flour, salt, and ¼ teaspoon ground red pepper. With pastry blender or 2 knives used scissor-fashion, cut in butter or margarine until mixture resembles coarse crumbs.

2. With fork, stir in cheese and water just until mixture forms a soft dough and leaves side of bowl. On lightly floured surface, with floured hands, pat dough into 6″ by 6″ square. Wrap dough with plastic wrap and chill in freezer 30 minutes for easier handling.

3. On lightly floured surface, roll chilled dough into 18″ by 8″ rectangle. Starting from one 8-inch end, fold one-third of dough over middle one-third; fold opposite one-third over both to make 8″ by 6″ rectangle.

4. Repeat rolling and folding as in step 3. Wrap in plastic wrap; freeze 30 minutes again.

5. Preheat oven to 375°F. Remove dough from freezer; roll and fold again as in step 3. Then, roll dough into 18″ by 12″ rectangle. Sprinkle dough rectangle lightly with ground red pepper; cut lengthwise in half. Cut each half crosswise into thirty-six 6″ by ½″ strips.

6. Place strips, ½ inch apart, on ungreased large cookie sheets, twisting each strip twice and pressing ends to cookie sheet. (This prevents strips from uncurling during baking.)

7. Bake cheese straws 15 minutes or until golden. Remove cheese straws from cookie sheets; cool completely on wire racks. Store in tightly covered container to use up within 1 week.

Cocktail Onion Crisps

TIME: about 1 hour or start up to 1 week ahead—YIELD: 128 pieces

1¾ cups all-purpose flour
½ cup yellow cornmeal
2 tablespoons sugar
¾ teaspoon salt
½ teaspoon baking soda
½ cup butter or margarine
½ cup water
2 tablespoons white vinegar
3 tablespoons dried onion flakes

1. Into large bowl, measure first 5 ingredients. With pastry blender or 2 knives used scissor-fashion, cut ¼ cup butter or margarine into flour mixture until mixture resembles coarse crumbs. Stir in water and vinegar. With hands, knead flour mixture until well blended.

2. Preheat oven to 375°F. Divide dough into 4 equal pieces. On well floured surface with floured rolling pin, roll 1 piece of dough into 12" by 12" square.

3. In small saucepan over low heat, melt remaining ¼ cup butter or margarine. With pastry brush, lightly brush dough with some melted butter or margarine; sprinkle evenly with some dried onion flakes. With rolling pin, lightly press onion flakes into dough. Cut dough into eight 1½-inch-wide strips; then cut crosswise into 3-inch lengths to make 32 rectangles.

4. With spatula, place rectangles, ½ inch apart, on large ungreased cookie sheet. Bake 8 minutes or until lightly browned; remove to wire racks to cool. Repeat with remaining dough.

5. Cool onion crisps completely on wire rack. Store in tightly covered container to use up within 1 week.

Middle Eastern Pork-and-Eggplant Dip

TIME: about 1 hour—SERVINGS: 12

1 medium eggplant (about 1¼ pounds)
½ pound ground pork
3 tablespoons salad oil
¼ cup water
2 tablespoons soy sauce
1½ teaspoons sugar
½ teaspoon salt
½ teaspoon ground ginger
⅛ teaspoon hot pepper sauce
2 6-inch pitas*
1 tablespoon minced red pepper (optional)
1 tablespoon chopped parsley (optional)

*A Pita is a Middle Eastern pocket bread available in most supermarkets.

1. Cut eggplant lengthwise in half. With spoon, scoop out eggplant pulp from one eggplant half, leaving a ¼-inch-thick shell. Cover shell, set aside. Chop remaining eggplant half and scooped out eggplant pulp.

2. In 3-quart saucepan over high heat, cook ground pork until all pan juices evaporate and meat is well browned, stirring frequently. Remove pork to small bowl.

3. In same saucepan over medium heat, in 2 tablespoons hot salad oil, cook chopped eggplant until lightly browned and tender, stirring occasionally. Add pork, water, and next 5 ingredients; over high heat, heat to boiling. Reduce heat to low. Cover and simmer 30 minutes or until eggplant is very tender, stirring occasionally. With back of spoon, press eggplant mixture to mash. Skim off fat from mixture.

4. Meanwhile, preheat broiler if manufacturer directs. Cut each pita into 8 triangles; separate each triangle into 2 pieces; place on cookie sheet. Broil 2 to 3 minutes until pita is lightly golden.

5. To serve, spoon eggplant mixture into reserved eggplant shell; garnish with red pepper and parsley, if desired. Serve toasted pita triangles with eggplant mixture. Makes about 2 cups.

Crisp Chinese Fried Walnuts

TIME: about 1½ hours or start up to 2 weeks ahead—YIELD: 4 cups

6 cups water
4 cups California walnuts
½ cup sugar
salad oil
salt

1. In 4-quart saucepan over high heat, heat water to boiling; add walnuts and heat to boiling; cook 1 minute. Rinse walnuts under running hot water; drain. Wash saucepan and dry well.

2. In large bowl with rubber spatula, gently stir warm walnuts with sugar until sugar is dissolved. (If necessary, let mixture stand 5 minutes to dissolve sugar.)

3. Meanwhile, in same saucepan over medium heat, heat about 1 inch salad oil to 350°F. on deep-fat thermometer or heat oil according to manufacturer's directions in deep-fat fryer set at 350°F. With slotted spoon, add about half of walnuts to oil; fry 5 minutes or until golden, stirring often.

4. With slotted spoon, place walnuts in coarse sieve over bowl to drain; sprinkle very lightly with salt; toss lightly to keep walnuts from sticking together. Transfer to paper towels to cool. Fry remaining walnuts. Store walnuts in tightly covered container to use up within 2 weeks.

Curried Almonds

TIME: about 1½ hours or start up to 1 week ahead—YIELD: 2 cups

2 4½-ounce cans blanched whole almonds (2cups)
1½ tablespoons butter or margarine
1 tablespoon curry powder
1½ teaspoons salt

Preheat oven to 375°F. In 15½″ by 10½″ jelly-roll pan, place all ingredients. Toast almond mixture in oven 15 minutes, stirring occasionally. Cool almonds completely in pan on wire rack. Store almonds in tightly covered container to use up within one week.

Crudités with Creamy Tarragon Dip

TIME: start early in day—SERVINGS: 8 to 10

6 large carrots
2 medium zucchini
1 small head cauliflower
¼ pound Chinese pea pods or sugar snap peas
1 small head romaine lettuce
1 small head red leaf lettuce
1 8-ounce package cream cheese, softened
½ cup mayonnaise
¼ cup milk
4 teaspoons tarragon vinegar
1 teaspoon sugar
¾ teaspoon tarragon
¾ teaspoon salt
⅛ teaspoon pepper

1. Prepare vegetables: Cut carrots lengthwise into ¼-inch-thick sticks. Cut zucchini crosswise into ¼-inch-thick slices. Cut cauliflower into flowerets. Remove stem ends and strings along both sides of Chinese pea pods or sugar snap peas (do not shell); rinse with cold water. Rinse romaine and red leaf lettuce leaves; pat dry with paper towels. Wrap vegetables separately in plastic wrap; refrigerate.

2. Prepare dip: In blender at low speed or in food processor with knife blade attached, blend cream cheese and remaining ingredients until smooth. Pour dip into small bowl; cover and refrigerate.

3. About 10 minutes before serving, line a large basket with a deep dish or foil. Arrange all vegetables and bowl of dip in basket.

NOTE: If dip becomes thick upon refrigeration, stir in a little milk until of dipping consistency.

Peppery Cheese Crackers

TIME: about 1½ hours or start up to 3 days ahead—
YIELD: about 3 dozen

1½ cups all-purpose flour
¾ cup butter or margarine,
  softened
1 teaspoon cracked pepper
¼ teaspoon salt
¾ pound Cheddar cheese,
  shredded (3 cups)
1 egg, slightly beaten

1. Preheat oven to 425°F. In large bowl, with hand, knead flour, butter or margarine, pepper, salt, and 2½ cups chredded Cheddar cheese until mixed.

2. Shape dough into 1-inch balls. Place balls, about 2 inches apart, on ungreased cookie sheets; flatten into ¼-inch-thick rounds. With pastry brush, lightly brush tops of dough rounds with beaten egg; sprinkle with remaining cheese. Bake 10 to 12 minutes until lightly browned. Remove crackers to wire racks; cool. Serve crackers as cocktail snack, with consommé or salad.

APPETIZERS

Pickled Shrimp Appetizer

TIME: start day ahead—SERVINGS: 24

3 pounds large shrimp
6 cups water
¼ cup cooking or dry sherry
¼ teaspoon peppercorns
1 bay leaf
salt
1 cup salad oil
⅔ cup lemon juice
½ cup white vinegar
3 tablespoons mixed pickling
  spice, tied in cheesecloth bag
2 teaspoons sugar
fresh dill

1. Shell and devein shrimp, leaving on tails and last shell segment.

2. In 4-quart saucepan over high heat, heat water, sherry, peppercorns, bay leaf, and 2 teaspoons salt to boiling. Add shrimp; heat to boiling. Shrimp should be done when water returns to boiling or cook 1 minute longer until they are tender and turn pink. Drain.

3. In large bowl, stir salad oil, lemon juice, vinegar, pickling spice, sugar, 2 sprigs dill, and 4 teaspoons salt. Add shrimp and toss well to coat with marinade. Cover and marinate shrimp in the refrigerator overnight, tossing occasionally.

4. To serve, arrange shrimp in chilled bowl; discard marinade. To keep shrimp well chilled, place bowl with shrimp in large bowl of crushed ice. Garnish with dill sprigs, if desired.

First-Course Spinach Pie

TIME: about 1 hour—SERVINGS: 12

1 cup milk
3 tablespoons butter or
  margarine
½ teaspoon salt
6 eggs
1 medium green onion, cut into
  1-inch pieces
1 10-ounce package frozen
  chopped spinach, thawed and
  squeezed dry
¼ pound Muenster cheese,
  shredded (1 cup)
thinly sliced radishes for garnish

1. Preheat oven to 375°F. Grease 12-inch quiche dish or 9″ by 9″ baking pan. In blender at high speed, blend milk, butter or margarine, salt, eggs, and green onion until smooth; pour into quiche dish. Stir spinach into egg mixture until evenly distributed.

2. Bake 20 minutes or until pie is set. Remove from oven; sprinkle with cheese. Bake 5 minutes longer or until cheese is melted. Cut pie into 12 wedges. Garnish each serving with a few radish slices.

FOR SIX MAIN-DISH SERVINGS: Prepare spinach pie as above, but serve with sliced cooked ham, Canadian bacon, sausage, or prosciutto.

Cocktail Meatballs

TIME: about 45 minutes—SERVINGS: about 10

1 pound ground beef
1 egg
2 teaspoons grated onion
1 teaspoon salt
¼ teaspoon pepper
dried bread crumbs
about 4 sweet gherkin pickles,
    cut into ¼-inch pieces
⅓ cup minced parsley
¼ cup minced celery leaves
cocktail picks

1. In medium bowl, mix ground beef, egg, onion, salt, pepper, and ½ cup bread crumbs. Divide meat mixture into 40 portions; shape each portion into a ball with a piece of gherkin pickle in center.

2. Preheat broiler if manufacturer directs. On sheet of waxed paper, mix parsley, celery leaves, and 2 tablespoons bread crumbs. Roll meatballs in parsley mixture to coat evenly; place on rack in broiling pan. Broil meatballs 8 to 10 minutes until browned on all sides, turning meatballs occasionally. Serve with cocktail picks.

Hot Mushroom Turnovers

TIME: about 2 hours—YIELD: about 3½ dozen

1 8-ounce package cream
    cheese, softened
all-purpose flour
butter or margarine, softened
½ pound mushrooms, minced
1 large onion, minced
¼ cup sour cream
1 teaspoon salt
¼ teaspoon thyme leaves
1 egg, beaten

1. In large bowl with mixer at medium speed, beat cream cheese, 1½ cups flour, and ½ cup butter or margarine until smooth; shape into ball; wrap; refrigerate 1 hour.

2. Meanwhile, in 10-inch skillet over meduim heat, in 3 tablespoons hot butter or margarine, cook mushrooms and onion until tender, stirring occasionally. Stir in sour cream, salt, thyme leaves, and 2 tablespoons flour; set aside.

3. On floured surface with floured rolling pin, roll half of dough ⅛ inch thick. With floured 2¾-inch round cookie cutter, cut out as many circles as possible. Repeat.

4. Preheat oven to 450°F. Onto half of each dough circle, place a teaspoon of mushroom mixture. Brush edges of dough circles with some egg; fold dough over filling. With fork, firmly press edges together to seal; prick tops. Place turnovers on ungreased large cookie sheet; brush turnovers with remaining egg. Bake 12 to 14 minutes until golden.

Pork Pâté

TIME: about 3 hours or start day ahead—YIELD: about 2 cups

1 pound ground pork
½ pound medium mushrooms
¼ cup chopped green onions
¾ teaspoon salt
⅛ teaspoon dill weed
1 small garlic clove, minced
½ cup dry vermouth
¼ teaspoon hot pepper sauce
¼ cup mayonnaise
2 tablespoons butter or
    margarine, cut up
1 medium cucumber, sliced
assorted crackers

1. In 12-inch skillet over medium-high heat, cook ground pork and next 5 ingredients until meat is lightly browned. Pour off drippings from skillet. Stir in dry vermouth and hot pepper sauce. Reduce heat to low; cover and simmer 10 minutes to blend flavors, stirring occasionally.

2. In food processor with knife blade attached or in blender at medium speed, blend pork mixture, mayonnaise, and butter or margarine until smooth, stopping processor or blender occasionally and scraping side with rubber spatula. Spoon pâté into small bowl or 2-cup crock. Cover and refrigerate 2 hours or until mixture is firm.

3. For easier spreading, let pâté stand at room temperature about 30 minutes before serving. Serve pâté with cucumber slices and assorted crackers.

Pâté Maison

TIME: start 1 to 3 days ahead—SERVINGS: 10

1 8-ounce package sliced bacon
2 tablespoons butter or
   margarine
1 small onion, minced
1 small garlic clove, minced
1 whole medium chicken breast
½ pound cooked ham
1 pound ground pork
1 pound ground veal
3 tablespoons brandy
4 teaspoons green peppercorns
2 teaspoons salt
½ teaspoon thyme leaves
½ teaspoon coarsely ground
   black pepper
⅛ teaspoon ground allspice
2 eggs

1. Line bottom and sides of 9″ by 5″ loaf pan with bacon slices, allowing slices to hang slightly over edges of pan. Set aside.

2. In 1-quart saucepan over medium heat, in hot butter or margarine, cook onion and garlic until tender, stirring occasionally. Meanwhile, remove skin and bones from chicken breast; cut meat into ½-inch-wide strips. Cut ham into ½-inch-wide strips.

3. In large bowl with wooden spoon, beat onion mixture, ground pork, and remaining ingredients except chicken and ham strips until well mixed and light.

4. Spread one third of ground-meat mixture in bottom of bacon-lined pan; top with ham strips, another one third of meat mixture, chicken strips, then remaining meat mixture. Press down firmly to pack mixture into loaf pan. Fold overhanging pieces of bacon over top.

5. Cover pan with foil and bake in 350°F. oven 1½ hours or until pâté shrinks from sides of pan and juices run clear. (To check color of escaping juices, press pâté firmly with back of spoon.)

6. Cool pâté slightly on wire rack until easy to handle. Drain off excess fat. Cover pâté in pan with foil or plastic wrap; place several soup cans on top to weigh down pâté; refrigerate overnight.

7. To serve, remove cans and foil from pâté. Unmold pâté onto cutting board or plate. (If necessary, dip pâté in pan in hot water to loosen bottom.) Scrape off any coagulated cooking juices and excess fat. Cut pâté into slices.

Holiday Chicken-Liver Pâté

TIME: about 2½ hours or start up to 2 days ahead—YIELD: 3 cups

butter or margarine
¾ pound chicken livers
½ pound mushrooms
¼ cup minced green onions
1 garlic clove, minced
¾ teaspoon salt
cooking or dry sherry
1 tablespoon green peppercorns,
   drained
parsley sprigs for garnish
1 2-ounce jar pimentos, drained,
   for garnish
¼ cup water
1 envelope unflavored gelatin

1. In 10-inch skillet over medium-high heat, in 4 tablespoons hot butter or margarine, cook chicken livers, mushrooms, green onions, garlic, and salt about 5 minutes or until chicken livers are lightly browned but still pink inside, stirring frequently. Stir in ⅓ cup sherry; cover and simmer 5 minutes to blend flavors.

2. In blender at medium speed or in food processor with knife blade attached, blend chicken-liver mixture and 6 tablespoons butter or margarine until smooth, stopping blender occasionally and scraping sides with rubber spatula. (Mixture will be thin.) Stir in green peppercorns. Pour mixture into six ½-cup crocks or 3-cup crock.

3. To decorate top of pâté: Arrange parsley sprigs on top of pâté to resemble a wreath. Cut some pimento into thin strips; arrange pimento strips on parsley wreath to resemble a bow. (Refrigerate remaining pimento to use in salad another day.)

4. In small saucepan, measure water and 2 tablespoons sherry; evenly sprinkle gelatin over sherry mixture. Cook over medium heat until gelatin is completely dissolved, stirring occasionally. Gently spoon gelatin mixture over pâté, being careful not to disturb garnish. Cover and refrigerate pâté 2 hours or until set. Serve pâté as a spread on crackers, party rye bread, sliced zucchini, or toast.

Country Pâté

TIME: start early in day or up to 1 week ahead—SERVINGS: 16

2 tablespoons salad oil
¼ pound mushrooms, chopped
1 medium onion, minced
1 small garlic clove, minced
¼ cup cooking or dry sherry
1 teaspoon salt
½ teaspoon cracked pepper
½ teaspoon thyme leaves
⅛ teaspoon ground nutmeg
½ pound ground pork
½ pound ground chicken (about 1 whole medium chicken breast)
¼ pound ground pork fat
¼ cup shelled pistachios
1 egg
⅓ cup chopped parsley
1 8-ounce package sliced bacon

1. In 3-quart saucepan over medium heat, in hot salad oil, cook mushrooms, onion, and garlic until tender, about 5 minutes, stirring occasionally. Add sherry, salt, pepper, thyme, and nutmeg; heat to boiling. Reduce heat to low; simmer 5 minutes, stirring occasionally. Remove saucepan from heat.

2. Stir in pork, chicken, pork fat, pistachios, egg, and 2 tablespoons parsley. Wrap remaining parsley with plastic wrap; refrigerate for garnish. With wooden spoon, beat until well mixed.

3. Line bottom and sides of 8½″ by 4½″ loaf pan with bacon, letting bacon slices hang over sides of pan. Reserve some bacon slices for top of loaf.

4. Spoon meat mixture evenly into pan, packing firmly to press out air pockets. Fold bacon over meat mixture; top with remaining bacon. Bake in 350°F. oven 1¼ hours. Remove from oven; cover and refrigerate overnight.

5. Just before serving, dip pan in 2 inches hot water for 15 seconds; lift from water and carefully run metal spatula between pâté and sides of pan; invert onto platter or cutting board. Carefully scrape excess fat from pâté. Garnish sides with reserved parsley. Makes about 2 pounds pâté.

FIRST-COURSE SOUPS

New England Clam Chowder

TIME: about 1 hour—SERVINGS: 9

12 large hard-shell (chowder) clams or two 10-ounce cans whole baby clams
water
¼ pound salt pork, diced
1 medium onion, diced
1 tablespoon all-purpose flour
½ teaspoon salt
⅛ teaspoon pepper
3 medium potatoes (1 pound), peeled and diced
4 cups half-and-half
1 tablespoon butter or margarine
paprika

1. With stiff brush, scrub clams under running cold water until free of sand. In 4-quart saucepan over high heat, heat 1 cup water to boiling. Add clams; heat to boiling. Reduce heat to low; cover and simmer just until clams open, about 5 minutes.

2. Remove clams; reserve clam broth. Cool clams until easy to handle; discard shells; coarsely chop clams; set aside.

3. Clam broth can be sandy at times. Let broth stand awhile until sand settles at the bottom of saucepan. Carefully pour clear broth into measuring cup; add water to make 2 cups if necessary.

4. If using canned clams, drain clams, reserving clam liquid; add water to make 2 cups if necessary.

5. In same saucepan over medium heat, cook salt pork until lightly browned. Add onion; cook until tender, stirring occasionally. Stir in flour, salt, and pepper until blended; cook 1 minute. Gradually stir in clam liquid until smooth; add potatoes; heat to boiling. Reduce heat to low; cover and simmer 15 minutes or until potatoes are tender. Stir in half-and-half and clams; heat through.

6. Stir in butter or margarine; sprinkle chowder with paprika. Makes 9 cups.

Corn Chowder

TIME: about 45 minutes—SERVINGS: 9

6 tablespoons butter or
    margarine
2 small potatoes (½ pound),
    peeled and diced
2 celery stalks, minced
1 small green pepper, minced
1 small onion, minced
1½ teaspoons salt
2 tablespoons all-purpose flour
2 tablespoons paprika
1½ cups water
2 chicken-flavor bouillon cubes
    or envelopes
1 16- to 20-ounce package
    frozen whole-kernel corn
2 pints half-and-half

1. In 4-quart saucepan over medium heat, in hot butter or margarine, cook potatoes, celery, green pepper, onion, and salt until vegetables are tender, about 10 minutes, stirring frequently. Stir in flour and paprika until blended; cook 1 minute.

2. Stir in water and bouillon; over medium heat, cook, stirring constantly, until mixture is smooth and thickened, about 5 minutes.

3. Stir in corn kernels and half-and-half. Cook, stirring frequently, until corn is tender and mixture is heated through, about 10 minutes. Makes about 9 cups.

Vegetable Borscht

TIME: about 1½ hours or start day ahead—SERVINGS: 10

¼ cup salad oil
3 medium carrots, shredded
1 large potato, diced
1 medium onion, diced
½ small head cabbage,
    shredded
8 cups water
1 16-ounce can tomatoes
1 pound beets, shredded
3 beef-flavor bouillon cubes or
    envelopes
2 teaspoons sugar
1½ teaspoons salt
¼ teaspoon pepper
sour cream for garnish
    (optional)

1. In 5-quart Dutch oven or saucepot over medium heat, in hot salad oil, cook carrots, potato, onion, and cabbage until lightly browned, stirring occasionally. Add water, tomatoes with their liquid, beets, bouillon, sugar, salt, and pepper; over high heat, heat to boiling. Reduce heat to low; cover and simmer 35 to 40 minutes until vegetables are very tender, stirring occasionally.

2. Serve soup hot or cover and refrigerate to serve chilled later. Garnish each serving with some sour cream, if desired. Makes about 12 cups.

Chilled Watercress Soup

TIME: about 2¼ hours or start early in day—SERVINGS: 10

3 tablespoons butter or
    margarine
1 small onion, thinly sliced
1 medium celery stalk, thinly
    sliced
2 cups water
1 teaspoon salt
⅛ teaspoon white pepper
1 medium potato, thinly sliced
1 chicken-flavor bouillon cube or
    envelope
1 large bunch watercress
2 cups half-and-half

1. In 3-quart saucepan over medium heat, in hot butter or margarine, cook onion and celery until tender, stirring occasionally. Add water, salt, pepper, potato, and bouillon; over high heat, heat to boiling. Reduce heat to low; cover and simmer 10 minutes.

2. Meanwhile, set aside 10 small watercress sprigs for garnish. Discard stems from remaining watercress; add watercress leaves to saucepan; continue cooking 5 minutes longer or until potato is very tender.

3. In blender at medium speed, blend watercress mixture until smooth. Pour mixture into large bowl; stir in half-and-half. Cover and refrigerate at least 1½ hours or until chilled. Garnish each serving with a watercress sprig. Makes about 5 cups.

Minestrone

TIME: about 1½ hours—SERVINGS: 10

2 tablespoons olive or salad oil
1 large carrot, diced
1 large celery stalk, thinly sliced
1 medium onion, diced
1 small garlic clove, cut in half
¼ pound green beans, cut into 1-inch pieces
6 cups water
1½ teaspoons salt
½ teaspoon oregano leaves
¼ small head cabbage, shredded (3 cups)
1 medium zucchini, diced
1 8-ounce can tomatoes
2 beef-flavor bouillon cubes or envelopes
¼ cup tubettini macaroni
½ 10-ounce bag spinach, coarsely shredded
1 10½- to 16-ounce can white kidney beans (cannellini), drained
1 8- to 10½-ounce can red kidney beans, drained
grated Parmesan or Romano cheese (optional)

1. In 4-quart saucepan over medium-high heat, in hot olive oil, cook carrot, celery, onion, garlic, and green beans until vegetables are lightly browned, about 15 minutes, stirring occasionally. Discard garlic.

2. Add water, salt, oregano, cabbage, zucchini, tomatoes with their liquid, and bouillon; over high heat, heat to boiling, stirring to break up tomatoes. Reduce heat to low; cover and simmer 25 minutes or until vegetables are tender.

3. Stir in tubettini, spinach, and beans; cook 10 minutes longer or until tubettini is very tender and soup is slightly thickened. Serve with grated cheese. Makes about 12 cups.

MAIN-DISH SOUPS

Zuppa di Pesce (Fish Soup)

TIME: about 45 minutes—SERVINGS: 6

1 16-ounce package frozen cod or flounder fillets
2 tablespoons olive or salad oil
1 medium onion, diced
1 small garlic clove, minced
1 28-ounce can tomatoes
2 cups water
⅓ cup cooking or dry white wine
2 tablespoons minced parsley
¾ teaspoon salt
½ teaspoon basil
¼ teaspoon pepper
1 dozen large mussels (about 1 pound)
12 littleneck clams

1. Let frozen fish fillets stand at room temperature about 15 minutes to thaw slightly.

2. Meanwhile, in 5-quart Dutch oven over medium heat, in hot olive oil, cook onion and garlic until tender, stirring occasionally. Add tomatoes with their liquid, water, wine, parsley, salt, basil, and pepper; heat to boiling. Reduce heat to low; cover and simmer 15 minutes to blend flavors.

3. Remove beards from mussels. With stiff brush, scrub mussels and clams under running cold water to remove any sand. With sharp knife, cut frozen fish into bite-sized chunks.

4. Add mussels, clams, and fish chunks to tomato mixture; over high heat, heat to boiling. Reduce heat to low; cover and simmer 10 minutes or until mussels and clams open and fish flakes easily when tested with a fork, stirring occasionally.

5. Serve in soup bowls, with forks and spoons.

Salmon Bisque

TIME: about 30 minutes—SERVINGS: 4

4 tablespoons butter or
  margarine
1 medium onion, diced
1 medium celery stalk, diced
2 tablespoons all-purpose flour
2 teaspoons paprika
1 cup water
1 chicken-flavor bouillon cube or
  envelope
¾ teaspoon salt
⅛ teaspoon dill weed
1 7¾-ounce can salmon, drained
  and flaked
1 pint half-and-half
1 tablespoon cooking or dry
  sherry
celery leaves for garnish

1. In 2 quart saucepan over medium heat, in hot butter or margarine, cook onion and celery until vegetables are tender, stirring occasionally. Stir in flour and paprika until blended; cook 1 minute. Stir in water, bouillon, salt, and dill; over medium heat, cook, stirring constantly, until mixture is thickened and smooth. Remove saucepan from heat; stir in salmon.

2. In blender at medium speed, blend salmon mixture until very smooth. Return blended salmon mixture to same saucepan; stir in half-and-half and sherry. Over medium heat, heat bisque until hot, stirring frequently. Garnish bisque with celery leaves. Makes about 4 cups.

Chunky Fish Soup au Gratin

TIME: about 40 minutes—SERVINGS: 4

1 16-ounce package frozen
  flounder, sole, or ocean perch
  fillets
2 medium celery stalks
1 medium zucchini
1 medium potato
1 small onion
4 tablespoons butter or
  margarine
3 cups water
¼ cup dry white wine
2 teaspoons salt
½ teaspoon Worcestershire
1 chicken-flavor bouillon cube or
  envelope
1 10-ounce package frozen
  mixed vegetables
1 small loaf Italian bread
1 cup shredded Monterey Jack
  cheese (4 ounces)

1. Remove frozen fish fillets from freezer; let stand at room temperature 15 minutes to thaw slightly.

2. Meanwhile, slice celery. Dice zucchini, potato, and onion.

3. In 4-quart saucepan over medium heat, in hot butter or margarine, cook celery, zucchini, potato, and onion until lightly browned, stirring occasionally. Add water, wine, salt, Worcestershire, and bouillon; over high heat, heat to boiling.

4. With sharp knife, cut frozen fish fillets into 1-inch chunks. Add fish and frozen mixed vegetables to mixture in saucepan; heat to boiling. Reduce heat to low; cover and simmer 10 to 15 minutes until fish flakes easily when tested with a fork and vegetables are tender.

5. While soup is simmering, preheat oven to 450°F. Cut four ½-inch thick slices from Italian bread. (Reserve remaining bread to serve another day.) Place bread slices in jelly-roll pan; toast bread in oven, about 3 minutes on each side or until golden. Remove pan from oven; set aside.

6. When soup is done, ladle soup into four 12-ounce oven-safe bowls. Place a toasted bread slice on top of soup in each bowl. Sprinkle each bread slice with ¼ cup cheese. Arrange bowls in jelly-roll pan for easier handling. Bake cheese-topped soup until cheese is melted and lightly browned, about 3 minutes.

Quick Beef-and-Vegetable Soup

TIME: about 45 minutes—SERVINGS: 6

1½ pounds ground beef
1 medium onion, sliced
1 16-ounce can stewed tomatoes
2 beef-flavor bouillon cubes or envelopes
7 cups water
½ cup regular long-grain rice
2 teaspoons salt
½ teaspoon basil
¼ teaspoon pepper
1 16-ounce package frozen mixed vegetables (broccoli, carrots, and cauliflower)

1. In 5-quart Dutch oven over high heat, cook ground beef and onion until all pan juices evaporate and meat is well browned, stirring frequently. Add stewed tomatoes and next 6 ingredients; heat to boiling. Reduce heat to low; cover and simmer 15 minutes, stirring occasionally.

2. Add frozen mixed vegetables; over high heat, heat to boiling. Reduce heat to low; cover and simmer 10 minutes longer or until vegetables are tender, stirring occasionally. Makes about 12 cups.

Beef-Vegetable Soup

TIME: about 3 hours—SERVINGS: 8

2 tablespoons salad oil
4 beef shank cross cuts (about 4 pounds), each cut 1 inch thick
2 celery stalks, sliced
2 carrots, sliced
1 medium onion, diced
1 28-ounce can tomatoes
4 cups water
2 teaspoons salt
½ teaspoon marjoram
¼ teaspoon pepper
2 tablespoons minced parsley
1 10-ounce package frozen peas
1 10-ounce package frozen whole-kernel corn

1. In 8-quart Dutch oven over medium-high heat, in hot salad oil, cook beef shank cross cuts until browned on all sides. Remove meat from Dutch oven to cutting board. Cut meat into bite-sized pieces. Set meat and bones aside.

2. In drippings remaining in Dutch oven over medium heat, cook celery, carrots, and onion until vegetables are tender-crisp, stirring occasionally. Return meat and bones to Dutch oven. Stir in tomatoes with their liquid, water, salt, marjoram, pepper, and 1 tablespoon parsley; over high heat, heat to boiling. Reduce heat to low; cover and simmer 2¼ hours.

3. Skim off fat from liquid in Dutch oven; discard bones. Stir in frozen peas and corn; over high heat, heat to boiling. Reduce heat to low; cover and simmer 15 minutes or until meat and vegetables are tender. Sprinkle soup with remaining 1 tablespoon parsley. Makes about 14 cups.

Chunky Beef-and-Bean Soup

TIME: about 3½ hours—SERVINGS: 10

1 16-ounce package dry pinto beans
water
1 pound ground beef
1 medium onion, diced
½ cup cooking or dry red wine (optional)
1 tablespoon salt
1 teaspoon sugar
½ teaspoon thyme leaves
¼ teaspoon pepper
1 9-ounce package frozen French-style green beans
1 8-ounce can tomato sauce

1. Rinse beans in running cold water and discard any stones or shriveled beans. In 5-quart Dutch oven over high heat, heat beans and 8 cups water to boiling; cook 3 minutes. Remove Dutch oven from heat; cover; let stand 1 hour. Drain and rinse beans; set aside.

2. In same Dutch oven over medium-high heat, cook ground beef and onion until pan juices evaporate and meat is browned, stirring occasionally. Return beans to Dutch oven; stir in wine (if not using wine, substitute ½ cup water), salt, sugar, thyme, pepper, and 6 cups water; over high heat, heat to boiling. Reduce heat to low; cover; simmer 1¾ hours, stirring occasionally.

3. Stir in frozen beans and tomato sauce; over high heat, heat to boiling. Reduce heat to low; cover; simmer 15 minutes or until beans are tender, stirring often. Makes about 13 cups.

11

Black-Bean Soup

TIME: about 3½ hours—SERVINGS: 8

1 16-ounce package dry black beans
water
1 ham bone with about 2 cups meat left on
2 large celery stalks, diced
1 large onion, diced
1 large carrot, diced
1 medium garlic clove, cut in half
1 bay leaf
½ teaspoon pepper
⅛ teaspoon ground cloves
salt
dry sherry
2 hard-cooked eggs, chopped
1 medium lemon, thinly sliced

1. Rinse beans in running cold water and discard any stones or shriveled beans. In 5-quart Dutch oven over high heat, heat beans and 8 cups water to boiling; cook 3 minutes. Remove Dutch oven from heat; cover and let stand 1 hour. Drain and rinse beans.

2. Return beans to Dutch oven. Add 8 cups water, ham bone, and next 7 ingredients; over high heat, heat to boiling. Reduce heat to low; cover and simmer 2 hours or until beans are tender, stirring occasionally.

3. Discard garlic and bay leaf. Remove ham bone from soup to cutting board. Cut meat from bone into bite-sized pieces; set aside. Discard bone. With slotted spoon, mash beans slightly. Return ham pieces to soup; add salt to taste. Over medium heat, heat through.

4. To serve, spoon soup into large bowls. For each serving, let each person stir in sherry to taste; top with some chopped hard-cooked egg and a lemon slice. Makes about 10½ cups.

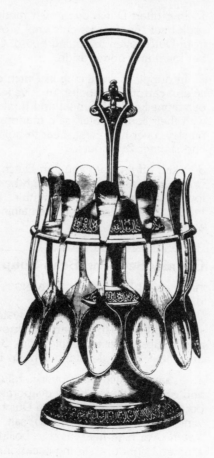

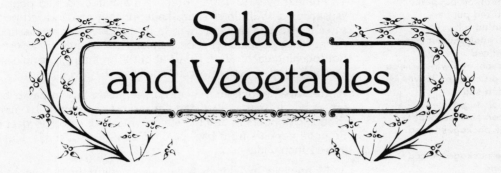

Salads and Vegetables

SALADS

Boston Lettuce Wedges with Pimento Dressing

TIME: about 10 minutes—SERVINGS: 4

3 tablespoons olive or salad oil
3 tablespoons red wine vinegar
1 tablespoon minced pimento
1 teaspoon sugar
½ teaspoon salt
¼ teaspoon pepper
1 head Boston lettuce, quartered

1. In bowl, mix first 6 ingredients.

2. On each of 4 salad plates, place a lettuce wedge. Spoon dressing over lettuce.

Pasta-Asparagus Salad

TIME: about 1¾ hours or start early in day—SERVINGS: 8

½ 16-ounce package ziti macaroni
olive or salad oil
1 pound fresh asparagus, cut into 1-inch pieces
½ pound mushrooms, thinly sliced
2 medium red peppers, thinly sliced
1 small garlic clove, cut in half
1 medium lemon
½ cup pitted small ripe olives
2 tablespoons capers
1 teaspoon salt
½ teaspoon sugar
⅛ teaspoon cracked pepper
⅛ teaspoon oregano leaves

1. Prepare ziti as label directs; drain. Place ziti in large bowl; toss with 2 tablespoons olive oil.

2. Meanwhile, in 10-inch skillet over medium heat, in 2 tablespoons hot olive oil, cook asparagus, mushrooms, peppers, and garlic until tender, about 15 minutes, stirring occasionally; discard garlic.

3. From lemon, grate 1 tablespoon peel and squeeze 2 tablespoons juice. To ziti in bowl, add asparagus mixture, lemon peel, juice, olives, and remaining ingredients; toss to coat well.

4. Cover and refrigerate at least 1 hour to blend flavors.

13

Antipasto

TIME: start early in day or day ahead—SERVINGS: 8

3 medium green peppers
3 medium red peppers
olive or salad oil
½ pound small mushrooms,
 thinly sliced
3 tablespoons red wine vinegar
½ teaspoon oregano leaves
½ teaspoon salt
¼ teaspoon sugar
⅛ teaspoon cracked pepper
2 8-ounce packages sliced
 salami
2 8-ounce packages sliced
 provolone
½ pound sliced prosciutto
lettuce leaves

1. Preheat oven to 450°F. Prepare marinated roasted peppers and mushrooms: With tip of sharp knife, prick green and red peppers in several places to prevent them from exploding when roasting in oven. Place peppers on cookie sheet, making sure that peppers are not touching each other. Roast about 20 minutes or until skin puckers, turning peppers occasionally so they won't burn.

2. Remove peppers to a medium-size, clean brown paper bag; fold top of bag to seal and let stand at room temperature 10 minutes. (Keeping peppers in bag to "steam" makes it easier to peel off skin.) Remove peppers from bag; peel off skin; discard seeds. Cut peppers into ½-inch-wide strips.

3. Meanwhile, in 10-inch skillet over medium heat, heat 1 tablespoon olive or salad oil; add mushrooms; cook until tender, stirring occasionally.

4. In a large bowl, combine mushrooms, pepper strips, red wine vinegar, oregano leaves, salt, sugar, cracked pepper and ¼ cup olive or salad oil. Cover and refrigerate at least 4 hours to blend flavors.

5. About 15 minutes before serving drain salad; arrange with salami, provolone, prosciutto, and lettuce leaves on large platter.

Jeweled Beet Salad

TIME: start early in day or day ahead—SERVINGS: 16

3 medium beets (¾ pound)
water
¼ cup sugar
¼ teaspoon salt
3 envelopes unflavored gelatin
1 medium carrot
1 8¼-ounce can crushed
 pineapple
⅓ cup red wine vinegar

1. In 3-quart saucepan over high heat, heat unpeeled beets and enough water to cover to boiling. Reduce heat to low; cover; simmer 25 to 30 minutes until beets are tender; drain. Cool beets slightly until easy to handle; peel.

2. Meanwhile, in 2-quart saucepan, mix sugar, salt, and 3 cups water. Evenly sprinkle gelatin over mixture. Cook over medium heat until gelatin is completely dissolved, stirring frequently; set aside at room temperature.

3. From carrot, cut 16 thin slices. With small flower-shaped canapé cutter, cut carrot slices to resemble flower shapes. From beets, cut 16 thin slices. Shred remaining beets.

4. Into 8″ by 8″ baking dish, pour ¼-inch layer of gelatin mixture; refrigerate about 20 minutes or until set.

5. Arrange carrot flowers on top of gelatin in dish so that when salad is cut later, carrots will be in the center of each of 16 servings. Place a beet slice on each carrot flower. Spoon a thin layer of gelatin over beet slices; refrigerate 30 minutes or until gelatin is set.

6. Into remaining gelatin mixture, stir crushed pineapple with its juice, vinegar, and shredded beets. Spoon beet mixture over gelatin in pan; refrigerate until salad is set, about 3 hours.

7. To serve, unmold gelatin onto chilled platter.

Do-Ahead Company Green Salad

TIME: about 30 minutes or start day ahead—SERVINGS: 12

1 10-ounce package frozen peas
boiling water
1 16-ounce can diced beets
1 medium head iceberg lettuce
1 large cucumber
1 8-ounce container sour cream
1 cup mayonnaise
¾ cup shredded Monterey Jack
　cheese (3 ounces)
3 tablespoons chopped
　watercress
1½ teaspoons sugar
½ teaspoon salt
¼ teaspoon pepper

1. Place frozen peas in small bowl; cover with boiling water; let stand 5 minutes to "cook" peas; drain.

2. Meanwhile, drain beets; pat dry with paper towels. Coarsely shred lettuce. Thinly slice cucumber.

3. Place beets in 13" by 9" baking dish; then top with lettuce, peas, and half of cucumber slices.

4. Prepare dressing: In medium bowl, mix sour cream, mayonnaise, cheese, watercress, sugar, salt, and pepper. Spoon dressing evenly over salad mixture in baking dish. Garnish top of salad with remaining cucumber slices.

5. Serve salad immediately or cover and refrigerate salad to serve within 24 hours. With knife, cut salad into 12 portions; lift each portion of salad with pancake turner to salad plate.

Fancy Coleslaw Vinaigrette

TIME: about 1½ hours or start early in day—SERVINGS: 6

1 medium head green cabbage
　(about 2 pounds)
1 large red pepper
⅓ cup olive or salad oil
¼ cup red wine vinegar
1 tablespoon sugar
1 teaspoon salt
½ teaspoon caraway seeds,
　crushed
⅛ teaspoon pepper
2 tablespoons chopped parsley

1. With sharp knife, cut out and discard tough ribs from cabbage leaves; finely shred cabbage to make about 6 cups; cut red pepper into very thin strips.

2. In large bowl with fork or wire whisk, mix olive oil, vinegar, sugar, salt, crushed caraway seeds, and pepper; add cabbage, red pepper, and parsley; toss gently to coat well with dressing.

3. Cover and refrigerate at least 1 hour to blend flavors.

Lettuce with Hot Bacon Dressing

TIME: about 30 minutes—SERVINGS: 8

8 cups firmly packed lettuce
　leaves
4 slices bacon, diced
1 small onion, minced
¼ cup cider vinegar
1½ teaspoons sugar
¾ teaspoon salt
¼ teaspoon dry mustard
⅛ teaspoon pepper
1 egg

1. Into large salad bowl, tear lettuce into bite-sized pieces; set aside.

2. In 2-quart saucepan over medium-low heat, cook bacon until browned. With slotted spoon, remove bacon to paper towels to drain. In bacon drippings remaining in saucepan over medium heat, cook onion until tender, stirring occasionally; stir in vinegar, sugar, salt, mustard, and pepper.

3. In small bowl with fork, beat egg slightly. Into egg, stir small amount of hot onion mixture; slowly pour egg mixture back into remaining onion mixture, stirring rapidly to prevent lumping. Cook, stirring constantly, until mixture is slightly thickened (do not boil).

4. Pour dressing mixture over lettuce; add bacon; toss gently to coat lettuce well. Serve immediately.

Zesty Lima-Bean Salad

TIME: about 2½ hours or start early in day—SERVINGS: 8

2 10-ounce packages frozen
    baby lima beans
¼ cup salad oil
1 medium green pepper, diced
1 small onion, diced
¼ cup cider vinegar
2 tablespoons sugar
½ teaspoon salt

1. In 12-inch skillet, prepare lima beans as labels direct but prepare both packages together. Drain and set aside.

2. In same skillet over medium heat, in hot salad oil, cook green pepper and onion until tender, stirring occasionally.

3. In medium bowl, combine cooked lima beans, green-pepper mixture, vinegar, sugar, and salt.

4. Cover and refrigerate about 2 hours to blend flavors, stirring occasionally.

Oriental Summer Salad

TIME: about 2¼ hours or start early in day—SERVINGS: 8

3 large cucumbers, thinly sliced
2 teaspoons salt
3 tablespoons minced green
    onions
⅓ cup salad oil
1 4-ounce package alfalfa
    sprouts
1 cup loosely packed watercress
    leaves

1. In medium bowl, toss cucumbers and salt; cover and let stand at room temperature 1 hour.

2. Tipping bowl over sink, press cucumbers with hand to drain liquid. Stir in green onions.

3. In small saucepan over high heat, heat salad oil until very hot and it begins to smoke. Slowly and evenly pour hot oil over cucumber mixture; toss with fork to mix well.

4. Cover; refrigerate at least 1 hour.

5. To serve, in large bowl, toss alfalfa sprouts with watercress. Arrange cucumber mixture and alfalfa-sprout mixture on chilled platter.

Pasta Salad

TIME: about 45 minutes or start early in day—SERVINGS: 12

1 16-ounce package rotelle or
    shell macaroni
1 cup frozen peas
boiling water
1 small bunch broccoli
1 large carrot
1 medium garlic clove
3 tablespoons salad oil
¾ teaspoon crushed red pepper
salt
½ cup milk
½ cup mayonniase
2 tablespoons cider vinegar

1. Prepare macaroni as label directs; drain.

2. Meanwhile, in small bowl, place frozen peas; cover with boiling water and let stand 5 minutes to "cook" peas; drain.

3. Cut broccoli into 2″ by 1″ pieces; cut carrot into 2″ by ⅛″ sticks; cut garlic clove in half. In 10-inch skillet over medium-high heat, heat salad oil and garlic until oil is hot. Add broccoli, carrot, crushed red pepper, and ¾ teaspoon salt; cook, stirring frequently, until vegetables are tender-crisp; discard garlic. Remove skillet from heat.

4. In large bowl with wire whisk or spoon, beat milk, mayonnaise, cider vinegar, and ½ teaspoon salt until smooth. Add macaroni, peas, and broccoli mixture; toss gently to coat with dressing.

5. Serve at room temperature or cover and refrigerate to serve chilled later.

Fiesta Salad

TIME: about 2½ hours or start early in day—SERVINGS: 10

1 20-ounce bag frozen peas
1 10-ounce package frozen
  whole-kernel corn
1 15½- to 20-ounce can
  garbanzo beans, drained
⅓ cup salad oil
¼ cup mayonnaise
3 tablespoons red wine vinegar
1¾ teaspoons sugar
1½ teaspoons salt
¼ teaspoon oregano leaves
⅛ teaspoon ground red pepper
lettuce leaves

1. Prepare peas and corn as labels direct but omit salt; drain.

2. In large bowl, combine peas, corn, and remaining ingredients except lettuce; toss to mix well.

3. Cover and refrigerate about 2 hours to blend flavors, stirring occasionally.

4. To serve, arrange lettuce leaves on large platter; spoon vegetable mixture on top of lettuce leaves.

Sweet-and-Sour Tomato and Cucumber Slices

TIME: about 1 hour—SERVINGS: 4

3 medium tomatoes
1 large cucumber
lettuce leaves
¼ cup cider vinegar
2 tablespoons olive or salad oil
1 tablespoon sugar
¾ teaspoon salt
½ teaspoon dry mustard
½ teaspoon basil
⅛ teaspoon pepper

1. Slice tomatoes and cucumbers; arrange on lettuce-lined platter, overlapping slices; set aside.

2. In small bowl with wire whisk or spoon, mix vinegar, olive oil, sugar, salt, mustard, basil, and pepper.

3. Spoon dressing over tomato and cucumber slices; cover and refrigerate until serving time.

Lettuce and Endive Salad with Avocado Dressing

TIME: about 30 minutes—SERVINGS: 8

2 large heads Bibb lettuce
1 small head Boston lettuce
2 large Belgian endives
½ bunch watercress
1 6-ounce bag radishes, sliced
1 ripe medium avocado (about 8
  ounces)
⅓ cup milk
3 tablespoons white wine
  vinegar
2 tablespoons salad oil
2 tablespoons mayonnaise
½ teaspoon salt
½ teaspoon sugar
⅛ teaspoon tarragon leaves

1. Into large bowl, tear lettuce into bite-sized pieces. Separate endives into leaves; cut large leaves in half. Add endives, watercress, and radishes to lettuce in bowl.

2. Prepare dressing: Remove peel and pit from avocado; cut avocado into chunks. In blender or food processor, blend avocado, milk, white wine vinegar, salad oil, mayonnaise, salt, sugar, and tarragon leaves until smooth.

3. Toss salad gently with dressing to coat.

Noodle Salad with Peanut Sauce

TIME: about 45 minutes or start early in day—SERVINGS: 8

1 16-ounce package spaghetti
1 6-ounce package radishes
¾ cup hot tap water
½ cup creamy peanut butter
¼ cup soy sauce
¼ cup sesame-seed oil or salad oil
2 tablespoons cider vinegar
1½ teaspoons sugar
¼ teaspoon ground red pepper
lettuce leaves
1 tablespoon minced green onion for garnish

1. Prepare spaghetti as label directs.

2. Meanwhile, thinly slice 5 radishes for garnish. Dice remaining radishes. In large bowl with wire whisk or fork, stir hot water, peanut butter, soy sauce, sesame-seed oil, cider vinegar, sugar, ground red pepper, and diced radishes until blended.

3. Drain spaghetti. Add spaghetti to peanut-butter mixture; with rubber spatula, toss gently to coat well.

4. Line large platter with lettuce leaves. Spoon spaghetti mixture onto lettuce leaves. Garnish with sliced radishes and green onion. Serve spaghetti at room temperature or cover and refrigerate to serve chilled later.

Garden-Vegetable Salad

TIME: about 45 minutes or start early in day—SERVINGS: 10

1 pound green beans
salt
water
½ cup mayonnaise
2 tablespoons cider vinegar
1 tablespoon minced green onion
1 tablespoon prepared mustard
1 tablespoon milk
¼ teaspoon tarragon
¼ teaspoon hot pepper sauce
4 medium zucchini, thinly sliced
3 medium carrots, thinly sliced
2 celery stalks, thinly sliced

1. In 2-quart saucepan over high heat, heat green beans, 1 teaspoon salt, and 1 inch water to boiling. Reduce heat to low; cover and simmer 5 to 10 minutes until beans are tender-crisp; drain.

2. In large bowl, stir mayonnaise, vinegar, green onion, mustard, milk, tarragon, hot pepper sauce, and ½ teaspoon salt. Add beans, zucchini, carrots, and celery; toss gently to coat with dressing.

3. Serve salad at room temperature or cover and refrigerate to serve chilled later.

New-Potato Salad Vinaigrette

TIME: about 2 hours or start early in day—SERVINGS: 8

4 pounds small red potatoes
water
⅓ cup olive or salad oil
¼ cup red wine vinegar
2 tablespoons chopped parsley
1 tablespoon chopped fresh chives or ½ teaspoon thyme leaves
1½ teaspoons salt
1¼ teaspoons sugar
2 teaspoons prepared mustard
⅛ teaspoon coarsely ground black pepper
3 large celery stalks, thinly sliced

1. In 5-quart saucepot over high heat, heat unpeeled potatoes and enough water to cover to boiling. Reduce heat to medium-low; cover and cook about 15 minutes or until potatoes are fork-tender; drain. Cool potatoes until easy to handle; cut each potato into quarters or bite-sized pieces (do not peel).

2. Meanwhile, in large bowl with fork or wire whisk, mix oil and next 7 ingredients. Add potatoes and celery; with rubber spatula, gently toss to mix well.

3. Cover and refrigerate at least 1 hour to blend flavors, tossing occasionally.

Tomato Slices with Lemon Dressing

TIME: about 40 minutes—SERVINGS: 4

2 medium tomatoes
lettuce leaves
1 medium lemon
⅓ cup olive or salad oil
1 teaspoon minced parsley
½ teaspoon salt
½ teaspoon sugar
⅛ teaspoon pepper

1. Slice tomatoes; arrange on lettuce-leaf-lined platter.

2. From lemon, grate ½ teaspoon peel and squeeze 1 tablespoon juice.

3. In small bowl with wire whisk or fork, mix lemon peel, juice, olive oil, and remaining ingredients.

4. Spoon dressing over tomatoes; cover; refrigerate.

SALADS WITH FISH OR MEAT

Shrimp Salad in Avocado Halves

TIME: about 40 minutes—SERVINGS: 4

2 eggs
1 pound medium shrimp
water
salt
1 large celery stalk, diced
½ cup mayonnaise
1 tablespoon milk
1 tablespoon lemon juice
½ teaspoon paprika
lettuce leaves
2 medium avocados
1 medium tomato, cut into 8 wedges

1. Hard-cook eggs.

2. Meanwhile, peel and devein shrimp. In 2-quart saucepan over high heat, heat 2 inches water and 1 teaspoon salt to boiling. Add shrimp; heat to boiling. Reduce heat to low; cook shrimp 1 minute or until tender; drain. Place shrimp in large bowl.

3. Remove shell from eggs. Dice eggs; place in large bowl with shrimp. With rubber spatula, gently stir in celery, mayonnaise, milk, lemon juice, paprika, and ¾ teaspoon salt until blended.

4. Line 4 chilled salad plates with lettuce leaves. Cut each avocado lengthwise in half; remove seed and peel. Place one avocado half on each plate. Spoon shrimp salad into avocado halves. Arrange 2 tomato wedges alongside each serving of avocado.

Tuna-Bulgur Salad

TIME: about 2½ hours or start early in day—SERVINGS: 5

½ cup bulgur (cracked wheat)
2 cups cold water
1 10-ounce package frozen baby lima beans
1 6½- to 7-ounce can tuna, drained
3 medium tomatoes, diced
½ cup chopped parsley
3 tablespoons mayonnaise
2 tablespoons salad oil
2 tablespoons lemon juice
½ teaspoon salt
¼ teaspoon pepper
small romaine leaves

1. In large bowl, stir bulgur with water; let stand 2 hours. Drain bulgur well.

2. Prepare lima beans as label directs; drain. Place lima beans in bowl with bulgur; add tuna and remaining ingredients except romaine; mix well.

3. Line platter with romaine leaves. Spoon bulgur mixture onto romaine leaves.

4. Serve salad at room temperature or refrigerate to serve chilled later. (To eat Middle Eastern style, use romaine leaves to pick up salad mixture and eat with fingers.)

Tuna and Cabbage Salad

TIME: about 30 minutes—SERVINGS: 4

⅓ cup cider vinegar
¼ cup olive or salad oil
1¼ teaspoons salt
½ teaspoon pepper
1 6½- to 7-ounce can tuna,
    drained and flaked
1 head red cabbage (1 pound),
    diced
½ cup pitted ripe olives, sliced
¼ cup minced parsley
½ small head Boston lettuce,
    separated into leaves
4 hard-cooked eggs, cubed

1. In small bowl with wire whisk, mix cider vinegar, olive oil, salt, and pepper.

2. In large bowl, combine tuna, diced cabbage, olive slices, and parsley.

3. Drizzle two-thirds of the vinegar mixture over tuna mixture; gently mix well.

4. Line platter with lettuce leaves. Arrange eggs in a single layer on lettuce; drizzle with remaining vinegar mixture. Spoon tuna salad over eggs.

Tuscany White-Bean and Tuna Salad

TIME: about 20 minutes—SERVINGS: 4

1 16-to 20-ounce can white
    kidney beans (cannellini),
    drained
1 6½-to 7-ounce can tuna,
    drained and coarsely flaked
3 tablespoons olive or salad oil
2 tablespoons chopped parsley
1 tablespoon lemon juice
¼ teaspoon salt
1 medium red onion, thinly sliced
freshly ground black pepper

1. In medium bowl, combine first 6 ingredients. Toss gently to mix well.

2. On chilled platter, arrange red-onion slices; top with bean mixture.

3. Serve as main dish with freshly ground black pepper.

Spring Beef Salad

TIME: about 40 minutes—SERVINGS: 4

4 medium potatoes (about 1½
    pounds)
water
3 eggs
1 beef top round steak, cut 1
    inch thick (about 1 pound)
salt
¼ cup salad oil
3 tablespoons red wine vinegar
1 tablespoon prepared mustard
1 teaspoon sugar
¼ teaspoon cracked pepper
¼ teaspoon basil
1 small head lettuce
1 medium zucchini, thinly sliced
1 6-ounce bag radishes, cut into
    roses

1. In 2-quart saucepan over high heat, heat unpeeled potatoes and enough water to cover to boiling. Reduce heat to medium-low; cover and cook 25 to 30 minutes until potatoes are fork-tender. Cut unpeeled potatoes into slices. In small saucepan, hard-cook eggs.

2. Meanwhile, preheat broiler if manufacturer directs. Place beef top round steak on rack in broiling pan; sprinkle with ¾ teaspoon salt. Broil steak 10 minutes for rare or until of desired doneness, turning steak once. Remove steak to cutting board. With knife held in slanting position, slice steak into ⅛-inch-thick slices.

3. Remove shell from hard-cooked eggs. Separate yolks from whites; coarsely chop whites; set aside. In blender at medium speed, blend hard-cooked egg yolks, salad oil, vinegar, mustard, sugar, pepper, basil, and ½ teaspoon salt until dressing is smooth.

4. To serve, arrange lettuce leaves, sliced steak, sliced potatoes, chopped egg whites, zucchini slices, and radish roses on 4 dinner plates. Pour dressing into 4 small glasses. Serve dressing with salad.

Pasta-and-Steak Salad

TIME: about 1 hour or start early in day—SERVINGS: 6

½ 16-ounce package rotelle or elbow macaroni
1 9-ounce package frozen cut green beans
salad oil
1 medium onion, sliced
1 beef top round steak, cut ¾ inch thick (about 1 pound)
1 6-ounce bag radishes, thinly sliced
2 tablespoons chopped parsley
1 tablespoon red wine vinegar
1¼ teaspoons salt
1 teaspoon sugar
½ teaspoon thyme leaves
¼ teaspoon coarsely ground black pepper

1. Prepare rotelle macaroni as label directs; drain.

2. Meanwhile, in 10-inch skillet, prepare frozen cut green beans as label directs. Drain beans and place in large bowl. In same skillet over medium heat, in 2 tablespoons hot salad oil, cook onion until tender, about 5 minutes. With slotted spoon, remove onion to bowl with green beans.

3. In oil remaining in skillet over medium-high heat, cook beef top round steak 5 to 8 minutes for rare, turning steak once. (If medium or well-done meat is preferred, cook 2 to 3 minutes longer.) Remove steak to cutting board. With knife held in slanting position, slice steak into ⅛-inch-thick slices. Place steak in bowl with beans.

4. To mixture in bowl, add macaroni, radishes, remaining ingredients, and 3 tablespoons salad oil; toss gently to mix well.

5. Serve salad at room temperature or cover and refrigerate to serve chilled later.

FRUITS SERVED AS VEGETABLES

Melon with Gingered Cream Cheese

TIME: about 15 minutes or start early in day—SERVINGS: 8

1 8-ounce package cream cheese, softened
⅓ cup milk
3 tablespoons minced crystallized ginger
1 medium honeydew melon

1. In small bowl with mixer at low speed, beat cream cheese with milk until smooth. Stir in 2 tablespoons minced ginger. If not using right away, cover and refrigerate.

2. To serve, cut honeydew melon into 8 wedges; discard seeds. Cut pulp loose from rind, leaving pulp in place, then slash the pulp of wedges criss-cross into bite-sized pieces. Spoon cream-cheese mixture on wedges; sprinkle with remaining ginger.

Spiced Apple Rings

TIME: about 1 hour or start up to 1 week ahead—YIELD: 2 cups

1 cup water
¾ cup apple cider
¾ cup sugar
¾ teaspoon ground cinnamon
¼ teaspoon ground ginger
¼ teaspoon ground allspice
3 lemon slices
3 red medium cooking apples

1. In 12-inch skillet over high heat, heat all ingredients except apples to boiling. Reduce heat to low; cover and simmer 5 minutes to blend flavors.

2. Meanwhile, core apples; cut apples crosswise into ¼-inch rings. For even cooking, add half amount of apple rings to skillet; simmer until tender but firm, 3 to 5 minutes; remove to small bowl. Repeat with remaining apple rings.

3. Discard lemon slices; pour liquid over apple rings in bowl. Cover and refrigerate to use up within 1 week.

4. Serve apple rings with roast chicken, pork, duckling.

Spiced Nectarine Slices

TIME: start early in day—SERVINGS: 16

1½ cups water
¾ teaspoon whole cloves
¼ teaspoon ground cinnamon
¼ teaspoon ground ginger
¼ teaspoon salt
4 large nectarines, peeled and thinly sliced
½ cup sugar
3 tablespoons lemon juice

1. In 10-inch skillet over medium heat, heat first 5 ingredients to boiling; boil 2 minutes.

2. Add nectarine slices; cook until tender, about 10 minutes, stirring occasionally. Toward end of cooking time, stir in sugar and lemon juice. Refrigerate.

Assorted Fruit in Port Wine

TIME: start day ahead or up to 2 weeks ahead—SERVINGS: 12

2 16-ounce cans apricot halves in heavy syrup
2 16-ounce cans cling peach halves in heavy syrup
2 16-ounce cans pear halves in heavy syrup
1 17-ounce jar light sweet cherries
1 9.5-ounce jar preserved kumquats
10 maraschino cherries
5 3-inch long cinnamon sticks
½ teaspoon ground ginger
½ teaspoon ground allspice
¼ teaspoon whole cloves
2 cups white port wine

1. Into large bowl, drain syrup from apricots, peaches, and pears. Reserve 2½ cups syrup mixture; set aside. Drain cherries and kumquats; discard syrup. Place drained fruit and maraschino cherries in large bowl; set aside.

2. In 2-quart saucepan over high heat, heat cinnamon sticks, ginger, allspice, cloves, and reserved syrup mixture to boiling. Reduce heat to low; simmer 5 minutes to blend flavors. Pour syrup mixture over fruit in bowl; stir in port wine.

3. Cover and refrigerate at least 24 hours before serving. Store fruit in refrigerator to use up within 2 weeks.

4. Serve fruit as accompaniment to roast pork, ham, lamb, poultry.

VEGETABLE ACCOMPANIMENTS

Grandma's Tomato Pudding

TIME: about 1½ hours—SERVINGS: 10

15 medium tomatoes (about 5 pounds), peeled and quartered
1 6-ounce can tomato paste
1 cup packed dark brown sugar
1 teaspoon salt
6 slices white bread, cut into 1-inch cubes (about 3 cups)
1 cup butter or margarine, melted

1. In 3-quart saucepan over medium heat, heat tomatoes to boiling, stirring. Reduce heat to low; cover; simmer until tomatoes are soft, about 10 minutes.

2. Uncover saucepan and cook 15 to 20 minutes longer, until tomatoes are slightly thickened, stirring often. Stir in tomato paste, brown sugar, and salt.

3. Preheat oven to 375°F. Arrange bread cubes in 3-quart casserole. Pour melted butter over bread cubes; top with tomato mixture. Bake 35 to 40 minutes until hot.

Sliced Tomatoes Provençale

TIME: about 15 minutes or start early in day—SERVINGS: 8

1 cup mayonnaise
½ cup milk
basil
6 medium tomatoes, sliced

1. In medium bowl with wire whisk or fork, mix mayonnaise, milk, and ½ teaspoon basil until blended.

2. Spoon half of mayonnaise mixture evenly in bottom of 12" by 8" baking dish. Arrange tomato slices in rows in mixture, overlapping slices slightly. Spoon remaining mayonnaise mixture over tomatoes; sprinkle with ¼ teaspoon basil.

3. Serve immediately or cover and refrigerate to serve later.

Pepper-and-Tomato Sauté

TIME: about 30 minutes—SERVINGS: 5

2 tablespoons salad oil
3 large green peppers, cut into large chunks
1 medium onion, chopped
2 large tomatoes, peeled, and cut into large chunks
1 teaspoon salt
½ teaspoon basil

1. In 12-inch skillet over medium heat, in hot salad oil, cook green peppers and onion 10 minutes.

2. Add tomatoes, salt, and basil; reduce heat to low; cover and simmer until vegetables are tender, stirring occasionally, about 10 to 15 minutes.

Onion-and-Pepper Sauté

TIME: about 40 minutes or start early in day—SERVINGS: 8

¼ cup salad oil
4 large onions, cut into ¼-inch-thick slices
4 large red peppers, cut into ½-inch-wide strips
¾ teaspoon salt
½ teaspoon basil or thyme leaves

1. In 12-inch skillet over medium heat, in hot salad oil, cook all ingredients until vegetables are tender, about 20 minutes, stirring occasionally.

2. Serve hot or cover and refrigerate to serve cold later.

Baked Onions

TIME: about 1¾ hours—SERVINGS: 10

¾ cup water
1 envelope chicken-flavor bouillon
10 medium onions
2 tablespoons butter or margarine, cut up
salt
paprika

1. In 8" by 8" baking dish, mix water and bouillon.

2. Add onions; dot with butter or margarine; sprinkle lightly with salt.

3. Cover dish with foil and bake in 350°F. oven 1½ hours or until onions are tender, occasionally basting onions with liquid in dish; sprinkle with paprika.

Braised Peppers and Potatoes

TIME: about 45 minutes—SERVINGS: 6

3 large red peppers
3 large green peppers
3 medium onions
3 medium potatoes (1 pound)
½ pound mushrooms
¼ cup olive or salad oil
2 garlic cloves, crushed
¾ cup water
2 tablespoons red wine vinegar
1 teaspoon chicken-flavor instant
   bouillon
¾ teaspoon salt
½ teaspoon basil
parsley sprigs for garnish

1. Cut red and green peppers into ½-inch strips. Cut each onion into quarters. Cut potatoes into ½-inch-thick slices. If mushrooms are large, cut each into halves or quarters.

2. In 12-inch skillet over medium heat, in hot olive oil, cook peppers, onions, potatoes, mushrooms, and garlic until lightly browned, stirring often.

3. Stir in water and remaining ingredients except parsley sprigs; heat to boiling. Reduce heat to low; cover and simmer until vegetables are tender, stirring occasionally, about 15 to 20 minutes.

4. Spoon pepper mixture onto platter; garnish with parsley sprigs.

Skillet Potatoes

TIME: about 30 minutes—SERVINGS: 4

vegetable cooking spray
   (optional)
3 tablespoons butter or
   margarine
4 medium potatoes, unpeeled,
   cut into ½-inch-thick slices
1 small onion, chopped
1 small green pepper, chopped
¾ teaspoon salt
¼ teaspoon pepper

1. If desired, spray 12-inch skillet with vegetable cooking spray as label directs; place skillet over medium heat.

2. In skillet, melt butter or margarine; add potatoes; sprinkle with onion, green pepper, salt, and pepper.

3. Cover skillet and cook potato slices until tender and well browned on both sides, turning potatoes occasionally, about 15 to 20 minutes.

New Potatoes with Mock Caviar

TIME: about 20 minutes—SERVINGS: 4

4 small red potatoes
½ teaspoon salt
water
⅓ cup sour cream
4 large pitted ripe olives, minced

1. In 1-quart saucepan over high heat, heat unpeeled potatoes, salt, and enough water to cover to boiling. Reduce heat to medium-low; cover and cook 10 to 15 minutes until potatoes are fork-tender. Drain potatoes; cut each in half.

2. To serve, spoon a dollop of sour cream on each potato half; top with some minced ripe olives.

Crumb-Coated Potatoes

TIME: about 20 minutes—SERVINGS: 8

½ cup butter or margarine
½ cup dried bread crumbs
½ teaspoon salt
¼ teaspoon pepper
3 16-ounce cans whole white
   potatoes, drained

1. In 12-inch skillet over medium heat, into hot butter or margarine, stir dried bread crumbs, salt, and pepper.

2. Add potatoes, shaking skillet to coat potatoes evenly with bread crumbs. Cook until potatoes are golden and heated through, about 15 minutes, shaking skillet occasionally.

Saratoga Chips

TIME: about 1½ hours or start early in day—SERVINGS: 8

salad oil
4 large potatoes (about 3
    pounds)
salt

1. In 2-quart saucepan over medium heat, heat about 1½ inches salad oil to 375°F. on deep-fat thermometer or heat oil in deep-fat fryer set at 375°F.

2. Meanwhile, peel potatoes. Cut potatoes into thin slices (or, for easier slicing, use food processor with slicing disk attached; or use a mandoline); pat dry with paper towels.

3. Fry potato slices in hot oil, a few at a time, until golden, about 5 minutes. With slotted spoon, remove potato chips to paper towels to drain. Sprinkle potato chips with salt to taste.

4. Serve warm as potato to accompany main dish or cool to serve as snack. Makes 12 cups.

Mashed Potatoes with Cabbage

TIME: about 45 minutes—SERVINGS: 4

6 medium potatoes (2 pounds)
water
1 medium head green cabbage
    (about 2 pounds)
5 tablespoons butter or
    margarine
1 small onion, diced
¾ cup milk
1 teaspoon salt
⅛ teaspoon pepper

1. In 4-quart saucepan over high heat, heat potatoes and enough water to cover to boiling. Reduce heat to medium-low; cover and cook 25 to 30 minutes until potatoes are fork-tender.

2. Meanwhile, discard tough outer leaves from cabbage; carefully remove 4 large leaves and reserve. Chop remaining cabbage. In 10-inch skillet over medium heat, in hot butter or margarine, cook chopped cabbage and onion until very tender, about 25 minutes, stirring occasionally.

3. When potatoes are done, drain and peel potatoes. In large bowl with mixer at low speed, beat potatoes, milk, salt, and pepper until light and fluffy. With rubber spatula, fold in cabbage mixture.

4. To serve, line platter or bowl with reserved cabbage leaves; spoon potato mixture on cabbage leaves.

Candied Sweet-Potato Slices

TIME: about 1½ hours—SERVINGS: 8

6 large sweet potatoes (about 3
    pounds)
water
salt
½ cup packed brown sugar
4 tablespoons butter or
    margarine, cut into small
    pieces

1. In 4-quart saucepan over high heat, heat unpeeled sweet potatoes and enough water to cover to boiling. Reduce heat to low; cover and simmer 25 to 30 minutes until potatoes are tender. Drain potatoes; let cool slightly until easy to handle.

2. Preheat oven to 375°F. Grease 12″ by 8″ baking dish. Peel potatoes; cut into ¼-inch-thick slices. Arrange one-third of potato slices in baking dish; lightly sprinkle with some salt; then sprinkle with one-third of brown sugar; dot with one-third of butter or margarine. Repeat with remaining potato slices, salt, brown sugar, and butter to make 3 layers in all.

3. Cover baking dish with foil; bake 30 minutes or until potatoes are heated through and sugar and butter are melted.

Creamy Sweet Potatoes

TIME: about 1¼ hours—SERVINGS: 16

9 medium sweet potatoes (about
  4½ pounds)
water
⅓ cup milk
3 tablespoons brown sugar
½ teaspoon salt
butter or margarine, softened

1. In 8-quart saucepot over high heat, heat sweet potatoes and enough water to cover to boiling. Reduce heat to medium-low; cover and cook 35 to 40 minutes until potatoes are fork-tender; drain; peel.

2. In large bowl with mixer at low speed, beat sweet potatoes, milk, brown sugar, salt, and 6 tablespoons butter or margarine until smooth, scraping bowl often with rubber spatula. Increase speed to high; beat potatoes until light and fluffy.

3. Spoon potatoes into warm large bowl; top mixture with 2 tablespoons butter or margarine.

Summer-Squash and Pepper Slaw

TIME: about 2½ hours or start day ahead—SERVINGS: 10

5 medium yellow straight-neck
  squash (10 ounces each)
5 medium red peppers
1 medium onion
⅔ cup salad oil
⅓ cup cider vinegar
2¼ teaspoons salt
2 teaspoons sugar
¼ teaspoon basil
¼ teaspoon marjoram leaves
¼ teaspoon crushed red pepper

1. Cut squash and red peppers into matchstick-thin strips; thinly slice onion. Place vegetables in large heat-safe bowl; set aside.

2. In 1-quart saucepan over high heat, heat salad oil and remaining ingredients to boiling. Pour hot mixture over vegetables in bowl, tossing to mix well.

3. Cover and refrigerate about 2 hours to blend flavors, stirring occasionally.

Oven-Baked Squash

TIME: about 1 hour—SERVINGS: 2

1 medium acorn squash
2 tablespoons butter or
  margarine
2 tablespoons dark brown sugar

1. Preheat oven to 350°F. Grease small roasting pan.

2. Cut squash lengthwise in half; with spoon, remove seeds. Place squash halves, cut-side down, in baking pan: bake 30 minutes.

3. Turn squash, cut-side up. Place half of butter or margarine and half of brown sugar into each cavity.

4. Bake 15 minutes longer or until squash is fork-tender and butter and brown sugar are melted.

Skillet-Baked Squash: About 30 minutes before serving, cut *1 medium acorn squash* lengthwise in half; remove seeds. Cut halves crosswise into ½-inch-thick slices. In 12-inch skillet over medium-low heat, melt *2 tablespoons butter* or margarine. Arrange squash slices in one layer in melted butter; cover skillet and cook about 20 minutes, turning occasionally, until browned on both sides and tender. Sprinkle with *2 tablespoons brown sugar;* cover skillet to melt sugar. Makes 2 accompaniment servings.

Zucchini with Mozzarella

TIME: about 40 minutes—SERVINGS: 8

2 tablespoons salad oil
1 medium onion, diced
1 medium green pepper, diced
1 small garlic clove, minced
1 16-ounce can tomatoes
4 medium zucchini (about 2 pounds), cut into ¼-inch slices
¾ teaspoon salt
½ teaspoon sugar
½ teaspoon oregano leaves
¼ teaspoon basil
1 8-ounce package mozzarella cheese, coarsely shredded

1. In 10-inch skillet over medium heat, in hot salad oil, cook onion, green pepper, and garlic until vegetables are tender, stirring occasionally.

2. Add tomatoes with their liquid and next 5 ingredients; heat to boiling. Reduce heat to low; cover and simmer until zucchini is tender-crisp, about 15 minutes, stirring occasionally to break up tomatoes.

3. When zucchini is done, sprinkle evenly with cheese; cover and simmer about 3 minutes or until cheese is melted.

Zucchini Strips Rémoulade

TIME: about 30 minutes—SERVINGS: 8

3 large zucchini (about 3 pounds)
¾ cup mayonnaise
1 tablespoon prepared mustard
1 tablespoon minced parsley
1 tablespoon capers, drained
½ teaspoon salt
¼ teaspoon tarragon

Cut each zucchini crosswise in half; then cut into matchstick-thin strips. In medium bowl, gently toss zucchini with remaining ingredients.

Zucchini-Tomato Skillet

TIME: about 30 minutes—SERVINGS: 6

3 tablespoons butter or margarine
2 tablespoons brown sugar
2 tablespoons prepared mustard
¼ teaspoon salt
2 medium zucchini, sliced
3 medium tomatoes

1. In 10-inch skillet over medium heat, heat butter or margarine, brown sugar, mustard, and salt until butter is melted.

2. Add zucchini slices; over high heat, heat to boiling. Reduce heat to medium-low; cover and simmer 20 minutes or until zucchini is tender, basting occasionally with liquid in skillet.

3. Slice tomatoes; cut each slice in half. Tuck tomato slices among zucchini slices; heat through.

Harvard Beets

TIME: about 20 minutes—SERVINGS: 6

2 16-ounce cans or jars sliced beets
⅓ cup vinegar
¼ cup sugar
1 tablespoon cornstarch
½ teaspoon salt
1 tablespoon butter or margarine

1. Drain beets, reserving ½ cup beet liquid.

2. In 2-quart saucepan, mix vinegar, sugar, cornstarch, salt, and reserved beet liquid until smooth; add butter or margarine; over medium heat, cook until thickened, stirring constantly.

3. Add beets and cook just until heated through, stirring occasionally.

Custard Corn Pudding

TIME: about 1½ hours—SERVINGS: 8

3 cups milk
3 tablespoons butter or
  margarine
5 eggs
2¼ teaspoons salt
2 teaspoons sugar
¼ teaspoon pepper
1 17-ounce can whole-kernel
  corn, well drained
hot water

1. In 1-quart saucepan over low heat, heat milk and butter or margarine until tiny bubbles form at edge and butter melts.

2. Meanwhile, in 2-quart casserole with wire whisk or fork, beat eggs, salt, sugar, and pepper until well mixed; stir in corn. Slowly add milk mixture to egg mixture, beating constantly with wire whisk.

3. Place casserole in 13″ by 9″ baking pan; fill pan with hot water to come halfway up side of casserole.

4. Bake in 325°F. oven 1 hour or until knife inserted in center comes out clean.

Cauliflower Polonaise

TIME: about 30 minutes—SERVINGS: 10

2 eggs
1 large head cauliflower (about
  2½ to 3 pounds)
water
salt
4 tablespoons butter or
  margarine
1 cup fresh bread crumbs (about
  2 slices white bread)
2 tablespoons chopped parsley
2 tablespoons lemon juice

1. Hard-cook eggs. Drain, peel, and chop eggs.

2. Meanwhile, with knife, remove leaves and core of cauliflower. In 5-quart saucepot over medium heat, in 1 inch boiling water, heat whole cauliflower and ½ teaspoon salt to boiling. Reduce heat to medium-low; cover saucepot and cook cauliflower 10 to 15 minutes until tender; drain. Place cauliflower on shallow platter; keep warm.

3. In small saucepan over medium heat, melt butter or margarine. Add bread crumbs and cook until bread crumbs are golden, stirring constantly. Stir in chopped eggs, parsley, lemon juice, and ½ teaspoon salt.

4. To serve, sprinkle bread-crumb mixture over cauliflower.

Creamed Cabbage

TIME: about 45 minutes—SERVINGS: 6

butter or margarine
1 slice white bread
1 medium head cabbage (about
  2 pounds)
water
salt
2 tablespoons all-purpose flour
¼ teaspoon caraway seeds
⅛ teaspoon pepper
1 cup milk

1. In 1-quart saucepan over medium-low heat, into 1 tablespoon hot butter or margarine, tear bread into small pieces. Cook bread crumbs until lightly browned, stirring frequently. Remove saucepan from heat; set aside.

2. Discard any tough outer leaves from cabbage. With knife, coarsely shred cabbage. In 3-quart saucepan over high heat, heat 1 inch water and ¼ teaspoon salt to boiling; add cabbage; cover and cook cabbage about 10 minutes or until tender. Drain cabbage in colander; set aside.

3. In same saucepan over medium-low heat, melt 2 tablespoons butter or margarine; stir in flour, caraway seeds, pepper, and ½ teaspoon salt until blended; cook 1 minute. Gradually stir in milk; cook, stirring constantly, until sauce is thickened and smooth. Return cabbage to saucepan; toss until well coated; heat through.

4. To serve, spoon cabbage mixture into bowl; top with bread crumbs.

Barley-Mushroom Casserole

TIME: about 2½ hours—SERVINGS: 8

½ pound mushrooms, sliced
1 medium carrot, sliced
1 small onion, diced
1 chicken-flavor bouillon cube or envelope
4 cups water
¾ cup medium barley
4 tablespoons butter or margarine, cut up
½ teaspoon salt
⅛ teaspoon pepper

1. In 2-quart casserole, combine all ingredients.

2. Bake casserole, covered, in 350°F. oven 2 hours, stirring occasionally.

Braised Hearts of Celery

TIME: about 30 minutes—SERVINGS: 8

2 large bunches celery
water
1 medium onion, chopped
2 chicken-flavor bouillon cubes or envelopes
3 tablespoons butter or margarine
¾ teaspoon oregano leaves
½ teaspoon salt
1 2-ounce jar diced pimentos, drained

1. Remove outer rows of celery ribs; trim root ends. Cut tops and leaves from celery 6 to 8 inches from root ends. (Save outer ribs, tops, and leaves for soup or salad another day.) Cut each bunch of celery lengthwise into quarters.

2. In 12-inch skillet over high heat, in 1 inch boiling water, heat celery, onion, and bouillon to boiling. Reduce heat to medium; cover and cook 15 minutes or until celery is fork-tender; drain well. Stir in butter or margarine and remaining ingredients.

Sautéed Beet Greens

TIME: about 15 minutes—SERVINGS: 2

6 cups packed tender beet greens
2 tablespoons salad oil
½ teaspoon cider vinegar (optional)
salt

1. Wash beet greens well under running cold water. Trim any tough stems.

2. In 4-quart saucepan over high heat, in hot salad oil, cook beet greens until tender, about 3 minutes, stirring occasionally.

3. Add vinegar, if desired; stir in salt to taste.

Braised Celery Bites

TIME: about 20 minutes—SERVINGS: 4

1 cup water
1 bunch celery, cut into 2-inch pieces
1 chicken-flavor bouillon cube or envelope
¼ teaspoon dry mustard
¼ teaspoon sugar
3 tablespoons butter or margarine

In 10-inch skillet over high heat, in boiling water, heat celery and next 3 ingredients to boiling. Reduce heat to medium; cover and cook 8 to 10 minutes until celery is tender-crisp. Drain celery; return to skillet. Stir in butter or margarine until melted.

Caponata

TIME: start early in day or day ahead—SERVINGS: 16

olive or salad oil
2 medium eggplants (about 1½
    pounds each), cut into bite-
    sized pieces
½ cup water
4 medium celery stalks, sliced
2 medium onions, sliced
1 6-ounce can pitted small ripe
    olives, drained
1 3- to 3½-ounce bottle capers,
    drained
3 tablespoons sugar
1 tablespoon salt
3 tablespoons red wine vinegar
¾ teaspoon oregano leaves
¼ teaspoon basil
¼ teaspoon pepper
4 medium tomatoes, cut into bite-
    sized pieces
parsley sprigs for garnish

1. In 8-quart Dutch oven over medium heat, in ½ cup hot olive oil, cook eggplant and water until eggplant is tender, about 15 minutes, stirring often; remove to large bowl; set aside.

2. In same Dutch oven over medium heat, in ¼ cup more olive oil, cook celery and onions until tender, about 10 minutes, stirring frequently.

3. Add eggplant, olives, capers, sugar, salt, vinegar, oregano, basil, and pepper; over high heat, heat to boiling. Reduce heat to low; cover and simmer 15 minutes.

4. Add tomatoes; over high heat, heat to boiling. Reduce heat to low; cover and simmer 5 minutes longer or until vegetables are tender, stirring often. Spoon mixture into large bowl. Cover; refrigerate until well chilled.

5. To serve, spoon Caponata onto platter; garnish with parsley sprigs.

Easy Country Vegetables

TIME: about 1 hour—SERVINGS: 10

salad oil
1 bunch green onions, cut into
    2-inch pieces
4 large carrots, thinly sliced
2 medium celery stalks, cut into
    ¼-inch-thick slices
salt
1 small bunch broccoli, cut into
    2" by 1" pieces
1 small head cauliflower, cut into
    flowerets
½ pound green beans, cut into
    2-inch pieces
½ cup water
3 medium potatoes (1 pound),
    unpeeled and cut into bite-
    sized chunks
3 tablespoons butter or
    margarine
2 tablespoons lemon juice
1 teaspoon prepared mustard
½ teaspoon oregano leaves
⅛ teaspoon pepper

1. In 8-quart Dutch oven over medium-high heat, in 2 tablespoons hot salad oil, cook green onions, carrots, celery, and ¼ teaspoon salt until vegetables are tender-crisp, about 10 minutes, stirring frequently. With slotted spoon, remove green-onion mixture to large bowl.

2. In same Dutch oven in 1 more tablespoon hot oil, stir broccoli, cauliflower, and green beans to coat lightly with oil; add water and ½ teaspoon salt. Cover and cook 5 to 10 minutes until vegetables are tender-crisp, stirring occasionally. With slotted spoon, remove broccoli mixture to bowl with onion mixture.

3. In same Dutch oven over medium heat, in 2 more tablespoons hot oil, add potatoes and ¼ teaspoon salt; cover Dutch oven and cook until potatoes are browned on all sides and tender, turning occasionally.

4. Return all vegetables to Dutch oven; add butter or margarine and remaining ingredients; heat through, gently tossing vegetables to coat with butter mixture.

Succotash

TIME: about 1 hour—SERVINGS: 10

4 slices bacon
6 medium potatoes (about 2 pounds), peeled and diced
1 medium green pepper, diced
1 small onion, minced
2 medium tomatoes, chopped
1 10-ounce package frozen baby lima beans
1 10-ounce package frozen whole-kernel corn
¾ cup water
2 teaspoons salt
1½ teaspoons sugar
⅛ teaspoon pepper

1. In 5-quart Dutch oven or saucepot over medium-low heat, cook bacon until browned; remove to paper towels to drain. Crumble bacon; reserve for garnish.

2. In drippings remaining in Dutch oven over medium heat, cook potatoes, green pepper, and onion until pepper and onion are tender, stirring often.

3. Add tomatoes and remaining ingredients; over high heat, heat to boiling. Reduce heat to medium-low; cover; simmer 20 minutes, stirring occasionally, until vegetables are tender and mixture thickens slightly.

4. To serve, spoon vegetable mixture into large bowl; sprinkle with reserved crumbled bacon.

Vegetable Mélange

TIME: about 30 minutes—SERVINGS: 8

4 medium celery stalks
3 medium carrots
2 medium zucchini (about 6 ounces each)
4 tablespoons butter or margarine
1 pound Chinese pea pods or 2 6-ounce packages frozen Chinese pea pods, thawed
1 teaspoon salt
1 teaspoon Worcestershire
⅛ teaspoon ground red pepper

1. Cut celery, carrots, and zucchini into matchstick-thin strips.

2. In 12-inch skillet over medium heat, in hot butter or margarine, cook celery and carrots about 5 minutes, stirring occasionally.

3. Add zucchini, pea pods, salt, Worcestershire, and ground red pepper. Continue cooking, stirring occasionally, until vegetables are tender-crisp.

Summer Vegetable Mélange

TIME: about 1 hour or start early in day—SERVINGS: 10

salad oil
3 medium onions, sliced
3 medium green peppers, cut into ½-inch strips
2 large carrots, sliced
1 garlic clove, crushed
½ pound medium mushrooms
½ pound Chinese pea pods
1 medium eggplant, cut into 3" by ½" strips
4 medium tomatoes, cut into wedges
1 tablespoon red wine vinegar
1½ teaspoons salt
½ teaspoon fennel seeds, crushed
¼ teaspoon pepper

1. In 8-quart Dutch oven over medium heat, in 2 tablespoons hot salad oil, cook onions, green peppers, carrots, and garlic until tender, about 10 minutes, stirring occasionally. With slotted spoon, remove onion mixture to medium bowl.

2. In same Dutch oven, in 2 more tablespoons hot oil, cook mushrooms and pea pods until tender, about 10 minutes, stirring occasionally. Remove mushrooms and pea pods to bowl with onion mixture.

3. In same Dutch oven, in ⅓ cup more hot oil, cook eggplant until lightly browned and tender, about 10 minutes, stirring occasionally and adding more oil if necessary.

4. Return vegetables to Dutch oven; add tomato wedges, wine vinegar, salt, crushed fennel seeds, and pepper; heat through.

5. Serve hot or cover and refrigerate to serve cold later.

Mushrooms and Green Onions in Lettuce Cups

TIME: about 20 minutes—SERVINGS: 2

2 tablespoons butter or
  margarine
¾ pound mushrooms, sliced
2 green onions, minced
⅛ teaspoon salt
⅛ teaspoon pepper
2 large lettuce leaves

1. In 2-quart saucepan over medium heat, in hot butter or margarine, cook mushrooms, green onions, salt, and pepper until mushrooms are tender, stirring occasionally.

2. On each lettuce leaf, spoon half of mushroom mixture.

Marinated Vegetables

TIME: start day ahead—SERVINGS: 14

water
1 medium bunch broccoli, cut
  into flowerets
1 medium head cauliflower, cut
  into flowerets
4 large carrots, thinly sliced
½ pint cherry tomatoes
¾ cup salad or olive oil
2 tablespoons sugar
3 tablespoons lemon juice
3 tablespoons red wine vinegar
2½ teaspoons salt
¾ teaspoon chervil
¼ teaspoon oregano leaves
¼ teaspoon ground red pepper

1. In 8-quart Dutch oven or saucepot over high heat, in 1 inch boiling water, heat broccoli, cauliflower, and carrots to boiling. Reduce heat to low; cover and simmer 10 minutes until vegetables are tender-crisp, stirring occasionally.

2. Drain vegetables; spoon into large bowl; add cherry tomatoes and remaining ingredients; mix well.

3. Cover and refrigerate at least 24 hours to blend flavors, tossing occasionally.

4. To serve, spoon vegetables onto large platter or into salad bowl.

Marinated Green Beans

TIME: about 2½ hours or start early in day—SERVINGS: 8

water
1 pound green beans
salad oil
1 small onion, thinly sliced
1 4-ounce jar pimentos
¼ cup cider vinegar
2 tablespoons sugar
1 teaspoon salt

1. In 2-quart saucepan over high heat, heat 1 inch water and green beans to boiling. Reduce heat to low; cover and simmer 5 to 10 minutes until beans are tender-crisp; drain; set aside.

2. In same saucepan over medium heat, in 1 tablespoon hot salad oil, cook onion until tender, stirring occasionally.

3. Drain pimentos, reserving 2 tablespoons liquid. Cut pimentos into thin strips; set aside.

4. In medium bowl with spoon, mix vinegar, sugar, salt, ¼ cup salad oil, and reserved pimento liquid. Add pimentos, cooked onion, and green beans; gently toss to coat with dressing.

5. Cover and refrigerate about 2 hours to blend flavors, stirring occasionally.

Plantain Chips

TIME: about 1½ hours or start day ahead—YIELD: about 4 cups

salad oil
2 unripe plantains (about 1
   pound each)
salt

1. In 2-quart saucepan over medium heat, heat about 1 inch salad oil to 400°F. on deep-fat thermometer or heat oil in deep-fat fryer set at 400°F.

2. Meanwhile, peel plantains; cut into paper-thin slices.

3. Fry plantain slices in hot oil, a few pieces at a time, until crisp, about 30 seconds. With slotted spoon, remove Plantain Chips to paper towels to drain.

4. Sprinkle Plantain Chips with salt to taste.

VEGETABLE MAIN DISHES

Harvest-Time Stuffed Vegetables

TIME: about 1¾ hours—SERVINGS: 8

1 cup regular long-grain rice
1¾ pounds ground beef
1 large onion, diced
1 medium eggplant (about 1
   pound)
2 tablespoons salad oil
4 medium tomatoes
4 small green peppers
2½ teaspoons sugar
1½ teaspoons salt
1 teaspoon oregano leaves
¼ teaspoon ground red pepper
1 32-ounce jar spaghetti sauce
2 cups water
½ 8-ounce package mozzarella
   cheese, shredded

1. Prepare rice as label directs.

2. Meanwhile, in 12-inch skillet over high heat, cook ground beef and onion until all pan juices evaporate and meat is well browned, stirring occasionally. Remove meat mixture to large bowl.

3. Cut eggplant lengthwise in half. With spoon, scoop out eggplant pulp from both halves, leaving a ¼-inch-thick shell; chop pulp. In same skillet over medium-high heat, in hot salad oil, cook chopped eggplant until lightly browned and tender, stirring occasionally. Remove eggplant to bowl with meat.

4. Cut a thin slice from stem end of each tomato; scoop out pulp, leaving a ¼-inch-thick shell; dice pulp. Cut off top of each green pepper; discard seeds. Into meat mixture in bowl, stir sugar, salt, oregano, ground red pepper, diced tomato pulp, cooked rice, and 2 cups spaghetti sauce.

5. Preheat oven to 375°F. In large open roasting pan (about 17¼" by 11½"), combine water and remaining spaghetti sauce. Fill each vegetable shell with some ground-beef mixture. If any meat mixture remains after filling vegetable shells, sprinkle the leftover into spaghetti-sauce mixture in roasting pan.

6. Arrange stuffed vegetables in roasting pan. Cover pan with foil; bake 50 to 60 minutes until vegetable shells are tender, basting frequently with sauce in roasting pan.

7. To serve, sprinkle tops of stuffed vegetables with shredded cheese.

Saucy Broccoli-Liver Bake

TIME: about 1 hour—SERVINGS: 6

1 pound beef liver
all-purpose flour
salt
butter or margarine
½ pound mushrooms, sliced
1 medium onion, diced
1½ cups milk
1 10-ounce package frozen
   chopped broccoli
1 8-ounce package pasteurized
   process cheese spread, diced
toasted English muffins or
   warmed biscuits

1. Trim any membrane from beef liver. Cut liver into ¼-inch-thick slices. On waxed paper, combine 3 tablespoons flour and ½ teaspoon salt; coat liver with flour mixture.

2. In 12-inch skillet over medium heat, in 2 tablespoons hot butter or margarine, cook liver until browned; remove to shallow 2½-quart baking dish; set aside.

3. Preheat oven to 350°F. In same skillet in 2 more tablespoons butter, cook mushrooms and onion until tender, stirring occasionally. Into mixture, stir 2 tablespoons flour and ½ teaspoon salt; cook 1 minute. Gradually stir in milk; cook, stirring, until thickened and smooth.

4. Add frozen chopped broccoli, separating broccoli with fork; stir in pasteurized process cheese spread until smooth. Pour mixture over liver in baking dish.

5. Bake 20 minutes or until liver is tender and mixture is hot. Serve over toasted English muffins or warmed biscuits.

Bacon-Potato Frittata

TIME: about 45 minutes—SERVINGS: 4

1 8-ounce package sliced bacon
2 medium potatoes, sliced (about
   ¾ pound)
4 eggs
2 medium green onions, chopped
¾ cup milk
½ teaspoon salt
⅛ teaspoon pepper
⅛ teaspoon oregano leaves

1. In 10-inch skillet over medium-low heat, cook bacon until browned; remove to paper towels to drain. Crumble bacon; set aside. Pour off all but 3 tablespoons bacon drippings from skillet.

2. Over medium heat, heat drippings in skillet until hot. Add potatoes; cover skillet and cook potatoes until tender and lightly browned on both sides, turning potatoes occasionally, about 15 minutes.

3. In small bowl, with fork or wire whisk, beat eggs and remaining ingredients until blended. Pour egg mixture into skillet over potatoes; sprinkle with crumbled bacon; cook until eggs begin to set around edge. With metal spatula, gently lift edge as it sets, tilting pan to allow uncooked portion to run under, shaking pan occasionally to keep egg mixture moving freely in pan. Reduce heat to low; cover and cook 10 minutes.

4. Serve immediately.

Vegetables and Pork Tenderloin Stir-Fry

TIME: about 30 minutes—SERVINGS: 4

1 pork loin tenderloin, whole
(about 1 pound)
3 tablespoons soy sauce
1 tablespoon cooking or dry
sherry
2 teaspoons minced, peeled
ginger root or ½ teaspoon
ground ginger
1¼ teaspoons sugar
¼ teaspoon hot pepper sauce
salad oil
2 medium red peppers, cut into
½-inch-thick strips
2 green onions, chopped
1 large bunch broccoli, cut into
bite-sized pieces
1 small garlic clove, minced
½ pound mushrooms, sliced
¼ teaspoon salt
⅓ cup water

1. With knife held in slanting position, almost parallel to the cutting surface, cut pork loin tenderloin crosswise into ⅛-inch-thick slices. In medium bowl, mix pork with next 5 ingredients.

2. In 12-inch skillet over high heat, in 3 tablespoons hot salad oil, cook red peppers, green onions, broccoli, garlic, mushrooms, and salt, stirring quickly and frequently (stir-frying) until vegetables are coated with oil. Add water and stir-fry until vegetables are tender-crisp. Spoon vegetables into bowl.

3. In same skillet over high heat, in 2 more tablespoons hot salad oil, cook pork mixture until pork loses its pink color, about 2 to 3 minutes, stirring quickly and frequently.

4. Return vegetables to skillet and stir-fry until heated through.

Sausage Ratatouille

TIME: about 1 hour—SERVINGS: 6

1¼ pounds hot or sweet Italian
sausage links
¼ cup water
3 tablespoons salad oil
2 medium green peppers, cut
into bite-sized pieces
1 medium eggplant (about 1
pound), cut into bite-sized
chunks
1 medium onion, sliced
1 28-ounce can tomatoes
2 medium zucchini, cut into bite-
sized chunks
1 teaspoon sugar
½ teaspoon salt
½ teaspoon thyme leaves
1 16- to 20-ounce can garbanzo
or white kidney beans, drained

1. In 12-inch skillet over medium heat, heat sausages and water to boiling. Cover; simmer 5 minutes. Remove cover; continue cooking, turning sausages frequently, until sausages are well browned, about 10 minutes. Remove sausages to paper towels to drain. Slice sausages into ½-inch pieces.

2. To drippings in skillet, add oil. Over medium heat, heat oil until hot; add green peppers, eggplant, and onion; cook until vegetables are browned on all sides, stirring occasionally.

3. Return sausages to skillet. Add tomatoes with their liquid, zucchini, sugar, salt, and thyme leaves; over high heat, heat to boiling. Reduce heat to low; cover and simmer 30 minutes, stirring occasionally. Stir in garbanzo beans; heat through.

Meat-and-Kasha-Filled Red Cabbage Leaves

TIME: about 1¾ hours—SERVINGS: 4

1 egg
½ cup medium kasha
(buckwheat groats)
butter or margarine
2 medium onions, chopped
1 chicken-flavor bouillon cube or
envelope
water
¾ pound ground beef
3 tablespoons catchup
1 8-ounce container sour cream
salt
pepper
1 medium head red or green
cabbage (2 pounds)
1 tablespoon cider vinegar
1 large carrot, cut into
matchstick-thin strips for
garnish
2 tablespoons all-purpose flour
⅛ teaspoon caraway seeds,
crushed
1¼ cups milk

1. In small bowl, stir egg and kasha until egg is completely absorbed by kasha; set aside.

2. In 2-quart saucepan over medium heat, in 2 tablespoons hot butter or margarine, cook onions until tender, stirring occasionally. With spoon, remove half of onion mixture to 1-quart saucepan; set aside for sauce.

3. To onion mixture in 2-quart saucepan, add kasha mixture; cook over medium heat until kasha is dry, separated, and lightly browned, about 2 minutes, stirring constantly. Add bouillon and 1 cup water; over high heat, heat to boiling. Reduce heat to low; cover and simmer 15 minutes or until kasha is tender and all liquid is absorbed.

4. Meanwhile, in 10-inch skillet over high heat, cook ground beef until all pan juices evaporate and meat is well browned, stirring occasionally. Add ½ cup water, stirring to loosen brown bits from bottom of skillet. Remove skillet from heat; stir in kasha, catchup, ¼ cup sour cream (reserve remaining sour cream for sauce), ¾ teaspoon salt, and ¼ teaspoon pepper; set aside.

5. Discard tough outer leaves from cabbage; with sharp knife, remove core. Fill 4-quart saucepan three-fourths full with water; add vinegar; heat to boiling. Place cabbage in water, cut-side up. Using 2 large spoons, gently separate leaves as outer leaves soften slightly. Remove 8 large leaves from cabbage; drain in colander. (Save remaining cabbage for use in soup or salad another day.) Trim rib of each reserved leaf very thin.

6. On center of each cabbage leaf, place about ½ cup ground-beef mixture. Fold 2 sides of cabbage leaf toward center over meat mixture, overlapping edges. From one narrow edge, roll jelly-roll fashion. In same 10-inch skillet, place filled cabbage leaves, seam-side down. Add ¾ cup water; over high heat, heat to boiling. Reduce heat to low; cover and simmer 40 minutes or until very tender.

7. While filled cabbage leaves are cooking, in small saucepan over high heat, heat ½ inch water and carrot strips to boiling. Reduce heat to medium; cook 3 to 5 minutes until carrot is tender. Drain; keep carrot warm for garnish.

8. About 10 minutes before cabbage is done, prepare sauce: In 1-quart saucepan containing cooked onion mixture, over medium heat, melt 2 tablespoons butter or margarine. Stir in flour, crushed caraway, ½ teaspoon salt, and ⅛ teaspoon pepper until blended; cook 1 minute. Gradually stir in milk; cook, stirring constantly, until slightly thickened and smooth. Stir in reserved sour cream until blended and heated through. Spoon sauce into warm deep platter; arrange stuffed-cabbage leaves in sauce. Garnish with carrot strips.

Celery-Ham Brunch

TIME: about 45 minutes—SERVINGS: 4

2 medium bunches celery
3 cups water
2 chicken-flavor bouillon cubes
  or envelopes
3 tablespoons butter or
  margarine
1 small onion, finely chopped
3 tablespoons all-purpose flour
¼ teaspoon thyme leaves
1 8-ounce can tomatoes
¾ cup milk
1 tablespoon cooking or dry
  sherry
2 4-ounce packages sliced
  cooked ham, cut into thin
  strips
1 cup frozen peas

1. Remove outer row of celery ribs; trim root ends. About 6 inches from root ends, cut tops and leaves from celery. (Use outer ribs, tops, and leaves for salad or soup another day.) Cut each celery bunch lengthwise in half.

2. In 12-inch skillet over high heat, heat water and bouillon to boiling. Add celery; heat to boiling. Reduce heat to medium; cover and cook 15 minutes or until celery is fork-tender. When celery is done, drain well, reserving ¾ cup cooking liquid. Keep celery warm.

3. In same skillet over medium heat, in hot butter or margarine, cook onion until tender. Stir in flour and thyme until blended; cook 1 minute.

4. Gradually stir in tomatoes with their liquid, milk, sherry, and reserved celery cooking liquid; cook, stirring constantly, until thickened and smooth.

5. Reserve about ½ cup ham strips. Stir frozen peas and remaining ham into sauce; cook, stirring occasionally, until peas are tender and ham is heated through.

6. To serve, spoon sauce into four deep luncheon plates; arrange celery on top of sauce. Garnish with reserved ham strips.

Dinner Salad for a Crowd

TIME: about 45 minutes—SERVINGS: 12

1 pound green beans
water
Oregano-Vinaigrette Dressing
  (right)
1 12-ounce can luncheon meat
1 pound provolone, Port du
  Salut, or Swiss cheese
1 pound sharp Cheddar cheese
2 large cucumbers
2 large tomatoes
1 medium red onion
2 medium heads iceberg lettuce
  (about 1½ pounds each)
1 7- to 8-ounce jar pimento-
  stuffed olives, drained

1. Trim ends from green beans; cut into bite-sized pieces. In 2-quart saucepan over high heat, in 1 inch boiling water, heat green beans to boiling. Reduce heat to low; cover and simmer 5 to 10 minutes until beans are tender-crisp, stirring occasionally. Drain; refrigerate.

2. Prepare Oregano-Vinaigrette Dressing.

3. Cut luncheon meat, cheeses, and cucumbers into bite-sized pieces. Thinly slice tomatoes and red onion. Cut iceberg lettuce into ½-inch chunks.

4. In large open roasting pan (about 17¼″ by 11½″), mix green beans, luncheon meat, cheeses, cucumbers, iceberg lettuce, and olives. Arrange sliced tomatoes and red onion slices on top of salad to make a pretty border. Pour dressing evenly over salad.

Oregano-Vinaigrette Dressing: In medium bowl, mix ¾ cup *salad oil, ½ cup red wine vinegar, 1 tablespoon sugar, 1 tablespoon minced parsley, 1 teaspoon oregano leaves, and 1 teaspoon salt.*

Summer Dinner Salad

TIME: about 45 minutes—SERVINGS: 8

3 medium potatoes (1 pound)
water
¾ pound liverwurst
¾ pound Fontina cheese
2 medium zucchini
3 medium kohlrabi
1 medium yellow straightneck
   squash
4 medium tomatoes
¼ pound mushrooms or 1
   4-ounce bag enoki mushrooms
1 large head red-leaf or Boston
   lettuce
1 bunch watercress
⅔ cup salad oil
⅓ cup cider vinegar
4 teaspoons prepared mustard
¾ teaspoon salt
⅛ teaspoon pepper

1. In 2-quart saucepan over medium heat, heat potatoes and enough water to cover to boiling. Reduce heat to low; cover and simmer 25 to 30 minutes until potatoes are tender; drain. Cool potatoes until easy to handle; slice.

2. Meanwhile, cut liverwurst, cheese, and zucchini into thin strips. Peel and thinly slice kohlrabi; thinly slice yellow squash. Cut each tomato into 8 wedges. Slice mushrooms. If using enoki mushrooms, rinse with running cold water and pat dry with paper towels.

3. Line chilled platter with lettuce leaves and watercress; arrange liverwurst, cheese, and vegetables on greens.

4. In small bowl, mix salad oil and remaining ingredients. Serve dressing over salad.

Deluxe Layered Chef's Salad

TIME: about 1 hour—SERVINGS: 8

4 eggs
½ 10-ounce bag spinach
½ small head iceberg lettuce
½ pound Swiss cheese
½ pound cooked ham
2 medium tomatoes
1 large green pepper
½ cup mayonnaise
¼ cup salad oil
2 tablespoons milk
2 tablespoons red wine vinegar
¾ teaspoon sugar
½ teaspoon salt
¼ teaspoon basil
packaged seasoned croutons for
   garnish

1. In 2-quart saucepan, place eggs and enough water to come 1 inch above tops of eggs; over high heat, heat to boiling. Remove saucepan from heat; cover and let eggs stand in hot water 15 minutes; drain. Carefully peel eggs under running cold water. Thinly slice hard-cooked eggs crosswise; set aside.

2. Meanwhile, coarsely shred spinach and lettuce. Cut Swiss cheese and ham into ½-inch cubes. Cut tomatoes into wedges; dice green pepper.

3. Place shredded spinach in bottom of 2½-quart glass bowl; top with cheese cubes, then with layers of lettuce, tomato, green pepper, and ham.

4. In small bowl, with fork or wire whisk, mix mayonnaise and next 6 ingredients until blended. Pour dressing over salad in bowl. Arrange egg slices on top of salad. Garnish salad with croutons.

Meat, Poultry, Fish, and Seafood

BEEF

Barbecued Beef and Vegetable Kabobs

TIME: about 2 hours or start early in day—SERVINGS: 4

1 cup regular long-grain rice
1 cup frozen peas, thawed
¼ cup mayonnaise
¼ cup milk
¼ teaspoon salt
1 pound beef for kabobs, cut into
   1-inch cubes
1 onion, quartered and separated
   into pieces
3 tablespoons soy sauce
1 tablespoon dry sherry
1 tablespoon salad oil
1 tablespoon chili sauce
¼ teaspoon ground ginger
1 medium zucchini
1 medium yellow straightneck
   squash
1 red or green pepper
½ pound medium mushrooms
¼ cup bottled Italian dressing

1. Prepare rice as label directs; refrigerate. When rice is cool, toss with next 4 ingredients. Cover and refrigerate.

2. Meanwhile, in medium bowl, mix beef for kabobs and next 6 ingredients; cover and refrigerate at least 1 hour.

3. About 1 hour before serving, prepare outdoor grill for barbecuing. Cut zucchini and squash into 1-inch chunks. Cut pepper into 1-inch pieces. On 2 skewers (each 14 inches long), alternately thread zucchini, squash, pepper, and mushrooms. On 2 more skewers, alternately thread beef and onion. Reserve marinade.

4. Place vegetable kabobs on grill over medium heat; cook 10 minutes, basting often with Italian dressing and turning skewers occasionally. Place meat kabobs on grill; cook 5 minutes or until meat is of desired doneness, basting often with marinade.

5. Serve kabobs with rice salad.

TO BROIL IN OVEN: Prepare rice salad and marinate beef as in steps 1 and 2 above. About 30 minutes before serving, preheat broiler if manufacturer directs. Cut vegetables and arrange vegetables and meat for kabobs as above but use 4 all-metal skewers. Place vegetable kabobs on rack in broiling pan; about 5 to 7 inches from source of heat (or at 450°F.), broil about 15 minutes, turning skewers and basting often with Italian dressing. Place beef kabobs on rack in same broiling pan; broil 10 minutes, turning skewers and basting often with marinade.

Barbecued Ribs

TIME: about 2½ hours—SERVINGS: 8

2 tablespoons salad oil
1 garlic clove, cut in half
4 pounds beef chuck short ribs
1 medium onion, diced
2 teaspoons chili powder
1 8-ounce can tomato sauce
1½ cups water
¼ cup cider vinegar
3 tablespoons brown sugar
1 tablespoon Worcestershire
1½ teaspoons salt
2 tablespoons chopped parsley
   for garnish

1. In 5-quart Dutch oven over medium heat, in hot salad oil, cook garlic until golden; discard garlic. In same oil in Dutch oven over medium-high heat, cook beef chuck short ribs, several pieces at a time, until well browned, removing pieces as they brown.

2. Spoon off all but 2 tablespoons drippings from Dutch oven. In drippings remaining in Dutch oven over medium heat, cook onion and chili powder until onion is tender, stirring frequently. Stir in tomato sauce, water, vinegar, brown sugar, Worcestershire, and salt. Return short ribs to Dutch oven; heat to boiling.

3. Cover Dutch oven and bake in 350°F. oven 2 hours or until short ribs are fork-tender.

4. To serve, remove ribs from Dutch oven to warm, deep serving dish. Skim off fat from sauce. Pour sauce over ribs; sprinkle with parsley.

Family Short-Ribs-and-Beans Supper

TIME: about 4 hours—SERVINGS: 8

1 16-ounce package dry pea
   (navy) beans
water
¼ pound salt pork, diced
2 pounds beef chuck short ribs,
   cut into serving pieces
1 medium onion, diced
2 teaspoons chili powder
4 teaspoons brown sugar
1 teaspoon salt
1 16-ounce bag carrots, cut into
   2-inch pieces
1 16-ounce can tomato puree
2 tablespoons cider vinegar
½ teaspoon hot pepper sauce

1. Rinse beans in running cold water and discard any stones or shriveled beans. In 8-quart Dutch oven or saucepot over high heat, heat beans and 8 cups water to boiling; cook 3 minutes. Remove Dutch oven from heat; cover and let stand 1 hour. Drain and rinse beans; set aside.

2. In same Dutch oven over medium-high heat, cook salt pork until lightly browned. With slotted spoon, remove salt pork to paper towels to drain.

3. In drippings remaining in Dutch oven, cook beef short ribs, a few pieces at a time, until browned on all sides, removing them to plate as they brown. Spoon off all but 2 tablespoons drippings in Dutch oven. In drippings, over medium heat, cook onion until tender, stirring occasionally. Add chili powder; cook 1 minute.

4. Return beans, short ribs, and salt pork to Dutch oven; add brown sugar, salt, and 6 cups water; over high heat, heat to boiling. Reduce heat to low; cover and simmer 2 hours, stirring mixture occasionally.

5. Skim off fat from liquid in Dutch oven. Stir in carrots, tomato puree, vinegar, and hot pepper sauce; over high heat, heat to boiling. Reduce heat to low; cover and simmer 45 minutes longer or until beans, meat, and carrots are tender, stirring occasionally. Serve in soup bowls.

Barbecued Steak with Sweet-Pepper Sauce

TIME: about 1¼ hours—SERVINGS: 8

1 4-ounce jar roasted sweet red
   peppers, drained and minced
¼ cup catchup
2 tablespoons soy sauce
2 teaspoons sugar
1 beef top round steak, cut 1¼
   inches thick (about 2 pounds)

1. Prepare outdoor grill for barbecuing.

2. In small bowl with fork, mix peppers, catchup, soy sauce, and sugar; set aside. Place beef top round steak on grill over medium heat; grill 20 minutes for rare or until of desired doneness, turning steak occasionally. During last 5 minutes of cooking, brush steak with pepper sauce.

TO BROIL STEAK IN OVEN: About 40 minutes before serving, preheat broiler if manufacturer directs. Meanwhile, prepare sweet-pepper sauce. Place steak on rack in broiling pan. Broil steak 20 minutes for rare or until of desired doneness; turn steak once and during last 5 minutes of cooking, brush with sauce.

New England Boiled Dinner

TIME: about 4 hours—SERVINGS: 10

1 4- to 5-pound package corned-
   beef brisket
1 garlic clove
½ teaspoon peppercorns
water
1 medium rutabaga (about 2
   pounds), cut into 2-inch
   chunks
about 10 small red potatoes
about 10 small white onions
6 medium carrots, cut into 2-inch
   pieces
1 medium head cabbage (about
   2 pounds), cut into wedges

1. Prepare corned-beef brisket as label directs, or in 8-quart Dutch oven or saucepot over high heat, heat corned beef, garlic, peppercorns, and enough water to cover meat to boiling. Reduce heat to low; cover and simmer about 3 hours or until meat is fork-tender. Remove corned beef from Dutch oven; keep warm.

2. Taste corned-beef cooking liquid; if too salty, discard some of liquid and replace with fresh water to desired salt level. Add rutabaga, potatoes, onions, and carrots; over high heat, heat to boiling. Reduce heat to low; cover and simmer 20 minutes. Add cabbage; cook 10 minutes longer or until all vegetables are tender.

3. To serve, arrange corned beef and vegetables on large warm platter.

Corned Beef and Cabbage Buns

TIME: about 45 minutes—SERVINGS: 4

2 tablespoons salad oil
2 cups sliced cabbage
1 small onion, sliced
1 carrot, sliced
1 12-ounce can corned beef,
   diced
½ cup shredded Swiss cheese
⅓ cup water
2½ teaspoons prepared mustard
1 8-ounce package refrigerated
   crescent dinner rolls
celery leaves for garnish

1. In 10-inch skillet over medium heat, in hot oil, cook cabbage, onion, and carrot until tender. Stir in corned beef, cheese, water, and mustard.

2. Preheat oven to 350°F. Separate crescent dough into 4 rectangles; press perforations together on rectangles. Spoon one-fourth of beef mixture onto center of each rectangle. Pull corners of each rectangle to center over meat mixture; twist together to seal. Bake 18 to 20 minutes until golden. Garnish with celery leaves.

Chuck Roast in Wine Sauce

TIME: about 2½ hours—SERVINGS: 10

1 cup water
1 cup cooking or dry red wine
¼ cup minced green onions
4 tablespoons butter or
  margarine
1 teaspoon brown sugar
¾ teaspoon beef-flavor instant
  bouillon
1 large carrot, minced
1 celery stalk, minced
1 beef chuck blade roast, cut 2
  inches thick (about 4 pounds)
½ teaspoon basil
¼ teaspoon pepper
salt

1. In 8-quart Dutch oven, combine water, wine, green onions, butter or margarine, brown sugar, bouillon, carrot, and celery; set aside.

2. Trim excess fat from beef chuck blade roast. Place roast in Dutch oven; sprinkle top with basil and pepper; cover and bake in 350°F. oven 1½ to 2 hours until meat is fork-tender, basting roast occasionally with liquid in Dutch oven.

3. Arrange roast on warm large platter; sprinkle roast with salt to taste. Skim off fat from sauce in Dutch oven; spoon some sauce on roast; serve remaining sauce in small bowl.

Yankee Pot Roast

TIME: about 4 hours—SERVINGS: 12

2 tablespoons salad oil
1 4- to 4½-pound beef chuck
  cross rib pot roast, boneless
2 teaspoons salt
1 teaspoon sugar
½ teaspoon pepper
½ teaspoon thyme leaves
1 bay leaf
water
8 medium potatoes, peeled and
  halved
8 medium carrots, cut into 3-inch
  pieces
1 pound small white onions
¼ cup all-purpose flour
parsley sprigs for garnish

1. In 8-quart Dutch oven over medium-high heat, in hot salad oil, cook beef chuck cross rib pot roast until well browned on all sides. Stir in salt, sugar, pepper, thyme leaves, bay leaf, and 3 cups water; heat to boiling. Reduce heat to low; cover and simmer 2¼ hours. Add potatoes, carrots, and onions; over high heat, heat to boiling. Reduce heat to medium-low; cover and cook 45 minutes or until meat and vegetables are fork-tender.

2. Remove strings from meat. Arrange meat and vegetables on warm large platter; keep warm. Skim off fat from liquid in Dutch oven; discard bay leaf.

3. In small bowl, stir flour and ½ cup water until blended; gradually stir into liquid in Dutch oven. Cook over medium heat, stirring, until gravy is thickened.

4. Serve gravy in gravy boat. Garnish platter with parsley.

Rib Roast with Yorkshire Pudding

TIME: about 3½ hours—SERVINGS: 12

1 3-rib beef rib roast, small end,
  with chine bone removed
2 slices white bread
1 cup mayonnaise
3 tablespoons minced parsley
2 tablespoons minced green
  onion
2 tablespoons prepared mustard
1 tablespoon lemon juice
½ teaspoon salt
Yorkshire Pudding (page 43)

1. In 17¼" by 11½" open roasting pan, place beef rib roast, fat-side up. Insert meat thermometer into center of roast, being careful that pointed end of thermometer does not touch bone or fat. Roast meat in 325°F. oven until thermometer reaches 140°F. for medium-rare, (about 20 minutes per pound) or until of desired doneness.

2. About 40 minutes before roast is done, prepare coating: Into small bowl, tear bread into small pieces; stir in mayonnaise, parsley, green onion, mustard, lemon juice, and salt. Remove roast from oven; evenly spread mayonnaise mixture on top of roast. Roast 25 minutes longer or until coating is golden and roast is of desired doneness.

3. When roast is done, place on warm large platter and let stand at room temperature 20 to 30 minutes for easier carving. Reserve drippings. Prepare Yorkshire Pudding.

4. To serve, cut Yorkshire Pudding into serving pieces; arrange pudding on platter with roast.

Yorkshire Pudding: In small bowl with wire whisk or fork, beat *1 cup all-purpose flour, 1 cup milk, ½ teaspoon salt,* and *2 eggs* until smooth. Spoon *2 tablespoons beef drippings* into pudding batter; pour off all but ¼ *cup beef drippings* from roasting pan. Return pan to oven; turn oven control to 450°F.; heat until very hot, about 3 to 5 minutes. Quickly pour batter onto hot drippings in pan; bake 10 minutes. Turn oven control to 350°F.; bake 20 minutes longer or until pudding is lightly browned and puffed.

Beef Tenderloin with Flavored Butters

TIME: start early in day—SERVINGS: 10

Herb, Roquefort, Wine, and
  Lemon Butters (right)
2 1½-pound beef tenderloin
  roasts (large end)
salt
pepper
parsley sprigs or holly sprigs for
  garnish

1. Prepare Herb, Roquefort, Wine, and Lemon Butters.*

2. About 40 minutes before serving, preheat boiler if manufacturer directs. Sprinkle beef tenderloin roasts lightly with salt and pepper. Place both pieces of meat on rack in broiling pan; broil 30 minutes for rare or until of desired doneness, turning meat once.

3. To serve, unmold all 4 butter molds onto a small wooden board or chilled plate. Cut meat into thick slices; arrange on warm platter; garnish with parsley sprigs. Select and spread butter on meat slices.

Herb Butter: In small bowl with mixer at low speed, beat ½ *cup butter* or margarine, softened, *2 teaspoons frozen chopped chives,* ½ *teaspoon dill weed,* and ⅛ *teaspoon salt* until well blended. Spoon mixture into a 4-ounce butter mold or small custard cup. Cover and refrigerate until well chilled, at least 1½ hours.

Roquefort Butter: In small bowl with mixer at low speed, beat ½ *cup butter* or margarine, softened, *3 ounces Roquefort* or blue cheese, crumbled, and ⅛ *teaspoon caraway seeds* until well blended. Spoon mixture into a 4-ounce butter mold or small custard cup. Cover and refrigerate until well chilled, at least 1½ hours.

Wine Butter: In small bowl with mixer at low speed, beat ½ *cup butter* or margarine, softened, *2 tablespoons dry red wine, 2 teaspoons minced parsley,* ⅛ *teaspoon cracked black pepper,* and ⅛ *teaspoon salt* until well blended. Spoon mixture into a 4-ounce butter mold or small custard cup. Cover and refrigerate until well chilled, at least 1½ hours.

Lemon Butter: From *1 medium lemon,* grate ½ teaspoon peel and squeeze 1 tablespoon lemon juice. In small bowl with mixer at low speed, beat ½ *cup butter* or margarine, softened, lemon peel, lemon juice, *2 teaspoons minced parsley,* ⅛ *teaspoon salt,* and ⅛ *teaspoon ground red pepper,* until well blended. Spoon mixture into a 4-ounce butter mold or small custard cup. Cover and refrigerate until well chilled, at least 1½ hours.

*Refrigerate leftover butters to use within 1 week on broiled steaks, hamburgers, fish fillets, or broiler-fryers.

Beef-and-Potato Pie

TIME: about 3 hours—SERVINGS: 8

salad oil
2 pounds beef for stew, cut into
    1-inch chunks
½ pound mushrooms, each cut in
    half
1 pound small white onions
3 medium carrots, sliced
3 medium celery stalks, sliced
2½ cups water
¾ teaspoon thyme leaves
½ teaspoon salt
¼ teaspoon pepper
1 beef-flavor bouillon cube or
    envelope
instant mashed potato flakes for
    8 servings
piecrust mix for one 9-inch
    piecrust
1 egg

1. In 5-quart Dutch oven over medium-high heat, in 2 tablespoons hot salad oil, cook beef for stew until well browned on all sides. With slotted spoon, remove meat to plate; set aside. In drippings remaining in Dutch oven (add 1 tablespoon salad oil if necessary), over medium heat, cook mushrooms 5 minutes; with slotted spoon, remove mushrooms to medium bowl; set aside.

2. In same Dutch oven over medium heat, in 2 more tablespoons hot salad oil, cook onions, carrots, and celery until vegetables are browned, stirring frequently. Stir in water, thyme, salt, pepper, and bouillon. Return meat to Dutch oven; over high heat; heat to boiling. Reduce heat to low; cover and simmer 1½ hours or until meat is fork-tender, stirring occasionally.

3. When meat is done, prepare mashed potatoes as label directs. Spoon mashed potatoes evenly into 13" by 9" baking dish.

4. Skim off fat from liquid in Dutch oven; stir in mushrooms. Spoon meat mixture evenly over potatoes in baking dish.

5. Preheat oven to 400°F. Prepare piecrust mix as label directs. On lightly floured surface with floured rolling pin, roll dough into 15" by 11" rectangle. Gently place pastry over meat mixture. With kitchen shears, trim pastry edge, leaving 1-inch overhang. Fold overhang under and press gently all around baking dish rim to make a decorative edge. With knife, score piecrust deeply to mark 8 rectangular servings. If you like, with hands, roll pastry trimmings into thin ropes to decorate rectangles.

6. In cup with fork, beat egg. With pastry brush, brush top of pie with egg. Bake pie 25 minutes or until crust is golden and mixture is heated through.

Deviled Beef Stew

TIME: about 2 hours—SERVINGS: 8

2 pounds beef for stew, cut into
    1½-inch chunks
all-purpose flour
¼ cup salad oil
2 medium celery stalks, sliced
1 medium onion, sliced
1½ cups water
1 cup tomato juice
2 tablespoons prepared mustard
1 tablespoon sugar
1 teaspoon salt
1 16-ounce bag carrots, cut into
    1-inch pieces
1 15½- or 20-ounce can
    garbanzo beans, drained

1. On waxed paper, coat beef with 2 tablespoons flour. In 12-inch skillet over medium-high heat, in hot salad oil, cook beef, several pieces at a time, until well browned, removing pieces as they brown to deep 3-quart casserole.

2. Into drippings in skillet (add salad oil if necessary), stir 2 tablespoons flour; cook, stirring constantly, until flour is browned. Add celery and onion; cook over medium heat until vegetables are tender, stirring occasionally. Stir in water, tomato juice, mustard, sugar, and salt; over high heat, heat to boiling.

3. Pour sauce over beef in casserole; add carrots. Bake casserole, covered, in 350°F. oven 1½ hours, stirring occasionally.

4. Skim off fat from liquid in casserole. Add garbanzo beans; cover and bake 10 minutes longer or until beans are heated through and meat and vegetables are fork-tender.

"Hot" Stir-Fried Beef

TIME: about 1 hour—SERVINGS: 6

1 1½-pound beef flank steak or top round steak
1 bunch green onions, cut into 3-inch pieces
3 tablespoons soy sauce
3 tablespoons catchup
2 tablespoons cooking or dry sherry
1 tablespoon cornstarch
1 tablespoon minced, peeled ginger root or 1 teaspoon ground ginger
½ teaspoon ground red pepper
4 medium carrots
4 medium celery stalks
salad oil
½ teaspoon salt

1. With sharp knife, cut beef flank steak lengthwise in half. With knife held in slanting position, almost parallel to the cutting surface, slice across width of each half into ⅛-inch-thick slices; cut slices into ⅛-inch strips.

2. In medium bowl, mix meat strips, green onions, soy sauce, catchup, sherry, cornstarch, ginger, and ground red pepper; set aside. With knife, cut carrots and celery into 3-inch-long matchstick-thin strips.

3. In 5-quart Dutch oven or 10-inch skillet over medium-high heat, in 3 tablespoons hot salad oil, cook carrots, celery, and salt, stirring quickly and frequently (stir-frying), until vegetables are tender-crisp, about 3 minutes. Spoon vegetables into medium bowl.

4. In same Dutch oven over high heat, in ¼ cup more hot salad oil, stir-fry meat mixture about 3 minutes or until meat loses its pink color and is tender, stirring frequently. Remove Dutch oven from heat; stir in vegetables. Spoon meat mixture onto warm large platter.

Beef Scallops with Fresh Tomato Sauce

TIME: about 45 minutes—SERVINGS: 8

2 1-pound beef top round steaks, each cut about ¼ inch thick
water
5 medium tomatoes
¼ cup salad oil
2 tablespoons chopped green onions
1 tablespoon sugar
1½ teaspoons salt
1 teaspoon basil
1 tablespoon cornstarch

1. On cutting board with meat mallet or dull edge of French knife, pound each beef top round steak to ⅛-inch thickness. Cut steaks into about 6″ by 3″ pieces.

2. In 3-quart saucepan over high heat, heat 3 inches water to boiling; add tomatoes; cook 30 seconds. With slotted spoon, remove tomatoes to large bowl of cold water; remove from water and slip off skins; cut out stem end. Chop 3 tomatoes; slice remaining 2 tomatoes; set aside.

3. In 12-inch skillet over medium-high heat, in hot salad oil, cook steak, a few pieces at a time, until browned on both sides, with pancake turner, removing pieces to warm platter as they brown; keep steaks warm.

4. Reduce heat to medium. To same skillet, add chopped tomatoes, green onions, sugar, salt, and basil. In cup with spoon, mix cornstarch and ½ cup water until smooth; gradually stir cornstarch mixture into tomato mixture, and cook, stirring constantly, until mixture thickens and boils; cook 1 minute. Add sliced tomatoes; heat through. Gently spoon tomato mixture over and around steaks.

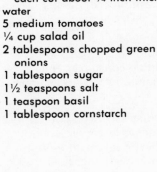

Beefsteak Pie with Whole-Wheat Crust

TIME: about 2½ hours—SERVINGS: 6

1 1½-pound beef chuck shoulder
    steak, boneless
salad oil
1 pound mushrooms, each cut in
    half
1 pound small white onions
½ cup catchup
1 tablespoon Worcestershire
2 teaspoons brown sugar
½ teaspoon basil
¼ teaspoon pepper
water
salt
½ cup whole-wheat flour
all-purpose flour
⅓ cup shortening
1 10-ounce package frozen
    broccoli spears

1. Trim excess fat from beef chuck shoulder steak; cut steak into 1-inch chunks; set aside.

2. In 12-inch skillet over medium heat, in 2 tablespoons hot salad oil, cook mushrooms until browned, stirring occasionally. Remove mushrooms to bowl.

3. In same skillet over medium heat, in 3 more tablespoons hot salad oil, cook onions until browned, stirring occasionally. Remove onions to bowl with mushrooms; set aside.

4. In drippings remaining in skillet over high heat, cook beef chunks until well browned on all sides. Return mushrooms and onions to skillet. Stir in catchup, Worcestershire, brown sugar, basil, pepper, 2 cups water, and 1 teaspoon salt; over high heat, heat to boiling, stirring to loosen brown bits from bottom of skillet. Reduce heat to low; cover and simmer 1 hour or until meat and vegetables are fork-tender.

5. Prepare piecrust: In medium bowl with fork, mix whole-wheat flour, ½ cup all-purpose flour, and ½ teaspoon salt. With pastry blender or 2 knives used scissor-fashion, cut shortening into flour until mixture resembles coarse crumbs. Sprinkle 3 tablespoons water, a tablespoon at a time, into flour mixture, mixing lightly after each addition until pastry is just moist enough to hold together. Shape pastry into ball.

6. Skim off fat from liquid in skillet. Cut frozen broccoli spears crosswise in half; add to simmering liquid in skillet, separating spears with fork.

7. In cup, mix 1 tablespoon all-purpose flour and 2 tablespoons water. Stir into liquid in skillet and cook, stirring constantly, until mixture is slightly thickened. Spoon beef mixture into deep 2½-quart casserole.

8. Preheat oven to 400°F. On lightly floured surface with floured rolling pin, roll pastry into a circle about 2 inches larger all around than top of casserole. Place pastry loosely over beef mixture. With kitchen shears trim pastry edge, leaving 1-inch overhang. Fold overhang under and press gently all around casserole rim to make a stand-up edge. With tip of knife, cut several slits in pastry top. Bake 25 minutes or until crust is golden and mixture is heated through.

Saucy Steak and Peppers

TIME: about 2 hours—SERVINGS: 8

3 tablespoons salad oil
1 beef top round steak, cut 1
    inch thick (about 2 pounds)
1 tablespoon all-purpose flour
2 medium celery stalks, thinly
    sliced

1. In 12-inch skillet over medium-high heat, in hot salad oil, cook beef top round steak until well browned on both sides. Remove steak to 12″ by 8″ baking dish.

2. Into hot drippings in skillet, stir flour; cook, stirring constantly, until flour is dark brown. Add celery and onion; cook over medium

1 medium onion, thinly sliced
1 cup water
½ teaspoon salt
⅛ teaspoon ground red pepper
2 medium green peppers, cut
    into bite-sized pieces

heat until vegetables are tender, stirring occasionally. Stir in water, salt, and ground red pepper; over high heat, heat to boiling.

3. Pour sauce over steak in baking dish. Cover baking dish with foil; bake in 350°F. oven 1¼ hours. Remove foil from baking dish; add green peppers to steak mixture. Bake, uncovered, about 15 minutes longer or until steak is fork-tender, occasionally basting steak with sauce in baking dish. Skim off fat from sauce.

Stuffed Beef Roll

TIME: about 2 hours—SERVINGS: 10

1 beef top round steak, cut 1
    inch thick (about 1¼ pounds)
½ pound ground beef or veal
1 egg
1 cup fresh bread crumbs (2
    slices white bread)
2 tablespoons chopped parsley
1 tablespoon grated onion
salt
1 4-ounce package sliced salami
½ 8-ounce package mozzarella
    cheese, cut into ¼-inch-thick
    strips
2 hard-cooked eggs, each cut
    lengthwise into 4 wedges
½ cup frozen peas
2 tablespoons olive or salad oil
2 medium carrots, sliced
1 medium onion, sliced
1 16-ounce can tomatoes
½ cup cooking or dry white wine
½ teaspoon basil

1. Butterfly beef top round steak: Holding knife parallel to work surface and starting from a long side of steak, cut steak horizontally almost but not all the way through; spread steak open to form 1 large piece. With meat mallet or dull edge of French knife, pound steak to about ¼-inch thickness.

2. In medium bowl, mix ground beef, egg, bread crumbs, parsley, grated onion, and ½ teaspoon salt. Spread ground-beef mixture over steak.

3. Place salami slices along center in lengthwise row over ground-beef mixture, overlapping slices if necessary. Place cheese strips along one side of salami; place egg wedges along other side of salami; sprinkle with peas. Starting at a long side, roll steak, jelly-roll fashion. With string, tie roll crosswise in several places.

4. In 8-quart Dutch oven over medium-high heat, in hot olive or salad oil, cook beef roll until browned on all sides. Reduce heat to medium; add carrots and onion. Cook until vegetables are lightly browned and tender, stirring occasionally. Stir in tomatoes with their liquid, wine, basil, and ¾ teaspoon salt, stirring to break up tomatoes; over high heat, heat to boiling. Reduce heat to low; cover; simmer 1 hour or until meat is tender, stirring often.

5. To serve, arrange beef roll in deep platter; discard strings; from Dutch oven spoon sauce over roll.

Steaks with Mustard Butter

TIME: about 15 minutes—SERVINGS: 2

butter or margarine
2 beef top loin or rib eye steaks,
    each cut about ¾ inch thick
1½ teaspoons lemon juice
1½ teaspoons prepared mustard
salt
pepper

1. In 12-inch skillet over medium-high heat, in 1 tablespoon hot butter or margarine, cook beef top loin steaks until browned on both sides, about 8 minutes for rare or until of desired doneness.

2. Meanwhile, in cup, mix lemon juice, mustard, and 3 tablespoons softened butter or margarine.

3. When steaks are done, sprinkle with salt and pepper to taste and top with mustard butter.

47

Chuck Steak Paisano

TIME: about 1¼ hours—SERVINGS: 5

2 tablespoons salad oil
¾ pound beef chuck shoulder
  steak, boneless
1 medium onion, diced
1 medium green pepper, thinly
  sliced
1 16-ounce can tomatoes
2 tablespoons sweet pickle relish
½ teaspoon basil
¼ teaspoon salt
1 16- to 20-ounce can white
  kidney beans (cannellini),
  drained

1. In 10-inch skillet over medium-high heat, in hot salad oil, cook beef chuck shoulder steak until well browned on both sides. Remove steak to plate.

2. In drippings remaining in skillet over medium heat, cook onion and green pepper until tender, stirring occasionally. Return steak to skillet; stir in tomatoes with their liquid and next 3 ingredients; over high heat, heat to boiling. Reduce heat to low; cover and simmer 45 minutes or until steak is tender. Stir in white kidney beans; heat through.

Braised Steak, Ranch Style

TIME: about 1¾ hours—SERVINGS: 6

2 tablespoons salad oil
1 beef chuck arm steak, cut ½
  inch thick (about 1½ pounds)
1 garlic clove, crushed
2 cups water
½ cup chili sauce
1 teaspoon sugar
¼ teaspoon salt
1 beef-flavor bouillon cube or
  envelope
1 pound small white onions
2 10-ounce packages frozen
  Fordhook lima beans

1. In 12-inch skillet over medium-high heat, in hot salad oil, cook beef chuck arm steak until well browned on both sides. Add garlic; cook over medium heat until golden. Stir in water, chili sauce, sugar, salt, and bouillon; over high heat, heat to boiling. Reduce heat to low; cover and simmer 45 minutes, turning steak occasionally. Skim off fat from liquid in skillet.

2. Add onions and frozen lima beans; over high heat, heat to boiling. Reduce heat to low; cover and simmer 40 minutes longer or until meat and vegetables are tender, stirring occasionally.

Sherried Steak Dinner

TIME: about 30 minutes—SERVINGS: 4

butter or margarine
2 16-ounce cans whole carrots,
  drained
1 tablespoon brown sugar
4 beef cubed steaks (about 1
  pound)
3 tablespoons minced green
  onions
⅓ cup cooking or dry sherry
¼ teaspoon salt
⅛ teaspoon pepper
1 tablespoon chopped parsley

1. In 2-quart saucepan over medium heat, melt 1 tablespoon butter or margarine; add carrots and brown sugar; heat through, stirring occasionally; keep warm.

2. If beef cubed steaks are large, cut each in half. In 12-inch skillet over medium-high heat, in 2 tablespoons hot butter or margarine, cook 2 or 3 pieces of steak at a time, until browned on both sides and tender, about 5 minutes. Remove steaks to dinner plates; keep warm.

3. In drippings remaining in skillet over medium heat, in 2 more tablespoons hot butter or margarine, cook green onions until tender, stirring occasionally. Stir in sherry, salt, and pepper; cook until mixture boils, stirring to loosen brown bits from skillet.

4. Pour sauce over steaks. Toss carrots with chopped parsley. Serve carrots with steaks.

Celebration Filets Mignons

TIME: about 45 minutes—SERVINGS: 4

¼ pound medium mushrooms
1 large or 2 medium tomatoes
butter or margarine
1 large onion, cut into ¾-inch-
   thick slices
4 beef loin tenderloin steaks,
   each cut 1 inch thick
½ cup water
2 tablespoons prepared mustard
4 teaspoons capers, drained
watercress sprigs for garnish

1. If desired, flute mushrooms; set aside.

2. Cut 4 thick center slices from tomatoes; reserve any leftover tomatoes to use in salad another day. In 10-inch skillet over medium heat, in 1 teaspoon hot butter or margarine, cook tomato slices until heated through. Remove to warm large platter.

3. Meanwhile, in 12-inch skillet over medium heat, in 2 tablespoons hot butter or margarine, cook onion until tender, stirring occasionally. Remove to bowl. In drippings remaining in skillet over medium-high heat, cook mushrooms and beef loin tenderloin steaks about 5 minutes for medium or until of desired doneness, turning steaks once. Remove steaks and mushrooms to platter, placing one steak on each tomato slice; keep warm.

4. Into drippings remaining in skillet, stir water, mustard, and capers; over medium heat, cook until mixture boils and thickens slightly, stirring constantly. Return onions to skillet; heat through.

5. Pour sauce over and around steaks. Garnish platter with watercress sprigs.

Meatballs Stroganoff

TIME: about 1 hour—SERVINGS: 6

1½ pounds ground beef
1 egg
¾ cup dried bread crumbs
1 tablespoon grated onion
¼ teaspoon pepper
salt
2 tablespoons salad oil
½ pound mushrooms, sliced
1½ cups water
2 tablespoons all-purpose flour
¼ cup cooking or dry sherry
½ teaspoon paprika
1 cup sour cream
1 tablespoon chopped parsley for
   garnish

1. In large bowl, mix ground beef, egg, bread crumbs, onion, pepper, and 1 teaspoon salt. Shape beef mixture into 1-inch meatballs.

2. In 12-inch skillet over medium-high heat, in hot salad oil, cook meatballs, half at a time, until well browned on all sides, removing meatballs to bowl as they brown. Pour off all but 2 tablespoons drippings from skillet.

3. In drippings remaining in skillet over medium heat, cook mushrooms until tender, about 5 minutes.

4. In small bowl, blend water with flour. Return meatballs to skillet; stir in flour mixture, sherry, paprika, and ½ teaspoon salt; over high heat, heat to boiling. Reduce heat to low; cover and simmer 10 minutes, stirring occasionally. Stir in sour cream; heat through. (Do not boil, or mixture may curdle.)

5. To serve, garnish meatballs with parsley.

Danish Meatballs

TIME: about 35 minutes—SERVINGS: 6

1 pound ground beef
½ pound ground pork
½ cup dried bread crumbs
1 tablespoon grated onion
1 egg
salt
2 tablespoons butter or
    margarine
2 tablespoons all-purpose flour
¼ teaspoon pepper
1 cup milk
1 cup water

1. In large bowl, mix ground beef, ground pork, bread crumbs, onion, egg, and 1 teaspoon salt. Shape mixture into 1½-inch meatballs.

2. In 10-inch skillet over medium-high heat, in hot butter or margarine, cook meatballs until browned on all sides, removing meatballs to bowl as they brown. Pour off all but 2 tablespoons drippings from skillet.

3. Into drippings in skillet over medium heat, stir flour, pepper, and 1 teaspoon salt; cook 1 minute. Gradually stir in milk and water; cook until thickened, stirring. Return meatballs to skillet; over high heat, heat to boiling. Reduce heat to low; cover; simmer 10 minutes.

Milan-Style Meatballs

TIME: about 1 hour—SERVINGS: 6

1½ pounds ground meat for
    meat loaf (ground beef, pork,
    and/or veal)
¾ cup dried bread crumbs
¼ cup water
⅛ teaspoon pepper
1 egg
salt
2 tablespoons salad oil
1 medium onion, diced
1 medium carrot, diced
1 medium celery stalk, diced
1 16-ounce can tomatoes
¼ cup cooking or dry white wine
½ teaspoon basil
1 tablespoon minced parsley
2 teaspoons grated lemon peel

1. In large bowl, mix ground meat, bread crumbs, water, pepper, egg, and 1 teaspoon salt. Shape meat mixture into 6 large meatballs.

2. In 10-inch skillet over medium-high heat, in hot salad oil, cook meatballs until browned on all sides, removing meatballs to plate as they brown. In drippings remaining in skillet over medium heat, cook onion, carrot, and celery until lightly browned and tender, stirring occasionally.

3. Return meatballs to skillet. Stir in tomatoes with their liquid, white wine, basil, and ¾ teaspoon salt, stirring to break up tomatoes; over high heat, heat to boiling. Reduce heat to low; cover and simmer 30 minutes, stirring occasionally.

4. When meatballs are done, skim off fat from liquid in skillet. Spoon meatballs with their sauce into warm deep platter. Sprinkle with parsley and lemon peel.

Hearty Italian-Style Meatballs

TIME: about 1 hour—SERVINGS: 6

salad oil
1 small onion, minced
1 small green pepper, minced
1 pound lean ground beef
1 cup wheat germ
¼ cup water
½ teaspoon salt
¼ teaspoon pepper
1 16-ounce jar Italian cooking
    sauce
1 20-ounce bag frozen Italian
    green beans

1. In 10-inch skillet over medium heat, in 2 tablespoons hot salad oil, cook onion and green pepper until tender, stirring occasionally. In large bowl, mix onion mixture, ground beef, wheat germ, water, salt, and pepper. Shape beef mixture into 12 meatballs.

2. In same skillet over medium-high heat, in 2 more tablespoons hot salad oil, cook meatballs, half at a time, until well browned on all sides, removing meatballs to large bowl as they brown. Pour off drippings from skillet. Return meatballs to skillet; add Italian cooking sauce; heat to boiling. Reduce heat to low; cover and simmer 15 minutes, stirring occasionally.

3. Meanwhile, prepare Italian green beans as label directs.

4. Serve beans with meatballs.

Swedish Meatballs

TIME: about 1¼ hours—SERVINGS: 12

butter or margarine
1 medium onion, minced
3 pounds ground beef
2 cups fresh bread crumbs
⅛ teaspoon ground mace
2 eggs
2 cups half-and-half
salt
¼ cup all-purpose flour
1 teaspoon sugar
⅛ teaspoon pepper
1 cup water
chopped parsley for garnish

1. In 12-inch skillet over medium heat, in 2 tablespoons hot butter or margarine, cook onion until tender, stirring occasionally.

2. In large bowl, mix onion, ground beef, bread crumbs, mace, eggs, ¾ cup half-and-half, and 2 teaspoons salt. Shape beef mixture into 1-inch meatballs.

3. In same skillet over medium-high heat, in 2 more tablespoons hot butter or margarine, cook meatballs, one-fourth at a time, until browned on all sides, removing meatballs to bowl as they brown and adding more butter or margarine if necessary.

4. Into drippings in skillet over medium heat, stir flour, sugar, pepper, and ½ teaspoon salt until blended. Gradually stir in water and remaining 1¼ cups half-and-half, stirring to loosen brown bits from bottom of skillet; cook, stirring constantly, until mixture is thickened and boils. Return meatballs to skillet; simmer, covered, about 15 minutes to blend flavors, stirring occasionally.

5. Spoon meatballs into chafing dish. Sprinkle with chopped parsley.

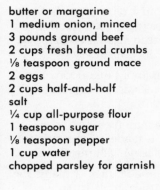

Pepper Burgers

TIME: about 30 minutes—SERVINGS: 4

Sautéed Escarole (right)
2 slices white bread
3 tablespoons minced parsley
2 tablespoons butter or margarine, softened
1 teaspoon cracked pepper
1 pound ground beef
1 tablespoon Worcestershire

1. Prepare Sautéed Escarole; keep warm.

2. Meanwhile, preheat broiler if manufacturer directs. Prepare burger topping: Into small bowl, tear bread into very small pieces. Add parsley, butter or margarine, and pepper; with hand, mix until well blended; set aside.

3. In medium bowl, mix ground beef and Worcestershire. Shape beef mixture into four ½-inch-thick round patties. Place patties on rack in broiling pan; broil 3 minutes on each side for medium-rare or until of desired doneness.

4. Remove broiling pan from oven; spoon topping mixture on patties. Broil 1 minute longer or until topping is lightly browned.

5. To serve, spoon escarole onto 4 dinner plates; arrange patties on escarole.

Sautéed Escarole: Cut *1 large head escarole* (about 1¾ pounds) into bite-sized pieces. Thinly slice *1 small onion.* In 5-quart Dutch oven over high heat, in *3 tablespoons hot salad oil,* cook escarole and onion, stirring constantly, until well coated with oil. Add ¾ *teaspoon salt* and ¼ *teaspoon sugar;* reduce heat to medium; continue cooking about 3 minutes or until vegetables are tender, stirring frequently.

Curried Meatballs with Pasta

TIME: about 45 minutes—SERVINGS: 6

salad oil
1 medium onion, minced
1 medium celery stalk, minced
¾ pound ground pork or beef
½ cup fresh bread crumbs (1
  slice white bread)
2 tablespoons water
1 egg
salt
1 medium bunch broccoli, cut
  into 2" by ½" pieces
2 tablespoons butter or
  margarine
2 tablespoons all-purpose flour
1 teaspoon curry powder
2½ cups milk
½ 16-ounce package bow-tie
  macaroni

1. In 2-quart saucepan over medium heat, in 1 tablespoon hot salad oil, cook onion and celery until tender, stirring occasionally. Remove saucepan from heat; stir in ground meat, bread crumbs, water, egg, and ½ teaspoon salt. Shape mixture into 1-inch meatballs.

2. In 10-inch skillet over medium-high heat, in 2 tablespoons hot salad oil, cook meatballs until browned on all sides, removing meatballs to medium bowl as they brown.

3. In drippings remaining in skillet over medium-high heat, cook broccoli and ½ teaspoon salt until broccoli is tender-crisp, stirring quickly and frequently. Remove broccoli to bowl with meatballs.

4. In 2-quart saucepan over medium heat, melt butter or margarine; stir in flour, curry powder, and ½ teaspoon salt; cook 1 minute. Gradually stir in milk; cook, stirring constantly, until mixture is thickened and smooth. Return meatballs and broccoli to saucepan; heat through.

5. Meanwhile, prepare bow-tie macaroni as label directs; drain.

6. To serve, toss bow-tie macaroni with meatball mixture.

Hamburgers Roquefort Style

TIME: about 20 minutes—SERVINGS: 4

1 pound ground beef
¼ pound Roquefort or blue
  cheese, crumbled
2 tablespoons prepared mustard
1 tablespoon butter or margarine
½ teaspoon salt
¼ teaspoon pepper

1. Shape ground beef into four ½-inch-thick patties. Heat 10-inch skillet over medium-high heat until hot; add patties, and cook about 4 minutes for medium or until of desired doneness, turning patties once.

2. Meanwhile, in small bowl, mix Roquefort cheese, mustard, butter, salt, and pepper until smooth.

3. Top each patty in skillet with one-fourth Roquefort-cheese mixture. Cover skillet and cook over medium-low heat until cheese mixture is melted.

Beef Patties à la Dijonnaise

TIME: about 30 minutes—SERVINGS: 4

1 pound ground beef
½ teaspoon chervil
salt
3 tablespoons butter or
  margarine
½ pound medium mushrooms,
  sliced
2 medium green onions, sliced
¼ cup sauterne wine
3 tablespoons water
2 tablespoons Dijon-style
  mustard

1. In medium bowl, mix ground beef with chervil and ½ teaspoon salt. Shape beef mixture into four 4-inch round patties.

2. Over high heat, heat 10-inch skillet until hot. Add patties and cook until browned on both sides, about 5 minutes for medium-rare, turning patties once. Remove patties to platter.

3. In drippings in skillet (you should have 1 tablespoon drippings), over medium heat, melt butter or margarine; cook mushrooms and green onions until tender. Stir in sauterne, water, mustard and ¼ teaspoon salt. Return patties and meat juice in platter to skillet; heat through, stirring frequently.

Hamburgers Holstein

TIME: about 40 minutes—SERVINGS: 4

1 pound ground beef
½ teaspoon seasoned salt
3 tablespoons butter or
   margarine
4 eggs
seasoned pepper
4 English muffins
1 2-ounce can anchovy fillets,
   drained
2 green onions, cut into 3-inch
   pieces

1. Preheat broiler if manufacturer directs. Shape ground beef into four patties, each about 4 inches in diameter. Sprinkle patties with seasoned salt. In 12-inch skillet over high heat, cook patties 5 minutes for medium-rare or until of desired doneness, turning once; remove patties from skillet; keep warm.

2. Pour off any drippings remaining in skillet; wipe skillet clean. In same skillet over medium heat, melt butter or margarine. One at a time, break eggs into saucer, then slip into skillet, cooking 2 eggs at a time. Reduce heat to low; cook eggs to desired firmness; sprinkle eggs with seasoned pepper; keep warm.

3. Meanwhile, place muffin halves, split-side up, on rack in broiling pan; broil 2 to 3 minutes until golden.

4. For each serving, on dinner plate, place a patty on 2 muffin halves; top with an egg. Garnish each egg-topped patty with a few anchovy fillets and a few pieces of green onion.

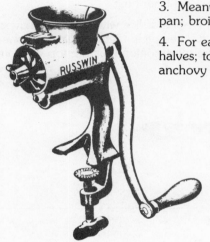

Springtime Burgers in Lettuce Cups

TIME: about 45 minutes—SERVINGS: 4

Radish-Pickle Relish (right)
⅓ cup mayonnaise
3 tablespoons catchup
1 tablespoon prepared mustard
⅛ teaspoon sugar
1 pound ground beef
1 teaspoon salt
2 tablespoons butter or
   margarine
lettuce leaves
1 small tomato, sliced
1 medium cucumber, thinly
   sliced

1. Prepare Radish-Pickle Relish; set aside.

2. In small bowl with wire whisk or fork, mix mayonnaise, catchup, mustard, and sugar. In medium bowl, mix ground beef, salt, and 2 tablespoons mayonnaise mixture. Shape beef mixture into four ¾-inch-thick round patties.

3. In 10-inch skillet over high heat, in hot butter or margarine, cook patties 5 minutes for medium-rare or until of desired doneness, turning patties once.

4. To serve, line 4 dinner plates with lettuce leaves. Spoon half of relish on lettuce; place a patty on top of each and top with 1 or 2 tomato slices. Spoon 2 tablespoons mayonnaise mixture on each and sprinkle with remaining relish.

5. Garnish servings with cucumber slices.

Radish-Pickle Relish: In small bowl with fork, mix *½ cup minced radishes, ⅓ cup minced dill pickles,* and *1 hard-cooked egg,* minced.

Deluxe Open-Faced Cheeseburgers

TIME: about 45 minutes—SERVINGS: 4

1 small avocado
3 tablespoons mayonnaise
2 teaspoons lemon juice
salt
2 tablespoons salad oil
1 medium onion, sliced
1 small green pepper, cut into thin rings
1 pound ground beef
½ teaspoon chili powder
2 ounces Monterey Jack cheese, shredded (½ cup)
4 slices whole-wheat bread, toasted
4 lettuce leaves
1 small tomato, sliced
2 tablespoons bottled taco sauce

1. In small bowl, with back of spoon, mash avocado. Stir in mayonnaise, lemon juice, and ½ teaspoon salt; set aside.

2. In 12-inch skillet over medium heat, in hot salad oil, cook onion and green pepper until tender, stirring occasionally. Remove onion mixture to another small bowl; set aside.

3. In medium bowl, mix ground beef with chili powder and ¾ teaspoon salt. Shape beef mixture into 4 patties, each about 4 inches in diameter. In same skillet over high heat, cook patties 5 minutes for medium-rare or until of desired doneness, turning once. Top each patty with some cheese; cover skillet and cook until cheese melts, about 2 minutes. Remove skillet from heat.

4. For each serving, spread a bread slice with one-fourth avocado mixture; top with meat patty, then with a lettuce leaf, and one-fourth tomato slices; spoon on one-fourth onion mixture; top with one-fourth taco sauce.

Meat-and-Potato Loaf

TIME: about 2 hours—SERVINGS: 6

3 medium potatoes (about 1 pound)
water
1 tablespoon salad oil
1 medium green pepper, diced
1½ pounds ground beef
2 cups fresh bread crumbs (4 slices white bread)
½ teaspoon basil
1 egg
salt
pepper
3 tablespoons milk
4 tablespoons butter or margarine
2 large onions, sliced
2 ounces Swiss cheese, shredded (½ cup)

1. In 2-quart saucepan over high heat, heat unpeeled potatoes and enough water to cover to boiling. Reduce heat to low; cover and simmer 25 to 30 minutes until potatoes are fork-tender.

2. Meanwhile, in 12-inch skillet over medium heat, in hot salad oil, cook green pepper until tender, stirring occasionally. Remove skillet from heat; stir in ground beef, bread crumbs, basil, egg, ¼ cup water, 1½ teaspoons salt, and ¼ teaspoon pepper. In deep 1½-quart oven-safe bowl, press ground-beef mixture to line inside of bowl, leaving a 1-inch shell.

3. Peel potatoes. In medium bowl, mash potatoes until smooth; stir in milk and ½ teaspoon salt. Spoon potatoes into center of ground-beef mixture, pressing firmly. Bake in 350°F. oven 1 hour and 15 minutes.

4. About 15 minutes before loaf is done, in 10-inch skillet over medium-high heat, in hot butter or margarine, cook onions and ¼ teaspoon salt until onions are tender, stirring occasionally.

5. To serve, carefully pour off fat from bowl. Invert bowl onto oven-safe platter. Sprinkle loaf with shredded Swiss cheese. Bake loaf 3 minutes or until cheese is melted.

6. Garnish platter with onions.

Picadillo "Salad"

TIME: about 45 minutes—SERVINGS: 4

¼ cup slivered blanched
  almonds
1 pound ground beef or pork
1 medium onion, diced
1 medium green pepper, diced
1 8-ounce can tomato sauce
½ cup dark seedless raisins
¼ cup water
¼ cup salad olives or chopped
  pimento-stuffed olives
¾ teaspoon salt
¼ teaspoon ground cumin
⅛ teaspoon pepper
½ 10-ounce bag spinach,
  shredded

1. In 10-inch skillet over medium heat, toast almonds until lightly browned, stirring frequently. Remove almonds to plate; set aside.

2. In same skillet over high heat, cook ground meat, onion, and green pepper until all pan juices evaporate and meat is well browned, stirring frequently. Stir in tomato sauce and remaining ingredients except spinach; heat to boiling. Reduce heat to low; cover; simmer 10 minutes to blend flavors.

3. Serve meat mixture hot or cold on shredded spinach. Sprinkle with toasted almonds

Salisbury Steaks with Onions and Peppers

TIME: about 35 minutes—SERVINGS: 4

2 tablespoons butter or
  margarine
4 medium onions, sliced
2 medium green peppers, cut
  into 2″ by ½″ strips
1 pound ground beef
1 cup soft bread crumbs (2 slices
  white bread)
1 egg
salt
pepper
1 tablespoon all-purpose flour
1 cup water
2 tablespoons catchup
1 tablespoon cooking or dry
  sherry
½ teaspoon soy sauce

1. In 12-inch skillet over medium heat, in hot butter or margarine, cook onions and green peppers until tender, stirring frequently. Remove onion mixture to warm platter; keep warm.

2. Meanwhile, in medium bowl with fork, mix ground beef, bread crumbs, egg, ½ teaspoon salt, and ¼ teaspoon pepper. Shape mixture into four ½-inch-thick oval patties.

3. In same skillet over medium-high heat, cook patties about 5 minutes for medium or until of desired doneness, turning patties once. Arrange patties on platter with onions and peppers; keep warm.

4. Into drippings in skillet over medium heat, stir flour, ¼ teaspoon salt, and ⅛ teaspoon pepper; cook 1 minute. Add water, catchup, sherry, and soy sauce; cook, stirring constantly, until mixture is slightly thickened; pour sauce over patties.

Filled Meat-Loaf Roll

TIME: about 1½ hours—SERVINGS: 8

2 slices white bread
1½ pounds ground meat for
  meat loaf (ground beef, pork,
  and/or veal)
1 medium onion, minced
2 tablespoons catchup
1 teaspoon salt
¼ teaspoon pepper
1 8-ounce package sliced salami
1 10-ounce package frozen
  chopped spinach, thawed and
  squeezed dry
2 ounces Monterey Jack cheese,
  shredded (½ cup)

1. Into medium bowl, tear bread into small pieces. Add ground meat for meat loaf, onion, catchup, salt, and pepper; mix well. On waxed paper, pat meat mixture into 12″ by 8″ rectangle.

2. On meat rectangle, arrange salami slices to cover meat; top with spinach and cheese. Starting at narrow end, roll meat mixture, jelly-roll fashion, lifting waxed paper to help shape roll.

3. Place rolled loaf, seam-side down, in 12″ by 8″ baking dish. Bake meat loaf in 350°F. oven 1 hour and 10 minutes.

4. When meat loaf starts to brown, cover loosely with a tent of folded foil to prevent over-browning.

Meat-and-Macaroni Casserole with Italian Vegetables

TIME: about 1 hour—SERVINGS: 8

1 16-ounce package elbow
    macaroni
3 medium green peppers
3 medium onions
½ pound mushrooms
3 tablespoons salad oil
salt
1½ pounds ground meat for
    meat loaf (ground beef, pork,
    and/or veal)
1 garlic clove, minced
1 28-ounce can tomatoes
¼ teaspoon pepper
1 8-ounce package mozzarella
    cheese, shredded

1. Prepare macaroni as label directs; drain; spoon into 13" by 9" baking dish; keep warm.

2. Meanwhile, cut green peppers into thin strips. Thinly slice onions and mushrooms.

3. In 2-inch skillet over medium heat, in hot salad oil, cook green peppers, onions, mushrooms, and ½ teaspoon salt until vegetables are tender, stirring occasionally. With slotted spoon, spoon ⅓ cup vegetable mixture into cup; set aside for garnish; keep warm. Spoon remaining vegetable mixture into baking dish with macaroni.

4. Preheat oven to 350°F. In drippings remaining in Dutch oven over high heat, cook ground meat for meat loaf and garlic until all pan juices evaporate and meat is browned. Stir in tomatoes with their liquid, pepper, half of shredded cheese, and 1 teaspoon salt. Spoon meat mixture into baking dish with macaroni and vegetables; toss gently to mix. Sprinkle with remaining cheese.

5. Bake 20 minutes or until cheese is melted and mixture is hot. Garnish with reserved vegetables.

Beef-Macaroni Pita Pockets

TIME: about 1¼ hours—SERVINGS: 8

¼ cup salad oil
1 medium eggplant (about 1
    pound), cut into ¾-inch pieces
1 pound ground beef
1 medium onion, diced
1 small garlic clove, minced
1 16-ounce can tomatoes
1 cup elbow macaroni
¾ cup water
1½ teaspoons salt
½ teaspoon oregano leaves
¼ teaspoon sugar
⅛ teaspoon ground red pepper
4 6-inch pitas*
lettuce leaves
hot pepper sauce (optional)

*A Pita is a Middle Eastern pocket
bread, available in most
supermarkets.

1. In 12-inch skillet over medium heat, in hot salad oil, cook eggplant until tender, stirring occasionally, about 15 minutes; remove to bowl.

2. In same skillet over medium-high heat, cook beef, onion, and garlic until pan juices evaporate and meat is browned, stirring often.

3. Return eggplant to skillet; add tomatoes their liquid and next 6 ingredients; over high heat, heat to boiling. Reduce heat to low; cover; simmer 20 minutes or until macaroni is tender.

4. Meanwhile, cut each pita in half; place on large cookie sheet. Heat pitas in 350°F. oven until warm, about 5 minutes.

5. To serve, tuck a lettuce leaf into each pita half. Spoon meat mixture into pitas. Serve hot pepper sauce to sprinkle on meat mixture, if desired.

Beef-Broccoli Strudel

TIME: about 1½ hours—SERVINGS: 6

1 pound ground beef
1 medium onion, diced
1 10-ounce package frozen
  chopped broccoli, thawed and
  squeezed dry
½ 8-ounce package mozzarella
  cheese, shredded
½ cup sour cream
¼ cup dried bread crumbs
1¼ teaspoons salt
¼ teaspoon pepper
½ pound phyllo (strudel leaves)*
½ cup butter or margarine,
  melted

*Phyllo is available in Greek pastry
shops or in the frozen-food section of
most supermarkets.

1. In 10-inch skillet over high heat, cook ground beef and onion until all pan juices evaporate and meat is well browned, stirring occasionally. Remove skillet from heat; stir in broccoli, mozzarella cheese, sour cream, bread crumbs, salt, and pepper.

2. Preheat oven to 350°F. On waxed paper, place 1 sheet of phyllo (about 16" by 12" rectangle; cut phyllo to fit if necessary); brush with some melted butter or margarine. Continue with some melted butter or margarine. Starting along a short side of phyllo, evenly spoon ground-beef mixture to cover about half of rectangle. From ground-beef mixture side, roll phyllo, jelly-roll fashion.

3. Place roll, seam-side down, on cookie sheet; brush with remaining butter or margarine. Bake 45 minutes or until golden. For easier slicing, cool strudel about 15 minutes on cookie sheet on wire rack.

Scalloped Beef and Potatoes

TIME: about 1¾ hours—SERVINGS: 8

1 pound ground beef
1 medium onion, chopped
salt
1 15¼- to 20-ounce can red
  kidney beans, drained
3 tablespoons butter or
  margarine
3 tablespoons all-purpose flour
2 cups milk
6 medium potatoes (about 2
  pounds), thinly sliced
paprika for garnish

1. In 12-inch skillet over high heat, cook ground beef, onion, and ½ teaspoon salt until all pan juices evaporate and meat is well browned, stirring frequently. Remove skillet from heat; stir in kidney beans; set aside.

2. In 2-quart saucepan over medium heat, melt butter or margarine; stir in flour and ¾ teaspoon salt until blended; cook 1 minute. Gradually stir in milk; cook, stirring constantly, until mixture is slightly thickened and smooth.

3. Preheat oven to 375°F. In 2½-quart casserole, arrange one-third potato slices; top with one-third sauce, then one-half ground-beef mixture. Repeat layering, ending with sauce. Sprinkle with paprika.

4. Cover casserole and bake 45 minutes. Uncover and bake 15 minutes longer or until potato slices are tender.

Beef-and-Vegetable Pizza

TIME: about 1 hour—SERVINGS: 8

1 pound ground beef
1 medium onion, diced
1 medium green pepper, diced
1 medium zucchini (about 8
  ounces), diced
¾ teaspoon salt
½ teaspoon rubbed sage
¼ teaspoon cracked pepper
1 13¾-ounce package hot-roll
  mix
1 cup water
1 8-ounce package mozzarella
  cheese, shredded
¼ cup pimento-stuffed olives,
  sliced

1. In 10-inch skillet over high heat, cook ground beef, onion, green pepper, zucchini, salt, sage, and cracked pepper until meat is lightly browned and vegetables are tender, stirring frequently; set aside.

2. Preheat oven to 425°F. Grease 14-inch pizza pan. Prepare hot-roll mix as label directs but use 1 cup water and omit egg; do not let dough rise. Pat dough evenly onto bottom of pizza pan. Spread ground-beef mixture evenly over dough; sprinkle with cheese; top with sliced olives.

3. Bake pizza on bottom rack of oven 20 minutes or until crust is browned and crisp.

Ground Beef and Zucchini Custard

TIME: about 1½ hours—**SERVINGS:** 6

4 medium zucchini
1½ pounds ground beef
2 tablespoons butter or
  margarine
1 medium onion, chopped
½ teaspoon curry powder
2 teaspoons salt
½ teaspoon pepper
2 slices white bread, cut into
  ½-inch cubes
4 eggs
2¾ cups milk

1. With sharp knife, cut 8 thin slices from zucchini; reserve for garnish. Dice remaining zucchini; set aside.

2. In 12-inch skillet over medium-high heat, cook ground beef until all pan juices evaporate and meat is well browned, stirring occasionally. Spoon meat into 12″ by 8″ baking dish; set aside.

3. In same skillet over medium heat, melt butter or margarine; add onion and diced zucchini; cook until onion is tender, stirring occasionally. Stir in curry powder; cook 1 minute.

4. Preheat oven to 350°F. Add vegetables to meat mixture; stir in salt, pepper, and bread cubes.

5. In small bowl with wire whisk or fork, beat eggs and milk; pour egg mixture over meat mixture. Bake, uncovered, 55 to 60 minutes until custard is set and top is golden brown.

6. To serve, arrange reserved zucchini slices on center of custard to resemble a flower.

Beef-Zucchini Pie

TIME: about 1 hour—**SERVINGS:** 6

1 10-ounce package refrigerated
  biscuits
1 pound ground beef
2 medium zucchini, diced
2 medium celery stalks, diced
1 small onion, diced
1½ teaspoons salt
1 teaspoon dry mustard
¼ teaspoon pepper
⅓ cup milk
2 eggs
2 ounces Cheddar cheese,
  shredded (½ cup)

1. Grease 9-inch pie plate. On lightly floured surface with floured rolling pin, roll each biscuit ⅛ inch thick; then cut each in half. Arrange biscuit halves on bottom and up side of pie plate, so that rounded side of biscuit comes up to rim. With fingers, gently press edges of biscuits together to make a piecrust; set aside.

2. In 12-inch skillet over high heat, cook ground beef and next 6 ingredients until pan juices evaporate and meat is well browned, stirring occasionally. Remove skillet from heat.

3. Preheat oven to 350°F. In small bowl with wire whisk or fork, beat milk and eggs until well blended. Stir egg mixture into meat mixture; spoon into biscuit-lined pie plate. Sprinkle cheese on top.

4. Bake 20 minutes or until biscuit crust is golden.

Beef-Filled Artichokes with Lemon Butter

TIME: about 1¼ hours—**SERVINGS:** 4

1 large lemon
1 pound ground beef
1 medium onion, diced
1 garlic clove, minced
water
4 slices white bread
1 medium tomato, diced
¼ cup grated Parmesan cheese
2 tablespoons mayonnaise
1 teaspoon salt

1. From lemon, grate ¾ teaspoon peel and squeeze 2 tablespoons juice. Cut lemon shells in half. Set aside peel, juice, and cut-up shells.

2. In 12-inch skillet over high heat, cook ground beef, onion, and garlic until all pan juices evaporate and meat is well browned, stirring frequently. Add ¾ cup water, stirring to loosen brown bits from bottom of skillet. Remove skillet from heat.

3. Into meat mixture in skillet, tear bread into small pieces. Stir in

¼ teaspoon pepper
¼ teaspoon ground sage
4 large artichokes
½ cup butter or margarine

lemon peel, tomato, cheese, mayonnaise, salt, pepper, and sage; set aside.

4. Prepare artichokes: With knife, cut off stem and 1 inch straight across top of each artichoke. Pull off any small, loose, or discolored leaves around bottom of artichokes. With kitchen shears, trim thorny tips off leaves.

5. Gently spread center of artichokes open and remove leaves from center to expose fuzzy and prickly portions (choke). With tip of spoon, carefully scrape out and discard the choke. Rinse artichokes well under running cold water; drain. Spoon some beef mixture into center of each artichoke. Spread leaves of artichokes apart and spoon remaining beef mixture between leaves.

6. Place artichokes on stem end in 8-quart Dutch oven; add 1 inch water and cut-up pieces of lemon shell; over high heat, heat to boiling. Reduce heat to low; cover and simmer artichokes about 35 minutes or until a leaf can be pulled off easily and filling is hot.

7. About 5 minutes before artichokes are done, prepare lemon-butter sauce: In 1-quart saucepan over medium-low heat, heat lemon juice, butter or margarine, and ¼ cup water until butter melts and mixture is hot.

8. To serve, pour lemon-butter sauce into 4 small bowls. Remove artichokes from water to dinner plates. Let each person use artichoke leaves to scoop up beef filling or dip leaves in lemon-butter sauce.

Mock Tournedos with Herbed Hollandaise

TIME: about 45 minutes—SERVINGS: 4

1 16-ounce package frozen
  crinkle-cut fried potatoes
2 slices white bread
1 pound ground beef
1 small onion, minced
2 tablespoons cooking or dry red
  wine
2 tablespoons water
1½ teaspoons prepared mustard
¾ teaspoon salt
¼ teaspoon basil
¼ teaspoon marjoram
¼ teaspoon pepper
8 slices bacon
Herbed Hollandaise (right)
1 medium tomato, cut into 8
  wedges for garnish
parsley sprigs for garnish

1. Prepare frozen potatoes in skillet as label directs; keep warm.

2. Meanwhile, preheat broiler if manufacturer directs. Into medium bowl, tear bread into small pieces; add ground beef and next 8 ingredients; mix well. Shape meat mixture into four 1-inch-thick patties. Wrap 2 bacon slices around side of each patty; secure with toothpicks.

3. Place patties on rack in broiling pan; broil 6 minutes for medium-rare or until of desired doneness, turning patties once.

4. While patties are broiling, prepare Herbed Hollandaise.

5. To serve, remove toothpicks from bacon-wrapped patties. Arrange patties and potatoes on 4 warm dinner plates; garnish with tomato wedges and parsley sprigs. Spoon a dollop of hollandaise on each plate; serve remaining hollandaise in small bowl.

Herbed Hollandaise: In small saucepan over low heat, melt ½ *cup butter* or margarine. In blender at low speed, blend *3 egg yolks, 2 tablespoons lemon juice,* ¼ *teaspoon basil,* and ⅛ *teaspoon ground red pepper.* With blender running, gradually add hot butter or margarine; blend until thickened.

Layered Beef and Cabbage Casserole

TIME: about 1¼ hours—SERVINGS: 8

1 large head green cabbage
  (about 4 pounds)
¼ cup salad oil
¾ teaspoon salt
1 pound ground beef
1 small onion, minced
1 32-ounce jar spaghetti sauce
1 cup water
⅓ cup regular long-grain rice
1 8-ounce package mozzarella
  cheese, coarsely shredded

1. With knife, cut off and discard tough ribs from cabbage leaves; coarsely shred cabbage leaves. In 5-quart Dutch oven over medium heat, in hot salad oil, cook cabbage and salt until very tender, stirring occasionally.

2. Meanwhile, prepare meat sauce: In 12-inch skillet over high heat, cook ground beef and onion until pan juices evaporate and meat is well browned, stirring occasionally. Add spaghetti sauce, water, and rice; heat to boiling. Reduce heat to low; cover and simmer 20 minutes, until rice is tender, stirring occasionally.

3. Preheat oven to 350°F. Into 13" by 9" baking dish, spoon ½ cup meat sauce. Top with one-half of cabbage, one-half remaining meat sauce, and one-half of cheese. Repeat layering with remaining cabbage, meat sauce, and cheese.

4. Bake 20 minutes or until heated through.

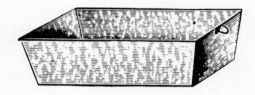

Polenta

TIME: about 2 hours—SERVINGS: 10

8 cups water
salt
2½ cups yellow cornmeal
1 pound ground beef
1 medium onion, diced
1 15½-ounce jar spaghetti sauce
4 tablespoons butter or
  margarine
3 tablespoons all-purpose flour
¼ teaspoon pepper
2½ cups milk
1 8-ounce package mozzarella
  cheese, shredded

1. Prepare polenta: Grease 15½" by 10½" jelly-roll pan. In 5-quart Dutch oven or saucepot over high heat, heat water and 2½ teaspoons salt to boiling. Reduce heat to medium; gradually pour in cornmeal, stirring constantly with wooden spoon. Cook over low heat until mixture is very thick and leaves side of pan, about 20 minutes, stirring frequently. Spoon mixture evenly into jelly-roll pan; cover with plastic wrap and refrigerate until cool and firm, about 1 hour.

2. Meanwhile, prepare meat sauce: In 10-inch skillet over high heat, cook ground beef and onion until pan juices evaporate and meat is well browned, stirring occasionally. Add spaghetti sauce; heat to boiling. Reduce heat to low; cover and simmer 10 minutes, stirring often.

3. Prepare white sauce: In 2-quart saucepan over medium heat, melt butter or margarine. Stir in flour, pepper, and ½ teaspoon salt until blended; cook 1 minute. Gradually stir in milk; cook, stirring constantly, until mixture is thickened. Remove saucepan from heat.

4. Preheat oven to 375°F. In 13" by 9" baking dish, place half of polenta mixture. Top with half of meat sauce, half of white sauce, and half of mozzarella. Repeat layering. Bake 35 minutes or until heated through. Let stand 15 minutes for easier cutting.

Zesty Beef Turnovers

TIME: about 30 minutes—SERVINGS: 4

1 pound ground beef
½ 8-ounce package mozzarella cheese, thinly sliced
1 8- or 8¼-ounce jar or bottle taco sauce
2 tablespoons butter or margarine
2 teaspoons lemon juice
1 small head lettuce, shredded
1 small tomato, cut into wedges
1 avocado, cut into wedges
2 tablespoons sliced pitted ripe olives

1. Shape ground beef into four 5-inch round patties. On center of each patty, place quarter of cheese and 2 teaspoons taco sauce. Fold each patty over in half to form a turnover, pressing edges with fingers to seal.

2. In 12-inch skillet over high heat, in hot butter or margarine, cook turnovers about 7 minutes or until meat is well browned, turning once.

3. In small bowl, mix remaining taco sauce with lemon juice. On platter, place shredded lettuce. Arrange turnovers, tomato, avocado, and olives on lettuce.

4. Serve salad and turnovers with taco-sauce mixture.

"Burrito" Pie

TIME: about 1 hour—SERVINGS: 6

¼ cup salad oil
4 8-inch flour tortillas
½ pound ground beef
1 medium onion, diced
1 small garlic clove, minced
1 4-ounce can chopped green chilies, drained
1 8-ounce can refried beans
⅓ cup hot taco sauce
¼ teaspoon salt
½ pound Monterey Jack cheese, shredded (2 cups)
1 cup shredded lettuce
1 medium tomato, diced
5 large pitted ripe olives, sliced

1. In 10-inch skillet over medium heat, in hot salad oil, fry 1 tortilla at a time, about 30 seconds on each side until lightly browned and blistered. With tongs, remove tortilla to paper towels to drain. Discard any remaining oil.

2. Preheat oven to 350°F. In same skillet over high heat, cook ground beef, onion, and garlic until all pan juices evaporate and meat is well browned, stirring occasionally. Remove skillet from heat; stir in green chilies, refried beans, taco sauce, and salt.

3. In 9-inch pie plate, place 1 tortilla; top with one-fourth of bean mixture and one-fourth of cheese. Repeat 3 times. Bake pie 30 minutes or until heated through. Sprinkle pie with shredded lettuce, diced tomato, and olives.

Mexican Beef Pie

TIME: about 35 minutes—SERVINGS: 6

½ pound ground beef
1 medium onion, diced
1 teaspoon chili powder
1 15¼- to 20-ounce can red kidney beans, drained
1 12-ounce can whole-kernel corn, drained
1 8-ounce can tomato sauce
1¼ teaspoons salt
½ teaspoon sugar
1 12- to 15-ounce package corn-muffin mix
1 cup shredded Cheddar cheese (4 ounces)

1. In 10-inch skillet over high heat, cook ground beef and onion until all pan juices evaporate and meat is well browned, stirring occasionally. Stir in chili powder; cook 1 minute. Remove skillet from heat. Stir in kidney beans, corn, tomato sauce, salt, and sugar.

2. Preheat oven to 350°F. Generously grease 12-inch pizza pan. Prepare corn-muffin batter as label directs. With back of spoon, spread corn-muffin batter in pizza pan, making rim slightly higher than center. Spoon meat mixture over corn-muffin batter in pizza pan, leaving a 1-inch rim of corn-muffin batter.

3. Sprinkle cheese over meat mixture. Bake 20 minutes or until corn-muffin mixture is golden and toothpick inserted in corn-muffin crust comes out clean.

Beef Empanadas

TIME: about 1 hour—SERVINGS: 4

¾ pound ground beef
1 small onion, diced
2 teaspoons chili powder
1 8-ounce can tomato sauce
1 2-ounce can chopped green
  chilies, drained
1 teaspoon sugar
salt
1 cup all-purpose flour
½ cup yellow cornmeal
½ cup shredded Cheddar cheese
  (2 ounces)
¼ cup shortening
cold water

1. In 10-inch skillet over high heat, cook ground beef and onion until all pan juices evaporate and meat is well browned, stirring occasionally. Spoon off fat in skillet if any. Stir in chili powder; cook 1 minute. Stir in tomato sauce, green chilies, sugar, and ¼ teaspoon salt; over high heat, heat to boiling. Reduce heat to low; cover and simmer 15 minutes, stirring occasionally.

2. Meanwhile, in medium bowl, stir flour, cornmeal, and ½ teaspoon salt. With pastry blender or 2 knives used scissor-fashion, cut cheese and shortening into flour mixture to resemble coarse crumbs. Sprinkle 5 to 6 tablespoons cold water, a tablespoon at a time, into mixture, mixing lightly after each addition until pastry is just moist enough to hold together. Shape pastry into a ball.

3. On lightly floured surface with floured rolling pin, roll half of pastry about ⅛ inch thick. Using 5-inch round plate as guide, cut 4 circles from pastry. Repeat with remaining pastry, rerolling scraps if necessary.

4. Preheat oven to 400°F. Onto one-half of a pastry circle, spoon some beef filling. Brush edges lightly with water; fold dough over filling. With fork, firmly press edges together to seal. Place on ungreased cookie sheet. Repeat with remaining pastry circles and beef filling to make 8 empanadas in all. Bake 15 minutes or until golden.

Spicy Mexican Roll-Ups

TIME: about 1¼ hours—SERVINGS: 10

2 tablespoons salad oil
4 medium celery stalks, thinly
  sliced
1 pound ground beef
1 medium onion, chopped
1 16-ounce can refried beans
1 4-ounce can chopped green
  chilies, drained
½ cup hot taco sauce
½ teaspoon salt
1 12½-ounce package flour
  tortillas (10 tortillas)
¼ pound Monterey Jack cheese,
  shredded (1 cup)
3 medium tomatoes, cut into
  wedges
1 6-ounce can pitted ripe olives,
  drained

1. In 10-inch skillet over medium heat, in hot salad oil, cook celery until tender, stirring occasionally. Remove celery to plate; set aside.

2. In same skillet over high heat, cook ground beef and onion until all pan juices evaporate and meat is well browned, stirring frequently. Reduce heat to medium. Stir in refried beans, green chilies, taco sauce, and salt until heated through; keep warm.

3. Meanwhile, steam tortillas as label directs. Or, in 12-inch skillet in ½ inch water, place 3 inverted 6-ounce custard cups. Arrange tortillas in pie plate; set plate on top of custard cups; over high heat, heat water to boiling. Reduce heat to low; cover and steam tortillas 5 minutes or until soft and hot.

4. Spread scant ½ cup bean mixture in lengthwise strip in center of each steamed tortilla. Top each with some sautéed celery and Arrange Monterey Jack cheese. Fold left and right sides of each tortilla over mixture.

5. Serve with tomato wedges and olives.

Mexican Beef Skillet Melt

TIME: about 45 minutes—SERVINGS: 6

¾ pound ground beef
1 small onion, diced
1¼ teaspoons chili powder
½ teaspoon salt
½ teaspoon sugar
⅛ teaspoon crushed red pepper
1 16-ounce can tomatoes
1 15¼- to 20-ounce can red
kidney beans, drained
1 8-ounce package tortilla chips
½ cup shredded Cheddar cheese
(2 ounces)

1. In 10-inch skillet over medium-high heat, cook ground beef and onion until all pan juices evaporate and meat is well browned, stirring frequently. Stir in chili powder; cook 1 minute. Add salt, sugar, crushed red pepper, and tomatoes with their liquid, stirring to mix well and break up tomatoes; heat to boiling. Reduce heat to low; cover and simmer 10 minutes to blend flavors.

2. Stir beans into ground-beef mixture; heat through. Remove skillet from heat; tuck some tortilla chips into beef mixture; sprinkle with cheese. Cover skillet; let stand 5 minutes to melt cheese. Serve with remaining tortilla chips.

Party Tacos with Two Fillings

TIME: about 2½ hours—SERVINGS: 12

Shredded-Beef Taco Filling (right)
1 small head iceberg lettuce
½ pound Cheddar cheese
3 large tomatoes
Scrambled-Egg-and-Pepper Taco
Filling (right)
3 medium avocados
2 4½-ounce packages taco shells
1 16-ounce jar mild or hot taco
sauce

1. Prepare Shredded-Beef Taco Filling; keep warm. Meanwhile, shred lettuce and cheese; dice tomatoes. Cover and refrigerate.

2. About 30 minutes before serving, prepare the Scrambled-Egg-and-Pepper Taco Filling. Dice avocados.

3. To serve, spoon scrambled-egg mixture and shredded-beef mixture into warm bowls. lettuce, Cheddar cheese, tomatoes, and avocados in separate piles on large platter with taco shells for taco accompaniments. Let each person spoon some beef or egg mixture into a taco shell, then top with taco accompaniments and taco sauce.

Shredded-Beef Taco Filling: In 10-inch skillet over medium-high heat, in *1 tablespoon hot salad oil*, cook *one 1½-pound boneless beef chuck shoulder steak*, cut into 1-inch chunks, *1 large onion*, diced, and *¼ teaspoon cumin* until meat is browned and onion is tender, stirring occasionally. Add *¾ cup water, 1 teaspoon salt, ¼ teaspoon cracked pepper*, and half of *one 4-ounce can diced green chilies*, drained, stirring to loosen brown bits from bottom of skillet; heat to boiling. Reduce heat to low; cover and simmer until meat is very tender and begins to fall apart and all the liquid is absorbed, about 1½ hours, stirring occasionally (adding more water during simmering if liquid is evaporating too quickly). Remove skillet from heat. With 2 forks, pull meat into shreds. Stir in remaining green chilies. Over medium heat, heat through. Makes enough filling for 12 tacos.

Scrambled-Egg-and-Pepper Taco Filling: In 12-inch skillet over medium heat, melt *2 tablespoons butter* or margarine; add *2 medium red or green peppers*, diced, and *3 green onions*, sliced; cook until tender, stirring often.
   In large bowl with wire whisk or fork, beat *12 eggs, ½ cup milk*, and *1¼ teaspoons salt* until just blended. Add egg mixture to peppers and green onions in skillet and cook over medium-high heat until eggs are set but still moist, stirring occasionally. Makes enough filling for 12 tacos.

Beef Patties en Croûte

TIME: about 45 minutes—SERVINGS: 5

1 pound ground beef
½ teaspoon salt
1 tablespoon butter or margarine
1 10-ounce package refrigerated
  biscuits
¼ pound liverwurst, cut into 5
  slices
2½ teaspoons prepared mustard
1 2½-ounce jar sliced
  mushrooms, drained

1. Shape ground beef into five 1-inch-thick round patties; sprinkle with salt. In 10-inch skillet over high heat, in hot butter or margarine, cook patties 5 minutes or until browned on both sides, turning once. Remove patties to paper towels to drain.

2. Preheat oven to 450°F. On lightly floured surface with floured rolling pin, roll one piece of biscuit dough into a 4-inch round. Place a liverwurst slice on center of dough round; top with a beef patty, ½ teaspoon mustard, and some mushrooms. Then roll another piece of biscuit dough into 5-inch round; arrange dough-round on top of beef patty; press edges together to seal. If you like, cut a small piece of dough from edge of round to make a pretty design to decorate top of biscuit-wrapped patty. Repeat to make 5 in all.

3. Place biscuit-wrapped patties on cookie sheet. Bake 10 minutes or until crust is golden.

VEAL

Meat Patties Italiano

TIME: about 1¼ hours—SERVINGS: 6

1 medium eggplant (about 1½
  pounds)
salt
pepper
salad oil
1 large onion
1½ pounds ground veal or
  ground turkey
1 cup dried bread crumbs
¾ cup water
1 egg
2 tablespoons chopped parsley
1 small garlic clove, minced
1 16-ounce can tomatoes
1 teaspoon sugar
¼ teaspoon basil
¼ pound Fontina or mozzarella
  cheese, shredded

1. Cut eggplant diagonally into 12 slices. Rub eggplant slices with 1 teaspoon salt and ¼ teaspoon pepper. In 12-inch skillet over medium heat, in 2 tablespoons hot salad oil, cook eggplant, a few slices at a time, until tender and browned on both sides, adding more oil as needed. Remove slices as they brown to paper towels to drain.

2. From onion, grate enough to make 1 tablespoon. Chop remaining onion; reserve for sauce. In medium bowl, mix grated onion, ground veal, bread crumbs, water, egg, 1 tablespoon chopped parsley, and ½ teaspoon salt. Shape veal mixture into six ¾-inch-thick patties. In same skillet over medium heat, in 2 tablespoons more hot salad oil, cook patties, half at a time, 5 minutes on each side, until golden and well done. Remove patties to plate; keep warm. Discard all but 1 tablespoon drippings from skillet.

3. Into drippings remaining in skillet over medium heat, cook garlic and reserved chopped onion until tender, stirring occasionally. Stir in tomatoes with their liquid, sugar, basil, remaining 1 tablespoon chopped parsley, ¼ teaspoon salt, and ⅛ teaspoon pepper. Cook 5 minutes to blend flavors, stirring to break up tomatoes. Keep sauce warm.

4. Preheat broiler if manufacturer directs. Place 6 eggplant slices on rack in broiling pan; top each with a veal patty, then with another eggplant slice; sprinkle with Fontina cheese. Broil eggplant-veal patties 1 minute or until cheese is melted.

5. To serve, spoon tomato sauce into warm deep platter. Arrange eggplant-veal patties on sauce.

Veal Scallops with Prosciutto and Sage

TIME: about 30 minutes—SERVINGS: 4

1 pound thin sliced veal cutlets
5 tablespoons all-purpose flour
½ teaspoon rubbed sage
butter or margarine
olive or salad oil
1 cup water
¼ cup cooking or dry sherry
¾ teaspoon chicken-flavor
  instant bouillon
¼ pound sliced prosciutto or 1
  4-ounce package sliced cooked
  ham,* cut into ½-inch-wide
  strips
⅛ teaspoon cracked pepper
2 teaspoon minced parsley

*If sliced cooked ham is used you
may need to add salt to adjust flavor.

1. With meat mallet or dull edge of French knife, pound each veal cutlet to about ⅛-inch thickness. If cutlets are very large, cut cutlets into 5" by 4" pieces. On waxed paper, mix flour and sage. Evenly coat cutlets with flour mixture.

2. In 12-inch skillet over medium-high heat, heat 2 tablespoons butter or margarine and 2 tablespoons olive or salad oil until hot. Add veal cutlets, a few pieces at a time; cook until browned on both sides, about 2 minutes, removing cutlets as they brown and adding more butter or oil if necessary.

3. To drippings remaining in skillet, add water, sherry, and bouillon; over high heat, heat to boiling, stirring to loosen brown bits from bottom of skillet. Return cutlets to skillet; add prosciutto; heat through.

4. Arrange meat and sauce on warm platter; sprinkle with pepper and parsley.

Veal Roman Style

TIME: about 30 minutes —SERVINGS: 2

½ pound thin sliced veal cutlets
¼ 4-ounce package sliced
  cooked ham
¼ 4-ounce package sliced
  Muenster cheese
¼ teaspoon ground sage
1 egg
¼ cup all-purpose flour
¼ teaspoon salt
⅛ teaspoon pepper
2 tablespoons butter or
  margarine
1 tablespoon salad oil
¼ cup water

1. With meat mallet or dull edge of French knife, pound veal cutlets to about ⅛-inch thickness. Cut cutlets into about 3" by 2" pieces.

2. Arrange ham on half of veal pieces, cutting ham to fit and making sure that ham pieces are slightly smaller than veal. Top with cheese, cutting the same as for ham. Sprinkle ham-and-cheese-topped veal with sage; top with remaining veal pieces. With meat mallet or dull edge of French knife, pound edges of each stack to seal in ham and cheese.

3. In pie plate with fork, beat egg. On waxed paper, combined flour, salt, and pepper. Dip veal stacks into egg, then coat with flour mixture.

4. In 12-inch skillet over medium-high heat, heat butter or margarine and salad oil until hot. Cook veal until browned on both sides, about 3 to 4 minutes. Add water, stirring to loosen brown bits from bottom of skillet.

5. Serve pan drippings over veal.

Veal Forestier

TIME: about 50 minutes—SERVINGS: 4

1 pound veal cutlets, each cut about ¼ inch thick
¼ cup all-purpose flour
4 tablespoons butter or margarine
½ pound mushrooms, sliced
½ cup dry vermouth
2 tablespoons water
¾ teaspoon salt
dash pepper
1 tablespoon chopped parsley
sautéed cherry tomatoes
parsley sprigs for garnish

1. On cutting board with meat mallet or dull edge of French knife, pound veal cutlets to ⅛-inch thickness. Cut cutlets into about 3″ by 2″ pieces. On waxed paper, coat cutlets lightly with flour.

2. In 10-inch skillet over medium-high heat, in hot butter or margarine, cook meat, a few pieces at a time, until lightly browned on both sides, removing pieces as they brown, adding more butter or margarine if necessary.

3. Add mushrooms, vermouth, water, salt, and pepper to skillet; heat to boiling. Reduce heat to low; cover and simmer 5 minutes or until mushrooms are tender. Return meat to skillet; heat through. Stir in chopped parsley.

4. Arrange meat on platter with sautéed cherry tomatoes. Garnish with parsley sprigs, if desired.

Veal Chops Paprika with Herbed Spaetzle

TIME: about 1 hour —SERVINGS: 8

2 tablespoons salad oil
8 veal rib chops, each cut ¾ inch thick
1 large onion, diced
1 tablespoon paprika
1¼ cups water
1¼ teaspoons salt
1 teaspoon sugar
⅛ teaspoon pepper
1 medium tomato, diced
Herbed Spaetzle (right)
1 8-ounce container sour cream

1. In 8-quart Dutch oven over medium-high heat, in hot salad oil, cook veal rib chops, a few at a time, until browned on both sides, removing veal chops to large plate as they brown.

2. In drippings remaining in Dutch oven, cook onion until tender. Stir in paprika; cook 1 minute. Return veal chops to Dutch oven; add water, salt, sugar, pepper, and tomato; over high heat, heat to boiling. Reduce heat to low; cover and simmer 20 minutes or until veal is fork-tender, turning chops occasionally.

3. Meanwhile, prepare Herbed Spaetzle; keep warm.

4. When veal is done, remove chops to large deep platter; keep warm. Skim off fat from liquid in Dutch oven. Stir in sour cream; over medium heat, heat through, stirring occasionally. (Do not boil, or mixture may curdle.) Spoon sauce over veal chops. Serve with spaetzle.

Herbed Spaetzle: In 6-quart saucepot over high heat, heat *4 quarts water* to boiling. Meanwhile, in medium bowl with spoon, beat *3 cups all-purpose flour, ¾ cup water, ¼ cup minced parsley, ¾ teaspoon salt, ½ teaspoon caraway seeds,* crushed, and *4 eggs* until smooth.

Reduce heat to medium. Over simmering water, with rubber spatula, press batter through spaetzle maker (or, colander or grater with large holes). Stir water gently so spaetzle do not stick together. Cook 2 to 3 minutes until tender but firm (*al dente*); drain.

Veal Chops in Creamy Anchovy Sauce

TIME: about 35 minutes—SERVINGS: 4

2 tablespoons butter or
  margarine
1 garlic clove, halved
4 veal rib chops, each cut ½
  inch thick
½ cup water
2 tablespoons dry vermouth
2 teaspoons lemon juice
½ 2-ounce can anchovy fillets,
  drained and chopped
3 tablespoons milk
1 tablespoon all-purpose flour
2 tablespoons minced parsley

1. In 12-inch skillet over medium-high heat, in hot butter or margarine, cook garlic until browned; discard garlic. In butter remaining in skillet. cook veal rib chops until well browned on both sides. Add water, vermouth, lemon juice, and anchovy fillets; heat to boiling. Reduce heat to low; cover and simmer 15 minutes or until chops are fork-tender, turning occasionally.

2. Place chops on warm platter; keep warm. In cup with fork, mix milk and flour until blended. Gradually stir flour mixture into hot liquid in skillet; cook over medium heat, stirring, until sauce is slightly thickened. Stir in parsley.

3. Pour anchovy sauce over chops.

Veal and Chestnut Braisés

TIME: about 1½ hours—SERVINGS: 8

2 tablespoons salad oil
2 pounds veal for stew, cut into
  1½-inch chunks
1 large onion, diced
1 medium rutabaga (about 1¾
  pounds), cut into bite-sized
  pieces
2 teaspoons salt
½ teaspoon sugar
¼ teaspoon pepper
1 chicken-flavor bouillon cube or
  envelope
water
1 pound chestnuts
2 tablespoons all-purpose flour
2 tablespoons minced parsley for
  garnish
4 cups hot cooked wild rice

1. In 5-quart Dutch oven over medium-high heat, in hot salad oil, cook veal for stew and onion until veal is browned on all sides and onion is tender. Stir in rutabaga, salt, sugar, pepper, bouillon, and 3 cups water; over high heat, heat to boiling. Reduce heat to low; cover and simmer 35 minutes or until veal is almost tender, stirring occasionally.

2. Meanwhile, in 2-quart saucepan over high heat, heat chestnuts and enough water to cover to boiling. Reduce heat to medium, cover and cook 15 minutes. Remove saucepan from heat. Immediately, with slotted spoon, remove 4 chestnuts from water. With kitchen shears, carefully cut each chestnut on flat side through shell. With fingers, peel off shell and skin, keeping chestnuts whole if possible. Repeat with remaining chestnuts. (Chestnuts will be difficult to peel when cool.)

3. Gently stir chestnuts into veal mixture; continue cooking until veal, rutabaga, and chestnuts are tender, about 15 minutes.

4. When veal mixture is ready, skim off fat from liquid in Dutch oven. In cup with spoon, stir flour and ¼ cup water until blended. Gradually stir flour mixture into veal mixture in Dutch oven; cook over medium heat, stirring, until mixture is slightly thickened. Spoon veal mixture into warm bowl; garnish with parsley. Serve with rice.

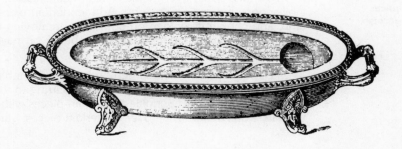

PORK

Spicy Pork and Tofu

TIME: about 45 minutes—SERVINGS: 6

1 pork loin tenderloin, whole
 (about ¾ pound)
¼ cup soy sauce
1 tablespoon cornstarch
3 tablespoons cooking or dry
 sherry
1 teaspoon minced, peeled
 ginger root or ¼ teaspoon
 ground ginger
½ teaspoon sugar
¼ teaspoon ground red pepper
4 medium celery stalks
2 medium carrots
1 small onion
1 16-ounce container firm tofu
 (soybean curd)*
salad oil
¼ teaspoon salt

*Available in many supermarkets or
at Oriental stores.

1. With knife held in slanting position, almost parallel to the cutting surface, cut pork loin tenderloin crosswise into ⅛-inch-thick slices. In medium bowl, mix pork, soy sauce, cornstarch, sherry, ginger, sugar, and ground red pepper; set aside.

2. Cut celery into 3-inch-long matchstick-thin strips. Thinly slice carrots and onion. Set vegetables aside. Drain tofu and pat dry with paper towels; cut tofu lengthwise in half; then cut each half crosswise into ½-inch slices; set aside.

3. In 5-quart Dutch oven or 12-inch skillet over medium-high heat, in 2 tablespoons hot salad oil, cook celery, carrots, onion, and salt, stirring quickly and frequently, until vegetables are tender-crisp, about 3 minutes. Spoon vegetables into bowl.

4. In same Dutch oven over high heat, in 3 tablespoons more hot salad oil, cook pork mixture about 3 minutes or until pork loses its pink color and is tender, stirring quickly and frequently. Add vegetables and tofu to Dutch oven; stir gently until mixture is heated through. If mixture is too thick, stir in a little water to thin to desired consistency. (Stir gently because the texture of tofu is very tender and will break easily.)

Pork Scallops alla Francese

TIME: about 30 minutes—SERVINGS: 4

1 pork loin tenderloin whole
 (about 1 pound)
⅓ cup all-purpose flour
salt
pepper
2 eggs
¼ cup milk
2 tablespoons salad oil
butter or margarine
1 tablespoon lemon juice
1 lemon, sliced, for garnish

1. With knife held in slanting position, almost parallel to the cutting surface, cut pork loin tenderloin crosswise into ¼-inch slices. With meat mallet or dull edge of French knife, pound each pork tenderloin slice to about ⅛-inch thickness. On waxed paper, combine flour, ¼ teaspoon salt, and ⅛ teaspoon pepper. In pie plate with fork, beat eggs and milk just until blended. Dip tenderloin pieces into flour mixture, then into egg mixture to coat.

2. In 12-inch skillet over medium heat, heat salad oil and 2 tablespoons butter or margarine. Add tenderloin pieces, a few at a time, and cook until golden on both sides, removing pieces to warm platter as they brown and adding more butter or margarine if needed; keep warm.

3. Into drippings in skillet, stir lemon juice and 4 tablespoons butter or margarine; cook until butter is melted, stirring to loosen brown bits from bottom of skillet. Sprinkle tenderloin pieces with salt and pepper to taste. Pour butter sauce over tenderloin pieces; garnish with lemon slices.

Pork Tenderloin with Hearts of Palm

TIME: about 30 minutes—SERVINGS: 4

1 pork loin tenderloin, whole
  (about 1 pound)
2 eggs
½ cup all-purpose flour
2 tablespoons salad oil
butter or margarine
½ cup water
⅓ cup dry vermouth
1 teaspoon instant chicken-flavor
  bouillon
¼ teaspoon salt
⅛ teaspoon white pepper
1 14-ounce can hearts of palm,
  drained
1 2-ounce jar diced pimentos,
  drained
lettuce leaves
1 small lemon, thinly sliced, for
  garnish

1. With knife held in slanting position, almost parallel to the cutting surface, cut pork loin tenderloin crosswise into ¼-inch slices. With meat mallet or dull edge of French knife, pound each pork tenderloin slice to about ⅛-inch thickness. In pie plate with fork, beat eggs. Onto waxed paper, measure flour. Dip tenderloin pieces into egg, then coat with flour.

2. In 12-inch skillet over medium heat, heat salad oil and 4 tablespoons butter or margarine until hot. Add tenderloin pieces, a few at a time, and cook until lightly browned on both sides, removing pieces as they brown to warm platter and adding more butter or margarine if needed; keep warm.

3. Into drippings in skillet, stir water, vermouth, bouillon, salt, and pepper, stirring to loosen brown bits from bottom of skillet. Cut hearts of palm lengthwise in half; add hearts of palm and pimentos to liquid in skillet; heat through.

4. Arrange lettuce leaves and hearts of palm on one-half of platter. Arrange pork on other half of platter. Spoon sauce over meat; garnish with lemon slices.

King-Sized Pork-And-Polenta Pie

TIME: about 2½ hours—SERVINGS: 16

1 5-pound pork shoulder blade
  roast, boneless*
¼ cup salad oil
2 medium onions, chopped
1 garlic clove, minced
3 tablespoons paprika
1 32-ounce package or can
  sauerkraut, drained
1 16-ounce can tomatoes
1 chicken-flavor bouillon cube or
  envelope
water
salt
3 cups yellow cornmeal
⅓ cup minced parsley

*Also called boneless pork butt roast,
boneless rolled butt roast, or
boneless pork butt.

1. Trim fat from pork shoulder blade roast; cut pork into 1-inch pieces.

2. In 8-quart Dutch oven over medium-high heat, in hot salad oil, cook pork, several pieces at a time, until browned on all sides, in Dutch oven over medium heat, cook onions and garlic until tender, stirring occasionally. Stir in paprika; cook 1 minute.

3. Return meat to Dutch oven; stir in sauerkraut, tomatoes with their liquid, bouillon, 3½ cups water, and 1 teaspoon salt; over high heat, heat to boiling. Reduce heat to low; cover and simmer 1 hour or until pork is fork-tender.

4. Prepare polenta: In medium bowl, mix cornmeal, 3 cups water, and 2½ teaspoons salt; set aside. In 4-quart saucepan over high heat, heat 3 cups water to boiling. Reduce heat to medium; stir cornmeal mixture into boiling water. Cook, stirring constantly, until mixture is thickened, about 4 minutes. Remove pan from heat; stir in parsley.

5. Preheat oven to 350°F. Skim off fat from liquid in Dutch oven; spoon mixture into 17¼" by 11½" roasting pan. With spoon, spread polenta evenly over top of pork mixture. Bake 35 minutes or until polenta is golden.

Pork Roast Blanquette

TIME: about 3½ hours—SERVINGS: 12

1 4- to 4½-pound pork shoulder
   blade roast, boneless*
2 teaspoons salt
½ teaspoon seasoned pepper
¼ teaspoon thyme leaves
water
1 16-ounce bag carrots, each
   halved crosswise
1 pound small white onions
1 pound medium mushrooms
2 tablespoons all-purpose flour
1 10-ounce package frozen peas
2 egg yolks

*Also called boneless pork butt roast,
boneless rolled butt roast, or
boneless pork butt.

1. In 8-quart Dutch oven over medium-high heat, cook pork shoulder blade roast until browned on all sides. Add salt, pepper, thyme, and 2 cups water; heat to boiling. Reduce heat to low; cover and simmer 1¼ hours.

2. Add carrots and onions; cover and simmer 30 minutes. Add mushrooms; cover and simmer 15 minutes longer or until vegetables and pork are tender. When pork is done, place on warm large platter with vegetables; keep warm.

3. In cup, stir flour and 2 tablespoons water until blended. Gradually stir flour mixture into liquid in Dutch oven; cook, stirring constantly, until gravy is slightly thickened. Add peas; heat through. In bowl with fork, beat egg yolks; stir in small amount of hot gravy. Slowly pour egg mixture back into gravy, stirring rapidly to prevent lumping; cook, stirring constantly, until gravy is thickened (do not boil).

4. To serve, pour some gravy over pork and vegetables. Pass remaining gravy in gravy boat.

Orange-Glazed Pork with Potatoes

TIME: about 2½ hours—SERVINGS: 12

2 3-pound smoked pork shoulder
   rolls
¼ teaspoon peppercorns
1 bay leaf
water
4 pounds potatoes
1 medium onion, diced
6 tablespoons butter or
   margarine
1 10- to 12-ounce jar orange
   marmalade
2 tablespoons prepared
   horseradish
salt
watercress sprigs for garnish

1. Prepare smoked pork shoulder rolls: Leave stockinette casing on pork rolls during simmering so pork rolls will hold their shape. In 8-quart Dutch oven or saucepot over high heat, heat pork rolls, peppercorns, bay leaf, and enough water to cover to boiling. Reduce heat to low; cover and simmer 1½ hours or until meat is fork-tender.

2. About 1 hour before pork rolls are done, peel potatoes and cut into 1½-inch chunks. In 17¼" by 11½" roasting pan in 450°F. oven, melt butter or margarine; add potatoes, turning to coat with melted butter. Bake potatoes 25 minutes, turning occasionally. Add onion; cook 20 minutes longer or until potatoes are tender and golden brown, turning occasionally; keep warm.

3. When pork rolls are done, cool slightly until easy to handle. Meanwhile, in small bowl, mix marmalade and horseradish. Carefully, remove casings from pork rolls; arrange rolls in 13" by 9" baking pan. Bake pork rolls 20 minutes, brushing occasionally with marmalade mixture.

4. To serve, cut pork roll into slices. Sprinkle potatoes with salt to taste. Arrange potatoes and pork rolls on warm large platter. Garnish with watercress sprigs.

Corn-Bread-Topped Pork Pie

TIME: about 2 hours—SERVINGS: 8

salad oil
1 medium onion, diced
2 garlic cloves, minced
2 pounds pork pieces, cut into
   1-inch chunks
1 28-ounce can tomatoes
1 4-ounce can chopped green
   chilies, drained
½ cup water
2 teaspoons brown sugar
salt
½ cup all-purpose flour
½ cup cornmeal
2 tablespoons sugar
1½ teaspoons double-acting
   baking powder
⅓ cup milk
1 egg

1. In 12-inch skillet over medium heat, in 2 tablespoons hot salad oil, cook onion and garlic until tender, stirring occasionally. With slotted spoon, remove onion mixture to small bowl.

2. In drippings remaining in skillet over medium-high heat, cook pork chunks until well browned on all sides. Return onion mixture to skillet. Stir in tomatoes with their liquid, green chilies, water, brown sugar, and ¾ teaspoon salt; over high heat, heat to boiling, stirring to loosen brown bits from bottom of skillet.

3. Spoon pork mixture into 2½-quart deep casserole. Cover casserole and bake in 350°F. oven 1 hour.

4. About 5 minutes before pork is done, prepare corn-bread topping: Into medium bowl, measure flour, cornmeal, sugar, baking powder, and ¼ teaspoon salt. With fork, stir in milk, egg, and 2 tablespoons salad oil just until blended. Remove casserole from oven. Skim off fat from liquid in casserole. With spoon, gently spread corn-bread batter evenly over top of pork mixture in casserole.

5. Bake 20 minutes or until golden and toothpick inserted into corn bread comes out clean and meat is fork-tender. Corn-bread topping will absorb liquid in casserole upon standing, so serve immediately.

Easy Pork Pasties

TIME: about 1½ hours—SERVINGS: 4

1 pound ground pork
1 small onion, diced
¾ teaspoon salt
½ teaspoon thyme leaves
⅛ teaspoon cracked pepper
½ cup water
2 tablespoons all-purpose flour
1 tablespoon salad oil
1 small carrot, diced
1 small potato, diced
1 small turnip, diced
piecrust mix for one 9-inch
   piecrust
1 egg, slightly beaten

1. In 10-inch skillet over medium-high heat, cook ground pork, onion, salt, thyme, and pepper until all pan juices evaporate and meat is well browned, stirring frequently.

2. In small bowl with fork, mix water and flour until blended. Stir flour mixture into ground-pork mixture in skillet; cook, stirring constantly, until mixture is slightly thickened. Remove ground-pork mixture to medium bowl; set aside.

3. In same skillet over medium heat, in hot salad oil, cook carrot, potato, and turnip until tender, about 10 minutes, stirring occasionally. Remove vegetables to medium bowl with ground-pork mixture; mix well.

4. Preheat oven to 400°F. Grease small cookie sheet.

5. Prepare piecrust mix as label directs. On lightly floured surface with floured rolling pin, roll dough ⅛ inch thick. Using 7-inch plate as guide, cut 4 circles from pastry, rerolling scraps if necessary.

6. Onto one-half of a pastry circle, spoon one-fourth pork mixture. Brush pastry edge with egg; fold dough over filling. With fork, firmly press edges together to seal. Place on cookie sheet. Repeat with remaining pastry circles and pork mixture to make 4 pasties in all. Brush pasties with egg; prick lightly with fork.

7. Bake 20 minutes until golden.

Pork Loaf

TIME: about 2 hours—SERVINGS: 6

4 eggs
2 tablespoons salad oil
3 medium celery stalks, diced
1 medium onion, diced
1½ pounds ground pork
1 cup fresh rye-bread crumbs
    (about 2 slices)
⅓ cup water
2 tablespoons minced parsley
½ teaspoon salt
bottled chili sauce
parsley sprigs for garnish

1. Hard-cook 3 eggs; remove shells; set aside.

2. Meanwhile, in 10-inch skillet over medium heat, in hot salad oil, cook celery and onion until tender, stirring occasionally.

3. In large bowl, mix celery mixture, ground pork, bread crumbs, water, parsley, salt, 2 tablespoons chili sauce, and remaining egg.

4. In 12″ by 8″ baking pan, form half of pork mixture into 8″ by 4″ rectangle. Arrange hard-cooked eggs in lengthwise row on top; top with remaining pork mixture and shape into an 8″ by 4″ oval loaf, pressing firmly. Brush top and side of loaf with 1 tablespoon chili sauce. Bake loaf in 350°F. oven 1½ hours.

5. To serve, place pork loaf on warm platter; brush with 1 tablespoon chili sauce. If you desire, garnish with parsley sprigs.

Pork-Stuffed Cabbage Leaves

TIME: about 2 hours—SERVINGS: 8

½ cup regular long-grain rice
1 small head cabbage (about
    2 pounds)
1 pound ground pork
salt
pepper
2 tablespoons salad oil
1 15- to 16-ounce can tomato
    sauce
1¼ cups water
2 tablespoons brown sugar
2 tablespoons red wine vinegar
1 tablespoon soy sauce

1. Prepare rice as label directs.

2. Meanwhile, discard tough green outer leaves from cabbage; with sharp knife, remove core. Fill 4-quart saucepan three-fourths full with water; heat to boiling. Reduce heat to medium. Place cabbage in simmering water, cut-side up. Using 2 large spoons, gently separate leaves as outer leaves soften slightly; remove 16 large leaves from cabbage and let drain in colander. Coarsely shred remaining cabbage; set aside. Trim rib of each reserved leaf very thin.

3. In medium bowl with fork, mix rice, ground pork, 1 teaspoon salt, and ⅛ teaspoon pepper.

4. On center of each cabbage leaf, place a scant ¼ cupful ground-pork mixture. Fold 2 sides of cabbage leaf toward center over meat, overlapping edges. From one narrow edge, roll jelly-roll fashion.

5. In 12-inch skillet over medium heat, in hot salad oil, cook reserved shredded cabbage 3 minutes. Stir in tomato sauce, water, brown sugar, vinegar, soy sauce, ¾ teaspoon salt, and ⅛ teaspoon pepper.

6. Place stuffed-cabbage leaves, seam-side down, in sauce in skillet. Over medium heat, heat to simmering. Reduce heat to low; cover and simmer 45 minutes or until cabbage is tender.

Pork-Cabbage Pie

TIME: about 2½ hours—SERVINGS: 6

¾ cup all-purpose flour
4 tablespoons butter or
   margarine, softened
¼ cup sour cream
2 tablespoons salad oil
1¼ pounds pork pieces, cut into
   ½-inch chunks
1 medium onion, diced
1 small head cabbage (about
   2 pounds)
1¼ cups water
1 tablespoon sugar
3 tablespoons cider vinegar
1½ teaspoons salt
¼ teaspoon dry mustard
⅛ teaspoon pepper
¼ teaspoon caraway seeds
1 egg, slightly beaten

1. Into medium bowl, measure flour. With pastry blender or 2 knives used scissor-fashion, cut butter or margarine and sour cream into flour until mixture resembles coarse crumbs. With hands, shape pastry into a ball; wrap with plastic wrap and refrigerate.

2. In 12-inch skillet over medium-high heat, in hot salad oil, cook pork pieces until browned, stirring occasionally. With slotted spoon, remove pork pieces to small bowl; set aside.

3. In drippings remaining in skillet over medium heat, cook onion until tender, stirring occasionally.

4. Cut cabbage into 1-inch pieces to make about 9 cups. Return pork to skillet; add cabbage and next 6 ingredients; over high heat, heat to boiling. Reduce heat to low; cover and simmer 1 hour or until meat is fork-tender. Remove cover; over medium heat, cook until almost all pan juices evaporate; stir in caraway seeds. Spoon pork mixture into 1½-quart casserole.

5. On lightly floured surface with floured rolling pin, roll pastry 1½ inches larger all around than top of casserole. Place pastry loosely over pork mixture. With kitchen shears, trim pastry edge, leaving 1-inch overhang; fold overhang under and press gently all around casserole rim.

6. Preheat oven to 425°F. Reroll pastry trimmings ⅛ inch thick; with knife, cut out decorative design. Brush top of pie with some beaten egg. Arrange pastry design on pie; brush with egg. Make several slits in piecrust for steam to escape during removing pieces as they brown to bowl. In drippings remaining baking.

7. Bake 30 minutes or until piecrust is golden brown and pork mixture is hot.

Skillet Pork with Dumplings

TIME: about 45 minutes—SERVINGS: 4

1 pound ground pork
1 medium onion, diced
1 medium green pepper, diced
2 teaspoons chili powder
1 16-ounce can tomatoes
2 teaspoons sugar
1 teaspoon salt
1 cup buttermilk-baking mix
¾ cup milk
¼ cup yellow cornmeal
chopped parsley for garnish

1. In 10-inch skillet over high heat, cook ground pork, onion, and green pepper until all pan juices evaporate and vegetables are tender, stirring occasionally. Stir in chili powder; cook 1 minute. Stir in tomatoes with their liquid, sugar, and salt, stirring to break up tomatoes; over high heat, heat to boiling. Reduce heat to low; cover and simmer 15 minutes to blend flavors, stirring occasionally. Skim off fat from liquid in skillet.

2. In medium bowl with fork, stir buttermilk-baking mix, milk, and cornmeal just until blended. Drop dumplings into 4 mounds on simmering pork mixture in skillet; cook, uncovered, 10 minutes. Cover skillet and cook until dumplings are set, about 10 minutes longer.

3. Garnish with chopped parsley.

Herb-and-Spice Meatballs with Waffles

TIME: about 45 minutes—SERVINGS: 4

2 slices white bread
1 pound ground pork
1 egg
1 tablespoon minced onion
1 teaspoon salt
½ teaspoon fennel seeds, crushed
¼ teaspoon pepper
⅛ teaspoon ground allspice
⅛ teaspoon ground cinnamon
1 tablespoon salad oil
1 10- to 11-ounce package frozen waffles
1 pint strawberries
1 medium orange, cut into wedges
maple or maple-flavor syrup

1. Into medium bowl, tear bread into small pieces. Add ground pork, egg, onion, salt, crushed fennel seeds, pepper, allspice, and cinnamon; mix well. Shape meat mixture into 1-inch meatballs.

2. In 12-inch skillet over medium heat, in hot salad oil, cook meatballs until well browned on all sides, about 15 minutes.

3. Meanwhile, prepare frozen waffles as label directs.

4. To serve, arrange meatballs, waffles, strawberries, and orange wedges on large platter.

5. Serve with maple syrup for breakfast, brunch, or supper.

Stuffed Pork Chops Deluxe

TIME: about 2¼ hours—SERVINGS: 6

½ cup regular long-grain rice
3 tablespoons butter or margarine
¼ pound mushrooms, sliced
2 medium celery stalks, minced
1 small onion, minced
6 pork loin rib chops, each cut about 1¼ inches thick
1 teaspoon paprika
¾ teaspoon salt
¼ teaspoon pepper
1 chicken-flavor bouillon cube or envelope
¼ teaspoon thyme leaves
water
2 tablespoons all-purpose flour
celery leaves for garnish

1. Prepare rice as label directs.

2. Meanwhile, in 12-inch skillet over medium heat, in hot butter or margarine, cook mushrooms, celery, and onion until tender, stirring occasionally. Remove skillet from heat; stir in cooked rice.

3. With knife, trim several pieces of fat from edge of pork loin rib chops; reserve fat. Cut each pork chop, from rib side, parallel to the surface of the chop, to form a pocket. Stuff pockets with rice mixture. Rub pork chops with paprika, salt, and pepper.

4. In same skillet over medium-high heat, heat reserved pork fat until lightly browned; using spoon, press and rub fat over bottom of skillet to grease it well; discard fat. Add 3 chops to skillet; over medium-high heat, cook until well browned on both sides, removing chops from skillet as they brown. Repeat with remaining chops.

5. Return chops to skillet; add bouillon, thyme, and 1½ cups water; over high heat, heat to boiling. Reduce heat to low; cover and simmer 1¼ hours or until pork chops are fork-tender, basting pork chops occasionally with liquid in skillet. Remove pork chops to large platter; keep warm.

6. Skim off fat from liquid in skillet. In cup, mix flour and ¼ cup water until blended. Gradually stir flour mixture into liquid in skillet. Cook over medium heat, stirring constantly, until gravy is slightly thickened. Pour gravy into platter with pork chops. Garnish pork chops with celery leaves.

Pork Chops with Caper Sauce

TIME: about 35 minutes—SERVINGS: 4

2 tablespoons salad oil
4 pork loin blade chops, each cut ¾ inch thick
¾ cup water
1 teaspoon prepared mustard
½ teaspoon salt
⅛ teaspoon pepper
½ cup sour cream
2 teaspoons capers
parsley sprigs for garnish

1. In 12-inch skillet over medium heat, in hot salad oil, cook pork loin blade chops until well browned on both sides, about 10 minutes. Spoon off drippings in skillet.

2. To pork chops in skillet, add water, mustard, salt, and pepper; over high heat, heat to boiling. Reduce heat to low; cover and simmer 20 minutes or until chops are tender, turning occasionally. Stir in sour cream and capers; heat. (Do not boil, or mixture will curdle.)

3. To serve, place pork chops on warm platter; spoon sauce over chops. Garnish with parsley sprigs.

Spicy Oven Pork Chops

TIME: about 1¼ hours—SERVINGS: 8

¼ cup soy sauce
2 tablespoons cooking or dry sherry
2 tablespoons water
8 pork loin blade chops, each cut ½ inch thick (about 4 pounds)
2 tablespoons salad oil
1 small onion, diced
¾ cup catchup
3 tablespoons brown sugar
3 tablespoons red wine vinegar
1 tablespoon Worcestershire
1 4-ounce can chopped green chilies, drained

1. In large open roasting pan, mix soy sauce, sherry, and water. Place pork loin blade chops in soy-sauce mixture, turning each chop to coat well. Bake in 375°F. oven 40 minutes. With pastry brush, baste chops occasionally with soy-sauce mixture in pan.

2. Meanwhile, in 2-quart saucepan over medium heat, in hot salad oil, cook onion until tender, stirring occasionally. Stir in catchup and remaining ingredients; heat to boiling. Remove saucepan from heat. Brush chops with half of catchup mixture; cook 10 minutes.

3. Turn chops; brush with remaining catchup mixture. Bake 20 minutes longer or until chops are fork-tender.

Pork Chops in Wine

TIME: about 1¼ hours—SERVINGS: 4

3 tablespoons olive or salad oil
½ pound small mushrooms
1 medium onion, sliced
1 garlic clove, crushed
4 pork loin blade, rib, loin; or sirloin chops, each cut ¾ inch thick
¾ cup cooking or dry white wine
¾ cup water
½ teaspoon salt
½ teaspoon basil
⅛ teaspoon pepper
2 medium tomatoes, diced
1 tablespoon chopped parsley

1. In 12-inch skillet over medium heat, in hot olive oil, cook mushrooms, onion, and garlic until vegetables are tender, stirring occasionally. With slotted spoon, remove mushroom mixture to small bowl.

2. In drippings remaining in skillet (add oil if necessary), over medium-high heat, cook pork chops until browned on both sides. Add wine, water, salt, basil, and pepper; heat to boiling, stirring to loosen brown bits from bottom of skillet. Reduce heat to low; cover and simmer 45 minutes.

3. Return mushroom mixture to skillet; add tomatoes. Cover and cook until vegetables are heated through and meat is fork-tender, about 15 minutes longer. Skim off fat from liquid in skillet; sprinkle with parsley.

Pork Chops with Creamy Gravy

TIME: about 30 minutes—SERVINGS: 4

milk
all-purpose flour
salt
pepper
4 pork loin blade chops, each cut
   ¾ inch thick
3 tablespoons salad oil
½ cup water

1. Into pie plate, pour 2 tablespoons milk. On waxed paper, combine ¼ cup flour, ¼ teaspoon salt, and ⅛ teaspoon pepper. Dip pork chops in milk, then into flour mixture to coat well.

2. In 12-inch skillet over medium-high heat, in hot salad oil, cook pork chops until browned on both sides and fork-tender, about 15 minutes, turning occasionally. Remove chops to warm platter; keep warm.

3. In cup with fork, mix water with 2 tablespoons flour until smooth. Stir flour mixture into drippings in skillet, stirring and scraping to loosen brown bits from bottom of skillet. Gradually stir in 1 cup milk and ⅛ teaspoon pepper; cook, stirring constantly, until gravy is thickened and boils. Add salt to taste.

4. Serve pork chops with gravy.

Spareribs with Peach Sauce

TIME: about 1¾ hours—SERVINGS: 6

½ cup soy sauce
¼ cup cooking or dry sherry
¼ cup water
6 pounds pork spareribs, cut into
   2-rib portions
1 28-ounce can cling peach
   halves, drained
⅓ cup chili sauce
2 tablespoons honey
2 teaspoons minced, peeled
   ginger root or ½ teaspoon
   ground ginger
¾ teaspoon salt
¼ teaspoon garlic powder

1. In large open roasting pan, mix soy sauce, sherry, and water. Place spareribs in soy-sauce mixture in one layer, turning ribs to coat well. Bake in 350°F. oven 1 hour. With pastry brush, baste ribs occasionally with soy-sauce mixture in pan.

2. Meanwhile, in covered blender at medium speed or in food processor with knife blade attached, blend peaches with remaining ingredients until smooth. Spoon mixture into small bowl; set aside.

3. Remove roasting pan from oven; spoon ½ cup soy-sauce mixture from pan into peach mixture. Turn ribs; return pan to oven; roast 20 minutes.

4. Brush ribs with some peach sauce. Roast 20 minutes longer or until ribs are fork-tender, brushing frequently with sauce.

5. To serve, place ribs on warm large platter. Spoon off fat from liquid remaining in roasting pan; spoon liquid over ribs.

Barbecued Spareribs, Oven-Style

TIME: about 2¼ hours—SERVINGS: 6

6 pounds pork spareribs, cut into
    1-rib portions
1 6-ounce can tomato paste
½ cup water
¼ cup packed brown sugar
¼ cup honey
¼ cup cider vinegar
2 tablespoons salad oil
1 tablespoon grated onion
2½ teaspoons salt
2 teaspoons chili powder
¼ teaspoon garlic powder

1. Arrange pork spareribs in large open roasting pan in one layer. Cover pan with foil and roast spareribs in 325°F. oven 1½ hours.

2. Meanwhile, prepare glaze: In medium bowl, mix tomato paste with remaining ingredients.

3. Remove roasting pan from oven; discard foil; spoon off fat. Brush ribs with some glaze. Return pan to oven and roast 30 minutes longer, until ribs are fork-tender, brushing ribs frequently with glaze.

HAM

Currant-Glazed Ham Steak

TIME: about 20 minutes—SERVINGS: 4

1 fully cooked smoked ham
    center slice, cut ¾ inch thick
    (about 1 pound)
⅓ cup red currant jelly
1 tablespoon port wine
¾ teaspoon dry mustard
salt
parsley sprigs for garnish

1. Trim several pieces of fat from edge of ham steak. In 10-inch skillet over medium-high heat, heat fat trimmings until lightly browned; using spoon, press and rub fat over bottom of skillet to grease it well; discard fat. Add ham to skillet; over medium-high heat, cook ham steak until well browned on both sides. Remove ham steak to platter; keep warm.

2. In same skillet over low heat, stir currant jelly, port wine, and dry mustard until jelly is melted and sauce is hot; add salt to taste if needed; pour over ham steak. Garnish with parsley.

Honeyed Ham Steak with Peach Halves

TIME: about 30 minutes—SERVINGS: 4

1 16-ounce can cling-peach
    halves in heavy syrup
1 fully cooked smoked ham
    center slice, cut 1 inch thick
    (about 1 pound)
½ cup orange juice
1 tablespoon honey
2 teaspoons prepared mustard
⅛ teaspoon ground allspice
2 tablespoons water
1 teaspoon cornstarch

1. Drain peach halves, reserving ½ cup syrup; set aside. Trim few small pieces of fat from ham steak. In 12-inch skillet over medium-high heat, heat pieces of fat until lightly browned, rubbing fat on bottom of skillet to grease it; discard fat. Cook ham in fat until lightly browned on both sides, about 5 minutes.

2. Into skillet with ham, stir orange juice, honey, mustard, allspice, and reserved peach syrup. Add peach halves; cook over medium heat until peaches are heated through, about 5 minutes. Place ham and peaches on warm platter, leaving liquid in pan.

3. In cup, stir water and cornstarch until blended; stir into hot liquid in skillet; cook over medium heat, stirring constantly, until mixture is thickened and boils; boil 1 minute. Spoon sauce over ham and peaches.

77

Baked Ham with Candied-Orange-Peel Glaze

TIME: about 4½ hours—SERVINGS: 20

1 10-pound fully cooked smoked
   whole ham
8 large oranges
water
¾ cup light corn syrup
¼ cup sugar
Holiday Potato Cones (right)
Spinach-Topped Tomatoes
   (page 79)

1. With sharp knife, remove skin and trim some fat from fully cooked smoked whole ham, leaving about ¼ inch fat. Place ham on rack in open roasting pan. Insert meat thermometer into center of ham, being careful that pointed end does not touch bone or fat. Bake ham in 325°F. oven 3 to 3½ hours until thermometer reaches 140°F. (about 15 to 18 minutes per pound). If ham browns too quickly, cover with tent of foil.

2. Meanwhile, prepare Glaze: With knife or vegetable peeler, cut peel from oranges into long strips. (Use fruit in salad another day.) Trim off white membrane from peel. Cut peel lengthwise into long, thin strips to make about 2 cups, firmly packed. In 3-quart saucepan over high heat, heat orange peels and 3 cups water to boiling; cook 15 minutes; drain; rinse. With 3 cups more water, cook peels 15 minutes again; drain.

3. In same saucepan over high heat, heat corn syrup and sugar until boiling and sugar is dissolved. Add peels to corn-syrup mixture; over medium heat, heat to boiling; reduce heat to low; simmer 10 minutes; keep warm.

4. About 1¼ hours before ham is done, prepare Holiday Potato Cones as in potato-cone recipe, but do not broil.

5. About 20 minutes before ham is done, prepare Spinach-Topped Tomatoes.

6. To serve, place ham on warm large platter, spoon orange-peel glaze to cover ham. Broil Holiday Potato Cones as directed in last paragraph of potato-cone recipe. Arrange Holiday Potato Cones and Spinach-Topped Tomatoes around ham.

Holiday Potato Cones: In 4-quart saucepan over high heat, heat *8 medium potatoes* (about 3 pounds) and enough *water* to cover to boiling. Reduce heat to medium-low; cover and cook about 35 minutes or until potatoes are fork-tender.
  Meanwhile, peel *4 large sweet potatoes* (about 3 pounds); cut ten ¾-inch thick diagonal center slices from sweet potatoes. (Reserve leftover sweet potatoes to make mashed potatoes next day.) In 12-inch skillet over medium heat, melt *3 tablespoons butter* or margarine; add sweet potato slices; cook until slices are golden on bottom. Reduce heat to low; cover and cook 5 minutes. With pancake turner, turn potatoes; cook over medium heat until browned on other side. Reduce heat to low; cover and cook 5 to 10 minutes longer until sweet potatoes are fork-tender. Sprinkle sweet potato slices with *1 tablespoon brown sugar;* cover skillet and heat until sugar is melted.
  When white potatoes are done, drain and peel. With mixer at low speed, beat white potatoes, *one 3-ounce package cream cheese,* ½ *cup milk, 4 tablespoons butter* or margarine, and *1 teaspoon salt* until smooth. With pancake turner, arrange sweet potato slices on cookie sheet. Using decorating bag and large rosette tube, pipe about ¾ cup mashed-potato mixture on top of each sweet potato slice to resemble a cone.

Preheat broiler if manufacturer directs. Broil potato cones until golden, about 8 to 10 minutes. Makes 10 servings. (For 20 servings, prepare recipe twice.)

Spinach-Topped Tomatoes: Cut *5 small tomatoes* into halves. In 12-inch skillet over medium heat, in *¼ inch boiling water,* arrange tomatoes, cut-side up; cook until tomato halves are heated through. Remove tomatoes from skillet; keep warm. Discard cooking liquid from skillet.

In same 12-inch skillet over medium heat, in *2 tablespoons hot salad oil,* cook *two 10-ounce bags spinach,* gradually adding spinach one-fourth at a time, until all spinach is wilted, stirring constantly; sprinkle with *¾ teaspoon salt.* Spoon sautéed spinach onto tomato halves. Makes 10 servings. (For 20 servings, prepare recipe twice.)

Oven Ham and Beans

TIME: about 35 minutes—SERVINGS: 6

4 teaspoons orange marmalade
2 teaspoons prepared mustard
2 16-ounce cans pork and beans in tomato sauce
1 fully cooked smoked ham center slice, cut about ¾ inch thick (about 1½ pounds)

1. In small bowl with spoon, mix marmalade and mustard.

2. Preheat oven to 325°F. Spoon beans into 12″ by 8″ baking dish. Cut ham slice into 6 equal portions; place on top of beans in baking dish. Brush ham with marmalade mixture.

3. Bake 35 minutes or until ham is heated through and beans are hot and bubbly.

SAUSAGES AND FRANKFURTERS

Skillet Sausage and Squash Supper

TIME: about 1¼ hours—SERVINGS: 6

1½ pounds hot Italian-sausage links
1½ pounds sweet Italian-sausage links
¼ cup water
4 medium potatoes, unpeeled and cut into bite-sized pieces
1 medium onion, chopped
2 tablespoons salad oil
2 medium zucchini (about 1 pound), cut into bite-sized pieces
2 medium yellow straightneck squash (about 1 pound), cut into bite-sized pieces
½ teaspoon salt
1½ teaspoons minced fresh basil or ½ teaspoon dried basil
fresh basil leaves for garnish

1. In 12-inch skillet over medium heat, heat sausages and water to boiling. Cover; simmer 5 minutes. Remove cover; continue cooking, turning sausages frequently, until sausages are well browned on all sides, about 20 minutes. Remove sausages to paper towels to drain. Slice sausages diagonally into bite-sized pieces. Discard all but 3 tablespoons drippings from skillet.

2. To same skillet over medium heat, in hot drippings, add potatoes and onion; cover skillet and cook until potatoes are browned on all sides and tender, turning occasionally, about 20 minutes.

3. Meanwhile, in 10-inch skillet over medium heat, in hot salad oil, cook zucchini, yellow squash, salt, and basil until vegetables are tender-crisp, stirring frequently, about 15 minutes.

4. When vegetables are done, add zucchini mixture and sausages to potato mixture; stir to mix well; cover skillet and cook over medium heat 3 to 5 minutes to blend flavors.

5. Spoon onto platter. Garnish with basil leaves.

Country Frank Sandwiches

TIME: about 30 minutes—SERVINGS: 6

1 16-ounce package chicken or other favorite frankfurters, cut into ¼-inch slices
3 tablespoons butter or margarine
1 large onion, sliced
1 medium green pepper, thinly sliced
1 medium red pepper, thinly sliced
¼ teaspoon basil
2 eggs, slightly beaten
¼ teaspoon salt
3 6-inch pitas*
6 large lettuce leaves

*A Pita is a Middle Eastern pocket bread, available in most supermarkets.

1. In 10-inch skillet over medium-high heat, cook frankfurters until browned on all sides, stirring frequently. Remove frankfurters to large bowl.

2. In same skillet over medium heat, in basil until vegetables are tender, stirring occasionally. With slotted spoon, remove vegetables to large bowl with frankfurters.

3. In drippings remaining in skillet over medium heat, cook eggs and salt, stirring, until eggs are set. Return frankfurters and vegetable mixture to skillet; heat.

4. To serve, cut each pita crosswise in half. Place a lettuce leaf in each half; then fill with frankfurter mixture.

Fried Knackwurst and Potatoes

TIME: about 45 minutes—SERVINGS: 6

4 eggs
salt
1 tablespoon salad oil
butter or margarine
1 16-ounce package knackwurst, cut into ½-inch pieces
6 medium potatoes (2 pounds), unpeeled and cut into ¼-inch-thick slices
1 medium onion, chopped
1 tablespoon chopped parsley for garnish

1. In small bowl with fork or wire whisk, beat eggs and ¼ teaspoon salt. In 12-inch skillet over medium heat, heat salad oil until hot. Pour egg mixture into hot oil, tilting skillet to coat bottom of skillet evenly with egg mixture. Cover and cook 3 to 5 minutes until egg mixture is set, occasionally tilting skillet and lifting edge of cooked egg to let uncooked egg run into skillet. Slide egg onto cutting board; cut into very thin strips; keep warm.

2. In same 12-inch skillet over medium heat, in 1 tablespoon hot butter or margarine, cook knackwurst until browned. Remove knackwurst to medium bowl; keep warm.

3. In same skillet, melt 5 tablespoons butter or margarine; add potatoes, onion, and ¼ teaspoon salt; cook potato slices until golden on bottom. Reduce heat to low; cover and cook 5 minutes. With pancake turner, turn potatoes; cook over medium heat until browned on other side. Reduce heat to low; cover and cook 5 to 10 minutes longer until potatoes are tender.

4. Return knackwurst to skillet; gently combine potatoes and knackwurst with pancake turner and heat through.

5. Arrange potato mixture on warm platter; arrange egg strips around potato mixture; sprinkle with parsley.

Kielbasa with Sauerkraut

TIME: about 30 minutes—SERVINGS: 4

1 1-pound kielbasa (smoked Polish sausage), cut into 2-inch pieces
2 tablespoons salad oil
1 small onion, diced
1 small green pepper, diced
1 16-ounce can or package sauerkraut, drained
¾ cup water
2 tablespoons brown sugar
¼ teaspoon salt
1 large red cooking apple, cut into thin wedges

1. In 10-inch skillet over medium-high heat, cook kielbasa until lightly browned; remove to plate.

2. In same skillet over medium heat, in hot salad oil, cook onion and green pepper until tender, stirring occasionally. Add sauerkraut, water, brown sugar, salt, and kielbasa; heat to boiling. Reduce heat to low; cover and simmer 15 minutes, stirring occasionally. Add apple wedges to sauerkraut mixture; simmer 5 minutes or until heated through.

LAMB

Basque Lamb Stew

TIME: about 2 hours—SERVINGS: 8

2 tablespoons salad oil
2 medium onions, sliced
1 garlic clove, crushed
1 pound lamb for stew, cut into 1-inch chunks
1 28-ounce can tomatoes
1 teaspoon salt
¼ teaspoon pepper
¼ teaspoon rosemary, crushed
water
1 8-ounce package elbow macaroni
4 large carrots
1 10-ounce package frozen Brussels sprouts, slightly thawed
1 15¼- to 20-ounce can red kidney beans
1 tablespoon all-purpose flour

1. In 5-quart Dutch oven over medium heat, in hot oil, cook onions and garlic until tender, stirring occasionally. With slotted spoon, remove mixture to small bowl.

2. In drippings remaining in Dutch oven over medium-high heat, cook lamb for stew until browned on all sides. Return onion mixture to Dutch oven; stir in tomatoes with their liquid, salt, pepper, rosemary, and 2¼ cups water; over high heat, heat to boiling. Reduce heat to low; cover and simmer 40 minutes.

3. Meanwhile, cook macaroni as label directs; drain.

4. Cut each carrot crosswise in half; cut each half lengthwise into 4 pieces; add to simmering liquid in Dutch oven. Cover and cook 30 minutes.

5. About 15 minutes before carrots are done, cut each Brussels sprout in half; add to stew; cover and cook until meat and vegetables are tender. Skim off fat from liquid in Dutch oven.

6. Add cooked macaroni and kidney beans with their liquid to stew. In cup, stir flour and 2 tablespoons water; stir into liquid in Dutch oven. Cook, stirring constantly, until liquid is slightly thickened and macaroni and beans are heated through.

Lamb Kabobs

TIME: about 30 minutes—SERVINGS: 4

1 pound lamb cubes for kabobs
½ cup cooking or dry red wine
2 tablespoons salad oil
½ teaspoon salt
½ teaspoon oregano leaves
⅛ teaspoon pepper
1 garlic clove, crushed
1 large green pepper
1 medium onion
1 4-ounce jar pimentos, drained
½ pound medium mushrooms

1. In medium bowl, mix first 7 ingredients; set aside.

2. Cut green pepper into 1½-inch pieces. Cut onion into quarters, then separate each quarter into pieces. Cut pimentos into 1½-inch pieces. Cut mushrooms in half, if they are large.

3. Preheat broiler if manufacturer directs. On four 14-inch all-metal skewers, alternately thread lamb and vegetables, reserving marinade. Place skewers on rack in broiling pan; brush with marinade. Broil 20 minutes, turning skewers occasionally and brushing with marinade.

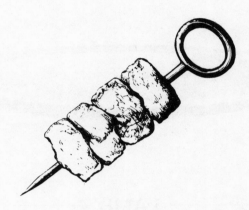

Roast Leg of Lamb with Herb Seasoning

TIME: about 2½ hours—SERVINGS: 8

⅓ cup chopped parsley
¼ cup olive or salad oil
2 teaspoons salt
2 teaspoons rosemary, crushed
½ teaspoon pepper
1 small garlic clove, crushed
1 4- to 4½-pound lamb leg shank half
8 medium potatoes (2½ pounds), peeled and cut into 1½-inch chunks

1. In small bowl, combine first 6 ingredients; set aside.

2. With knife, cut 3 crosswise slits on top (fat side) of lamb leg shank half, each about 4 inches long and ¼ inch deep. Lightly press some parsley mixture into slits; pat remaining parsley mixture onto top of lamb.

3. Place lamb, fat-side up, on small rack in 17¼" by 11½" open roasting pan. Insert meat thermometer into center of lamb, being careful that pointed end of thermometer does not touch bone or fat. Roast lamb in 325°F. oven until thermometer reaches 160°F. for medium (about 30 to 35 minutes per pound) or until of desired doneness.

4. About 35 minutes before lamb is done, add potatoes to roasting pan with meat, turning potatoes to coat on all sides with pan drippings; turn potatoes occasionally to brown on all sides.

5. When lamb is done, place on large platter; let stand 10 minutes for easier carving. Continue roasting potatoes about 10 minutes longer or until tender. Spoon potatoes around lamb.

Herb-Marinated Leg of Lamb

TIME: start day ahead—SERVINGS: 16

1 medium onion, chopped
1 large garlic clove, minced
1 cup dry red wine
¼ cup olive or salad oil
3 tablespoons prepared mustard
¾ teaspoon thyme leaves
⅛ teaspoon pepper
salt
rosemary
1 8-pound lamb leg, whole
1 bunch watercress
Lemon Cups for garnish (right)
water
3 tablespoons all-purpose flour

1. In large stainless steel, enamel, or glass pan, mix first 7 ingredients, 2 teaspoons salt, and ½ teaspoon rosemary. Add lamb leg and turn to coat with marinade. Cover and refrigerate at least 12 hours, turning lamb occasionally.

2. About 3½ hours before serving, place lamb, fat-side up, on rack in large open roasting pan; reserve marinade. Insert meat thermometer into center of lamb, being careful that pointed end of thermometer does not touch bone or fat. Roast lamb in 325°F. oven until thermometer reaches 160°F. for medium (about 25 to 30 minutes per pound) or until of desired doneness, basting occasionally with marinade. About 15 minutes before lamb is done, chop enough watercress to make ½ cup; reserve remaining sprigs for garnish. Carefully pat chopped watercress onto lamb. Return lamb to oven; continue roasting until done.

3. Meanwhile, prepare Lemon Cups; refrigerate.

4. When lamb is done, place on warm large platter or cutting board; let stand for 15 minutes for easier carving. While lamb is standing, prepare gravy: Remove rack from roasting pan; pour pan drippings into a 4-cup measure or medium bowl (set pan aside); let stand a few seconds until fat separates from meat juice. Skim 3 tablespoons fat from drippings into a 2-quart saucepan; skim off and discard any remaining fat. Add ¼ cup water to roasting pan; stir until brown bits are loosened; add to meat juice in cup with additional water to make 2½ cups. Into hot fat in saucepan over medium heat, stir flour, ½ teaspoon crushed rosemary, and ¼ teaspoon salt until blended; gradually stir in meat-juice mixture and cook, stirring constantly, until gravy thickens and boils; boil 1 minute.

4. Pour gravy into gravy boat. Serve gravy with lamb. Garnish with Lemon Cups and reserved watercress sprigs.

Lemon Cups: With knife, cut *2 medium lemons* crosswise in half. With spoon, scoop out pulp (reserve for juice another day). Cut a thin slice off the bottom of each lemon half so it can stand upright. Cut rim of each lemon half into sawtooth pattern. Fill each lemon cup with *red currant jelly*.

Lamb Chops Teriyaki

TIME: about 25 minutes—SERVINGS: 4

⅓ cup packed brown sugar
¼ cup soy sauce
2 tablespoons catchup
1 tablespoon lemon juice
½ teaspoon salt
½ teaspoon ground ginger
¼ teaspoon pepper
⅛ teaspoon garlic powder
4 lamb shoulder blade or arm
  chops, each cut ¾ inch thick
parsley sprigs for garnish

1. Preheat broiler if manufacturer directs.

2. Meanwhile, in small bowl, mix first 8 ingredients until sauce is smooth.

3. Place lamb shoulder chops on rack in broiling pan; broil 15 minutes for medium-rare or until of desired doneness, turning chops once, and brushing often with sauce.

4. Remove chops to platter. Garnish with parsley sprigs.

Lamb Noisettes

TIME: about 1 hour—SERVINGS: 4

8 pitted prunes
8 dried apricot halves
water
butter or margarine
2 slices white bread, diced
⅛ teaspoon thyme leaves
⅛ teaspoon basil
salt
4 lamb loin chops, each cut 1¼
   inches thick
8 slices bacon
pepper
Currant-Orange Sauce (right)
1 10-ounce package frozen
   asparagus spears
5 large carrots, peeled and cut
   into long sticks

1. In 1-quart saucepan over high heat, heat prunes, apricots, and 3 tablespoons water to boiling; remove saucepan from heat; let stand 10 minutes or until fruit is plump and all liquid is absorbed.

2. Meanwhile, in 2-quart saucepan over medium heat, melt 3 tablespoons butter or margarine; add bread, thyme, basil, 1 teaspoon salt, and 2 teaspoons water; toss to mix well.

3. To remove bones from lamb chops: With knife, starting at one side of back bone, cut through meat along bone, keeping knife blade against bone; cut along both sides of bone just far enough to separate bone from meat, making sure that meat remains in one piece.

4. Preheat broiler if manufacturer directs. To stuff boned lamb chops, trim excess fat from chops. Fill each chop where the bone is removed with one-fourth of bread mixture, 2 prunes, and 2 apricot halves; push meat tightly around filling. Wrap 2 bacon slices tightly around side of each orange peel, chop; secure with toothpicks.

5. Place lamb chops on rack in broiling pan; sprinkle lightly with salt and pepper. Broil lamb chops 8 minutes; with pancake turner, gently turn lamb chops; broil about 8 minutes longer for medium-rare or until of desired doneness; keep warm.

6. While lamb chops are broiling, prepare Currant-Orange Sauce; keep warm. Meanwhile, prepare asparagus spears as label directs. Also, in 12-inch skillet over medium heat, in 1 inch boiling water, heat carrots and ¾ teaspoon salt to boiling; reduce heat to low; cover and simmer 10 minutes or until carrot sticks are tender-crisp. Drain; return carrots to skillet; toss with 1 tablespoon butter or margarine to coat well.

7. To serve, place lamb chops on warm platter; arrange asparagus spears and buttered carrot sticks on platter with lamb chops. Pass Currant-Orange Sauce in small bowl to serve over chops.

Currant-Orange Sauce: From *1 medium orange*, grate 2 teaspoons peel and squeeze ½ cup juice. In 1-quart saucepan, mix orange peel, orange juice, *¼ cup red currant jelly,* and *1 teaspoon honey;* over medium heat, heat to boiling. Reduce heat to low; simmer, uncovered, 5 minutes, stirring frequently.

Glazed Lamb Chops with Skillet Potatoes

TIME: about 30 minutes—SERVINGS: 2

vegetable cooking spray
(optional)
2 tablespoons butter or
margarine
2 medium potatoes, unpeeled
and cut into ½-inch-thick
slices
1 small onion, chopped
salt
2 teaspoons minced parsley
¼ cup apricot preserves
2 teaspoons prepared mustard
2 teaspoons minced preserved
ginger
2 lamb shoulder blade chops,
each cut ¾ inch thick
pepper
parsley sprigs for garnish

1. If desired, spray 10-inch skillet with vegetable cooking spray as label directs; place skillet over medium heat. In skillet, melt butter or margarine; add potatoes, onion, and ¼ teaspoon salt. Cover skillet and cook potato slices until well browned on both sides, turning occasionally, about 15 to 20 minutes. Sprinkle potatoes with chopped parsley.

2. Meanwhile, preheat broiler if manufacturer directs. In cup, mix apricot preserves, mustard, and ginger.

3. Lightly sprinkle lamb shoulder blade chops with salt and pepper. Place chops on rack in broiling pan. Broil chops 10 to 15 minutes for medium-rare or until of desired doneness, turning once and brushing occasionally with apricot mixture.

4. Arrange chops and potatoes on warm platter; garnish with parsley sprigs.

Spring Lamb and Vegetable Potpourri

TIME: about 1¼ hours—SERVINGS: 8

1½ pounds ground lamb
⅓ cup dried bread crumbs
1 small onion, minced
1 garlic clove, minced
1 egg
water
salt
pepper
ground coriander
salad oil
6 medium carrots, cut into 1½-
inch pieces
1 medium zucchini, cut crosswise
into ½-inch slices
1 large eggplant (2 pounds), cut
into 1½-inch chunks
½ pound mushrooms
1 28-ounce can tomatoes
1 tablespoon all-purpose flour
2 16- to 20-ounce cans white
kidney (cannellini) beans,
drained

1. In medium bowl, mix ground lamb, bread crumbs, onion, garlic, egg, 2 tablespoons water, 1 teaspoon salt, ¼ teaspoon pepper, and ¼ teaspoon coriander. Shape mixture into 1½-inch meatballs.

2. In 8-quart Dutch oven over high heat, in 2 tablespoons hot oil, cook meatballs until well browned on all sides, removing them to large bowl as they brown.

3. In drippings remaining in Dutch oven over medium heat, cook carrots and zucchini until browned on all sides, stirring occasionally; with slotted spoon, remove to bowl with meatballs.

4. In same Dutch oven, in 3 more tablespoons hot salad oil, cook eggplant and mushrooms until browned on all sides, stirring ocasionally. Stir in tomatoes with their liquid, ¾ cup water, ¾ teaspoon salt, ¼ teaspoon pepper, and ¼ teaspoon coriander.

5. Return meatballs and vegetables to Dutch oven; over high heat, heat to boiling. Reduce heat to low; cover and simmer until vegetables are fork-tender, about 35 minutes, stirring occasionally and being careful not to break up meatballs. Skim off fat from liquid in Dutch oven.

6. In cup, blend flour with 2 tablespoons water; gradually stir flour mixture into simmering liquid in Dutch oven. Cook, stirring constantly, until mixture is slightly thickened.

7. About 10 minutes before vegetables are done, prepare kidney beans: In 2-quart saucepan over medium heat, heat kidney beans, 1 tablespoon salad oil, ½ teaspoon salt, and ⅛ teaspoon pepper until hot.

8. To serve, spoon lamb mixture into center of warm deep platter; spoon bean mixture around lamb mixture.

RABBIT

Brunswick Stew

TIME: about 3 hours—SERVINGS: 10

¼ cup salad oil
3 celery stalks, sliced (1 cup)
2 medium onions, sliced
1 2½- to 3-pound package
   frozen rabbit, thawed*
2 pounds beef for stew, cut into
   1-inch chunks
1 28-ounce can tomatoes
3 medium potatoes (1 pound),
   peeled and grated
2 teaspoons salt
½ teaspoon basil
½ teaspoon crushed red pepper
¼ teaspoon pepper
1 10-ounce package frozen lima
   beans
1 10-ounce package frozen
   whole kernel corn

*Or, use one 2½- to 3-pound broiler-
fryer, cut up. Simmer only 35 minutes
in step 3.

1. In 8-quart Dutch oven over medium heat, in hot salad oil, cook celery and onion until lightly browned. With slotted spoon, remove vegetables to small bowl; set aside.

2. In hot oil remaining in Dutch oven, cook rabbit, then beef chunks, several pieces at a time, until well browned on all sides, removing pieces as they brown.

3. Return rabbit, beef, and onion mixture to Dutch oven; stir in tomatoes with their liquid and next 5 ingredients; heat to boiling. Reduce heat to low; cover and simmer 1 hour or until rabbit is fork-tender, stirring occasionally. Remove rabbit to plate; set aside. Continue cooking beef mixture until meat is fork-tender, about 1 hour longer, stirring occasionally.

4. Meanwhile, cool rabbit until easy to handle; discard bones and skin; cut meat into bite-sized pieces. When beef is done, return rabbit to Dutch oven. Stir in frozen beans and corn and cook until hot, about 10 minutes.

CHICKEN

Braised Chicken and Vegetables with Brown Rice

TIME: about 1¼ hours—SERVINGS: 7

1 cup brown rice
3 tablespoons salad oil
1 2½- to 3-pound broiler-fryer,
   cut up
½ pound small white onions
6 medium carrots, cut into 1-inch
   pieces
1 chicken-flavor bouillon cube or
   envelope
2 cups water
1 teaspoon salt
¼ teaspoon coarsely ground
   black pepper
⅛ teaspoon ground sage
1 medium bunch broccoli, cut
   into 3" by 1" pieces
½ cup milk
1 tablespoon all-purpose flour

1. Prepare brown rice as label directs.

2. Meanwhile, in 5-quart Dutch oven over medium heat, in hot salad oil, cook chicken, a few pieces at a time, until browned on all sides, removing pieces as they brown to medium bowl.

3. In drippings remaining in Dutch oven, cook onions until browned, stirring occasionally. Return chicken to Dutch oven. Add carrots, bouillon, water, salt, pepper, and sage. Over high heat, heat to boiling, stirring to loosen brown bits from bottom of pan. Reduce heat to low; cover and simmer 20 minutes. Add broccoli; cook 15 to 20 minutes longer until chicken and vegetables are tender.

4. Spoon rice onto warm platter. With slotted spoon, remove chicken and vegetables to platter with rice.

5. Skim off fat from liquid in Dutch oven. In cup, stir milk and flour; stir into simmering liquid in Dutch oven. Cook over medium heat until gravy is slightly thickened.

6. Serve gravy in small bowl to spoon over chicken, vegetables, and rice.

Creamy Chicken and Fettuccine

TIME: about 40 minutes—SERVINGS: 4

½ 12-ounce package fettuccine
  noodles
2 whole large chicken breasts
1 egg
all-purpose flour
salt
pepper
butter or margarine
¼ pound mushrooms, sliced
1½ cups milk
2 tablespoons cooking or dry
  sherry
¼ cup grated Parmesan cheese
1 tablespoon chopped parsley for
  garnish

1. In 6-quart saucepot, prepare fettuccine as label directs; drain; keep warm.

2. Meanwhile, cut each chicken breast in half; remove skin and bones. In small bowl with fork, beat egg slightly. On waxed paper, mix ¼ cup flour, ½ teaspoon salt, and ⅛ teaspoon pepper. Dip chicken pieces into beaten egg, then into flour mixture to coat evenly.

3. In 10-inch skillet over medium-high heat, in 2 tablespoons hot butter or margarine, cook chicken until tender and browned on both sides, about 10 minutes. Remove chicken to warm large platter; keep warm.

4. In drippings in skillet over medium heat, heat 2 more tablespoons butter or margarine; add mushrooms and cook until tender, stirring occasionally. Stir in 2 tablespoons flour, ½ teaspoon salt, and ⅛ teaspoon pepper; cook 1 minute. Gradually add milk and sherry; cook, stirring constantly, until thickened, about 5 minutes. Stir in cheese until melted. Reserve 1 cup sauce from skillet.

5. Add fettuccine to sauce remaining in skillet, tossing to coat well.

6. Arrange fettuccine on platter next to chicken. Pour reserved sauce over chicken pieces. Sprinkle fettuccine with parsley.

Chicken Stroganoff

TIME: about 1 hour—SERVINGS: 6

2 whole large chicken breasts
butter or margarine
1 medium onion, sliced
½ pound mushrooms, sliced
1 tablespoon all-purpose flour
1 chicken-flavor bouillon cube or
  envelope
1½ cups water
1 8-ounce container sour cream
½ 8-ounce package medium
  noodles
½ 8-ounce package spinach
  noodles

1. Cut each chicken breast in half; remove skin and bones. Then, with knife held in slanting position, almost parallel to the cutting surface, slice across width of each half into ⅛-inch-thick slices.

2. In 12-inch skillet over medium-high heat, in 2 tablespoons hot butter or margarine (be careful not to let butter burn), cook chicken, stirring constantly, until chicken is tender, about 2 to 3 minutes. Remove chicken to plate; set aside.

3. In same skillet over medium heat, in 2 more tablespoons hot butter or margarine, cook onion and mushrooms until vegetables are tender, stirring occasionally. Into vegetable mixture, stir flour and bouillon until blended; cook 1 minute. Gradually stir in water; cook, stirring constantly, until mixture is thickened and smooth.

4. Reduce heat to low. Stir sour cream into mixture in skillet; add chicken; heat through, stirring constantly. (Do not boil, or mixture may curdle.)

5. Meanwhile, prepare noodles: In 5-quart saucepot, heat 3 quarts water to boiling; stir in noodles; cook 5 to 10 minutes until tender; drain.

6. Serve noodles with chicken mixture.

Chicken-Bacon Nuggets

TIME: about 30 minutes—SERVINGS: 4

2 whole large chicken breasts
¼ cup orange marmalade
2 tablespoons soy sauce
½ teaspoon salt
½ teaspoon ground ginger
⅛ teaspoon garlic powder
1 8-ounce package sliced bacon
about 24 toothpicks

1. Cut each chicken breast lengthwise in half; remove skin and bones; then cut each half into 6 chunks. In medium bowl, mix chicken, marmalade, soy sauce, salt, ginger, and garlic powder; set aside.

2. Preheat broiler if manufacturer directs. Arrange bacon slices on rack in broiling pan. Broil bacon 4 minutes or until partially cooked, turning once. Cut each bacon slice crosswise in half.

3. Wrap each piece of chicken with a piece of bacon; secure with a toothpick. Place bacon-wrapped chicken on rack in broiling pan; broil 5 minutes or until chicken is fork-tender, turning nuggets once and brushing with marmalade mixture remaining in bowl. Remove toothpicks.

Plump Roast Chicken with Dressing

TIME: about 4 hours—SERVINGS: 6

Moist Bread Dressing (page 89)
1 5½- to 6 pound roasting
   chicken
salad oil
¼ teaspoon paprika
⅛ teaspoon pepper
salt
1 small onion, quartered
water
3 tablespoons all-purpose flour
parsley sprigs for garnish

1. Prepare Moist Bread Dressing.

2. Remove giblets and neck from chicken; reserve for gravy. Rinse chicken with running cold water and drain well. Spoon some of dressing lightly into neck cavity. (Do *not* pack dressing; it expands during cooking.) Fold neck skin over dressing; fasten neck skin to back with skewer. With chicken breast-side up, lift wings up toward neck, then fold under back of chicken so they stay in place.

3. Spoon remaining dressing lightly into body cavity.* Close by folding skin lightly over opening; skewer closed if necessary. With string, tie legs and tail together.

4. Place chicken, breast-side up, on rack in open roasting pan; brush with salad oil; sprinkle with paprika, pepper, and ½ teaspoon salt. Roast in 350°F. oven about 2½ hours. Start checking for doneness during last 30 minutes. (If you like, use a meat thermometer. Before placing chicken in oven, insert meat thermometer into thickest part of meat between breast and thigh, being careful that pointed end of thermometer does not touch bone.)

5. When chicken turns golden, cover loosely with a "tent" of folded foil. Remove foil during last of roasting time and, with pastry brush, brush chicken generously with pan drippings. Chicken is done when thickest part of leg feels soft when pinched with fingers protected by paper towels. (If using meat thermometer, chicken is done when thermometer reaches 175° to 180°F.)

6. While chicken is roasting, prepare giblets and neck to use in gravy: In 1-quart saucepan over high heat, heat giblets, neck, onion, 1 cup water, and ¼ teaspoon salt to boiling. Reduce heat to low; cover and simmer 30 minutes or until giblets are tender. Drain,

*Bake any leftover dressing in covered, greased small casserole during last 30 minutes of roasting chicken.

reserving broth; discard onion. Pull meat from neck; discard bones; coarsely chop neck meat and giblets; refrigerate.

7. When chicken is done, place on warm platter; keep warm.

8. Prepare gravy: Remove rack from roasting pan; pour pan drippings into a 2-cup measure or small bowl (set pan aside); let stand a few seconds until fat separates from meat juice. Skim 3 tablespoons fat from drippings into 1-quart saucepan; skim off and discard any remaining fat. Add reserved giblet broth to roasting pan; stir until brown bits are loosened; add to meat juice in cup to make 1½ cups (add water if necessary). Into fat in saucepan over medium heat, stir flour and ¼ teaspoon salt until blended; gradually stir in meat-juice mixture; cook, stirring constantly, until mixture is thickened. Add reserved giblets and meat; cook until heated through. Pour gravy into gravy boat.

9. To serve, arrange parsley sprigs around chicken. Serve with gravy.

Moist Bread Dressing: In 4-quart saucepan over medium heat, melt ½ *cup butter* or margarine; add *1 medium celery stalk*, diced, and *1 medium onion*, diced; cook until vegetables are tender, about 10 minutes, stirring frequently. Remove saucepan from heat. Stir in *2 tablespoons minced parsley*, ¾ *teaspoon salt*, ½ *teaspoon poultry seasoning*, and ¼ *teaspoon pepper*. Add *9 cups white-bread cubes*, ¼ *cup water*, and *1 egg*, slightly beaten; mix well.

Roast Chicken Paprika

TIME: about 1¼ hours—SERVINGS: 4

2 tablespoons butter or
  margarine
1 2½- to 3-pound broiler-fryer,
  quartered
paprika
salt
pepper

1. In broiling pan, in 350°F. oven, melt butter or margarine. Remove broiling pan from oven; place chicken, skin-side down, in melted butter or margarine. Bake chicken 40 minutes.

2. With pancake turner, loosen chicken from pan if necessary. Turn chicken skin-side up; with pastry brush, brush generously with pan drippings; lightly sprinkle with paprika, salt, and pepper. Bake 20 minutes longer or until chicken is fork-tender.

Saucy Chicken Livers

TIME: about 30 minutes—SERVINGS: 4

1 pound chicken livers
4 tablespoons butter or
  margarine
1 small onion, minced
1 16-ounce can tomatoes
2 tablespoons cooking wine
1½ teaspoons sugar
½ teaspoon basil
½ teaspoon salt
¼ teaspoon pepper
2 tablespoons milk
1 tablespoon all-purpose flour

1. Cut each chicken liver in half; remove white membrane.

2. In 10-inch skillet over medium heat, in hot butter or margarine, cook chicken livers and onion until livers are lightly browned and onion is tender. Add tomatoes with their liquid, wine, sugar, basil, salt, and pepper, stirring to break up tomatoes; heat to boiling. Reduce heat to low; cover; simmer 10 minutes.

3. In cup, mix milk and flour; gradually stir into mixture in skillet; cook over medium heat, stirring, until thickened.

Fried Chicken

TIME: about 50 minutes—SERVINGS: 4

salad oil
¼ cup milk
1 cup all-purpose flour
1 teaspoon salt
¼ teaspoon pepper
1 3-pound broiler-fryer, cut up

1. In 12-inch skillet over medium-high heat, heat ¼ inch salad oil until hot.

2. Meanwhile, into pie plate, pour milk. On sheet of waxed paper, combine flour, salt, and pepper; dip chicken pieces in milk, then coat well with flour mixture.

3. Carefully place chicken pieces, skin-side up, in hot oil. Cook about 5 minutes or until underside of chicken is golden; reduce heat to low; cook 5 minutes longer. With pancake turner, loosen chicken from pan bottom. Turn chicken, skin-side down. Cook over medium-high heat about 5 minutes or until skin-side of chicken is golden brown; reduce heat to low; cook 5 minutes longer or until chicken is fork-tender.

4. Remove chicken pieces, skin-side up, to paper towels to drain.

Chicken Milano

TIME: about 30 minutes—SERVINGS: 4

1 cup regular long-grain rice or orzo (rice-shaped pasta)
2 whole large chicken breasts
2 tablespoons butter or margarine
1 medium onion, sliced
1 small garlic clove, minced
1 10¾-ounce can condensed tomato soup
1 4-ounce jar sliced mushrooms, drained
2 medium zucchini (1¼ pounds), sliced
½ teaspoon basil
⅛ teaspoon crushed red pepper

1. Prepare rice or orzo as label directs.

2. Meanwhile, remove skin and bones from chicken breasts; cut breast meat into 1½-inch chunks.

3. In 10-inch skillet over medium heat, in hot butter or margarine, cook onion and garlic until onion is tender, stirring occasionally.

4. Add chicken chunks; cook until chicken is lightly browned on all sides, stirring frequently.

5. Stir in undiluted tomato soup and remaining ingredients; over high heat, heat to boiling. Reduce heat to low; cover and simmer 20 minutes, stirring occasionally.

6. To serve, spoon chicken mixture over rice in deep platter.

Chicken with Bulgur Pilaf

TIME: about 1¼ hours—SERVINGS: 6

3 tablespoons salad oil
1 2½- to 3-pound broiler-fryer, cut up
1 small onion, diced
1¼ cups bulgur (cracked wheat)
4½ cups water
1 cup regular long-grain rice
1 chicken-flavor bouillon cube or envelope
1½ teaspoons salt
⅛ teaspoon pepper

1. In 12-inch skillet over medium-high heat, in hot salad oil, cook chicken until browned on all sides. Remove chicken to bowl.

2. In drippings remaining in skillet over medium heat, cook onion and bulgur until bulgur is browned.

3. To bulgur in skillet, add water, rice, bouillon, salt, and pepper. Return chicken to skillet; over high heat, heat to boiling. Reduce heat to low; cover; simmer 35 minutes or until chicken and bulgar are tender.

90

From top: New England Clam Pies, page 11[?], [...] [...]3,
and Beef Empanadas, page 62

Beef Scallops with Fresh Tomato Sauce, page 45

Clockwise from top left: Fettuccine Alfredo, page 131; Fettuccine with White Clam Sauce, page 132; Fettuccine with Pesto Sauce, page 131; Ravioli with Meat Sauce, page 133; Tortellini in Escarole Soup, page 130, and Fettuccine Primavera, page 132

Easy Country Vegetables, page 30

Harvest-Time Stuffed Vegetables, page 33

Cinnamon Butterfly Rolls, page 157

Fried Indian Bread (Poori), page 161

Cracked-Wheat Rolls, page 149

Herbed Dinner Rolls, page 167

Chicken, Tofu, and Rice

TIME: about 1 hour—SERVINGS: 8

1 2½- to 3-pound broiler-fryer
¼ cup salad oil
1 medium onion, diced
3 cups water
1 16-ounce can tomatoes
2 cups regular long-grain rice
1 teaspoon salt
¼ teaspoon pepper
1 chicken-flavor bouillon cube or
  envelope
1 16-ounce container firm tofu
  (soybean curd)*
1 cup frozen peas
¼ cup grated Parmesan cheese
1 medium tomato, cut into thin
  wedges
1 3¼-ounce can pitted ripe
  olives, drained and each cut in
  half

*Available in many supermarkets or
at Oriental stores.

1. With poultry or kitchen shears, cut chicken into 16 pieces. In 5-quart Dutch oven over medium heat, in hot salad oil, cook chicken, a few pieces at a time, until browned on all sides, removing pieces as they brown to bowl.

2. In drippings remaining in Dutch oven, cook onion until tender, stirring occasionally.

3. Return chicken to Dutch oven; add water, tomatoes with their liquid, rice, salt, pepper, and bouillon; over high heat, heat to boiling, stirring to loosen brown bits from bottom of pan. Reduce heat to low; cover and simmer 30 minutes, stirring occasionally.

4. Drain tofu; cut tofu lengthwise into quarters, then cut each quarter crosswise into ¼-inch slices. Gently stir tofu, frozen peas, and Parmesan cheese into chicken mixture; top with tomato wedges; cover and cook 5 to 10 minutes longer until chicken and rice are tender and all liquid is absorbed. Garnish with olives.

Party Chicken and Shrimp

TIME: about 1 hour—SERVINGS: 6

1 pound medium shrimp
3 whole large chicken breasts,
  each cut in half
4 tablespoons butter or
  margarine
1 medium onion, diced
¼ cup minced parsley
1 8-ounce can tomato sauce
⅓ cup port wine
¼ cup water
¾ teaspoon salt
1 teaspoon basil
¼ teaspoon pepper
parsley sprig for garnish

1. Shell and devein shrimp. If you like, remove bones from chicken breasts; set shrimp and chicken aside.

2. In 12-inch skillet over medium heat, in hot butter or margarine, cook onion until tender, stirring occasionally. With slotted spoon, remove onion to small bowl.

3. In drippings remaining in skillet over medium-high heat, cook chicken breast halves until browned on both sides.

4. Into skillet with chicken, measure 3 tablespoons minced parsley; stir in onion, tomato sauce, wine, water, salt, basil, and pepper; over high heat, heat to boiling. Reduce heat to low; cover and simmer 10 minutes.

5. Add shrimp; cover and simmer 5 minutes or until chicken and shrimp are tender. Skim off fat from liquid in skillet.

6. Spoon mixture onto warm platter, sprinkle with remaining parsley. Garnish with parsley sprig.

Stir-Fried Chicken and Mushrooms

TIME: about 30 minutes—SERVINGS: 4

1 cup regular long-grain rice
2 whole large chicken breasts
2 tablespoons soy sauce
2 tablespoons cooking or dry
  sherry
2 teaspoons cornstarch
1 teaspoon minced ginger root or
  ¼ teaspoon ground ginger
¼ teaspoon sugar
⅛ teaspoon garlic powder
1 pound medium mushrooms
4 green onions
salad oil
1 cup frozen peas, thawed

1. Prepare rice as label directs; keep warm.

2. Meanwhile, cut each chicken breast lengthwise in half; remove skin and bones. Then, with knife held in slanting position, almost parallel to the cutting surface, slice across width of each half into ⅛-inch-thick slices. In medium bowl, mix chicken, soy sauce, sherry, cornstarch, ginger root, sugar, and garlic powder; set aside.

3. Thinly slice mushrooms; cut each green onion crosswise into 3-inch pieces. In 12-inch skillet or wok over medium-high heat, in ¼ cup hot salad oil, cook mushrooms and green onions, stirring quickly and frequently, until mushrooms are tender, about 2 minutes. With spoon, remove mushroom mixture to bowl.

4. In same skillet or wok over high heat, in 3 more tablespoons hot salad oil, cook chicken mixture, stirring quickly and frequently, until chicken is tender, about 2 to 3 minutes. Return mushroom mixture to skillet; add peas; heat through.

5. Serve with rice.

Szechwan Chicken

TIME: about 30 minutes—SERVINGS: 4

2 whole large chicken breasts
2 tablespoons soy sauce
2 tablespoons cooking or dry
  sherry
2 teaspoons cornstarch
¼ teaspoon sugar
¼ teaspoon ground ginger
¼ teaspoon crushed red pepper
⅛ teaspoon garlic powder
6 green onions
2 medium green peppers
salad oil
½ cup dry roasted peanuts

1. Cut each chicken breast in half; remove skin and bones. Then, with knife held in slanting position, almost parallel to the cutting surface, slice across width of each half into ⅛-inch-thick slices. In medium bowl, mix chicken and next 7 ingredients; set aside.

2. Cut green onions crosswise into 2-inch pieces; cut green peppers into bite-sized pieces. In 12-inch skillet over medium-high heat, in 2 tablespoons hot salad oil, cook green onions and peppers, stirring quickly and frequently, until vegetables are tender-crisp, about 2 minutes. With slotted spoon, remove vegetables to small bowl.

3. In same skillet over medium heat, in 3 more tablespoons hot salad oil, cook peanuts until lightly browned, stirring frequently. With slotted spoon, remove peanuts to bowl with vegetables.

4. In salad oil remaining in skillet over high heat, cook chicken mixture, stirring quickly and frequently, until chicken is tender, about 2 to 3 minutes. Return vegetables with any juices in bowl and peanuts to skillet; heat through.

Country Chicken

TIME: about 1 hour—SERVINGS: 6

4 medium potatoes (about 1½ pounds), cut into bite-sized chunks
1 pound hot Italian sausage links, cut into 1½-inch pieces
1 tablespoon salad oil
1 2½- to 3-pound broiler-fryer, cut up
4 medium green or red peppers, cut into bite-sized pieces
1 large onion, quartered and separated into pieces
½ cup water
½ teaspoon salt
½ teaspoon oregano leaves
1 10-ounce package frozen whole green beans

1. In large open roasting pan, mix potatoes, sausages, and salad oil. Bake in 425°F. oven 15 minutes.

2. Cut each piece of chicken breast in half; add with next 5 ingredients to pan, tossing to mix with ingredients in pan. Bake 15 minutes.

3. Separate frozen green beans under running warm water; drain on paper towels. Sprinkle green beans over chicken mixture; bake 15 to 20 minutes longer until chicken and vegetables are tender, stirring occasionally.

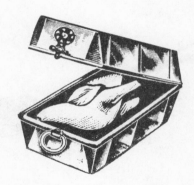

Sunday Chicken Salad

TIME: about 1½ hours—SERVINGS: 5

1 3- to 3½-pound broiler-fryer
salt
water
¼ pound cooked ham
1 large celery stalk, thinly sliced
⅓ cup mayonnaise
2 tablespoons milk
1 tablespoon lemon juice
⅛ teaspoon pepper
1 large avocado

1. Cook chicken: Rinse chicken, its giblets, and neck with running cold water. Place chicken, breast-side down, in 5-quart saucepot or Dutch oven; add giblets, neck, 1 teaspoon salt, and 2 inches water; over high heat, heat to boiling. Reduce heat to low; cover and simmer 35 minutes or until chicken is fork-tender.

2. Remove chicken to large bowl; refrigerate 20 minutes or until easy to handle. (Save broth for use in soup or gravy another day.) Discard skin and bones; cut meat and giblets into bite-sized pieces.

3. Dice ham. In large bowl, mix ham, chicken pieces, celery, mayonnaise, milk, lemon juice, pepper, and ½ teaspoon salt.

4. Cut avocado lengthwise in half; remove seed and peel. Carefully cut avocado into bite-sized pieces; gently stir avocado into chicken mixture.

Big Chicken Burger

TIME: about 30 minutes—SERVINGS: 2

1 8- to 8¾-ounce can red kidney
   beans, drained
1 tablespoon red wine vinegar
1 teaspoon sugar
salad oil
salt
2 slices white bread
1 5- to 6¾-ounce can chunk
   chicken, drained and flaked
1 egg
1 medium carrot, finely shredded
   (about ½ cup)
2 teaspoons grated onion
1 small tomato, cut into wedges
2 medium lettuce leaves

1. In small bowl, mix kidney beans, vinegar, sugar, 1 tablespoon salad oil, and ¾ teaspoon salt.

2. Into medium bowl, tear bread into small pieces. Add chicken, egg, carrot, onion, and ½ teaspoon salt; mix well. With hands, shape chicken mixture into two 3-inch-round patties.

3. In 10-inch skillet over medium heat, in 1 tablespoon hot salad oil, cook patties until browned on both sides, about 8 to 10 minutes.

4. For each serving, on plate, place a chicken patty and half of tomato wedges. On same plate with patty, spoon half of bean mixture onto a lettuce leaf.

Chicken Fricassee with Dumplings

TIME: about 1 hour—SERVINGS: 4

¼ cup all-purpose flour
2 teaspoons salt
1 teaspoon paprika
⅛ teaspoon pepper
1 2½- to 3-pound broiler-fryer,
   cut up
3 tablespoons salad oil
2 medium celery stalks, thinly
   sliced
2 medium carrots, thinly sliced
1 small onion, sliced
1 10¾-ounce can condensed
   cream of chicken soup
milk
1 cup buttermilk-baking mix

1. On waxed paper, combine flour, salt, paprika, and pepper; coat chicken with flour mixture. In 12-inch skillet over medium-high heat, in hot salad oil, cook chicken, a few pieces at a time, until browned on all sides, removing pieces to plate as they brown.

2. In drippings remaining in skillet over medium heat, cook celery, carrots, and onion until tender, stirring occasionally.

3. Return chicken to skillet; stir in undiluted soup and 1½ cups milk; heat to boiling. Reduce heat to low; cover and simmer 25 minutes.

4. In small bowl with fork, stir buttermilk-baking mix and ⅓ cup milk just until blended. (Dough will be soft.) Drop dumpling dough by heaping tablespoons onto simmering liquid in skillet. Cover skillet and cook 10 minutes or until chicken is tender and dumplings are set.

Party Chicken in Herbed Pastry Tray

TIME: about 2½ hours—SERVINGS: 6

Herbed Pastry Tray (right)
salad oil
3 whole large chicken breasts,
　boned and each cut in half
1 pound small white onions
6 medium carrots, sliced
1½ cups water
2 tablespoons cooking or dry
　sherry
1¼ teaspoons salt
¼ teaspoon pepper
1 chicken-flavor bouillon cube or
　envelope
2 9-ounce packages frozen
　artichoke hearts
¼ cup frozen peas
½ cup milk
3 tablespoons all-purpose flour
½ 10-ounce bag spinach

1. Prepare Herbed Pastry Tray.

2. In 5-quart Dutch oven over medium-high heat, in 2 tablespoons hot salad oil, cook chicken breasts until browned on all sides. With tongs, remove chicken to medium bowl.

3. In same Dutch oven over medium heat, in 1 more tablespoon hot salad oil, cook onions and carrots until lightly browned, stirring occasionally.

4. Return chicken to Dutch oven. Add water, sherry, salt, pepper, and bouillon; over high heat, heat to boiling, stirring to loosen brown bits from bottom of pan. Reduce heat to low; cover; simmer 25 minutes. Skim off fat. Add frozen artichoke hearts and peas.

5. In cup, stir milk and flour; gradually stir into liquid in Dutch oven. Cook over medium heat 10 minutes longer, stirring constantly, until chicken and vegetables are tender and sauce is thickened and smooth.

6. To serve, line Herbed Pastry Tray with uncooked spinach leaves; spoon chicken mixture over spinach. Stand a pastry braid at each narrow end of Herbed Pastry Tray for form handles.

Herbed Pastry Tray: Into large bowl, measure *3¾ cups all-purpose flour, 1 cup cold butter or margarine,* cut into ¼-inch pieces, *¾ teaspoon ground sage,* and *½ teaspoon thyme leaves.* With fingertips, blend flour and butter or margarine until mixture resembles coarse crumbs. In cup with fork, beat *3 egg yolks* with *¾ cup iced water;* add to flour mixture, stirring with fork to mix well. Shape pastry into ball.

Preheat oven to 400°F. On floured surface with floured rolling pin, roll three-fourths of pastry into 20″ by 14″ rectangle. Line 15½″ by 10½″ jelly-roll pan with pastry. Trim pastry edge, leaving 1-inch overhang. Gently press pastry to bottom and up sides of pan. Fold overhang under and press gently all around to make stand-up edge; flute. With fork, gently prick pastry in many places, being careful not to make holes large, or sauce in chicken mixture will seep through. Line pastry with foil, pressing foil to bottom and up sides of pastry. Roll remaining pastry into 12″ by 3″ rectangle; cut into six 12″ by ½″ strips. Braid pastry strips into 2 braids, using 3 strips for each braid. Place braids on small cookie sheet; shape each braid into curved handle.

Bake Herbed Pastry Tray 10 minutes; discard foil; again prick pastry with fork. Bake 25 minutes longer or until pastry is lightly browned and crisp. (If pastry puffs up again, gently press pastry to bottom of pan with spoon.) Bake pastry braids 15 minutes or until lightly browned. Cool Herbed Pastry Tray in pan on wire rack 10 minutes. Cool pastry braids on wire rack 10 minutes. With knife, gently loosen Herbed Pastry Tray from sides of pan; carefully remove to large platter.

Chicken in Anchovy Sauce

TIME: about 40 minutes—SERVINGS: 6

2 tablespoons olive or salad oil
3 whole large chicken breasts, each cut in half
½ pound small white onions
¾ cup water
½ cup cooking or dry white wine
2 tablespoons white wine vinegar
½ teaspoon oregano leaves
1 chicken-flavor bouillon cube or envelope
1 7-ounce jar roasted sweet red peppers, drained, and cut into ½-inch-thick strips
½ cup pitted small ripe olives, each cut in half
½ 2-ounce can anchovy fillets, drained and chopped

1. In 12-inch skillet over medium-high heat, in hot olive oil, cook chicken breasts until browned on all sides. Remove chicken breasts to plate.

2. In drippings remaining in skillet over medium heat, cook onions until browned, stirring occasionally. Return chicken to skillet; stir in water, wine, vinegar, oregano, and bouillon; over high heat, heat to boiling. Reduce heat to low: cover and simmer 20 minutes or until chicken is fork-tender, turning chicken once.

3. Skim off fat from liquid in skillet. Add roasted peppers, olives, and anchovies to chicken mixture in skillet; heat through.

ROCK CORNISH HENS AND CAPONS

Rock Cornish Hens with Sausage Stuffing

TIME: about 1¾ hours—SERVINGS: 4

2 1½- to 2-pound fresh or frozen (thawed) Rock Cornish hens
1 8-ounce package pork sausage meat
salad oil
1 10-ounce bag spinach
1 small onion, diced
2 slices white bread
1 egg
⅛ teaspoon pepper
salt
lettuce leaves for garnish
½ 14-ounce jar spiced crab apples, drained
½ 9.5-ounce jar kumquats, drained

1. Remove giblets and necks from Rock Cornish hens; reserve to use in soup another day. Rinse hens with running cold water; pat dry with paper towels. Cut each hen in half; refrigerate.

2. Prepare stuffing: In 10-inch skillet over medium-high heat, cook pork sausage meat until browned. With slotted spoon, remove sausage to medium bowl; set aside. In same skillet over medium heat, in drippings and 2 tablespoons hot salad oil, cook spinach and onion until tender, about 10 minutes, stirring occasionally. Remove skillet from heat.

3. Into spinach mixture, tear bread into small pieces; stir in egg, pepper, and cooked sausage.

4. Preheat oven to 400°F. Carefully loosen skin on each hen half by pushing fingers between skin and meat to form a pocket; spoon some stuffing into each pocket. Place hen halves, breast-side up, in 13″ by 9″ baking pan. Brush hens with salad oil; sprinkle lightly with salt. Bake hens 55 to 60 minutes until fork-tender.

5. Arrange hens on warm large platter; garnish with lettuce leaves, spiced apples, and kumquats.

Six Golden Hens

TIME: about 2½ hours—SERVINGS: 6

½ cup regular long-grain rice
1 chicken-flavor bouillon cube or envelope
6 1-pound fresh or frozen (thawed) Rock Cornish hens
water
3 tablespoons butter or margarine
¼ pound mushrooms, chopped
1 small onion, diced
1 10-ounce package frozen chopped spinach, thawed and squeezed dry
1 tablespoon cooking or dry sherry
salt
pepper
Holiday Vegetables (right)
1 16-ounce can whole-berry cranberry sauce
1 8- to 8½-ounce can sliced pears, drained and chopped

1. Prepare rice as label directs, except add bouillon to water.

2. Meanwhile, remove giblets and necks from Rock Cornish hens. Rinse hens with running cold water; pat dry with paper towels; refrigerate.

3. Prepare stuffing: In 1-quart saucepan over high heat, heat giblets, neck, and enough water to cover to boiling. Reduce heat to low; cover and simmer 15 minutes or until giblets are tender; drain. (Refrigerate broth to use in soup another day.) Pull meat from neck; discard bones; chop neck meat and giblets.

4. In 3-quart saucepan over medium heat, in hot butter or margarine, cook mushrooms and onion until tender, stirring occasionally. Remove saucepan from heat; stir in cooked rice, chopped neck meat and giblets, spinach, sherry, ¼ teaspoon salt, and ¼ teaspoon pepper.

5. Spoon some stuffing lightly into body cavity of each hen. Fold neck skin to back; lift wings up toward neck, then fold under back. With string, tie legs and tail of each hen together. Place hens, breast-side up, on rack in open roasting pan.

6. Sprinkle hens lightly with salt and pepper. Roast hens in 350°F. oven about 1¼ hours, brushing occasionally with drippings in pan. Hens are done when legs can be moved up and down easily, or when fork is inserted between leg and body cavity and juices that escape are not pink.

7. About 40 minutes before hens are done, prepare Holiday Vegetables.

8. When hens are done, discard strings. Place hens on warm large platter; keep warm.

9. Prepare sauce: In 1-quart saucepan over medium heat, heat cranberry sauce and chopped pears until heated through, stirring occasionally. Brush hens lightly with some cranberry-sauce mixture.

10. Spoon remaining sauce into bowl to serve with hens. Arrange vegetables on platter with hens.

Holiday Vegetables: In 3-quart saucepan, heat *1 inch water* and *1 teaspoon salt* to boiling. Add *1 pound green beans;* heat to boiling. Reduce heat to low; cover and simmer 5 minutes or until beans are tender. With slotted spoon, remove beans to large bowl; toss with *2 tablespoons butter* or margarine; keep warm.

In same water, heat *4 medium carrots,* cut into matchstick-thin strips, to boiling. Reduce heat to low; cover and simmer 3 minutes or until carrots are tender-crisp; drain. Return carrots to saucepan; toss with *2 tablespoons butter* or margarine; keep warm.

Broiled Rock Cornish Hens à L'Orange

TIME: about 40 minutes—SERVINGS: 4

2 1¾- to 2-pound fresh or frozen (thawed) Rock Cornish hens
1¼ teaspoons salt
¼ teaspoon pepper
4 tablespoons butter or margarine
4 teaspoons lemon juice
1 tablespoon soy sauce
½ cup orange marmalade

1. Preheat broiler if manufacturer directs. Remove giblets and necks from Rock Cornish hens; refrigerate to use in soup another day. Rinse hens in running cold water; pat dry with paper towels. With kitchen shears, cut each hen in half.

2. Sprinkle hens with salt and pepper. Place hen halves, skin-side down, in broiling pan (do not use rack). Place 1 tablespoon butter or margarine in each cavity; pour 1 teaspoon of lemon juice over each half. About 7 to 9 inches from source of heat (or at 450°F.), broil hen halves about 20 minutes. As soon as butter melts, move hen halves slightly to let butter run under so skin of hen will not stick to pan during broiling and brush hens with the melted butter. Turn hen halves skin-side up; broil about 15 minutes longer or until fork-tender, brushing with pan drippings occasionally.

3. During last 5 minutes of broiling hens, brush with soy sauce. About 1 minute before hens are done, brush with marmalade; broil until golden.

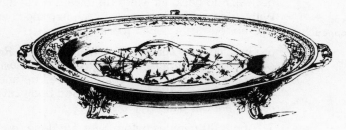

Braised Capon with Mushrooms, Potatoes, and Leeks

TIME: about 2½ hours—SERVINGS: 8

4 large leeks (about 3 pounds)
1 6- to 7-pound fresh or frozen (thawed) capon
2 tablespoons salad oil
paprika
6 medium potatoes (about 2 pounds), each cut into 6 chunks
1 pound medium mushrooms
¾ cup water
½ cup cooking or dry white wine
1½ teaspoons salt
½ teaspoon thyme leaves
¼ teaspoon pepper
1 chicken-flavor bouillon cube or envelope
¼ cup milk
2 tablespoons all-purpose flour
2 tablespoons chopped parsley for garnish

1. Cut off roots and trim leaf ends of leeks. Cut each leek crosswise into 3-inch pieces; then cut root end of each leek lengthwise in half. Rinse leeks well with running cold water to remove all sand; set aside.

2. Remove giblets and neck from inside of capon; reserve for soup another day. Rinse capon with running cold water; pat dry with paper towels.

3. In 8- to 12-quart Dutch oven over medium-high heat, in hot salad oil, cook capon until browned on all sides. Sprinkle capon lightly with paprika; add leeks, potatoes, mushrooms, water, white wine, salt, thyme, pepper, and chicken bouillon; heat to boiling. Cover Dutch oven and bake in 350°F. oven 1½ hours or until capon and vegetables are fork-tender, basting capon occasionally with liquid in Dutch oven.

4. Remove Dutch oven from oven. Skim off fat from liquid in Dutch oven. In cup, stir milk and flour until blended; gradually stir milk mixture into liquid in Dutch oven; cook over medium heat, stirring constantly, until slightly thickened.

5. To serve, lightly sprinkle capon with paprika, then parsley.

Roast Capon with Potato-Sausage Stuffing

TIME: about 3½ hours—SERVINGS: 8

Potato-Sausage Stuffing (right)
1 6- to 7-pound fresh or frozen
    (thawed) capon
salad oil
⅛ teaspoon pepper
salt
water
½ teaspoon instant chicken-
    flavor bouillon
3 tablespoons all-purpose flour
watercress for garnish

1. Prepare Potato-Sausage Stuffing.

2. Remove giblets and neck from inside of capon; reserve for soup another day. Rinse capon with running cold water; pat dry with paper towels.

3. Spoon some of stuffing lightly into neck cavity. (Do not pack stuffing; it expands during cooking.) Fold neck skin over stuffing; fasten neck skin to back with skewer. With capon breast-side up, lift wings up toward neck, then fold under back of capon so they stay in place. Spoon remaining stuffing lightly into body cavity.* Close, by folding skin lightly over opening; skewer closed if necessary. With string, tie legs and tail together.

4. Place capon, breast-side up, on rack in open roasting pan. Brush skin with salad oil; sprinkle with pepper and ½ teaspoon salt. Insert meat thermometer into thickest part of meat between breast and thigh, being careful that pointed end of the thermometer does not touch bone. Roast capon in 325°F. oven about 2½ hours. Start checking doneness during last 30 minutes of roasting.

5. When capon turns golden brown, cover loosely with a tent of foil. Remove foil during last of roasting time; with pastry brush, brush capon generously with pan drippings. Capon is done when thermometer reaches 175° to 180°F. and thickest part of drumstick feels soft when pressed with fingers protected with paper towels. Place capon on warm large platter; let stand 20 minutes for easier carving.

6. Meanwhile, prepare gravy: Remove rack from roasting pan; pour pan drippings into a 2-cup measure or small bowl (set pan aside); let stand a few seconds until fat separates from meat juice. Skim 3 tablespoons fat from drippings into a 1-quart saucepan; skim off and discard any remaining fat. Add 1 cup water to roasting pan; stir until brown bits are loosened; add to meat juice in cup along with chicken-flavor bouillon to make 1½ cups (add more water if necessary). Into fat in saucepan over medium heat, stir flour and ¼ teaspoon salt until blended; gradually stir in meat-juice mixture; cook, stirring constantly, until mixture is thickened. Pour gravy into gravy boat.

7. To serve, arrange watercress around capon. Serve with gravy.

Potato-Sausage Stuffing: In 12-inch skillet, prepare *one 16-ounce package pork-sausage links* as label directs. Remove sausages to paper towels to drain. Into drippings in skillet, stir *2 large celery stalks,* diced; cook over medium heat, until tender, stirring occasionally. Add *one 24-ounce or two 12-ounce packages frozen hash-brown potato nuggets,* ¼ teaspoon salt, and ¼ teaspoon thyme leaves; cook until potatoes are browned, stirring occasionally. Place potato mixture in large bowl. Cut sausage links into ¼-inch slices; place in bowl with potato mixture; mix well.

*Bake any leftover stuffing covered, in small, greased casserole during last 40 minutes of roasting time.

TURKEY

Roast Turkey with Pecan Stuffing, Giblet Gravy

TIME: about 6½ hours—SERVINGS: 16

1 cup butter or margarine
4 large celery stalks, thinly
   sliced
2 large onions, diced
1 6-ounce can pecans, toasted
   and chopped
14 cups white-bread cubes
   (about 22 slices)
¼ cup chopped parsley
1½ teaspoons poultry seasoning
¼ teaspoon pepper
3 eggs
salt
1 14-pound fresh or frozen
   (thawed) ready-to-stuff turkey
salad oil
water
⅓ cup all-purpose flour
2 bunches watercress
1 2-ounce jar pimento, drained
3 6-ounce jars pickled cocktail
   corn, drained

1. Prepare stuffing: In 8-quart Dutch oven over medium heat, in hot butter or margarine, cook celery and onions until tender, stirring occasionally. Remove Dutch oven from heat; stir in pecans, bread cubes, parsley, poultry seasoning, pepper, eggs, and 1½ teaspoons salt; mix well.

2. Remove giblets and neck from turkey; reserve for gravy. Rinse turkey with running cold water; drain well.

3. Spoon some of stuffing lightly into neck cavity. (Do not pack stuffing; it expands during cooking.) Fold neck skin over stuffing; fasten neck skin to back with 1 or 2 skewers. With turkey breast-side up, lift wings up toward neck, then fold under back of turkey so they stay in place.

4. Spoon some stuffing lightly into body cavity.* Close, by folding skin lightly over opening; skewer if necessary. Depending on brand of turkey, with string, tie legs and tail together; or push drumsticks under band of skin; or use stuffing clamp.

5. Place turkey, breast-side up, on rack in open roasting pan. Brush skin with salad oil. Insert meat thermometer into thickest part of meat between breast and thigh, being careful that pointed end of thermometer does not touch bone. Roast turkey in 325°F. oven about 4¾ hours. Start checking for doneness during last hour of roasting.

6. While turkey is roasting, prepare giblets and neck to use in gravy: In 2-quart saucepan over high heat, heat giblets, neck, and enough water to cover to boiling. Reduce heat to low; cover and simmer 1 hour or until giblets are tender. Drain, reserving broth. Pull meat from neck; discard bones. Coarsely chop neck meat and giblets; refrigerate.

7. When turkey turns golden brown, cover loosely with a tent of folded foil. Remove foil during last of roasting time and with pastry brush, brush turkey generously with pan dripping for attractive sheen. Turkey is done when thermometer reaches 180° to 185°F. and thickest part of drumstick feels soft when pressed with fingers protected by paper towels.

8. When turkey is done, place on warm platter; keep warm.

9. Prepare giblet gravy: Remove rack from roasting pan; pour drippings into a 4-cup measure or medium bowl (set pan aside); let stand a few seconds until fat separates from meat juice. Skim ⅓ cup fat from drippings into 2-quart saucepan; skim off and discard remaining fat. Add reserved giblet broth to roasting pan; stir until brown bits are loosened; add to meat juice in cup and enough water to make 4 cups.

10. Into fat in saucepan over medium heat, stir flour and 1 teaspoon

*Bake any leftover stuffing in covered, greased small casserole during last 40 minutes of roasting turkey.

salt until blended. Gradually stir in meat-juice mixture; cook, stirring constantly, until mixture is thickened. Stir in reserved giblets and neck meat; cook until heated through. Pour gravy into gravy boat.

11. To serve, garnish turkey platter with watercress. Slice pimento into strips. Wrap 3 ears of cocktail corn with a pimento strip. Arrange corn bundle on watercress. Repeat with remaining corn and pimento strips. Pass gravy in gravy boat.

Turkey Loaf with Zucchini Sauce

TIME: about 1¾ hours—SERVINGS: 6

4 tablespoons butter or
  margarine
2 medium celery stalks, diced
1 medium onion, diced
¼ pound medium mushrooms
1½ pounds ground turkey
1 cup fresh bread crumbs
½ cup water
½ teaspoon salt
¼ teaspoon pepper
Zucchini Sauce (right)
parsley sprigs for garnish

1. In 2-quart saucepan over medium heat, in 2 tablespoons hot butter or margarine, cook celery and onion until tender, stirring occasionally. With slotted spoon, remove mixture to large bowl; set aside. In same saucepan in 2 more tablespoons hot butter, cook mushrooms until tender, about 5 minutes, stirring often; remove from heat.

2. To celery mixture in bowl, add ground turkey, bread crumbs, water, salt, and pepper; mix well. In 12″ by 8″ baking dish, form half of turkey mixture into 8″ by 4″ rectangle. Arrange mushrooms, stem-side down, in lengthwise row on top; top with remaining turkey mixture and shape into 8″ by 4″ loaf, pressing firmly. Bake loaf in 350°F. oven 1 hour and 15 minutes.

3. About 15 minutes before loaf is done, prepare Zucchini Sauce.

4. To serve, place turkey loaf on warm platter. Garnish with parsley sprigs. Serve with Zucchini Sauce.

Zucchini Sauce: Coarsely shred *1 medium zucchini* (½ *pound*). In 2-quart saucepan over medium heat, melt *2 tablespoons butter* or margarine; add zucchini and cook until tender, about 2 minutes, stirring often. Stir in *1 tablespoon all-purpose flour;* cook 1 minute. Gradually stir in ½ *cup milk,* ½ *cup water,* and ½ *teaspoon instant chicken-flavor bouillon;* cook, stirring gently, until slightly thickened and hot.

Family-Style Turkey Loaf

TIME: about 2 hours—SERVINGS: 6

1 10-ounce package frozen rice
  with peas and mushrooms
2 tablespoons salad oil
1 medium onion, diced
1 small zucchini (6 ounces),
  shredded
1½ pounds ground turkey
1 teaspoon salt
¼ teaspoon pepper
parsley sprigs for garnish

1. Prepare frozen rice with peas and mushrooms as label directs. Meanwhile, in 3-quart saucepan over medium heat, in hot salad oil, cook onion until tender, stirring occasionally. Add zucchini; cook until tender, about 5 minutes longer, stirring often.

2. Remove saucepan from heat. To mixture in saucepan, add cooked rice mixture, ground turkey, salt, and pepper; mix well. In 12″ by 8″ baking dish, form mixture into 8″ by 4″ loaf, pressing firmly. Bake loaf in 350°F. oven 1¼ hours.

3. To serve, with 2 pancake turners, carefully place turkey loaf on warm platter. Garnish with parsley sprigs.

101

Sausage-Stuffed Turkey Loaf

TIME: about 2 hours—SERVINGS: 8

8 hot or mild Italian sausage
links (about 1¼ pounds)
water
4 tablespoons butter or
margarine
2 medium celery stalks, diced
1 medium onion, diced
1½ pounds ground turkey
1 cup fresh bread crumbs (about
2 slices white bread)
½ teaspoon salt
¼ teaspoon pepper
¼ cup California walnuts, finely
chopped
¼ cup coarsely chopped parsley

1. In 12-inch skillet over medium heat, heat sausages and 2 tablespoons water to boiling. Cover; simmer 5 minutes. Remove cover; continue cooking, turning sausages frequently, until sausages are well browned, about 30 minutes. Remove to paper towels to drain.

2. Meanwhile, in 3-quart saucepan over medium heat, in hot butter or margarine, cook celery and onion until tender, stirring occasionally. Remove saucepan from heat. To celery mixture in saucepan, add ground turkey, bread crumbs, salt, pepper, and ½ cup water; mix well. In small bowl, mix walnuts with parsley; set aside.

3. In 12″ by 8″ baking dish, form one-third of turkey mixture into 8″ by 4″ rectangle. Arrange 4 sausages in two rows on rectangle; top with another one-third of turkey mixture and remaining sausages. Cover loaf with remaining turkey mixture and shape into 8″ by 4″ loaf, pressing firmly. Pat walnut-parsley mixture into top of loaf.

4. Bake in 350°F. oven 1¼ hours.

Turkey Meatballs with Caper Sauce

TIME: about 45 minutes—SERVINGS: 6

1½ pounds ground turkey
1 small onion, grated
1 egg
½ cup dried bread crumbs
salt
4 tablespoons butter or
margarine
2 tablespoons all-purpose flour
⅛ teaspoon pepper
2 cups milk
2 tablespoons capers, drained
1 tablespoon chopped parsley for
garnish

1. In large bowl, mix ground turkey, grated onion, egg, bread crumbs, and 1 teaspoon salt. Shape mixture into 1-inch meatballs.

2. In 12-inch skillet over medium-high heat, in hot butter or margarine, cook meatballs, half at a time, until browned on all sides, removing meatballs to bowl as they brown.

3. Into drippings remaining in skillet over medium heat, stir flour, pepper, and ½ teaspoon salt; cook 1 minute. Gradually stir in milk and capers, and cook until slightly thickened, stirring constantly. Return meatballs to skillet; heat to boiling. Reduce heat to low; cover and simmer 10 minutes or until meatballs are tender, stirring occasionally.

4. Garnish with chopped parsley.

Almond-Crumb Turkey Cakes

TIME: about 30 minutes—SERVINGS: 4

1 pound ground turkey
¼ cup minced parsley
1 tablespoon grated onion
¾ teaspoon salt
⅛ teaspoon pepper
⅛ teaspoon marjoram
1 egg
butter or margarine, softened
⅓ cup whole almonds, ground
⅓ cup dried bread crumbs
2 medium pears, sliced
lettuce leaves
4 radish roses for garnish

1. In large bowl, mix first 7 ingredients with 3 tablespoons butter or margarine until well blended.

2. Shape turkey mixture into four ¾-inch-thick ovals. On waxed paper, combine almonds and bread crumbs. Dip each turkey oval into almond mixture to coat completely.

3. In 12-inch skillet over medium heat, in 3 tablespoons hot butter or margarine, cook turkey cakes until golden on both sides and well done, about 10 minutes, turning once.

4. Serve turkey cakes with pear slices and lettuce leaves. Garnish each serving with a radish rose.

Turkey Pot Pie

TIME: about 1½ hours—SERVINGS: 8

5 tablespoons butter or
  margarine
1 medium onion, diced
½ cup all-purpose flour
2½ cups milk
1 cup water
1 teaspoon salt
¼ teaspoon pepper
1 chicken-flavor bouillon cube or
  envelope
3 cups bite-sized chunks cooked
  turkey or chicken
3 medium potatoes (about 1
  pound), thinly sliced
¼ pound mushrooms, quartered
1 10-ounce package frozen
  mixed vegetables
piecrust mix for one 9-inch
  piecrust
1 egg, slightly beaten

1. In 4-quart saucepan over medium heat, in hot butter or margarine, cook onion until tender, stirring occasionally. Stir in flour until blended; cook 1 minute. Gradually stir in milk, water, salt, pepper, and bouillon; cook, stirring constantly, until mixture is slightly thickened.

2. Stir in turkey, potatoes, mushrooms, and frozen mixed vegetables, breaking up vegetables with fork. Spoon mixture into 13" by 9" baking dish.

3. Preheat oven to 375°F. Prepare piecrust mix as label directs. On lightly floured surface with floured rolling pin, roll dough into 15" by 11" rectangle. With knife, cut out and reserve 6" by 3" rectangle from center of pastry. Place larger pastry rectangle loosely over turkey mixture. Fold overhang under and press gently all around rim to make a scalloped edge. Pinch edges in center of pastry to form decorative edge.

4. From reserved cutout pastry rectangle, cut pretty designs. Brush top of pie with some beaten egg; arrange pastry designs on top; brush designs with egg. Bake pie 45 minutes or until crust is golden and vegetables are tender.

GOOSE AND DUCK

Roast Goose with Chestnut Stuffing, Sausage, and Apples

TIME: about 4½ hours—SERVINGS: 8

Chestnut Stuffing (page 105)
1 10-pound frozen goose,
  (thawed)
1 teaspoon salt
¼ teaspoon pepper
2 pounds pork sausage links or
  sweet Italian sausage links
water
3 large red cooking apples
butter or margarine
⅛ teaspoon ground ginger
½ cup apple jelly
1 tablespoon all-purpose flour
½ cup cooking or dry sherry
2 teaspoons chicken-flavor
  instant bouillon
1 teaspoon soy sauce

1. Prepare Chestnut Stuffing.

2. Remove giblets and neck from goose; refrigerate to use in soup another day. Discard fat from body cavity; rinse goose with running cold water and drain well. Spoon some stuffing into neck cavity. (Do not pack stuffing; it expands during cooking.) Fold neck skin over stuffing; fasten neck skin to back with 1 or 2 skewers. With goose breast-side up, lift wings up toward neck, then fold under back of goose.

3. Spoon stuffing lightly into body cavity.* Close, by folding skin over opening; skewer if necessary. With string, tie legs and tail together. With fork, prick skin of goose in several places.

4. Place goose, breast-side up, on rack in open roasting pan. Rub goose with salt and pepper. Insert meat thermometer into thickest part of meat between breast and thigh, being careful that pointed end of thermometer does not touch bone.

5. Roast goose in 350°F. oven about 3 hours. Start checking for doneness during last 30 minutes of roasting. Goose is done when thermometer reaches 190°F. and thickest part of leg feels soft when pinched with fingers protected by paper towels.

6. About 45 minutes before goose is done, prepare sausages: In 12-inch skillet over medium heat, heat sausages and ¼ cup water to boiling. Cover; simmer 5 minutes. Remove cover; continue cooking, turning sausages frequently, until sausages are well browned; keep warm.

7. Meanwhile, prepare apple rings: Core apples; cut into ½-inch-thick rings. In 10-inch skillet over medium heat, in 2 tablespoons hot butter or margarine, cook apple rings, a few at a time, about 5 minutes, until fork-tender, turning apple rings once during cooking, and adding more butter or margarine if needed. Remove apple rings to plate.

8. Into skillet, stir ginger and ⅓ cup apple jelly until melted; return apple rings to skillet, spooning apple-jelly mixture over rings to coat; heat through. With slotted spoon, remove apple rings to plate, leaving apple-jelly mixture in skillet; keep apple rings warm.

9. Into drippings remaining in skillet, stir flour; cook 1 minute. Add sherry, chicken-flavor bouillon, soy sauce, 1 cup water, and remaining apple jelly, stirring constantly, until slightly thickened and smooth.

10. To serve, remove skewers and strings from goose; place goose on warm large platter. Arrange sausages and apple rings around goose. Serve with sauce.

*Bake any leftover stuffing in covered, small greased casserole during last 40 minutes of roasting time.

Chestnut Stuffing: In 4-quart saucepan over high heat, heat *1½ pounds chestnuts* and enough *water* to cover to boiling. Reduce heat to medium; cover and cook 10 minutes. Remove saucepan from heat. With slotted spoon, remove 3 or 4 chestnuts at a time from water to cutting board. Cut each chestnut in half. With tip of small knife, scrape out chestnut meat from its shell. (Skin will stay in shell.) Chop any large pieces of chestnut meat; set aside. Discard chestnut cooking water in saucepan.

In same saucepan over medium heat, melt *½ cup butter* or margarine; add *2 medium celery stalks*, diced, and *1 medium onion*, diced; cook until vegetables are tender, about 10 minutes, stirring occasionally. Remove saucepan from heat; stir in *2 tablespoons minced parsley, 1 teaspoon salt, ½ teaspoon poultry seasoning*, and *¼ teaspoon pepper*. Add *9 cups white-bread cubes, ½ cup water, 1 egg*, slightly beaten, and reserved chestnuts; mix well.

Roast Duckling with Port-Wine Sauce

TIME: about 2½ hours—SERVINGS: 8

2 4½- to 5-pound fresh or frozen (thawed) ducklings
salt
pepper
water
¾ cup red port wine
½ cup orange juice
2 tablespoons lemon juice
1 teaspoon prepared mustard
¼ teaspoon ground ginger
¾ cup currant jelly
2 tablespoons all-purpose flour
3 small oranges, sliced for garnish
1 3½-ounce can pitted ripe olives, drained, for garnish

1. Remove giblets and necks from ducklings. Rinse ducklings, giblets, and necks with running cold water; pat ducklings dry with paper towels. Cut each duckling into quarters; trim excess fat and skin on pieces.

2. Place duckling quarters, skin-side down, on rack in large open roasting pan; sprinkle lightly with salt and pepper. Roast in 350°F. oven 1 hour; turn duckling quarters; sprinkle with salt and pepper. Roast about 45 minutes longer or until ducklings are fork-tender and thickest part of drumstick feels soft when pinched with fingers protected by paper towels.

3 Meanwhile, in 3-quart saucepan over high heat, heat giblets, necks, ¼ teaspoon salt, and enough water to cover to boiling. Reduce heat to low; cover and simmer 1 hour or until giblets are tender. Drain, reserving 1 cup broth. (Refrigerate giblets, necks, and remaining broth to use in soup another day.)

4. In 2-quart saucepan, combine port wine, orange juice, lemon juice, mustard, ginger, ½ teaspoon salt, ½ cup currant jelly, and reserved 1 cup broth; over medium heat, heat to boiling. Reduce heat to low; cover and simmer 10 minutes to blend flavors.

5. In cup, stir flour and ¼ cup water until smooth; gradually stir in simmering liquid in saucepan. Cook over medium heat until sauce is slightly thickened and smooth.

6. About 10 minutes before ducklings are done, in cup, stir ¼ cup currant jelly and 1 teaspoon water until smooth; brush duckling quarters with jelly mixture.

7. To serve, arrange duckling quarters on warm large platter; garnish with orange slices and olives. Serve sauce in small bowl.

Herbed Duckling with Strawberry Sauce

TIME: about 2 hours—SERVINGS: 8

2 4½- to 5-pound fresh or frozen
(thawed) ducklings
1½ teaspoons ground sage
½ teaspoon pepper
12 juniper berries, crushed
salt
2 pints strawberries
⅓ cup water
¼ cup orange-flavor liqueur
3 tablespoons sugar
2 teaspoons cornstarch
watercress sprigs for garnish

1. Remove giblets and necks from ducklings; refrigerate to use in soup another day. Rinse ducklings with running cold water; pat dry with paper towels. Cut each duckling into quarters; trim excess fat and skin on pieces. Place duckling pieces, skin-side down, on rack in large open roasting pan.

2. In cup, combine sage, pepper, crushed juniper berries, and 2 teaspoons salt. Evenly sprinkle half of sage mixture on duckling pieces. Roast in 350°F. oven 1 hour; turn duckling; sprinkle with remaining sage mixture and roast about 45 minutes longer or until duckling is fork-tender and thickest part of drumstick feels soft when pinched with fingers protected by paper towels.

3. About 15 minutes before duckling is done, prepare strawberry sauce: Reserve 6 strawberries for garnish. Hull remaining strawberries; thinly slice 6 hulled strawberries and set them aside. In blender at high speed or in food processor with knife blade attached, blend hulled whole strawberries, water, orange-flavor liqueur, sugar, cornstarch, and ½ teaspoon salt until smooth.

4. Pour strawberry mixture into 2-quart saucepan. Cook over medium heat, stirring constantly, until sauce is boiling; stir in sliced strawberries.

5. To serve, spoon some sauce onto warm platter; arrange duckling pieces on sauce; garnish with watercress sprigs and reserved whole strawberries. Spoon remaining sauce from small bowl.

Apple-Glazed Duckling

TIME: about 2 hours—SERVINGS: 4

1 4½- to 5-pound fresh or frozen
(thawed) duckling
¼ teaspoon pepper
salt
2 tablespoons butter or
margarine
2 large red cooking apples, cored
and cut into ¾-inch wedges
1 10-ounce jar apple jelly
⅛ teaspoon ground ginger
parsley sprigs for garnish

1. Remove giblets and neck from duckling; refrigerate to use in soup another day. Rinse duckling with running cold water; pat dry with paper towels. Cut duckling into quarters; trim excess fat and skin on pieces. Evenly sprinkle duckling pieces on all sides with pepper and 1¼ teaspoons salt.

2. Place duckling pieces, skin-side down, on rack in 14" by 10" open roasting pan. Roast in 350°F. oven 1 hour; turn duckling and roast about 45 minutes longer or until duckling is fork-tender and thickest part of drumstick feels soft when pinched with fingers protected by paper towels.

3. About 20 minutes before duckling is done, in 12-inch skillet over medium heat, in hot butter or margarine, cook apple wedges about 5 to 7 minutes until apples are fork-tender. With pancake turner, turn wedges once during cooking. Stir in half of apple jelly; heat through; keep warm.

4. Meanwhile, in small bowl, mix ginger, ½ teaspoon salt, and remaining apple jelly. During last 10 minutes of roasting, brush duckling pieces with apple-jelly mixture.

5. To serve, place duckling pieces on warm platter with apple wedges. Garnish with parsley sprigs.

Roast Goose with Mushroom Gravy

TIME: about 4½ hours—SERVINGS: 8

Pumpernickel-Apple Stuffing
   (right)
1 12-pound frozen goose
   (thawed)
1 teaspoon salt
½ teaspoon pepper
Mushroom Gravy (right)
parsley sprigs for garnish

1. Prepare Pumpernickel-Apple Stuffing.

2. Remove giblets and neck from goose. Refrigerate giblets and neck to use in soup another day. Discard fat from body cavity; rinse goose with running cold water and drain well. Spoon some stuffing into neck cavity. (Do not pack stuffing; it expands during cooking.) Fold neck skin over stuffing; fasten neck skin to the back with 1 or 2 skewers. With goose breast-side up, lift wings up toward neck, then fold under back of goose.

3. Spoon stuffing lightly into body cavity;* fold skin over opening; skewer closed if necessary. With string, tie legs and tail together. With fork, prick skin of goose in several places.

4. Place goose, breast-side up, on rack in open roasting pan. Rub goose with salt and pepper. Insert meat thermometer into thickest part of meat between breast and thigh, being careful that pointed end of thermometer does not touch bone. Roast goose in 350°F. oven about 3 hours. Start checking for doneness during last 30 minutes.

5. About 15 minutes before goose is done, prepare Mushroom Gravy.

6. Goose is done when thermometer reaches 190°F. and thickest part of leg feels soft when pinched with fingers protected by paper towels.

7. To serve, remove skewers and string; place goose on warm large platter; garnish with parsley sprigs. Serve goose with Mushroom Gravy.

Pumpernickel-Apple Stuffing: In 5-quart Dutch oven or saucepot over medium heat, melt *½ cup butter* or margarine. Add *4 celery stalks*, diced, *1 large red cooking apple*, peeled and diced, *1 medium onion*, diced; cook until vegetables are tender, stirring frequently. Remove Dutch oven from heat; stir in *5 cups pumpernickel-bread cubes, 5 cups white-bread cubes, 1¾ cups milk, 2 tablespoons minced parsley, ¾ teaspoon salt, ½ teaspoon thyme leaves*, and *¼ teaspoon rubbed sage*.

Mushroom Gravy: In 3-quart saucepan over medium heat, melt *3 tablespoons butter* or margarine. Add *½ pound mushrooms*, thinly sliced, and *1 green onion*, sliced; cook until vegetables are tender, stirring occasionally. Stir in *2 tablespoons all-purpose flour* until blended. Gradually stir in *2 cups milk*, then *1 chicken-flavor bouillon cube* or envelope, *¼ teaspoon salt*, and *⅛ teaspoon pepper*; cook, stirring frequently, until mixture is slightly thickened.

*Bake any leftover stuffing in covered, greased small casserole during last 40 minutes of roasting time.

FISH

Fish and Noodles

TIME: about 1¼ hours—SERVINGS: 8

1 8-ounce package wide noodles
1 16-ounce package frozen cod, flounder, or haddock fillets
4 tablespoons butter or margarine
½ pound mushrooms, sliced
2 tablespoons minced green onions
¼ cup all-purpose flour
1¼ teaspoons salt
¼ teaspoon pepper
3¼ cups milk
3 tablespoons cooking or dry sherry
1 10-ounce package frozen chopped spinach, thawed and squeezed dry

1. Cook noodles as label directs but omit salt; drain. Place noodles in 2½-quart casserole.

2. Meanwhile, let frozen fish stand at room temperature 15 minutes to thaw slightly; then cut into bite-sized chunks.

3. While fish is thawing, in 3-quart saucepan over medium heat, in hot butter or margarine, cook mushrooms and green onions until tender. Push vegetables to side of pan; stir in flour, salt, and pepper until blended; cook 1 minute. Gradually stir in milk and sherry; cook until mixture is slightly thickened and smooth, stirring frequently.

4. Preheat oven to 350°F. Add spinach and fish chunks to mixture in saucepan. Pour mixture into casserole with noodles; stir gently to mix. Bake casserole, covered, 45 minutes or until mixture is hot and bubbly and fish flakes easily when tested with a fork.

Flounder in Lemony Dill Sauce

TIME: about 30 minutes—SERVINGS: 4

3 tablespoons butter or margarine
1 tablespoon chopped fresh dill or ¾ teaspoon dill weed
1 tablespoon lemon juice
¼ teaspoon salt
1 medium green onion, thinly sliced
1 pound flounder fillets
lemon slices (optional)

1. In 10-inch skillet over medium-low heat, heat first 5 ingredients until butter or margarine is melted and hot, stirring occasionally.

2. If flounder fillets are large, cut into serving-size pieces. Add flounder to butter mixture in skillet; cover and cook 8 to 10 minutes until flounder flakes easily when tested with a fork, basting flounder occasionally with butter mixture in skillet.

3. Arrange flounder with its sauce in warm deep platter. If desired, flounder can be garnished with lemon slices.

Broiled Cod Steaks Montauk

TIME: about 20 minutes—SERVINGS: 4

½ cup mayonnaise
½ teaspoon prepared mustard
¼ teaspoon seasoned salt
⅛ teaspoon seasoned pepper
salad oil
4 small cod steaks, each cut ½ inch thick
1 small orange for garnish
1 small lemon for garnish

1. Preheat broiler if manufacturer directs.

2. Meanwhile, in small bowl, mix mayonnaise, mustard, seasoned salt, and seasoned pepper; set aside.

3. Lightly brush rack in broiling pan with salad oil. Place cod steaks on rack. About 7 to 9 inches from source of heat, broil cod steaks 7 minutes. Remove broiling pan from broiler; do not turn fish. Spread one-fourth of mayonnaise mixture on each cod steak. Return pan to broiler; broil about 3 to 5 minutes longer or until cod flakes easily when tested with a fork and topping is lightly browned and bubbly.

4. Thinly slice orange and lemon; cut each slice crosswise in half. Garnish cod steaks with fruit slices.

French-Quarter Fish Creole

TIME: about 45 minutes—SERVINGS: 6

2 tablespoons butter or
    margarine
water
salt
1½ cups regular long-grain rice
1 16-ounce package frozen
    flounder, cod, or haddock
    fillets
2 tablespoons salad oil
2 medium onions, diced
2 celery stalks, diced
1 large green pepper, cut into
    ½-inch strips
1 garlic clove, crushed
1 28-ounce can tomatoes
1½ teaspoons sugar
½ teaspoon hot pepper sauce
1 10-ounce package frozen peas

1. In 2-quart saucepan over high heat, heat butter or margarine, 3 cups water, and 1 teaspoon salt to boiling. Stir in rice; heat to boiling. Reduce heat to low; cover and simmer 20 minutes or until rice is tender and all liquid is absorbed. Fluff rice with fork; keep warm.

2. Meanwhile, let frozen fish stand at room temperature 15 minutes to thaw slightly. In 4-quart saucepan over medium heat, in hot oil, cook onions, celery, green pepper, and garlic until tender, stirring often.

3. Cut fish into 1-inch chunks. Add to vegetable mixture in saucepan with tomatoes with their liquid, sugar, hot pepper sauce, frozen peas, and 1 teaspoon salt; over high heat, heat to boiling. Reduce heat to low; cover and simmer 10 minutes or until fish flakes easily when tested with a fork and peas are tender.

4. Serve with rice.

Spinach-Stuffed Fish Fillets with Parsley Rice

TIME: about 45 minutes—SERVINGS: 6

1 cup regular long-grain rice
butter or margarine
1 10-ounce bag spinach
1 medium green onion, chopped
⅛ teaspoon pepper
1 slice white bread, cut into
    small pieces
paprika
salt
1 tablespoon cooking or dry
    white wine
1 teaspoon lemon juice
2 flounder or sole fillets (about
    ½ pound each)
2 tablespoons minced parsley
lemon wedges

1. Prepare rice as label directs; keep warm.

2. Meanwhile, in 10-inch skillet over medium heat, in 1 tablespoon hot butter or margarine, cook spinach and onion until tender, stirring occasionally. Remove skillet from heat; stir in pepper, bread, ¼ teaspoon paprika, and ¼ teaspoon salt.

3. Preheat oven to 350°F. Place 3 tablespoons butter or margarine in 13″ by 9″ baking pan; place in oven until butter melts. Remove baking pan from oven; stir in wine and lemon juice until blended.

4. Place one flounder fillet in butter mixture in pan; top with spinach mixture. Place second flounder fillet on top of spinach mixture. Sprinkle with ¼ teaspoon paprika and ¼ teaspoon salt. Bake 15 minutes or until fish flakes easily when tested with a fork, basting fish occasionally with butter mixture in pan.

5. To serve, toss rice with parsley. Serve rice with stuffed fish fillets and lemon wedges.

Flounder Florentine

TIME: about 30 minutes—SERVINGS: 4

butter or margarine
1 10-ounce bag spinach
1 16-ounce package frozen
  flounder fillets, thawed, or 1
  pound fresh flounder fillets
salt
paprika
1 tablespoon all-purpose flour
1 cup water
2 tablespoons lemon juice
¾ teaspoon chicken-flavor
  instant bouillon
lemon slices for garnish

1. In 12-inch skillet over medium heat, in 2 tablespoons hot butter or margarine, cook spinach until tender, about 3 minutes. Spoon spinach mixture onto large platter; keep warm.

2. Lightly sprinkle flounder fillets with salt and paprika. In same skillet over medium heat, in 2 more tablespoons hot butter or margarine, cook flounder fillets 2 to 3 minutes on each side until fish flakes easily when tested with a fork. With pancake turner, remove fish from skillet and arrange on top of spinach on platter.

3. In drippings remaining in skillet, melt 2 more tablespoons butter or margarine. Stir in flour until blended; cook 1 minute. Gradually stir in water, lemon juice, and bouillon; cook, stirring constantly, until slightly thickened.

4. Pour sauce over spinach and fish; garnish with lemon slices.

Open-Faced Salmon Sandwiches

TIME: about 30 minutes—SERVINGS: 4

2 eggs
1 7¾-ounce can salmon
4 tablespoons butter or
  margarine
¼ cup all-purpose flour
½ teaspoon salt
⅛ teaspoon pepper
2 cups milk
1 tablespoon lemon juice
1 10-ounce package frozen
  broccoli spears
4 slices pumpernickel bread

1. Hard-cook eggs.

2. Meanwhile, drain salmon, reserving liquid. In 3-quart saucepan over medium heat, melt butter or margarine; stir in flour, salt, and pepper until blended; cook 1 minute. Gradually stir in milk, lemon juice, and reserved salmon liquid; cook, stirring constantly, until mixture is thickened.

3. With knife, cut frozen broccoli crosswise in half. Add broccoli to mixture in saucepan; cook until fork-tender, stirring occasionally. Gently stir in salmon; heat through.

4. To serve, cut each slice of bread diagonally in half; arrange on 4 plates; spoon salmon mixture over bread. Slice hard-cooked eggs; top each serving with egg slices.

Salmon-Avocado Open-Faced Sandwiches

TIME: about 20 minutes—SERVINGS: 2

½ cup mayonnaise
2 tablespoons minced dill pickle
2 tablespoons chili sauce
½ teaspoon lemon juice
⅛ teaspoon hot pepper sauce
2 slices pumpernickel bread
1 7¾-ounce can salmon, drained
  and flaked
6 pitted ripe olives, sliced
1 small avocado, sliced
½ 16-ounce jar sliced pickled
  beets, drained
2 medium lettuce leaves

1. In small bowl, mix mayonnaise with next 4 ingredients.

2. For each serving, on dinner plate, place 1 slice bread; lightly spread bread with some mayonnaise mixture. On mayonnaise mixture, arrange half of salmon and top with half of olives.

3. On plate with sandwich, arrange hot butter or margarine, cook onion, peppers, and half of avocado slices and beets.

4. Spoon half of remaining mayonnaise mixture into a lettuce leaf; place on plate with sandwich.

Buffet Salmon with Three Sauces

TIME: start early in day or day ahead—SERVINGS: 12

7 cups water
1 cup dry white wine
2 medium celery stalks, sliced
1 medium onion, sliced
1 tablespoon salt
½ teaspoon peppercorns
1 envelope chicken-flavor
    bouillon
1 6-pound whole salmon or
    striped bass, dressed, with
    head and tail on
Confetti Sauce, Mustard Sauce,
    and Green Mayonnaise (right)
3 eggs
3 medium tomatoes
3 lemons
parsley sprigs for garnish

1. In 26-inch fish poacher,* over high heat, heat first 7 ingredients to boiling (the poacher will require 2 heating units).

2. Rinse salmon under running cold water. Place salmon on poaching rack; lower rack with salmon into boiling liquid in fish poacher; over high heat, heat to boiling. Reduce heat to low; cover and simmer 30 minutes or until fish flakes easily when tested with a fork. Remove rack from poacher. With 2 pancake turners, place salmon on large platter; cover and refrigerate until well chilled.

3. Meanwhile, prepare Confetti Sauce, Mustard Sauce, and Green Mayonnaise; cover and refrigerate.

4. Hard-cook eggs; refrigerate.

5. To serve, with knife or kitchen shears, carefully cut skin around top half of salmon; remove and discard skin. Slice tomatoes, lemons, and hard-cooked eggs; arrange on platter with salmon. If desired, salmon can be garnished with parsley sprigs. Serve with all three sauces.

Confetti Sauce: Drain and reserve ½ cup liquid from *one 16-ounce jar pickled mixed vegetables;* dice pickled mixed vegetables. In large bowl with fork, combine reserved liquid, *½ cup olive or salad oil, 4 teaspoons tarragon vinegar,* and *½ teaspoon salt* until well blended. Stir in diced vegetables; refrigerate until well chilled.

Mustard Sauce: In blender at medium speed or in food processor with knife blade attached, blend *½ cup mustard, ½ cup olive or salad oil, 2 tablespoons sugar, 3 tablespoons dry white wine, 1 tablespoon sour cream,* and *¼ teaspoon salt* until well blended. Stir in *1 teaspoon minced fresh dill* or ¼ teaspoon dill weed, and *1 teaspoon minced parsley;* refrigerate until well chilled.

Green Mayonnaise: In blender at medium speed or in food processor with knife blade attached, blend *1 cup mayonnaise, 2 tablespoons chopped parsley, 2 teaspoons tarragon vinegar, ¼ teaspoon salt,* and *1 green onion,* cut up, until smooth, stopping blender occasionally, scraping container with rubber spatula.

*Or, if you don't have a poacher, use a 12-inch skillet. Cut fish crosswise in half; cook as above but cook one piece of fish at a time. To serve, reassemble fish on large platter to make a whole fish.

Poached Salmon with Egg Sauce

TIME: about 1¼ hours—SERVINGS: 4

4 medium potatoes (about 1¼ pounds)
water
2 hard-cooked eggs
milk
butter or margarine
1 small onion, minced
1 tablespoon all-purpose flour
⅛ teaspoon hot pepper sauce
salt
3 tablespoons cooking or dry sherry
2 large salmon or cod steaks (each cut about ¾-inch thick and about ¾ pound)
1 10-ounce package frozen peas
1 tablespoon chopped parsley

1. In 3-quart saucepan over high heat, heat unpeeled potatoes and enough water to cover to boiling. Reduce heat to medium-low; cover and cook 25 to 30 minutes until potatoes are fork-tender.

2. Meanwhile, prepare egg sauce: coarsely chop egg whites. In small bowl with fork, mash egg yolks with 3 tablespoons milk until smooth; set eggs aside. In 2-quart saucepan over medium heat, in 2 tablespoons hot butter or margarine, cook onion until tender, stirring occasionally. Stir in flour, hot pepper sauce, and ½ teaspoon salt until blended; cook 1 minute. Gradually stir in 1 cup milk; cook, stirring constantly, until mixture is slightly thickened and smooth. Stir in egg whites and egg-yolk mixture; keep warm.

3. In 12-inch skillet over high heat, heat sherry, 4 cups water, and 1 teaspoon salt to boiling. Add salmon steaks to boiling water; heat to boiling. Reduce heat to low; cover and simmer 5 to 8 minutes until salmon flakes easily when tested with a fork. With slotted pancake turner, gently remove salmon steaks; carefully cut each salmon steak in half; discard bone; keep warm.

4. Prepare peas as label directs; keep warm.

5. When potatoes are done, drain; cut into quarters. Return potatoes to saucepan; with rubber spatula, gently toss potatoes with parsley, 1 tablespoon butter or margarine, and ¼ teaspoon salt.

6. To serve, arrange potatoes and peas on warm large platter with salmon steaks. Serve with egg sauce.

Baked Tuna Squares

TIME: about 1½ hours—SERVINGS: 6

2 tablespoons salad oil
2 large celery stalks, minced
1 medium onion, minced
1 12½- to 13-ounce can tuna, drained
½ cup quick-cooking oats, uncooked
¾ teaspoon salt
¼ teaspoon pepper
4 eggs, separated
milk
1 medium cucumber
½ cup mayonnaise
½ teaspoon dill weed
parsley sprigs for garnish

1. Preheat oven to 350°F. Generously grease 8″ by 8″ baking pan.

2. In 10-inch skillet over medium heat, in hot salad oil, cook celery and onion until tender, stirring occasionally. In large bowl with fork, finely flake tuna; add celery mixture, oats, salt, pepper, egg yolks, and ½ cup milk; mix until well blended. In small bowl with mixer at high speed, beat egg whites until stiff peaks form. Fold egg whites into tuna mixture. Spoon tuna mixture into prepared pan. Bake 50 minutes or until knife inserted in center comes out clean.

3. Meanwhile, from cucumber, chop enough to make ½ cup. Slice remaining cucumber for garnish; cover and refrigerate. In small bowl with fork, mix chopped cucumber, mayonnaise, dill weed, and 2 tablespoons milk. Cover and refrigerate.

4. When tuna mixture is done, cool in pan on wire rack 10 minutes for easier serving. Cut tuna mixture into 6 servings; remove from pan and place on warm platter. Garnish each serving with some parsley sprigs and reserved cucumber slices. Serve tuna squares with cucumber sauce.

Tuna Fish Pies

TIME: about 1 hour or start early in day—SERVINGS: 4

2 slices white bread
1 6½- to 7-ounce can tuna,
   drained and flaked
½ cup shredded sharp Cheddar
   cheese (2 ounces)
¼ cup milk
1 tablespoon cider vinegar
1 teaspoon grated onion
¼ teaspoon salt
⅛ teaspoon pepper
2 eggs
piecrust mix for two 9-inch
   piecrusts
Creamy Mushroom Sauce (right)

1. Into medium bowl, tear bread into small pieces. Stir in tuna, cheese, milk, vinegar, onion, salt, pepper, and 1 egg; set aside.

2. Prepare piecrust mix as label directs. On lightly floured surface with floured rolling pin, roll out half of pastry. With knife, cut pastry into four 8" by 4" fish shapes; place on large cookie sheet. Spoon one-fourth of tuna mixture onto center of each pastry. Roll out remaining pastry to make 4 more fish shapes for top crusts.

3. Preheat oven to 400°F. With pastry brush, lightly brush bottom-crust edges with water; gently place pastry tops over tuna mixture. With fork, press each pastry fish all around to seal. With shears, cut an eye and scales on each fish.

4. In cup with fork, beat remaining egg. With pastry brush, brush egg over entire surface of each fish. Bake 20 to 25 minutes until lightly browned.

5. Meanwhile, prepare Creamy Mushroom Sauce.

6. Serve fish warm with sauce. (If desired, fish can be refrigerated to be served cold later, with or without sauce.)

Creamy Mushroom Sauce: In 2-quart saucepan over medium heat, melt *2 tablespoons butter* or margarine. Add *¼ pound mushrooms,* thinly sliced, and cook until tender, stirring occasionally. Stir in *2 tablespoons all-purpose flour* and *½ teaspoon salt* until blended; cook 1 minute. Gradually stir in *1½ cups milk;* cook, stirring constantly, until mixture is slightly thickened. Remove saucepan from heat; stir in *¼ cup shredded sharp Cheddar cheese (1 ounce)* until smooth.

Tuna Logs

TIME: about 30 minutes—SERVINGS: 2

1 6½- to 7-ounce can tuna,
   drained
1 egg
¾ cup fresh bread crumbs
   (about 1½ slices white bread)
2 tablespoons bottled tartar
   sauce
1 tablespoon grated onion
⅛ teaspoon pepper
2 tablespoons salad oil
4 frankfurter rolls
shredded lettuce
chili sauce
pimento-stuffed olives
dill pickles
cherry peppers

1. In medium bowl with fork, finely flake tuna; stir in egg, bread crumbs, bottled tartar sauce, grated onion, and pepper. Shape mixture into four 5-inch-long logs.

2. In 10-inch skillet over medium heat, in hot salad oil, cook logs until browned all around, about 8 minutes, turning frequently with pancake turner.

3. Line frankfurter rolls with shredded lettuce; top with tuna logs and chili sauce.

4. Serve with pimento-stuffed olives, dill pickles, and cherry peppers.

Tuna Loaf Special

TIME: about 1 hour—SERVINGS: 5

1 12½- to 13-ounce can tuna,
   drained
2 cups fresh bread crumbs
½ cup milk
1 tablespoon lemon juice
¼ teaspoon dill weed
¼ teaspoon salt
¼ teaspoon hot pepper sauce
3 eggs, separated
lemon half-slices
fresh dill sprig (optional)
Creamy Pea Sauce (right)

1. In bowl, mix first 7 ingredients and egg yolks. With mixer, beat egg whites until stiff. Fold into tuna mixture; spoon into 8½" by 4½" greased loaf pan.

2. Bake in preheated 375°F. oven for 35 minutes or until knife inserted into loaf comes out clean.

3. Make Creamy Pea Sauce.

4. Garnish with lemon slices and dill.

Creamy Pea Sauce: In saucepan over medium heat, into *2 tablespoons hot butter*, stir *2 tablespoons all-purpose flour* and *½ teaspoon salt* until blended. Slowly stir in *1½ cups milk*; cook until thickened. Stir in *1 cup frozen peas*; heat through.

SEAFOOD

Insalata di Calamari

TIME: about 3 hours or start early in day—SERVINGS: 8

2 pounds fresh or frozen
   (thawed) squid
water
salt
2 medium celery stalks, thinly
   sliced
1 small garlic clove, crushed
½ cup olive or salad oil
⅓ cup chopped parsley
¼ cup red wine vinegar
1 tablespoon lemon juice
1 teaspoon basil
1 teaspoon oregano leaves
⅛ teaspoon crushed red pepper
lettuce leaves

1. Prepare squid: Pull off tentacles from squid body. Cut off and discard portion of tentacles containing sac. Remove thin transparent cartilage and all loose pieces from inside body; with fingertips, gently scrape and pull off thin dark outer skin from squid. Rinse tentacles and body under running cold water. Slice body crosswise into ¾-inch-thick rings. Cut tentacles into several pieces if they are large.

2. In 2-quart saucepan over high heat, heat 1 inch water and 1 teaspoon salt to boiling. Add squid; heat to boiling. Reduce heat to medium; cook 3 to 5 minutes until squid is tender and turns opaque; drain.

3. Place squid in medium bowl; add 1 teaspoon salt, celery, and remaining ingredients except lettuce leaves. Toss to mix well. Cover and refrigerate at least 2 hours to blend flavors, tossing occasionally.

4. To serve, arrange lettuce leaves on platter; spoon squid salad on top of lettuce.

Spinach-Filled Jumbo Shrimp

TIME: about 45 minutes—SERVINGS: 4

Parslied Rice Timbales (right)
1 pound jumbo shrimp (12 shrimp)
butter or margarine
1 green onion, minced
1 10-ounce package frozen chopped spinach, thawed and squeezed dry
1 lemon
2 slices white bread
1 egg
½ cup shredded Fontina or Swiss cheese (2 ounces)
pepper
2 tablespoons all-purpose flour
2 tablespoons salad oil
½ cup water
⅓ cup cooking or dry sherry
½ teaspoon instant chicken-flavor bouillon
red salmon caviar

1. Prepare Parslied Rice Timbales.

2. Remove shells from shrimp, leaving tail parts of shells on. With knife, cut each shrimp three-fourths of the way through, along center back; spread each shrimp open. Rinse shrimp under running cold water to remove vein. Pat shrimp dry with paper towels. With meat mallet or dull edge of French knife, lightly pound shrimp to flatten slightly.

3. In 12-inch skillet over medium heat, in 3 tablespoons hot butter or margarine, cook green onion until tender, stirring occasionally. Stir in spinach; heat through. Remove skillet from heat.

4. From half of lemon, cut 6 thin slices; cut each slice in half; cover and set aside for garnish. From remaining lemon half, squeeze 1 teaspoon juice. Tear bread into small pieces; add to spinach in skillet; stir in lemon juice, egg, cheese, and ⅛ teaspoon pepper.

5. Spoon some spinach mixture along center back of each shrimp. Bring cut edges of each shrimp up toward filling; firmly press shrimp to filling. Onto waxed paper, measure flour. Coat spinach-filled shrimp with flour.

6. Wipe skillet clean. In skillet over medium heat, heat salad oil and 4 tablespoons butter or margarine until hot. Add 6 shrimp; cook until shrimp turn pink and are lightly browned on both sides (about 1 to 2 minutes per side). Remove shrimp to platter next to rice timbales as they brown; keep warm. Repeat with remaining shrimp.

7. Into drippings remaining in skillet, measure water, sherry, bouillon, and ⅛ teaspoon pepper. Over medium-high heat, heat to boiling, stirring to loosen brown bits from bottom of skillet. Cook 1 minute to blend flavors. Pour sauce into small bowl.

8. To serve, garnish shrimp with lemon slices; top each timbale with some red salmon caviar. Serve sauce to pour over shrimp, if desired.

Parslied Rice Timbales: In 2-quart saucepan over high heat, heat *1½ cups water* to boiling; stir in *¾ cup regular long-grain rice, 2 teaspoons chicken-flavor instant bouillon,* and *1 teaspoon butter* or margarine. Over high heat, heat to boiling. Reduce heat to low; cover and simmer 20 minutes until rice is tender and all liquid is absorbed. Remove saucepan from heat; stir in *2 tablespoons chopped parsley.*

Divide rice into 4 portions. Gently pack one portion of rice at a time into a greased 4-ounce timbale mold or a small custard cup; unmold rice onto large warm platter, leaving room for shrimp. (Or, use an ice-cream scoop.) Keep warm.

Scallops and Asparagus in Cream

TIME: about 30 minutes—SERVINGS: 4

3 tablespoons butter or
    margarine
1 pound asparagus, cut
    diagonally into 1-inch pieces
½ pound medium mushrooms,
    sliced
1 small onion, thinly sliced
1 small garlic clove, cut in half
1 pound fresh or frozen (thawed)
    sea scallops
¼ cup cooking or dry white wine
¾ teaspoon salt
⅛ teaspoon pepper
½ cup half-and-half

1. In 12-inch skillet over medium heat, in hot butter or margarine, cook asparagus, mushrooms, onion, and garlic until vegetables are tender, about 10 minutes, stirring occasionally. Discard garlic; remove vegetables to medium bowl; set aside.

2. In same skillet over medium heat, cook scallops, wine, salt, and pepper, stirring frequently, until scallops are tender, about 5 minutes. Stir in half-and-half and vegetables; heat through.

Holiday Scallops with Julienne Vegetables

TIME: about 1 hour—SERVINGS: 4

1 small lemon
2 pounds fresh or frozen
    (thawed) sea scallops
⅛ teaspoon pepper
cooking or dry sherry
salt
butter or margarine
4 green onions, cut into 2-inch
    pieces
3 large carrots, cut into match-
    stick-thin strips
3 medium zucchini, cut into
    matchstick-thin strips
2 tablespoons all-purpose flour
½ teaspoon paprika
1 cup milk

1. Grate 1 teaspoon peel and squeeze 2 teaspoons juice from lemon. In medium bowl, combine lemon peel, lemon juice, scallops, pepper, ¼ cup sherry, and ½ teaspoon salt; set aside.

2. In 12-inch skillet over medium heat, in 4 tablespoons hot butter or margarine, cook green onions and carrots 5 minutes, stirring occasionally. Add zucchini and ¾ teaspoon salt; cook 5 minutes or until vegetables are tender, stirring occasionally. With slotted spoon, remove vegetables to warm platter; keep warm; discard drippings.

3. In same skillet over medium-high heat, in 2 tablespoons hot butter or margarine, cook scallop mixture, stirring frequently until scallops are tender, about 5 minutes. With slotted spoon, remove scallops to center of vegetables on platter.

4. In same skillet over medium heat, melt 2 tablespoons butter or margarine; stir in flour, paprika, and ½ teaspoon salt until blended; cook 1 minute. Gradually stir in milk and 1 tablespoon sherry; cook, stirring constantly, until mixture is slightly thickened.

5. Pour mixture over scallops on platter.

Oysters on Half Shell with Green-Peppercorn Sauce

TIME: about 15 minutes—SERVINGS: 8 first-course servings

1 tablespoon green peppercorns,
    drained
½ cup mayonnaise
3 tablespoons white wine
    vinegar
¼ teaspoon paprika
crushed ice
16 oysters on the half-shell

1. In small bowl with spoon, slightly crush peppercorns. Stir in mayonnaise, vinegar, and paprika until mixed.

2. Line 1 or 2 large chilled platters with crushed ice; arrange oysters on ice. Spoon some sauce on each oyster.

116

New England Clam Pie

TIME: about 1 hour—SERVINGS: 4

6 tablespoons butter or
   margarine
4 medium carrots, sliced
3 large potatoes (1½ pounds),
   diced
1 medium onion, diced
⅓ cup all-purpose flour
¾ teaspoon salt
⅛ teaspoon pepper
3 10-ounce cans whole baby
   clams
2 cups half-and-half
piecrust mix for two 9-inch
   piecrusts
1 egg
Pastry Clam Shells for garnish
   (right)

1. In 3-quart saucepan over medium heat, in hot butter or margarine, cook carrots, potatoes, and onion until tender, stirring occasionally. Stir in flour, salt, and pepper until blended; cook 1 minute, stirring constantly.

2. Drain 1 cup clam liquid into potato mixture in saucepan; discard remaining liquid; set clams aside. Into mixture in saucepan, stir half-and-half; cook over medium heat until mixture is slightly thickened, stirring. Stir in clams; heat through. Ladle clam mixture into four 12-ounce casseroles or oven-safe soup bowls.

3. Prepare piecrust mix as label directs. On lightly floured surface with floured rolling pin, roll pastry ⅛ inch thick. Cut out 4 pastry circles, ½ inch larger than top of casserole. (Reserve pastry trimmings for clam-shell garnish.) With floured ½-inch round cookie cutter, cut out center of each pastry circle for steam to escape during baking.

4. Preheat oven to 400°F. Moisten edges of casseroles with water. Firmly press a pastry circle on top of each casserole. In cup with fork, beat egg slightly; brush pastry circles with egg. Place casseroles in jelly-roll pan for easier handling. If desired, prepare Pastry Clam Shells. Bake pies 20 to 25 minutes until pastry is golden; bake Pastry Clam Shells 10 minutes.

5. Garnish pies with Pastry Clam Shells.

Pastry Clam Shells: You will need *small clam shells* or other seashells for this garnish. On lightly floured surface with floured rolling pin, roll pastry trimmings ⅛ inch thick. Cut out as many small pastry pieces as needed to fit on rounded sides of clam shells. Press pastry pieces firmly onto clam shells, trimming edges if necessary. Brush pastry with beaten egg. Place pastry-covered clam shells, pastry-side up, on small cookie sheet. Bake 10 minutes or until pastry is golden. Cool shells on wire rack 10 minutes. Carefully remove baked pastry shells from clam shells.

Mussels in Wine

TIME: about 30 minutes—SERVINGS: 4

3 dozen large mussels (about 3
   pounds)
3 tablespoons olive or salad oil
1 small onion, diced
2 garlic cloves, minced
1 16-ounce can tomatoes
¾ cup cooking or dry white wine
¼ teaspoon basil
2 tablespoons chopped parsley

1. With stiff brush, scrub mussels under running cold water to remove any sand; remove beards; set aside.

2. In 5-quart Dutch oven or saucepot over medium heat, in hot olive or salad oil, cook onion and garlic until tender, stirring occasionally. Stir in tomatoes with their liquid, wine, and basil; over high heat, heat to boiling.

3. Add mussels; heat to boiling. Reduce heat to low; cover and simmer until mussels open, about 5 minutes, stirring occasionally. Sprinkle with parsley.

4. Serve mussels in bowls with their broth.

117

SEAFOOD COMBINATIONS

Backyard Clambake

TIME: about 1½ hours—SERVINGS: 8

Yogurt-Watercress Sauce (right)
2 dozen littleneck clams
2 dozen large mussels (about 2 pounds)
cheesecloth
1 3-pound bluefish, dressed, with head and tail removed
1 pound seaweed (optional)
1 quart water
2 2½-pound broiler-fryers, quartered
8 ears corn, husks and silk removed
¾ cup butter or margarine
1 large lemon, cut into 8 wedges
watercress for garnish

1. Prepare the Yogurt-Watercress Sauce; cover and refrigerate.

2. With stiff brush, scrub clams and mussels under running cold water until free of sand. Tie clams loosely in a sheet of double-thickness cheesecloth; tie mussels loosely in another sheet of cheesecloth. Cut bluefish crosswise in half; wrap with double-thickness cheesecloth. Rinse seaweed thoroughly.

3. In 15- to 20-quart saucepot with water, arrange chicken quarters, clams, mussels, corn, bluefish, and seaweed, if used, in that order; over high heat, heat to boiling. Reduce heat to medium-high; cover and cook 25 to 30 minutes, until fish flakes easily when tested with a fork, chicken is fork-tender, and clams and mussels open.

4. In 1-quart saucepan over low heat, melt butter or margarine.

5. To serve, with tongs, remove seaweed and discard. Remove cheesecloth from clams, mussels, and bluefish; cut fish into serving pieces if desired. Strain broth in saucepot through double-thickness cheesecloth. Serve broth in mugs. Serve clambake with melted butter or margarine, Yogurt-Watercress Sauce, and lemon wedges; garnish with watercress.

Yogurt-Watercress Sauce: Peel *1 small cucumber.* Cut cucumber lengthwise in half; with spoon, remove seeds; chop cucumber. In small bowl, toss cucumber with *½ teaspoon salt;* cover and let stand 15 minutes.

Meanwhile, in blender at medium speed or in food processor with knife blade attached, blend *one 8-ounce container plain yogurt, ½ cup mayonnaise, ¼ cup loosely packed watercress leaves,* and *1 medium green onion,* cut up, just until green onion and watercress are finely chopped.

Drain cucumber; pat dry with paper towels. In small bowl, stir yogurt mixture and cucumber.

Fish-and-Shrimp Mousse with Paprika Mayonnaise

TIME: start early in day or day ahead—SERVINGS: 12

water
1 16-ounce package frozen shelled and deveined large shrimp
2 16-ounce packages frozen flounder, sole, or cod fillets
1½ cups mayonnaise
1 cup milk
1¾ teaspoons salt
4 teaspoons prepared white horseradish
¼ teaspoon white pepper
cooking or dry sherry
4 envelopes unflavored gelatin
1 chicken-flavor bouillon cube or envelope
vegetable cooking spray (optional)
1 cucumber
10 small watercress sprigs
Paprika Mayonnaise (right)

1. In 3-quart saucepan over high heat, heat 2 cups water to boiling. Add frozen shrimp; heat to boiling. Reduce heat to medium; cook 1 minute. Drain shrimp; cover and refrigerate.

2. Prepare fish mousse: In 12-inch skillet over high heat, heat 1½ cups water to boiling; add frozen fish; heat to boiling. Reduce heat to medium; cover and cook 10 to 15 minutes until fish flakes easily when tested with a fork. Drain fish, reserving ¾ cup cooking liquid. Place fish in large bowl; with fork, break into small pieces. Stir in mayonnaise, milk, salt, horseradish, pepper, ¼ cup sherry, and reserved cooking liquid until blended.

3. Into 1-quart saucepan, measure ¾ cup water; evenly sprinkle 3 envelopes gelatin over water. Cook over medium heat, stirring until gelatin is completely dissolved. Stir gelatin mixture into fish mixture in bowl.

4. In blender at medium speed, blend fish mixture, in small batches, until smooth. Pour pureed fish mixture into another large bowl; cover and refrigerate while preparing sherry aspic.

5. Prepare sherry aspic: In 1-quart saucepan, combine bouillon, 1½ cups water, and ¼ cup sherry; evenly sprinkle 1 envelope gelatin over sherry mixture. Cook over medium heat, stirring until gelatin is completely dissolved.

6. Spray 10-inch Bundt pan or 2½-quart mold with vegetable cooking spray. Pour half of sherry aspic into Bundt pan; refrigerate until set, about 20 minutes. Thinly slice cucumber. On aspic, arrange watercress sprigs, 5 cooked shrimp, and 5 cucumber slices to make a pretty design. (Wrap and refrigerate remaining cucumber slices for garnish.) Carefully pour remaining aspic into pan; refrigerate until set, about 20 minutes.

7. Dice remaining shrimp; stir into fish mixture in large bowl. Spoon fish mixture over aspic layer in pan; cover and refrigerate until set, about 3 hours.

8. To serve, prepare Paprika Mayonnaise. Unmold mousse onto chilled platter; garnish with remaining cucumber slices. Serve Paprika Mayonnaise in small bowl to spoon over mousse as desired.

Paprika Mayonnaise: In small bowl, stir *1 cup mayonnaise, 1 tablespoon cider vinegar,* and *1½ teaspoons paprika* until mixed.

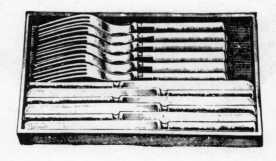

119

Party Paella

TIME: about 3 hours—SERVINGS: 12

2 dozen mussels
2 dozen littleneck clams
water
½ pound hot Italian sausage
links
olive or salad oil
1 pound large shrimp, shelled
and deveined
1 2- to 2½-pound broiler-fryer,
cut up
1 large garlic clove, minced
¾ teaspoon salt
½ teaspoon thyme leaves
1 large onion, chopped
1 large green pepper, cut into
½-inch strips
1 16-ounce can tomatoes
2¼ cups regular long-grain rice
½ cup cooking or dry white wine
½ teaspoon saffron
1 chicken-flavor bouillon cube or
envelope
1 9-ounce package frozen whole
or cut green beans, thawed

1. Scrub mussels and clams with stiff brush under running cold water; remove beards from mussels. In 8-quart Dutch oven over high heat, into 1 inch boiling water, add mussels and clams; heat to boiling. Reduce heat to medium-low; cover and cook until shells open.

2. Discard top shell from each mussel and clam; rinse mussel and clam on half shell in cooking broth to remove any sand. Place mussels and clams on plate; cover and refrigerate. Let broth stand awhile until sand settles at the bottom of Dutch oven. Pour 2 cups clear broth into measuring cup; discard remaining broth.

3. In same Dutch oven over medium heat, heat sausages and 2 tablespoons water to boiling. Reduce heat to low; cover; simmer 5 minutes. Remove cover; continue cooking, turning sausages frequently, until sausages are well browned, about 15 minutes. Remove sausages to paper towels to drain; cool slightly; cut sausages into 1-inch slices.

4. In drippings remaining in Dutch oven (adding 1 tablespoon olive oil if necessary), over medium heat, cook shrimp until pink and tender, about 3 minutes, stirring frequently. Remove shrimp to small bowl; set aside.

5. In medium bowl, mix chicken with garlic, salt, and thyme. In same Dutch oven over medium-high heat, in 2 tablespoons hot olive oil, cook chicken pieces until well browned on all sides. Remove chicken pieces to medium bowl; set aside.

6. In drippings remaining in Dutch oven over medium heat, cook onion and green pepper until tender, stirring occasionally. Add tomatoes with their liquid, rice, wine, saffron, bouillon, browned chicken, and 2 cups reserved broth; over high heat, heat to boiling. Reduce heat to low; cover and simmer until rice is tender and all liquid is absorbed, stirring occasionally, about 30 minutes.

7. Preheat oven to 350°F. Stir sausage, shrimp, and green beans into rice mixture. Tuck mussels and clams into rice. Cover and bake 30 minutes to heat through.

8. Serve paella from Dutch oven or transfer to large platter and serve.

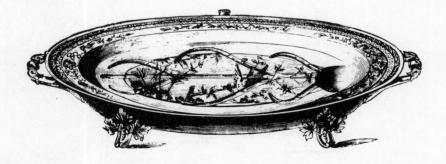

Beans, Rice, and Pasta

RICE AND BEAN MAIN DISHES

Rice and Bean Bake

TIME: about 1½ hours—SERVINGS: 6

1 7-ounce package precooked
   rice
2 tablespoons salad oil
3 medium zucchini (about 1½
   pounds), sliced
1 medium onion, chopped
1 16-ounce can tomatoes
1 teaspoon salt
½ teaspoon basil
½ pound American cheese,
   shredded (2 cups)
1 15¼- to 20-ounce can red
   kidney beans, drained

1. Prepare rice as label directs.

2. Meanwhile, in 10-inch skillet over medium heat, in hot salad oil, cook zucchini and onion until tender, stirring occasionally. Drain tomatoes; reserve liquid for soup another day. Add tomatoes, salt, and basil to zucchini mixture, stirring to break up tomatoes.

3. Grease 2½-quart deep glass casserole. Into casserole, spoon one-third of rice; top with zucchini mixture, another one-third of rice, then one-half of cheese. Spoon kidney beans over cheese; top with remaining rice; sprinkle with remaining cheese. Cover casserole and bake in 350°F. oven about 40 minutes or until heated through.

Hot-and-Spicy Chili

TIME: about 1¼ hours—SERVINGS: 6

1 pound ground beef
1 large green pepper, diced
1 medium onion, diced
1 small garlic clove, minced
2 tablespoons chili powder
¼ teaspoon ground cumin
1 15¼- to 20-ounce can red
   kidney beans
3 large tomatoes, chopped
1 6-ounce can tomato juice
½ cup water
1½ teaspoons salt
½ teaspoon crushed red pepper
¼ teaspoon sugar

1. In 12-inch skillet over high heat, cook ground beef, green pepper, onion, and garlic until all pan juices evaporate and beef is well browned, stirring frequently.

2. Stir in chili powder and cumin; cook 1 minute. Drain liquid from kidney beans into skillet; reserve beans.

3. Stir in tomatoes, tomato juice, water, salt, crushed red pepper, and sugar; over high heat, heat to boiling. Reduce heat to low; cover and simmer 30 minutes, stirring occasionally. Stir in reserved kidney beans; simmer, uncovered, 10 minutes longer to blend flavors.

Hungarian Pork and Beans

TIME: about 3½ hours—SERVINGS: 7

1 16-ounce package Great
    Northern beans
water
salad oil
½ pound pork pieces, cut into
    ¾-inch chunks
2 medium turnips (about ¾
    pound), cut into 1-inch pieces
2 medium carrots, cut into 1-inch
    pieces
1 medium onion, diced
1 medium green pepper, diced
2 tablespoons paprika
1¾ teaspoons salt
1 teaspoon sugar
1 medium tomato, diced
1 chicken-flavor bouillon cube or
    envelope
sour cream (optional)

1. Rinse beans in running cold water and discard any stones or shriveled beans. In 5-quart Dutch oven or saucepot over high heat, heat beans and 8 cups water to boiling; cook 3 minutes. Remove Dutch oven from heat; cover and let stand 1 hour. Drain and rinse beans; place in medium bowl; set aside.

2. In same Dutch oven over medium-high heat, in 1 tablespoon hot salad oil, cook pork pieces until browned on all sides. Remove pork to plate. In drippings remaining in Dutch oven (add 1 tablespoon salad oil if drippings are not enough), over medium heat cook turnips, carrots, onion, and green pepper until lightly browned, stirring occasionally. Stir in paprika; cook 1 minute.

3. Return beans and pork to Dutch oven; stir in salt, sugar, tomato, bouillon, and 4 cups water; over high heat, heat to boiling. Reduce heat to low; cover and simmer 1½ hours or until beans and pork are tender and most of liquid is absorbed. Serve with sour cream, if desired.

Cheesy Rice-Chicken Soufflé

TIME: about 1½ hours—SERVINGS: 8

⅓ cup regular long-grain rice
2 tablespoons butter or
    margarine
3 tablespoons all-purpose flour
¼ teaspoon salt
⅛ teaspoon pepper
¾ cup milk
½ pound Cheddar cheese,
    shredded (2 cups)
4 eggs, separated
1 5- to 6¾-ounce can chunk
    chicken, drained and flaked

1. Prepare rice as label directs; set aside.

2. Preheat oven to 325°F. In 2-quart saucepan over low heat, melt butter or margarine. Stir in flour, salt, and pepper until blended. Gradually stir in milk; cook until mixture is slightly thickened and smooth, stirring constantly. Stir in cheese; cook, stirring, just until cheese melts. Remove saucepan from heat.

3. In small bowl with fork, beat egg yolks slightly; stir in a small amount of hot cheese sauce. Slowly pour egg mixture back into sauce, stirring rapidly to prevent lumping. Cool slightly.

4. In large bowl with mixer at high speed, beat egg whites until stiff peaks form. With rubber spatula, gently fold cheese mixture, one third at a time, into egg whites just until blended. Gently fold rice and chicken into mixture.

5. Pour mixture into a 1½-quart ungreased soufflé dish. With back of spoon, about 1 inch from edge of dish, make 1-inch-deep indentation all around in soufflé mixture. (This makes a top-hat effect when the soufflé is done.) Bake 55 to 60 minutes until knife inserted under top hat comes out clean. Serve immediately.

Four-Bean and Barley Salad

TIME: about 3½ hours or start early in day—SERVINGS: 6

2½ cups water
1 cup medium barley
1 9-ounce package frozen cut green beans
1 15¼- to 20-ounce can red kidney beans, drained
1 16- to 20-ounce can white kidney beans (cannellini), drained
1 15½- to 20-ounce can garbanzo beans, drained
1 2-ounce jar diced pimento, drained
½ cup salad oil
¼ cup cider vinegar
2 teaspoons sugar
½ teaspoon salt
¼ teaspoon basil
¼ teaspoon oregano leaves
⅛ teaspoon pepper

1. In 4-quart saucepan over high heat, heat water and barley to boiling. Reduce heat to low; cover and simmer 1 hour or until barley is tender and all liquid is absorbed.

2. Meanwhile, prepare green beans as label directs but omit salt. Drain beans; place in large bowl. Add kidney beans and garbanzo beans; set aside.

3. When barley is done, add to bean mixture in bowl with pimento and remaining ingredients; toss gently to mix well.

4. Cover and refrigerate 2 hours to blend flavors, stirring occasionally.

RICE AND BEAN ACCOMPANIMENTS

Rice Pilaf

TIME: about 40 minutes—SERVINGS: 4

2 tablespoons butter or margarine
1 cup regular long-grain rice
1 small onion, diced
2 cups water
½ teaspoon salt
¼ teaspoon ground cardamom
⅛ teaspoon pepper
1 chicken-flavor bouillon cube or envelope

1. In 2-quart saucepan over medium heat, in hot butter or margarine, cook rice and onion until rice is golden, stirring frequently.

2. Add water and remaining ingredients; over high heat, heat to boiling. Reduce heat to low; cover; simmer 20 minutes or until rice is tender and liquid is absorbed; fluff with fork.

Rice-and-Bean Salad

TIME: about 45 minutes or start early in day—SERVINGS: 8

1 cup regular long-grain rice
salad oil
3 large celery stalks, thinly sliced
1 15¼-to 20-ounce can red kidney beans, drained
2 tablespoons red wine vinegar
¾ teaspoon salt
½ teaspoon sugar
⅛ teaspoon coarsely ground black pepper

1. Prepare rice as label directs; place in large bowl; set aside.

2. Meanwhile, in 10-inch skillet over medium heat, in 2 tablespoons hot salad oil, cook celery until tender, stirring occasionally. Spoon celery into bowl with rice. Add kidney beans, vinegar, salt, sugar, pepper, and 2 tablespoons salad oil, tossing to mix well. Serve salad at room temperature or cover and refrigerate to serve chilled later.

123

Risotto

TIME: about 1 hour—SERVINGS: 8

one 9-ounce package frozen
  artichoke hearts
7 cups water
2 tablespoons lemon juice
½ teaspoon salt
1 chicken-flavor bouillon cube or
  envelope
butter or margarine
1 small onion, minced
1½ cups Italian arborio rice
  (short-grain pearl rice)
1 cup frozen peas
2 ounces mozzarella cheese,
  shredded (½ cup)
1 tablespoon grated Parmesan
  cheese

1. Prepare frozen artichoke hearts as label directs; drain. Cut each artichoke heart lengthwise in half; set aside.

2. In 3-quart saucepan over high heat, heat water, lemon juice, salt, and bouillon to boiling. Reduce heat to medium-low to maintain simmer.

3. Meanwhile, in 5-quart Dutch oven or saucepot over medium heat, in 4 tablespoons hot butter or margarine, cook onion until tender, stirring occasionally. Add rice; cook until rice grains are opaque, stirring frequently.

4. Add 2 cups simmering bouillon mixture to rice, stirring until liquid is absorbed. Add remaining bouillon mixture, ½ cup at a time, stirring after each addition until liquid is absorbed.

5. Into rice, stir artichoke hearts, peas, mozzarella cheese, Parmesan cheese, and 4 tablespoons butter or margarine; cook, until vegetables are heated through and cheese and butter are melted, stirring often.

Risotto, American Style: In 5-quart Dutch oven or saucepot over medium heat, melt *4 tablespoons butter* or margarine; add *1 small onion*, minced; cook until tender, stirring occasionally. Stir in *3 cups water, 1 chicken-flavor bouillon cube or envelope, 2 tablespoons lemon juice,* and *½ teaspoon salt;* heat to boiling. Add *1½ cups regular long-grain rice;* heat to boiling. Reduce heat to low; cover and simmer 20 minutes or until rice is tender and all liquid is absorbed.

Meanwhile, prepare *one 9-ounce package frozen artichoke hearts* as label directs; drain. Cut each artichoke heart lengthwise in half; stir into rice. Add *1 cup frozen peas, ½ cup shredded mozzarella cheese, 4 tablespoons butter* or margarine, and *1 tablespoon grated Parmesan cheese;* cook until vegetables are heated through and cheese and butter are melted, stirring frequently.

Festive White and Wild Rice

TIME: about 1¼ hours—SERVINGS: 6

½ cup wild rice
water
butter or margarine
1 small onion, diced
1 chicken-flavor bouillon cube or
  envelope
1 cup regular long-grain rice
½ teaspoon salt
⅛ teaspoon pepper

1. Wash wild rice well; drain. In 2-quart saucepan over high heat, heat 1 cup water to boiling; stir in wild rice. Reduce heat to low; cover and simmer 45 minutes or until rice is tender and all liquid is absorbed.

2. About 30 minutes before wild rice is done, in 4-quart saucepan over medium heat, in 2 tablespoons hot butter or margarine, cook onion until tender, stirring occasionally. Add bouillon and 2 cups water; over high heat, heat to boiling; stir in regular long-grain rice. Reduce heat to low; cover and simmer 20 minutes or until rice is tender and all liquid is absorbed.

3. Stir wild rice into rice mixture in 4-quart saucepan; stir in salt, pepper, and 2 tablespoons butter or margarine until butter is melted.

Vermont Pork and Beans

TIME: about 4½ hours—SERVINGS: 16

2 16-ounce packages dry pea
  (navy) beans
water
½ pound pork for stew, cut into
  ½-inch chunks
1 large onion, diced
¾ cup packed dark brown sugar
⅓ cup dark molasses
5 teaspoons salt
1 tablespoon dry mustard

1. Rinse beans in running cold water and discard any stones or shriveled beans. In 5-quart Dutch oven over high heat, heat beans and 8 cups water to boiling; cook 3 minutes. Remove Dutch oven from heat; cover and let stand 1 hour. Drain and rinse beans; set aside.

2. In same Dutch oven over medium-high heat, cook pork and onion until pork is browned and onion is tender, stirring often. Return beans to Dutch oven; add 8 cups water; over high heat, heat to boiling. Reduce heat to low; cover and simmer 1 hour.

3. Add brown sugar, molasses, salt, and dry mustard; cover and simmer 2 hours longer or until beans are tender, stirring occasionally. Serve as accompaniment dish.

NOTE: If bean mixture becomes too thick on standing, add water, ½ cup at a time; cook over low heat, stirring occasionally, until of desired consistency.

PASTA MAIN DISHES

Pasta and Asparagus with Meatballs

TIME: about 1 hour—SERVINGS: 6

1 pound asparagus
salad oil
salt
1 8-ounce package spaghetti
1 small lemon
1 pound ground pork
1 egg
1½ cups fresh bread crumbs
  (about 3 slices white bread)
1 tablespoon chopped parsley
¼ teaspoon caraway seeds,
  crushed
water
4 teaspoons all-purpose flour
1 chicken-flavor bouillon cube or
  envelope

1. Cut asparagus into 2-inch pieces. In 12-inch skillet over medium-high heat, in 1 tablespoon hot salad oil, cook asparagus and ¼ teaspoon salt until asparagus are tender-crisp, about 3 minutes, stirring frequently. Remove asparagus from skillet to bowl; set aside.

2. Prepare spaghetti as label directs; drain.

3. Meanwhile, from lemon, grate 1¼ teaspoons peel and squeeze 1 tablespoon juice; set aside.

4. In large bowl, with fork, mix ground pork, egg, bread crumbs, parsley, caraway seeds, ¾ teaspoon salt, 1 teaspoon lemon peel, and ¼ cup water. Shape mixture into 1-inch meatballs.

5. In 12-inch skillet over medium-high heat, in 1 tablespoon hot salad oil, cook meatballs until browned on all sides, about 10 minutes, removing meatballs to bowl as they brown. Pour off all but 2 tablespoons drippings from skillet.

6. Into drippings in skillet over medium heat, stir flour and ¼ teaspoon salt; cook 1 minute. Gradually stir in bouillon, 2 cups water, reserved lemon juice, and remaining lemon peel; cook, stirring constantly, until slightly thickened.

7. Return meatballs and asparagus to sauce in skillet. Add spaghetti; gently toss until spaghetti, meatballs, and asparagus are well coated with sauce and heated through.

125

Fresh Tomato Sauce with Spaghetti

TIME: about 3 hours—SERVINGS: 6

6 medium tomatoes (2 pounds), peeled and chopped
1 medium green onion, minced
3 tablespoons minced parsley
2 teaspoons red wine vinegar
1 teaspoon salt
½ teaspoon sugar
1½ teaspoons minced fresh basil or ½ teaspoon dried basil
⅛ teaspoon pepper
¼ cup olive or salad oil
2 medium garlic cloves, sliced
1 8-ounce package spaghetti or linguine

1. In large bowl, mix first 8 ingredients.

2. In 1-quart saucepan over medium heat, in hot olive oil, cook garlic until golden; discard garlic. Pour hot oil over tomato mixture; mix well. Cover bowl and let stand 2 hours to blend flavors.

3. About 30 minutes before serving, in 6-quart saucepot, prepare spaghetti as label directs; drain. Return spaghetti to saucepot; add tomato sauce. Over medium-low heat, heat mixture just until tomato sauce is hot, tossing to mix well.

Beef-Noodle Paprikash

TIME: about 45 minutes—SERVINGS: 6

⅓ cup dried bread crumbs
3 tablespoons butter or margarine
1 16-ounce package fusilli (twisted spaghetti)
1 pound ground beef
1 medium onion, diced
1 tablespoon paprika
2 cups milk
1½ teaspoons salt
1 chicken-flavor bouillon cube or envelope
1 8-ounce container sour cream

1. In small saucepan over medium-low heat, heat bread crumbs and butter or margarine until bread crumbs are toasted, about 5 minutes, stirring occasionally; set aside.

2. Prepare fusilli as label directs.

3. Meanwhile, in 10-inch skillet over high heat, cook ground beef and onion until all pan juices evaporate and meat is well browned, stirring frequently. Stir in paprika; cook 1 minute. Add milk, salt, and bouillon; heat to boiling, stirring occasionally. Reduce heat to low; stir in sour cream; heat through. (Do not boil or mixture may curdle.)

4. Drain fusilli; spoon onto warm large platter. Pour meat sauce over fusilli; sprinkle with toasted bread crumbs.

Linguine with Ham-and-Cheese Sauce

TIME: about 30 minutes—SERVINGS: 4

1 8-ounce package linguine or thin spaghetti
4 tablespoons butter or margarine
1 small onion, chopped
1 tablespoon all-purpose flour
½ teaspoon salt
⅛ teaspoon cracked pepper
2 cups milk
1 10-ounce package frozen peas
1 4-ounce package sliced cooked ham, cut into thin strips
½ cup shredded Swiss cheese (2 ounces)

1. In 6-quart saucepot, prepare linguine as label directs; drain. Return linguine to saucepot; keep warm.

2. Meanwhile, in 2-quart saucepan over medium heat, in hot butter or margarine, cook onion until tender, stirring occasionally. Stir in flour, salt, and pepper until blended; cook 1 minute. Gradually stir in milk; cook, stirring constantly, until slightly thickened and smooth.

3. Stir in frozen peas, separating peas with fork; heat to boiling. Over low heat, cook mixture 2 to 3 minutes until peas are tender. Add ham; heat through. Remove saucepan from heat; stir in cheese until melted.

4. Gently toss linguine in saucepot with cheese sauce. Serve immediately.

Vermicelli with Cheese Sauce and Mushrooms

TIME: about 30 minutes—SERVINGS: 4

½ 16-ounce package vermicelli
  or thin spaghetti
butter or margarine
½ pound medium mushrooms,
  sliced
2 medium carrots, coarsely
  shredded
1 tablespoon all-purpose flour
¾ teaspoon salt
⅛ teaspoon pepper
1¾ cups milk
½ cup shredded Swiss cheese
  (2 ounces)
2 tablespoons grated Parmesan
  cheese
1 tablespoon minced parsley

1. In 6-quart saucepot, prepare vermicelli as label directs; drain. Return vermicelli to saucepot; keep warm.

2. Meanwhile, in 2-quart saucepan over medium heat, in 2 tablespoons hot butter or margarine, cook mushrooms until tender, stirring occasionally. Remove mushrooms to plate; keep warm.

3. In same saucepan over medium heat, in 2 tablespoons hot butter or margarine, cook carrots until tender, stirring occasionally. Stir in flour, salt, and pepper until blended; cook 1 minute. Gradually stir in milk; cook, stirring constantly, until mixture is slightly thickened. Stir in cheeses and parsley until cheese is melted.

4. Gently toss vermicelli in saucepot with cheese sauce; spoon mixture onto warm platter; top with mushrooms. Serve immediately.

Thai-Style Pork-Noodle Toss

TIME: about 45 minutes—SERVINGS: 8

½ 16-ounce package linguine or
  spaghetti
1 pork shoulder blade steak, cut
  ¾-inch thick (about 1 pound)
  or ¾ pound fresh boneless
  pork butt
¼ cup catchup
¼ cup soy sauce
1 tablespoon sugar
½ teaspoon crushed red pepper
¼ teaspoon ground ginger
2 eggs
¼ teaspoon salt
salad oil
3 medium green onions, cut into
  2-inch pieces
1 medium garlic clove, halved
¾ pound bean sprouts or
  1 16-ounce can bean sprouts,
  drained
¼ cup unsalted peanuts, finely
  chopped

1. Prepare linguine as label directs; drain.

2. Meanwhile, remove blade bone from pork shoulder blade steak. With knife held in slanting position, almost parallel to the cutting surface, slice pork crosswise into ⅛-inch-thick slices. In bowl, mix pork, catchup, soy sauce, sugar, crushed red pepper, and ginger; set aside.

3. In small bowl with fork, beat eggs with salt until blended. In 10-inch skillet over high heat, in 1 tablespoon hot salad oil, cook egg mixture, stirring, until eggs are the size of peas and leave side of skillet. Spoon eggs into large bowl.

4. In same skillet over medium heat, in 2 tablespoons hot salad oil, cook green onions and garlic until garlic is golden; discard garlic. With slotted spoon, remove green onions to bowl with eggs. In oil remaining in skillet, over medium-high heat, cook pork mixture until pork loses its pink color, stirring frequently. Add bean sprouts; cook until bean sprouts are slightly wilted, stirring to loosen brown bits.

5. Spoon pork mixture into bowl with eggs; toss with linguine and chopped peanuts.

Macaroni and Franks Casserole

TIME: about 1 hour—SERVINGS: 6

1 8-ounce package corkscrew
  macaroni
1 16-ounce package frankfurters,
  cut into ½-inch pieces
1 10¾-ounce can condensed
  tomato soup
2 medium celery stalks, minced
1 cup milk
2 tablespoons minced parsley
2 tablespoons butter or
  margarine

1. In 5-quart saucepot or Dutch oven, prepare macaroni as label directs, but *do not add salt*. Drain macaroni; return to saucepot.

2. Preheat oven to 350°F. To cooked macaroni, add frankfurters, undiluted tomato soup, celery, milk, minced parsley, and butter or margarine; toss mixture gently to mix well. Spoon macaroni mixture into 2-quart casserole. Bake casserole, covered, 30 minutes or until hot and bubbly.

Ziti with Mexican-Style Meat Sauce

TIME: about 35 minutes—SERVINGS: 6

1 pound ground beef
1 medium green pepper, cut into
  thin strips
1 small onion, diced
2 cups water
1 6-ounce can tomato paste
1 2-ounce jar pimentos, drained
  and cut into thin strips
1 1⅜- to 1⅝-ounce package
  enchilada-sauce mix
1 16-ounce package ziti
  macaroni

1. In 12-inch skillet over medium-high heat, cook ground beef, green pepper, and onion until meat is browned and pepper and onion are tender, stirring occasionally.

2. Stir in water, tomato paste, pimentos, and enchilada-sauce mix; over high heat, heat to boiling. Reduce heat to low; cover; simmer 15 minutes, stirring occasionally.

3. Meanwhile, prepare ziti as label directs; drain. Serve meat sauce over ziti.

Meatless Lasagna

TIME: about 1¾ hours—SERVINGS: 8

⅔ 16-ounce package lasagna
  noodles (about 14 noodles)
¼ cup all-purpose flour
salt
1 large eggplant (about 1½
  pounds), cut crosswise into
  ½-inch slices
salad oil
1 16-ounce package mozzarella
  cheese, shredded (4 cups)
1 15- to 16-ounce container
  ricotta cheese (2 cups)
¼ cup water
1 egg
1 15- to 15½-ounce jar spaghetti
  sauce

1. Prepare lasagna noodles as label directs; drain.

2. Meanwhile, on waxed paper, mix flour with ½ teaspoon salt. Coat eggplant slices with mixture. In 12-inch skillet over medium heat, in ¼ cup hot oil, cook eggplant, a few slices at a time, until browned on both sides, adding oil if needed; drain on paper towels.

3. Preheat oven to 375°F. Set aside 1 cup mozzarella. In medium bowl, combine ricotta, water, egg, and ½ teaspoon salt. In 13" by 9" baking dish, spoon half of spaghetti sauce; arrange half of noodles over sauce, overlapping to fit; top with half of ricotta mixture, half of remaining mozzarella, and half of eggplant slices. Repeat layering. Sprinkle with reserved mozzarella. Cover dish with foil and bake 40 minutes or until hot and bubbly.

Lasagna, Northern Style

TIME: about 2 hours—SERVINGS: 12

½ pound ground beef
½ pound ground pork
1 small onion, diced
1 28-ounce can tomatoes
1 6-ounce can tomato paste
¼ cup water
1 teaspoon basil
¼ teaspoon pepper
salt
1 16-ounce package mozzarella
  cheese, shredded
1 15- to 16-ounce container
  ricotta cheese (2 cups)
2 eggs
2 tablespoons chopped parsley
⅔ 16-ounce package lasagna
  noodles (about 14 noodles)
3 tablespoons butter or
  margarine
3 tablespoons all-purpose flour
¼ teaspoon ground nutmeg
1½ cups milk

1. In 4-quart saucepan over high heat, cook ground beef, ground pork, and onion until all pan juices evaporate and meat is well browned, stirring frequently. Add tomatoes with their liquid, tomato paste, water, basil, pepper, and 1¼ teaspoons salt; heat to boiling. Reduce heat to low; cover and simmer 10 minutes, stirring occasionally. Skim off fat from sauce; keep warm.

2. In medium bowl, mix mozzarella cheese, ricotta cheese, eggs, and parsley; set aside.

3. Prepare lasagna noodles as label directs; drain.

4. Meanwhile, in 2-quart saucepan over medium heat, melt butter or margarine; stir in flour, nutmeg, and ¼ teaspoon salt until blended; cook 1 minute. Gradually stir in milk; cook, stirring constantly, until white sauce is thickened and smooth; remove from heat.

5. Preheat oven to 375°F. In 13″ by 9″ baking dish, evenly spoon about ¾ cup meat sauce. Arrange half of noodles over sauce, overlapping to fit. Spoon half of cheese mixture over noodles; spread with half of white sauce; top with half of remaining meat sauce. Repeat layering with remaining noodles, cheese mixture, and sauces.

6. Bake lasagna 45 minutes or until heated through. Remove from oven; let stand 10 minutes for easier serving.

HOMEMADE PASTA

Gnocchi al Forno

TIME: about 1¼ hours—SERVINGS: 8

DOUGH:
water
salt
1 cup milk
½ cup butter or margarine
1 cup all-purpose flour
4 eggs

SAUCE:
2 tablespoons butter or
  margarine
2 tablespoons all-purpose flour
¼ teaspoon salt
2 cups milk
¼ cup grated Parmesan cheese

1. Prepare dough: Fill 6-quart Dutch oven or saucepot half full with water; add 2 teaspoons salt; heat to boiling. Meanwhile, in 2-quart saucepan over medium-high heat, heat milk, butter, and 1 teaspoon salt until butter melts and mixture boils; remove from heat. Immediately, with wooden spoon, stir in flour all at once until mixture forms a ball and leaves side of pan; then beat eggs into dough mixture until dough is smooth and shiny.

2. Spoon dough into large decorating bag with 1-inch opening at tip. Holding decorating bag over boiling water, gradually squeeze dough out, and with kitchen shears, cut dough off in 1-inch lengths; let dough drop into boiling water (or drop dough by teaspoonfuls into water). Cook dough 4 minutes or until puffy and tender. With slotted spoon, remove gnocchi to colander; drain well.

3. Make sauce: In 2-quart saucepan over medium heat, melt butter. Stir in flour and salt until blended; cook 1 minute. Gradually stir in milk; cook, stirring constantly, until mixture is slightly thickened and smooth. Reduce heat to low; stir in Parmesan cheese until cheese is melted.

4. Preheat oven to 350°F. In shallow 1½-quart casserole, combine sauce and gnocchi; bake 40 minutes or until bubbly and lightly browned on top.

Homemade Pasta Dough

TIME: about 40 minutes—YIELD: 1 pound

about 2¼ cups all-purpose flour
2 eggs
¼ cup water
1 tablespoon olive or salad oil
1 teaspoon salt

In large bowl, stir 2¼ cups flour with remaining ingredients to make a stiff dough. On well-floured surface, knead dough until smooth and not sticky, about 20 times. Wrap dough with plastic wrap and let rest 30 minutes for easier rolling. (Or, in food processor with knife blade attached, blend all ingredients 10 to 15 seconds to form a smooth ball. Do not knead dough; wrap and let rest for 30 minutes.)

Tortellini in Escarole Soup

TIME: about 3½ hours—SERVINGS: 8 (main-dish)

2 whole medium chicken breasts
water
salt
Homemade Pasta Dough
    (preceding recipe)
3 tablespoons minced parsley
2 tablespoons grated Parmesan
    cheese
1 egg
pepper
¼ cup olive or salad oil
1 medium onion, diced
2 large heads escarole (about
    1½ pounds each), torn into
    bite-size pieces
3 chicken-flavor bouillon cubes
    or envelopes

1. In 10-inch skillet over high heat, heat chicken breasts, 4 cups water, and 1 teaspoon salt to boiling. Reduce heat to low; cover and simmer 15 minutes or until chicken is fork-tender. Remove chicken breasts to bowl; refrigerate 20 minutes or until easy to handle. Reserve broth.

2. Meanwhile, prepare Homemade Pasta Dough.

3. When chicken is ready, discard skin and bones; cut chicken into large chunks. In blender at medium speed or in food processor with knife blade attached, blend chicken until finely ground. In bowl, mix ground chicken, parsley, Parmesan, egg, ½ teaspoon salt, and ⅛ teaspoon pepper; set aside.

4. Cut pasta dough into 3 pieces. On floured surface with floured rolling pin, roll 1 dough piece into 20" by 14" rectangle (keep remaining 2 pieces covered with plastic wrap). With 2-inch round cookie cutter, cut as many circles as you can. Remove trimmings; wrap and reserve.

5. Place scant ½ teaspoon chicken filling in center of each circle; brush edges with water. Fold each circle in half with edges not quite meeting; press edges to seal. To shape, place straight edge of half-circle at right angle to a finger; bend around finger until two ends meet to form a fan shape; press to seal ends. Place in single layer on clean cloth towel. Repeat with remaining dough, trimmings, and filling, making about 125 tortellini in all. Let tortellini dry 30 minutes.

6. Prepare escarole soup: In 8-quart Dutch oven over medium heat, in hot olive oil, cook onion until lightly browned and tender, stirring occasionally. Add escarole; cook, stirring constantly, until escarole is well coated with oil. Add bouillon, 8 cups water, reserved chicken broth, 1 tablespoon salt, and ¼ teaspoon pepper; over high heat, heat to boiling. Reduce heat to low; cover and simmer 20 minutes or until escarole is tender.

7. Meanwhile, cook tortellini: In 6-quart saucepot over high heat, heat 4 quarts water to boiling. Add tortellini; stir gently to separate pieces; heat to boiling. Reduce heat to medium-low; cook until tender but firm (al dente) about 5 minutes. Drain.

8. To serve, add the tortellini to the escarole soup; heat through. Makes 18 cups.

Fettuccine

YIELD: 1 pound

Homemade Pasta Dough
(page 130)

1. Prepare Homemade Pasta Dough.

2. Cut dough in half. On floured surface with floured rolling pin, roll one half of dough into 16″ by 12″ rectangle (dough should be about ¹⁄₁₆ inch thick). Fold dough in half into 8″ by 12″ rectangle; then fold in half again into 4″ by 12″ rectangle. With knife, cut folded dough crosswise into about ¼-inch-wide strips. Unfold strips; place in single layer on pasta drying rack or on clean cloth towel to dry. Repeat with remaining dough.

3. Dry noodles at least 1 hour before cooking. If not using noodles same day, wrap dried noodles with plastic wrap and refrigerate to use within 2 weeks.

Fettuccine Alfredo

TIME: about 2½ hours—SERVINGS: 4

1 pound Fettuccine (above)
6 quarts water
1 cup heavy or whipping cream
½ cup grated Parmesan cheese
6 tablespoons butter or
  margarine
½ teaspoon salt
¼ teaspoon cracked pepper

1. Prepare Fettuccine; dry 1 hour.

2. About 25 minutes before serving, cook noodles: In 8-quart saucepot over high heat, heat water to boiling. Add Fettuccine; with fork, gently stir to separate noodles; heat to boiling. Reduce heat to medium; cook noodles 3 minutes or until tender but firm (*al dente*). Drain.

3. Return noodles to saucepot; over low heat, gently toss noodles with heavy or whipping cream, grated Parmesan cheese, butter or margarine, salt, and cracked pepper until butter melts and mixture is heated through. Serve immediately. If desired, sprinkle more grated Parmesan cheese over each serving.

Fettuccine with Pesto Sauce

TIME: about 2½ hours—SERVINGS: 4

1 pound Fettuccine (above)
water
¾ cup loosely packed basil
  leaves
¼ cup grated Parmesan cheese
¼ cup olive or salad oil
1 tablespoon walnuts or pine
  nuts (optional)
¼ teaspoon salt
1 small garlic clove

1. Prepare Fettuccine; dry 1 hour.

2. About 25 minutes before serving, cook noodles: In 6-quart saucepot over high heat, heat 3 quarts water to boiling. Add ½ pound Fettuccine (wrap remaining dried noodles with plastic wrap and refrigerate to use within 2 weeks). With fork, gently stir to separate noodles; heat to boiling. Reduce heat to medium; cook noodles 3 minutes or until tender but firm (*al dente*). Drain.

3. Meanwhile, prepare pesto sauce: In blender at medium speed or in food processor with knife blade attached, blend basil leaves, grated Parmesan cheese, olive or salad oil, walnuts or pine nuts, salt, and garlic clove until almost smooth. (Do not overblend or mixture will separate.) If sauce is too thick, add 1 tablespoon hot water to sauce to thin slightly. Serve pesto sauce over noodles.

Fettuccine with White Clam Sauce

TIME: about 2½ hours—SERVINGS: 4

1 pound Fettuccine (page 131)
18 large cherrystone clams
water
¼ cup olive or salad oil
4 tablespoons butter or
  margarine
1 small garlic clove, thinly sliced
2 tablespoons minced parsley
salt

1.   Prepare Fettuccine; dry 1 hour.

2.   About 25 minutes before serving, from cherrystone clams, shucked and with liquid reserved, drain 2 cups clam liquid (add enough water to make 2 cups if clam liquid is not enough). Chop clams; set clams and liquid aside.

3.   In 2-quart saucepan over medium heat, in hot olive or salad oil and hot butter or margarine, cook garlic until lightly browned; discard garlic. Add clam liquid; heat to boiling. Reduce heat to low; cover and simmer 5 minutes to blend flavors. Add clams and minced parsley; cook until clams are heated through and just turn opaque, stirring occasionally. Add salt to taste.

4.   Meanwhile, cook noodles: In 8-quart saucepot over high heat, heat 6 quarts water to boiling. Add Fettuccine; with fork, gently stir to separate noodles; heat to boiling. Reduce heat to medium; cook noodles 3 minutes or until tender but firm (*al dente*). Drain; serve clam sauce over noodles.

Fettuccine Primavera

TIME: about 2½ hours—SERVINGS: 4

1 pound Fettuccine (page 131)
½ pound asparagus
¼ pound Chinese pea pods
¼ pound mushrooms
2 medium carrots
2 medium green onions
3 quarts water
olive or salad oil
½ cup frozen peas
1½ teaspoons salt
⅛ teaspoon coarsely ground
  black pepper
1 cup half-and-half
4 tablespoons butter or
  margarine
2 tablespoons grated Parmesan
  cheese

1.   Prepare Fettuccine; dry 1 hour.

2.   About 45 minutes before serving, cut asparagus into 1½-inch pieces; remove strings from Chinese pea pods; slice mushrooms; cut carrots into matchstick-thin strips. Cut green onions into 1½-inch pieces; set aside.

3.   Cook noodles: In 6-quart saucepot over high heat, heat water to boiling. Add ½ pound Fettuccine (wrap remaining dried noodles with plastic wrap and refrigerate to use within 2 weeks). With fork, gently stir to separate noodles; heat to boiling. Reduce heat to medium; cook noodles 3 minutes or until tender but firm (*al dente*).

4.   Meanwhile, in 12-inch skillet over medium-high heat, in 2 tablespoons more hot olive or salad oil, cook asparagus, carrots, and Chinese pea pods until tender-crisp, about 5 minutes, stirring frequently. With slotted spoon, remove vegetables to bowl; set aside. In same skillet in 2 tablespoons more hot olive or salad oil, cook mushrooms and green onions 3 to 5 minutes, stirring frequently. Return asparagus mixture to skillet; add frozen peas, salt, and coarsely ground black pepper. Cook over medium heat until vegetables are heated through, stirring occasionally; remove from heat.

5.   Drain noodles. Return noodles to sacucepot; over low heat, gently toss noodles with half-and-half, butter or margarine, grated Parmesan cheese, and vegetable mixture until butter melts and mixture is heated through and slightly thickened.

Ravioli

TIME: about 1½ hours—YIELD: 48 ravioli

Homemade Pasta Dough
  (page 130)
1¼ cups ricotta cheese
¼ cup minced parsley
2 teaspoons grated onion
½ teaspoon salt
1 egg
water

1. Prepare Homemade Pasta Dough.
    While pasta dough is resting, prepare filling: In small bowl, mix ricotta cheese, parsley, onion, salt, and egg; cover; set aside.

2. Cut pasta dough into 4 pieces. On floured surface with floured rolling pin, roll one piece of dough into 12″ by 8″ rectangle. (Keep remaining dough covered.) With dull edge of knife, lightly mark dough into twenty-four 2-inch squares; place a heaping teaspoon of filling in center of each. Roll second piece of dough into 13″ by 9″ rectangle; place over filling. Press around filling and along edges. With ravioli cutter or knife, cut into 24 ravioli; place on floured, clean cloth towel. Repeat with remaining dough and filling. Let ravioli dry 30 minutes. If not using ravioli immediately, cover and refrigerate.

Ravioli with Meat Sauce: About 3 hours before serving, prepare *Hearty Home-Style Meat Sauce* (see page 176); keep warm. Prepare *Ravioli* as above and let dry 30 minutes.
    About 25 minutes before serving, cook Ravioli: In 8-quart saucepot over high heat, heat *6 quarts water* to boiling. Add Ravioli; stir gently to separate pieces; heat to boiling. Reduce heat to medium; cook until tender but firm, about 5 minutes; drain. Serve Ravioli topped with meat sauce. Makes 8 main-dish servings.

Ravioli with Butter Sauce: About 2 hours before serving, prepare *Ravioli* as above and let dry 30 minutes.
    About 25 minutes before serving, cook Ravioli: In 8-quart saucepot over high heat, heat *6 quarts water* to boiling. Add Ravioli; stir gently to separate pieces; heat to boiling. Reduce heat to medium; cook until tender but firm, about 5 minutes; drain. Gently toss Ravioli with *4 tablespoons butter or margarine*. Makes 6 main-dish servings.

Eggs and Cheese

Tuna Quiche

TIME: about 1½ hours—SERVINGS: 6

piecrust mix for one 9-inch
   piecrust
butter or margarine
1 medium onion, diced
1 small green pepper, diced
1 6½- to 7-ounce can tuna,
   drained and coarsely flaked
4 eggs
1 cup half-and-half
½ teaspoon salt

1. Prepare piecrust mix as label directs; use to line 9-inch pie plate. Spread crust with 1 tablespoon softened butter or margarine.

2. Preheat oven to 425°F. In 2-quart saucepan over medium heat, in 3 tablespoons hot butter or margarine, cook onion and pepper until tender, stirring occasionally. Remove saucepan from heat; stir in tuna. Spoon mixture into piecrust.

3. In bowl, with fork, beat eggs, half-and-half, and salt. Pour egg mixture into piecrust. Bake 15 minutes; turn oven control to 325°F.; bake 35 minutes or until knife inserted in center comes out clean.

No-Crust Artichoke Quiche

TIME: about 40 minutes—SERVINGS: 6

2 6-ounce jars marinated
   artichoke hearts
¼ pound mushrooms, sliced
½ pound Muenster cheese,
   shredded (2 cups)
1¼ cups milk
½ teaspoon salt
⅛ teaspoon pepper
6 eggs

1. Preheat oven to 350°F. Drain artichokes, reserving marinade. Dice artichokes; set aside.

2. In 10-inch skillet over medium heat, heat 2 tablespoons reserved marinade; add mushrooms and cook until tender, about 5 minutes, stirring occasionally. Into bottom of 10-inch quiche dish or 9″ by 9″ baking dish, evenly distribute artichoke hearts, mushrooms, and cheese; set aside.

3. In large bowl, with wire whisk or fork, beat milk, salt, pepper, eggs, and 2 tablespoons reserved marinade.

4. Pour egg mixture over ingredients in quiche dish. Bake 30 minutes or until knife inserted in center comes out clean.

Salmon Quiche

TIME: about 1½ hours—SERVINGS: 6

piecrust mix for one 9-inch
    piecrust
1 tablespoon butter or margarine,
    softened
¼ pound Swiss cheese, shredded
1 7¾-ounce can salmon
4 eggs
2 cups half-and-half
¼ teaspoon salt
⅛ teaspoon pepper
½ cup sliced pitted ripe olives

1. Prepare piecrust mix as label directs; use to line 9-inch pie plate. Spread piecrust with butter or margarine. Sprinkle cheese on piecrust.

2. Preheat oven to 425°F. Drain salmon; pat dry with paper towels. In medium bowl with fork, beat eggs, half-and-half, salt, and pepper. Flake salmon; stir into egg mixture.

3. Pour mixture into piecrust; sprinkle with olives. Bake 15 minutes; turn oven control to 300°F.; bake 50 minutes longer or until knife inserted in center comes out clean.

Sausage Quiche

TIME: about 1½ hours—SERVINGS: 6 to 12

piecrust mix for one 9-inch
    piecrust
1 tablespoon butter or margarine,
    softened
1 16-ounce package pork-
    sausage meat
¼ pound Swiss cheese, shredded
    (1 cup)
4 eggs
2 cups heavy or whipping cream

1. Prepare piecrust mix as label directs; use to line 9-inch pie plate. Spread piecrust with butter or margarine.

2. In 10-inch skillet over medium heat, cook pork-sausage meat until well browned. With slotted spoon, remove sausage meat to paper towels to drain. Sprinkle sausage and cheese on piecrust.

3. Preheat oven to 425°F. In medium bowl, with fork, beat eggs and cream; pour into piecrust. Bake 15 minutes; turn oven control to 300°F.; bake 40 minutes longer or until knife inserted in center comes out clean. Sausage will stay at the bottom and leave custard layer on top.

Turkey and Broccoli Quiche

TIME: about 1½ hours—SERVINGS: 8

piecrust mix for one 9-inch
    piecrust
butter or margarine
½ pound ground turkey
1 small onion, chopped
1 teaspoon salt
4 eggs
2 cups half-and-half
¼ pound Swiss cheese, shredded
    (1 cup)
1 10-ounce package frozen
    chopped broccoli, thawed and
    squeezed dry

1. Prepare piecrust mix as label directs; use to line 9-inch pie plate. Spread piecrust with 1 tablespoon butter or margarine.

2. In 10-inch skillet over medium-high heat, in 2 tablespoons butter or margarine, cook ground turkey, onion, and salt until all pan juices evaporate, stirring frequently to break up turkey.

3. Preheat oven to 425°F. In large bowl, with fork, beat eggs and half-and-half; stir in turkey mixture, cheese, and broccoli; pour into piecrust. Bake 15 minutes; turn oven control to 300°F.; bake 40 minutes longer or until knife inserted in center comes out clean.

No-Crust Cheesy Salmon Pie

TIME: about 1 hour—SERVINGS: 6

1 7¾-ounce can salmon, well drained and flaked
1 medium zucchini (about ½ pound), shredded
1 2-ounce jar diced pimentos, well drained
½ 8-ounce package pasteurized process cheese spread, diced
1 tablespoon grated onion
1 cup milk
½ cup buttermilk baking mix
3 eggs

1. Preheat oven to 400°F. Grease 9-inch pie plate. In medium bowl, mix first 5 ingredients.

2. In small bowl, with wire whisk, beat milk, baking mix, and eggs until well mixed. Stir egg mixture into salmon mixture; pour into pie plate. Bake 35 to 40 minutes until pie is set and top is golden.

Cheesy Vegetable Pie

TIME: about 1½ hours—SERVINGS: 6

piecrust mix for one 9-inch piecrust
3 tablespoons salad oil
½ medium head green cabbage (about 1¼ pounds), shredded
¼ pound mushrooms, sliced
1 medium celery stalk, sliced
1 small onion, diced
4 eggs
¾ cup milk
½ teaspoon salt
⅛ teaspoon ground red pepper
½ pound longhorn or mild Cheddar cheese, shredded
6 cherry tomatoes, each cut in half

1. Prepare piecrust mix as label directs. On lightly floured surface with floured rolling pin, roll pastry into a circle about 2 inches larger all around than 9-inch pie plate. Line pie plate with pastry; trim pastry edge, leaving 1-inch overhang. Fold overhang under; pinch pastry to make a high fluted edge; set piecrust aside.

2. In 12-inch skillet over medium heat, in salad oil, cook cabbage, mushrooms, celery, and onion until vegetables are tender, about 15 minutes, stirring the mixture occasionally.

3. Preheat oven to 350°F. In medium bowl, with wire whisk or fork, beat eggs, milk, salt, and ground red pepper until well blended. Spoon cabbage mixture into piecrust; top with cheese; carefully pour egg mixture over ingredients in piecrust.

4. Arrange cherry tomatoes, cut-side down, around the edge of pie. Bake 40 to 45 minutes until pie is set and top is golden.

Salami-and-Eggplant Pie

TIME: about 45 minutes—SERVINGS: 6

salad oil
1 medium eggplant, sliced
1 8-ounce package refrigerated crescent dinner rolls
1 8-ounce can tomato sauce
4 ounces salami, diced
8 ounces mozzarella cheese, shredded
¼ cup grated Parmesan cheese
1 green pepper, cut into ¼-inch slices
¼ teaspoon oregano

1. In 12-inch skillet over medium-high heat, in ¼ cup hot oil, cook eggplant, few slices at a time, until tender, adding more oil as needed.

2. Preheat oven to 375°F. Separate crescent dough into 8 triangles; press into greased 9-inch pie plate. Arrange half of eggplant on dough. Top with half of tomato sauce, half salami, half mozzarella, half Parmesan; repeat.

3. Tuck green pepper into mixture; sprinkle with oregano. Bake 20 minutes or until pie is hot and crust is golden.

136

Cheese-and-Pepper Country Pie

TIME: about 1½ hours—SERVINGS: 8

1 large onion
2 tablespoons salad oil
2 medium green peppers, cut
  into 2" by ½" strips
2 medium red peppers, cut into
  2" by ½" strips
1 13¾-ounce package hot-roll
  mix
½ 15-ounce container ricotta
  cheese
1 egg
1 16-ounce package mozzarella
  cheese, coarsely shredded
1 4-ounce package sliced salami,
  diced (optional)

1. Cut a few paper-thin slices from onion; separate into rings; set aside. Dice remaining onion. In 10-inch skillet over medium heat, in hot salad oil, cook peppers and diced onion until tender, stirring occasionally.

2. Meanwhile, prepare hot-roll mix as label directs, but use 1 cup water and omit egg; do not let dough rise. Divide dough in half; keep dough covered with plastic wrap to prevent it from drying out. Grease large cookie sheet. Pat ½ of dough evenly on cookie sheet into a 10-inch round.

3. In small bowl, mix ricotta with egg until blended. Top dough with mozzarella, vegetable mixture, ricotta mixture, and (if desired) diced salami to within ½ inch from edge.

4. Preheat oven to 400°F. On lightly floured surface with floured hands, pat remaining dough into 11-inch round. Gently place dough over cheese-and-vegetable mixture; tuck top piece of dough under bottom dough all around to seal. Sprinkle reserved onion rings over top. Bake 20 to 25 minutes until pie is golden brown. Remove pie from oven; cool on wire rack 10 minutes for cheese to set slightly for easier slicing.

Greek Pie

TIME: about 1¾ hours—SERVINGS: 6

¾ pound ground beef
1 medium onion, diced
1 15- to 16-ounce container
  ricotta cheese
1 10-ounce package frozen
  chopped spinach, thawed and
  squeezed dry
1 8-ounce package mozzarella
  cheese, shredded
½ teaspoon salt
½ pound phyllo (strudel leaves)*
½ cup butter or margarine,
  melted

*Phyllo is available in Greek pastry shops or in the frozen-food section of most supermarkets.

1. In 10-inch skillet over high heat, cook ground beef and onion until all pan juices evaporate and meat is well browned, stirring occasionally. Spoon off any fat in skillet. Into large bowl, spoon beef mixture. Stir in ricotta, spinach, mozzarella, and salt; set aside.

2. On waxed paper, brush one sheet of phyllo with some melted butter or margarine; place in 9-inch pie plate, with edges overhanging. Brush second sheet of phyllo with some melted butter or margarine; place over first sheet with corners slightly away from corners of first sheet. Continue layering, brushing each sheet of phyllo with some butter or margarine and placing sheets so that corners are always slightly away from corners of sheet directly below.

3. Spoon beef mixture on phyllo in pie plate. Fold overhanging edges of phyllo over beef mixture until top of pie is completely closed. Brush top with remaining melted butter or margarine. Bake in 350°F. oven 1 hour or until pie is golden brown.

Italian Cheese-and-Escarole Pie

TIME: about 2½ hours—SERVINGS: 12

6 eggs
½ teaspoon oregano leaves
salt
olive or salad oil
1 large head escarole (about 1¼
   pounds), coarsely shredded
1 medium onion, sliced
1 garlic clove, minced
1 pound mushrooms, sliced
Pastry (right)
7 slices very thin white bread
1 pound Fontina or Bel Paese
   cheese, shredded
2 4-ounce cans or jars pimentos,
   well drained
1 teaspoon water

1. Prepare omelets: In small bowl with wire whisk or fork, beat 5 eggs and 1 egg white (reserve yolk to brush top of pie later), oregano, ¼ teaspoon salt. Brush bottom of 8-inch omelet pan or skillet with olive or salad oil. Over medium heat, heat pan. Pour half of egg mixture into hot pan; let set around edge. With metal spatula, lift edge as it sets, tilting pan to allow uncooked egg mixture to run under omelet. Shake pan occasionally to keep omelet moving freely in pan. When omelet is set but still moist on the surface, remove pan from heat and slide omelet onto cookie sheet. Repeat with remaining egg mixture to make 2 open-faced omelets; set omelets aside.

2. In 12-inch skillet over medium-high heat, in 2 tablespoons hot olive or salad oil, cook escarole, onion, and garlic until vegetables are tender and lightly browned, stirring occasionally. Remove escarole mixture to bowl; set aside.

3. In same skillet over medium-high heat, in 2 more tablespoons hot oil, cook mushrooms and ¼ teaspoon salt until mushrooms are tender and all liquid is absorbed, stirring occasionally. Remove skillet from heat; set aside.

4. Prepare Pastry. On lightly floured surface with floured rolling pin, roll larger pastry ball into a 16-inch circle. Lightly press pastry to bottom and side of 9″ by 3″ spring-form pan; with kitchen shears, trim pastry edge, leaving 1-inch overhang.

5. Arrange half of bread slices on pastry in bottom of pan, cutting bread to fit. Top with an omelet, half of escarole mixture, half of cheese, half of mushrooms, and all of the pimentos. Repeat layering, ending with mushrooms. Fold edge of pastry over filling. In cup, beat water with remaining egg yolk. Brush edge of pastry with some egg yolk mixture.

6. Preheat oven to 400°F. Roll remaining pastry ball into a 9-inch circle. Place pastry over filling, pressing around edge to seal. Make a small hole in center of pastry. With tip of knife, cut several slits from edge of pastry to center hole to make decorative design. Brush top with remaining yolk mixture. Bake pie 45 minutes or until crust is golden and filling is heated through.

7. To serve, let pie stand at room temperature 15 minutes for easier slicing. Loosen crust from side of pan; carefully remove pie from pan. Cut pie into wedges.

Pastry: In medium bowl with fork, stir *3 cups all-purpose flour* and *1 teaspoon salt*. With pastry blender or two knives used scissor-fashion, cut in *1¼ cup shortening* until mixture resembles coarse crumbs. Sprinkle *5 to 6 tablespoons cold water*, a tablespoon at a time, into flour mixture, mixing lightly after each addition until mixture is just moist enough to hold together. With hands, shape two-thirds of pastry into a large ball; shape remaining pastry into another ball.

Deluxe Whole-Wheat Pizzas

TIME: about 2 hours—SERVINGS: 12

Whole-Wheat Pizza Dough
(right)
olive or salad oil
¼ pound medium mushrooms,
sliced
1 medium zucchini, sliced
1 small onion, sliced
1 pound ground beef
1 14-ounce jar pizza sauce
1 7-ounce jar roasted sweet red
peppers, drained and cut into
bite-sized pieces
1 3½-ounce can pitted ripe
olives, drained and sliced
1 8-ounce package mozzarella
cheese, shredded

1. Prepare Whole-Wheat Pizza Dough.

2. Meanwhile, in 10-inch skillet over medium heat, in 2 tablespoons hot olive oil, cook mushrooms, zucchini, and onion until tender, stirring occasionally. Remove vegetables to bowl.

3. Prepare meat sauce: In same skillet over high heat, cook ground beef until all pan juices evaporate and meat is well browned, stirring frequently. Remove skillet from heat; stir in pizza sauce.

4. When dough is ready, preheat oven to 450°F. Grease two 14-inch pizza pans or two 15½″ by 10½″ jelly-roll pans. With greased hands, pat a pizza-dough half into each pizza pan, making a ½-inch rim. (Or, if using jelly-roll pans, pat dough onto bottom and sides.)

5. For each pizza, brush dough with 2 teaspoons olive oil; spread with half of meat sauce; top with half of vegetable mixture, half of red peppers, and half of olives; sprinkle with half of cheese.

6. Bake one pizza at a time on lowest rack in oven 15 minutes or until crust is browned and crisp. If desired, freeze unbaked pizzas to use up within 2 weeks.

Whole-Wheat Pizza Dough: In large bowl, combine *1¾ cups whole-wheat flour, ¼ cup all-purpose flour, 1 teaspoon salt, 1 teaspoon sugar,* and *1 package active dry yeast.* In 1-quart saucepan over low heat, heat *1½ cups water* and *2 tablespoons salad oil* until very warm (120° to 130°F.).

With mixer at low speed, gradually beat liquid into dry ingredients just until blended. Increase speed to medium; beat 2 minutes, occasionally scraping bowl with rubber spatula. Beat in *¼ cup all-purpose flour* to make a thick batter; continue beating 2 minutes, scraping bowl often. With spoon, stir in *¾ cup all-purpose flour* to make a soft dough.

Turn dough onto well-floured surface and knead about 5 minutes, working in *about ¼ cup more all-purpose flour* while kneading. Shape dough into a ball and place in greased large bowl, turning dough over so that top is greased. Cover and let rise in warm place (80° to 85°F.), away from draft, until doubled, about 45 minutes. (Dough is doubled when two fingers pressed lightly into dough leave a dent.) Punch down dough. Turn dough onto lightly floured surface; cut dough in half; cover with towel and let rest 15 minutes for easier shaping.

TO FREEZE AND SERVE UP TO 2 WEEKS LATER: Wrap unbaked pizza tightly with foil; label and freeze. To serve, about 35 minutes before serving, preheat oven to 450°F. Remove foil; bake pizza on lowest oven rack 20 minutes or until crust is browned and crisp.

Family-Style Pizza

TIME: about 1 hour—SERVINGS: 8

1 13¾-ounce package hot-roll
  mix
½ 14-ounce jar pizza sauce
1 medium tomato, diced
1 3- to 4-ounce jar sliced
  mushrooms, drained
1 16-ounce package mozzarella
  cheese, thinly sliced
1 4-ounce package sliced salami
1 medium green pepper, thinly
  sliced
4 pitted ripe olives, sliced
⅛ teaspoon crushed red pepper

1. Prepare hot-roll mix as label directs, but use 1 cup water and omit egg; do not let dough rise. Pat dough evenly onto bottom of 14-inch pizza pan. Spread pizza sauce evenly over dough; top with diced tomato, mushrooms, cheese, salami, green pepper, olives, and crushed red pepper.

2. Bake pizza in preheated 425°F. oven on bottom rack 30 minutes or until topping is hot and bubbly and crust is browned and crisp.

Skillet Macaroni and Cheese

TIME: about 25 minutes—SERVINGS: 4

½ 16-ounce package ziti or
  1 8-ounce package elbow
  macaroni
2 tablespoons butter or
  margarine
2 tablespoons all-purpose flour
½ teaspoon dry mustard
dash pepper
1¾ cups milk
8 ounces sharp Cheddar cheese,
  shredded
1 4-ounce package sliced cooked
  ham, diced
1 2-ounce jar diced pimento
1 tablespoon chopped parsley

1. Cook macaroni as label directs.

2. Meanwhile in 10-inch skillet over medium heat, melt butter or margarine; stir in flour, mustard, and pepper until blended; cook 1 minute. Gradually stir in milk; cook, stirring constantly, until thickened and smooth. Remove skillet from heat; stir in cheese until melted.

3. Drain macaroni; stir into cheese sauce in skillet with ham, pimento, and parsley. Over low heat, heat through.

Tuna-Stuffed Eggs

TIME: about 1¼ hours or start early in day—YIELD: 24 stuffed egg halves

12 eggs
water for cooking eggs
6 slices bacon
1 3¼- to 3½-ounce can tuna,
  drained and finely flaked
¾ cup mayonnaise
1 tablespoon lemon juice
¾ teaspoon salt
½ teaspoon hot pepper sauce

1. In 4-quart saucepan, place eggs and enough water to come 1 inch above tops of eggs; over high heat, heat to boiling. Remove saucepan from heat; cover tightly and let eggs stand in hot water 15 minutes; drain.

2. Meanwhile in 10-inch skillet over medium heat, cook bacon until browned; remove to paper towel to drain. Crumble bacon; set aside.

3. Carefully peel eggs under running cold water. Slice eggs lengthwise in half. Gently remove yolks and place in medium bowl. With fork, finely mash yolks. Stir in tuna and remaining ingredients until smooth.

4. With spoon, pile egg-yolk mixture into egg-white centers. Sprinkle stuffed eggs with crumbled bacon; cover and refrigerate.

Baked Eggs and Vegetables Niçoise

TIME: about 1½ hours—SERVINGS: 6

salad oil
1 medium onion, diced
1 medium green pepper, diced
1 medium red pepper, diced
1 garlic clove, crushed
1 large eggplant (about 1½ pounds), cut into ½-inch cubes
1 medium zucchini, cut into ¼-inch-thick slices
1 8-ounce can tomatoes
½ cup water
1½ teaspoons sugar
1¼ teaspoons salt
¼ teaspoon thyme leaves
1 15½- to 20-ounce can garbanzo beans, drained
3 ounces Cheddar cheese, shredded (¾ cup)
6 eggs

1. In 12-inch skillet over medium heat, in 2 tablespoons hot oil, cook onion, peppers, and garlic until tender, stirring occasionally. With slotted spoon, remove pepper mixture to small bowl; set aside.

2. In same skillet over medium heat, in ¼ cup more hot salad oil, cook eggplant and zucchini until tender, stirring occasionally, about 15 minutes. Return pepper mixture to skillet; add tomatoes with their liquid and next 4 ingredients; over high heat, heat to boiling. Reduce heat to low; simmer 15 minutes, stirring occasionally. Stir in garbanzo beans; heat through.

3. Preheat oven to 425°F. Spoon vegetable mixture into 2½-quart shallow baking dish. With spoon, make 6 deep indentations in vegetable mixture. Sprinkle 2 tablespoons Cheddar cheese into each indentation.

4. One at a time, break eggs into saucer and slip into indentations on top of cheese. Bake 12 minutes or until eggs are just set or of desired doneness.

Breakfast Tartlets

TIME: about 1¼ hours—SERVINGS: 4

piecrust mix for one 9-inch piecrust
¼ pound Gruyère or Swiss cheese, shredded (1 cup)
4 eggs
¼ cup heavy or whipping cream
2 tablespoons butter or margarine, cut into small pieces
ground red pepper
1 6-ounce package sliced cooked ham
1 16-ounce can pear halves, drained
lettuce leaves

1. Preheat oven to 400°F. Prepare piecrust mix as label directs. On lightly floured surface with floured rolling pin, roll dough about ⅛ inch thick. Using 6-inch round plate as guide, cut 4 circles from pastry, rerolling scraps if necessary.

2. Set each pastry circle loosely in a 6-ounce custard cup; place some foil in each pastry cup to keep sides from collapsing. Place cups in jelly-roll pan; bake 15 minutes or until pastry is golden brown. Cool pastry in cups 5 minutes. Remove pastry cups from custard cups; discard foil. Turn oven control to 350°F.

3. Into each pastry cup, sprinkle one-fourth of the cheese. Break 1 egg into each cup on top of cheese; top with 1 tablespoon heavy cream; dot with one-fourth of the butter or margarine. Sprinkle each lightly with some ground red pepper. Place pastry cups in jelly-roll pan. Bake about 15 minutes for soft-cooked eggs or until desired doneness.

4. To serve, on each breakfast plate, arrange 1 egg tartlet, 1 or 2 slices ham, 1 or 2 pear halves, and 1 lettuce leaf.

141

Skillet Cheese Toast

TIME: about 30 minutes—SERVINGS: 4

1 8-ounce package Muenster cheese, shredded
1 tablespoon prepared mustard
1 teaspoon Worcestershire
1 egg
4 tablespoons butter or margarine
8 1-inch-thick diagonal slices Italian bread
½ pint cherry tomatoes

1. Preheat broiler if manufacturer directs. In small bowl, mix cheese, mustard, Worcestershire, and egg.

2. In 12-inch skillet with broiler-safe handle (or, cover skillet handle with heavy-duty foil) over medium-low heat, in hot butter or margarine, cook bread until golden brown on one side. Remove skillet from heat. Turn bread; top each slice with some cheese mixture.

3. Place skillet in broiler; broil until cheese mixture is hot and bubbly, about 3 minutes; garnish with cherry tomatoes.

California Open-Faced Sandwiches

TIME: about 35 minutes—SERVINGS: 2

6 slices bacon
¼ cup olive or salad oil
¼ cup mayonnaise
1 tablespoon cider vinegar
½ teaspoon salt
1 small head iceberg lettuce
1 medium tomato, thinly sliced
¾ cup shredded Swiss cheese (3 ounces)

1. In 10-inch skillet over medium-low heat, cook bacon slices until browned; remove to paper towels to drain.

2. In small bowl with wire whisk or fork, mix olive oil, mayonnaise, vinegar, and salt until blended.

3. Preheat broiler if manufacturer directs. Cut two 1-inch-thick slices from head of lettuce. (Reserve remaining lettuce for salad another day.) Place lettuce slices on rack in broiling pan; top with dressing, tomato slices, bacon slices, then shredded cheese. Broil 2 to 3 minutes until cheese is melted.

4. Serve immediately.

Cheese-Vegetable Strata

TIME: about 1½ hours—SERVINGS: 9

8 slices white bread
3 tablespoons salad oil
1 medium bunch broccoli, cut into bite-sized pieces
1 medium onion, chopped
½ pound mushrooms, sliced
salt
1 8-ounce package Muenster cheese slices
6 eggs
4 cups milk
½ teaspoon dry mustard

1. With 3-inch flower-shaped cookie cutter, cut 6 rounds from bread slices; set aside. Tear remaining slices and trimmings into small pieces; place in bottom of greased 13" by 9" baking dish.

2. In 10-inch skillet over medium-high heat, in hot salad oil, cook broccoli, onion, mushrooms, and ½ teaspoon salt until vegetables are tender, stirring frequently. With slotted spoon, place vegetables on top of bread pieces in baking dish.

3. Preheat oven to 350°F. Place cheese slices over broccoli mixture in baking dish, overlapping slices if necessary.

4. In large bowl, with wire whisk or fork, beat eggs, milk, mustard, and 1 teaspoon salt until blended. Dip bread rounds into egg mixture; then place on top of cheese in baking dish.

5. Carefully pour remaining egg mixture over cheese in baking dish. With back of spoon, lightly press bread rounds into mixture. Bake 45 minutes or until knife inserted in center comes out clean.

NOTE: If bread browns too quickly, cover with foil during last 10 minutes of baking.

Golden Buck

TIME: about 40 minutes—SERVINGS: 4

4 tablespoons butter or
   margarine
¼ cup all-purpose flour
¼ teaspoon salt
⅛ teaspoon ground red pepper
1¼ cups milk
½ cup beer
6 ounces Cheddar cheese,
   shredded (1½ cups)
1 long loaf Italian bread
2 medium tomatoes, each cut
   into 4 slices
water
4 eggs
parsley sprigs for garnish

1. In 2-quart saucepan over medium heat, melt butter or margarine; stir in flour, salt, and ground red pepper until blended; cook 1 minute. Gradually stir in milk and beer; cook, stirring constantly, until thickened and smooth. Stir in cheese until melted; keep sauce warm.

2. Preheat oven to 200°F. Cut eight 1-inch-thick slices from bread (reserve remaining bread to use another day); toast bread slices. For each serving, arrange two toasted bread slices, side by side, on oven-safe plate. Top each serving with 2 tomato slices; keep warm in oven.

3. Poach eggs: In 10-inch skillet over high heat, heat 1 inch water to boiling. Reduce heat to low. One at a time, break eggs into saucer and slip into simmering water. Cook eggs 2 to 4 minutes until of desired firmness. With slotted spoon, carefully remove eggs from water. Drain each egg (still held in spoon) over paper towels.

4. Arrange eggs on tomatoes. Spoon some sauce over eggs; garnish servings with parsley. Serve remaining sauce in small bowl.

Quick Eggs and Peppers

TIME: 30 minutes—SERVINGS: 4

2 medium green or red peppers
2 medium onions
1 medium zucchini (about 8
   ounces)
½ pound medium mushrooms
butter or margarine
½ teaspoon salt
8 eggs
¼ cup milk
½ cup shredded Cheddar cheese
   (2 ounces)
4 slices whole-wheat bread,
   toasted

1. Cut peppers into ½-inch-wide strips. Cut onions into thin slices. Cut zucchini into ½-inch-thick slices; cut each slice in half. Cut each mushroom in half.

2. In 12-inch skillet over medium heat, in 4 tablespoons hot butter or margarine, cook peppers and onions about 5 minutes, stirring occasionally. Add zucchini, mushrooms, and salt; continue cooking until vegetables are tender, stirring occasionally. With slotted spoon, remove vegetables to platter; keep warm. Wipe skillet clean.

3. In medium bowl, beat eggs and milk. Into same skillet over medium heat, in 2 more tablespoons hot butter or margarine, pour egg mixture. As mixture begins to set, with spatula, stir cooked portion slightly so thin uncooked part flows to bottom. Cook until eggs are slightly set. Stir in cheese. Spoon eggs onto platter with vegetables. Cut each toasted bread slice in half; serve toast with egg mixture.

Breads

YEAST BREADS

Mother's Oatmeal Bread

TIME: about 4½ hours or start day ahead—YIELD: 2 loaves

2 teaspoons salt
2 packages active dry yeast
about 5½ cups all-purpose flour
2 cups water
1 cup old-fashioned oats, uncooked
½ cup light molasses
1 tablespoon butter or margarine

1. In large bowl, combine salt, yeast, and 2 cups flour. In 2-quart saucepan over low heat, heat water, oats, molasses, and butter or margarine until very warm (120° to 130°F.). (Butter or margarine does not need to melt completely.)

2. With mixer at low speed, gradually beat oatmeal mixture into dry ingredients just until blended. Increase speed to medium; beat 2 minutes, occasionally scraping bowl with rubber spatula. Beat in ¾ cup flour to make a thick batter; continue beating 2 minutes, scraping bowl often. With wooden spoon, stir in 2 cups flour to make a soft dough.

3. Turn dough onto well-floured surface and knead until smooth and elastic, about 10 minutes, working in about ¾ cup more flour while kneading. Shape dough into a ball and place in greased large bowl, turning dough over so that top is greased. Cover with towel and let rise in warm place (80° to 85°F.), away from draft, until doubled, about 1 hour. (Dough is doubled when two fingers pressed lightly into dough leave a dent.)

4. Grease two 1½-quart round casserole dishes. When dough is ready, punch down dough; turn dough onto lightly floured surface; cut dough in half. Shape one half of dough into a ball; place in casserole. Repeat. Cover loaves with towels and let dough rise in warm place until doubled, about 45 minutes. (Dough is doubled when one finger very lightly pressed against dough leaves a dent.)

5. Preheat oven to 350°F. With sharp knife, cut several slashes on top of each loaf. Bake 45 minutes or until loaves sound hollow when tapped with fingers. Remove loaves from casseroles immediately; cool on wire racks.

White Bread

TIME: about 4 hours or start up to 5 days ahead—YIELD: 2 loaves

3 tablespoons sugar
2½ teaspoons salt
1 package active dry yeast
5¾ to 6½ cups all-purpose flour
1½ cups water
½ cup milk
butter or margarine

1. In large bowl, combine sugar, salt, yeast, and 2 cups flour. In 1-quart saucepan over low heat, heat water, milk, and 3 tablespoons butter or margarine until very warm (120° to 130°F.). (Butter or margarine does not need to melt completely.)

2. With mixer at low speed, gradually beat liquid into dry ingredients until mixed. Increase speed to medium; beat 2 minutes, occasionally scraping bowl with rubber spatula. Beat in ½ cup flour or enough to make a thick batter; continue beating 2 minutes, occasionally scraping bowl. With spoon, stir in enough additional flour (about 3 cups) to make a soft dough.

3. Turn dough onto lightly floured surface and knead until smooth and elastic, about 10 minutes, adding more flour while kneading, if necessary. Shape dough into ball and place in greased large bowl, turning dough over so that top is greased. Cover with towel; let rise in warm place (80° to 85°F.), away from draft, until doubled, about 1 hour.

4. Punch down dough. Turn dough onto lightly floured surface; cut in half; cover with bowl for 15 minutes.

5. Grease two 8½" by 4½" loaf pans. On floured surface, with hands, pat one dough-half into an oval about 5 inches wide. Pick up both ends and, gently shaking dough, stretch it into a 15-inch-long strip. Fold ends over so they overlap slightly in center; press ends lightly together. Then, starting with a long edge nearest you, roll up dough, jelly-roll fashion, completely pressing out air as you roll; pinch edges together to seal. Place dough, seam-side down, in loaf pan. Repeat with remaining dough. Cover with towel; let rise in warm place until doubled, about 1 hour.

6. Preheat oven to 400°F. If desired, brush loaves with melted butter or margarine. Bake 25 to 30 minutes until loaves are golden and sound hollow when lightly tapped with fingers. Remove from pans immediately; cool on wire racks.

White Bread with Egg: Prepare as above but add *1 egg,* slightly beaten, to liquid ingredients. Makes 2 loaves.

Whole-Wheat Bread: In medium bowl, mix *2½ cups all-purpose flour* with *2½ cups whole-wheat flour.* Prepare bread as above but use flour mixture instead of all-purpose flour called for. If extra flour is needed, use all-purpose flour. Makes 2 loaves.

Herb Bread: Prepare bread as above but in step 1, add *½ cup grated Parmesan cheese* and *1 tablespoon dill weed* with dry ingredients. Makes 2 loaves.

Whole-Grain Bread

TIME: about 5 hours or start up to 3 days ahead—YIELD: 1 loaf

2 cups rye flour
1 cup unprocessed bran
½ cup wheat germ
about 4¼ cups whole-wheat
  flour
3 tablespoons sugar
4 teaspoons salt
2 packages active dry yeast
¾ cup milk
½ cup butter or margarine
⅓ cup dark molasses
water
2 eggs
2 tablespoons yellow cornmeal
1 teaspoon caraway seeds

1. In large bowl, combine rye flour, unprocessed bran, wheat germ, and 3 cups whole-wheat flour. In another large bowl, combine sugar, salt, yeast, and 3 cups flour mixture. In 2-quart saucepan over low heat, heat milk, butter or margarine, molasses, and 1 cup water until very warm (120° to 130°F.). (Butter or margarine does not need to melt completely.) With mixer at low speed, gradually beat liquid into dry ingredients until just blended. Increase speed to medium; beat 2 minutes, occasionally scraping bowl with rubber spatula. Reserve 1 egg white; beat in remaining eggs and 2 cups flour mixture; continue beating 2 minutes, occasionally scraping bowl. With spoon, stir in remaining flour mixture and additional whole-wheat flour (about ¾ cup) to make a soft dough.

2. Lightly flour surface with whole-wheat flour; turn dough onto surface; knead until smooth and elastic, about 10 minutes, adding more whole-wheat flour while kneading. Shape dough into ball; place in greased large bowl, turning dough to grease top. Cover; let rise in warm place (80° to 85°F.), away from draft, until doubled, about 1 hour.

3. Punch down dough; turn onto surface lightly floured with whole-wheat flour; cover with bowl for 15 minutes; let dough rest. Sprinkle cookie sheet with cornmeal.

4. Shape dough into oval, tapering ends; place on cookie sheet. Cover with towel; let rise in warm place until doubled, about 1 hour.

5. Preheat oven to 350°F. Cut 3 diagonal slashes on top of loaf. In cup, mix reserved egg white with 1 tablespoon water. With pastry brush, brush bread with egg-white mixture. Sprinkle bread with caraway seeds. Bake 50 to 60 minutes until loaf sounds hollow when lightly tapped. Cool on rack.

Parker House Rolls

TIME: about 3½ hours or start early in day—YIELD: 3 dozen

½ cup sugar
2 teaspoons salt
2 packages active dry yeast
about 6½ cups all-purpose flour
2 cups water
1 cup butter or margarine
1 egg

1. In large bowl, combine sugar, salt, yeast, and 2¼ cups flour. In 2-quart saucepan over low heat, heat water and ½ cup butter or margarine until very warm (120° to 130°F.). (Butter or margarine does not need to melt completely.)

2. With mixer at low speed, gradually beat liquid into dry ingredients just until blended; beat in egg. Increase speed to medium; beat 2 minutes, occasionally scraping bowl with rubber spatula. Beat in 1 cup flour to make a thick batter; continue beating 2 minutes, scraping bowl often. With wooden spoon, stir in 2¾ cups flour to make a soft dough.

3. Turn dough onto well-floured surface and knead until smooth and elastic, about 10 minutes, working in about ½ cup more flour while kneading. Shape dough into a ball and place in greased large bowl, turning dough over so that top is greased. Cover with towel and let

rise in warm place (80° to 85°F.), away from draft, until doubled, about 1 hour. (Dough is doubled when two fingers pressed lightly into dough leave a dent.)

4. Punch down dough. Turn dough onto lightly floured surface; cover with bowl and let rest for 15 minutes for easier shaping.

5. Meanwhile, grease 17¼" by 11½" roasting pan. In small saucepan over low heat, melt remaining ½ cup butter or margarine.

6. On lightly floured surface with floured rolling pin, roll dough ½ inch thick. With floured 3-inch round cookie cutter, cut dough into rounds. With dull edge of knife, make a crease across center of each dough round. Brush rounds lightly with some melted butter; fold in half along crease. Arrange folded dough in rows in pan, each nearly touching the other. Knead trimmings together; reroll and cut until all dough is used, making 36 rolls. Brush tops of rolls with remaining melted butter. Cover pan with towel and let rise in warm place until doubled, about 40 minutes. (Dough is doubled when one finger very lightly pressed against dough leaves a dent.)

7. Meanwhile, preheat oven to 425°F. Bake rolls 18 to 20 minutes until browned. Serve rolls warm.

8. To serve later, wrap rolls with foil in one layer. Just before serving, reheat rolls in 375°F. oven 10 minutes or until warm.

Italian Bread

TIME: start early in day or day ahead—YIELD: 2 loaves

1 tablespoon sugar
2 teaspoons salt
2 packages active dry yeast
about 5 cups all-purpose flour
1 tablespoon butter or margarine
water
cornmeal
salad oil
1 egg white

1. In large bowl, combine sugar, salt, yeast, and 2 cups flour. In small saucepan over low heat, heat butter or margarine and 1¾ cups water until very warm (120° to 130°F.). (Butter or margarine does not need to melt completely.)

2. With mixer at low speed, gradually beat liquid into dry ingredients until just blended. Increase speed to medium; beat 2 minutes, occasionally scraping bowl. Beat in ½ cup flour to make thick batter; continue beating 2 minutes, scraping bowl often. Stir in about 1¾ cups flour to make soft dough.

3. Turn dough onto floured surface; knead until smooth and elastic, about 10 minutes, adding about ¾ cup more flour while kneading. Cut dough in half; cover; let rest 20 minutes for easier shaping. Grease large cookie sheet; sprinkle with cornmeal.

4. On floured surface with floured rolling pin, roll one dough-half into 15" by 10" rectangle. Starting with 15-inch side, tightly roll dough, jelly-roll fashion; pinch seam to seal. Repeat. Place loaves, seam-side down, on cookie sheet; taper ends. Brush with salad oil; cover loosely with plastic wrap. Refrigerate 2 to 24 hours.

5. To bake, preheat oven to 425°F. Meanwhile, remove loaves from refrigerator; uncover and let stand 10 minutes. Cut 3 or 4 diagonal slashes on top of each loaf. Bake 20 minutes.

6. In small bowl, with fork, beat egg white with 1 tablespoon water. Remove loaves from oven; brush with mixture; return to oven and bake 5 minutes. Remove loaves from cookie sheet; cool on wire racks.

147

Swedish Limpa

TIME: start early in day or day ahead—YIELD: 2 loaves

2 cups rye flour
3½ to 4 cups all-purpose flour
¼ cup sugar
1 tablespoon salt
2 packages active dry yeast
1 cup milk
1 cup water
2 tablespoons light or dark
  molasses
2 tablespoons butter or
  margarine
2 teaspoons anise seeds
salad oil

1. On waxed paper, combine rye flour and 3½ cups all-purpose flour. In large bowl, combine sugar, salt, yeast, and 2 cups flour mixture. In small saucepan over low heat, heat milk, water, molasses, butter or margarine, and anise seeds until very warm (120° to 130°F.). (Butter or margarine does not need to melt completely.) With mixer at low speed, gradually beat liquid mixture into dry ingredients. Increase speed to medium; beat 2 minutes, occasionally scraping bowl with rubber spatula. Beat in ¾ cup flour mixture or enough to make a thick batter; beat 2 minutes, occasionally scraping bowl. With spoon, stir in remaining flour mixture and about ½ cup all-purpose flour to make soft dough.

2. Turn dough onto lightly floured surface and knead until smooth and elastic, about 10 minutes. Cut dough in half; cover with towel; let stand 20 minutes for easier shaping. Grease large cookie sheet.

3. Shape dough into 2 balls; with hands, flatten dough into ovals, each about 12″ by 4″. Place ovals at least 3 inches apart on cookie sheet; brush with salad oil. Cover loosely with plastic wrap and refrigerate 2 to 24 hours.

4. About 2 hours before serving, preheat oven to 375°F. Uncover loaves and let stand at room temperature 10 minutes. Bake 35 minutes or until loaves sound hollow when lightly tapped with fingers. Remove from cookie sheet and cool on wire racks.

Onion Flatbread

TIME: about 4½ hours or start day ahead—YIELD: 2 loaves

3 tablespoons sugar
2 teaspoons salt
1 package active dry yeast
about 5¾ cups all-purpose flour
2 cups milk
3 tablespoons butter or
  margarine
½ cup chopped green onions

1. In large bowl, combine sugar, salt, yeast, and 2 cups flour. In 1-quart saucepan over low heat, heat milk and butter or margarine until very warm (120° to 130°F.). (Butter or margarine does not need to melt completely.)

2. With mixer at low speed, gradually beat liquid into dry ingredients just until blended. Increase speed to medium; beat 2 minutes, occasionally scraping bowl with rubber spatula. Beat in ¾ cup flour to make a thick batter; continue beating 2 minutes, scraping bowl often. With wooden spoon, stir in green onions and 2¾ cups flour to make a soft dough.

3. Turn dough onto well-floured surface and knead until smooth and elastic, about 10 minutes, working in about ¼ cup more flour while kneading. Shape dough into a ball and place in greased large bowl, turning dough over so that top is greased. Cover with towel and let rise in warm place (80° to 85°F.), away from draft, until doubled, about 1 hour. (Dough is doubled when 2 fingers pressed lightly into dough leave a dent.)

4. Punch down dough. Turn dough onto lightly floured surface; cut dough in half; cover with bowl and let dough rest 15 minutes for easier shaping.

5. Preheat oven to 400°F. Grease 2 large cookie sheets. On 1

cookie sheet, roll 1 dough piece into ½-inch-thick round. Repeat with remaining dough. Cover cookie sheets with towels and let dough rise in a warm place until doubled, about 1 hour. (Dough is doubled when 1 finger pressed very lightly against dough leaves a dent.)

6. Bake breads 12 to 15 minutes until loaves are golden brown and sound hollow when lightly tapped with fingers. Remove breads from cookie sheets; cool on wire racks.

TO FREEZE AND SERVE UP TO 1 MONTH LATER: When loaves are cool, wrap each loaf tightly with foil or freezer wrap; seal, label, and freeze. To thaw, remove wrap; let bread stand at room temperature 2 hours.

Cracked-Wheat Rolls

TIME: start early in day or up to 3 days ahead—YIELD: 30 rolls

¾ cup bulgur (cracked wheat)
water
1 cup whole-wheat flour
½ cup sugar
2 teaspoons salt
2 packages dry active yeast
about 5 cups all-purpose flour
butter or margarine
1 egg
salad oil

1. In small saucepan over medium heat, heat bulgur and ¾ cup water to boiling. Reduce heat to low; simmer 5 minutes or until water is absorbed, stirring frequently. Remove saucepan from heat; set aside to cool.

2. In large bowl, combine whole-wheat flour, sugar, salt, yeast, and 1¼ cups all purpose flour. In 1-quart saucepan over low heat, heat 2 cups water and ½ cup butter or margarine until very warm (120° to 130°F.). (Butter or margarine does not need to melt completely.)

3. With mixer at low speed, gradually beat liquid into dry ingredients just until blended. Increase speed to medium; beat 2 minutes, occasionally scraping bowl with rubber spatula. Gradually beat in egg and ¾ cup flour to make a thick batter; continue beating 2 minutes, scraping bowl often. With wooden spoon, stir in cooled bulgur and 2½ cups flour to make a soft dough.

4. Turn dough onto well-floured surface and knead until dough is smooth and elastic, about 10 minutes, working in about ½ cup more flour while kneading. Shape dough into a ball and place in greased large bowl, turning dough over so that top is greased. Cover bowl with towel and let rise in warm place (80° to 85°F.), away from draft, until doubled, about 1½ hours. (Dough is doubled when two fingers pressed lightly into dough leave a dent.)

5. Punch down dough. Turn dough over; brush with salad oil. Cover bowl tightly with plastic wrap and refrigerate up to 3 days, punching down dough occasionally, until ready to use.

6. About 2 hours before serving: Remove dough from refrigerator; grease 15½" by 10½" open roasting pan. Cut dough into 30 equal pieces; shape into balls and place in pan. Cover with towel; let rise in warm place until doubled, about 1½ hours. (Dough is doubled when one finger very lightly pressed against dough leaves a dent.)

7. Preheat oven to 425°F. Bake rolls 15 to 20 minutes until golden. In small saucepan over low heat, melt 2 tablespoons butter or margarine. With pastry brush, lightly brush melted butter or margarine over hot rolls. Remove rolls from pan to serve or cool rolls on wire rack to serve later.

Pannetone (Italian Sweet Bread)

TIME: about 4½ hours or start day ahead—YIELD: 2 loaves

1 cup sugar
1 teaspoon salt
2 packages active dry yeast
about 9 cups all-purpose flour
1 cup butter or margarine
1½ cups milk
½ cup water
2 eggs
1 cup golden raisins
1 4-ounce container diced candied citron, chopped
5 teaspoons grated lemon peel

1. In large bowl, combine sugar, salt, yeast, and 2 cups flour. In 1-quart saucepan over low heat, heat butter or margarine, milk, and water until very warm (120° to 130°F.). (Butter or margarine does not need to melt completely.)

2. With mixer at low speed, gradually beat liquid into dry ingredients just until blended. Increase speed to medium; beat 2 minutes, occasionally scraping bowl with rubber spatula. Beat in eggs and 3 cups flour to make a thick batter; continue beating 2 minutes, scraping bowl often. With wooden spoon, stir in raisins, citron, lemon peel, and 3½ cups flour to make a soft dough.

3. Turn dough onto well-floured surface and knead until smooth and elastic, about 10 minutes, working in about ½ cup more flour while kneading. Shape dough into a ball and place in greased large bowl, turning dough over so that top is greased. Cover with towel and let rise in warm place (80° to 85°F.), away from draft, until doubled, about 1 hour. (Dough is doubled when 2 fingers pressed lightly into dough leave a dent.)

4. Meanwhile, prepare collars for two 2-quart soufflé dishes: From roll of foil, tear off two 25-inch strips; fold each strip lengthwise in half. Wrap each foil strip around outside of a soufflé dish so collar stands 3 inches above rim. Secure with cellophane tape. Grease dishes and collars.

5. Preheat oven to 350°F. Punch down dough. Turn dough onto lightly floured surface; cut dough in half and shape into 2 round loaves. Place each loaf into a prepared soufflé dish. Cover with towel and let dough rise in warm place until doubled, about 1 hour. (Dough is doubled when 1 finger very lightly pressed against dough leaves a dent.)

6. Cut a cross on top of each loaf. Bake 45 to 50 minutes until loaves are golden brown and sound hollow when lightly tapped with fingers. Remove loaves from soufflé dishes; cool on wire racks.

"Coffee Can" Batter Bread

TIME: about 4½ hours—YIELD: 1 loaf

3 tablespoons sugar
2 teaspoons salt
1 teaspoon ground ginger
1 package active dry yeast
4 to 4½ cups all-purpose flour
1½ cups half-and-half
¼ cup water
butter or margarine
1 2-pound coffee can*

*Or, use two 1-pound coffee cans and bake 50 minutes or until done.

1. In large bowl, combine sugar, salt, ginger, yeast, and 1 cup flour. In small saucepan over low heat, heat half-and-half, water, and 2 tablespoons butter or margarine until very warm (120° to 130°F.). (Butter or margarine does not need to melt completely.)

2. With mixer at low speed, gradually beat liquid into dry ingredients. Increase speed to medium; beat 2 minutes, occasionally scraping bowl with rubber spatula. Continue beating and add 2 cups flour, 1 cup at a time, beating well after each addition. With wooden spoon, beat in 1 to 1½ cups flour to make dough heavy and stiff, but not too sticky to knead.

3. Grease coffee can and its plastic lid. Place dough in coffee can; cover with lid.

4. Let covered can stand in warm place until dough rises and pops off the lid, about 1 to 1¼ hours. Meanwhile, preheat oven to 350°F. Discard lid. Bake dough for 65 to 70 minutes until bread sounds hollow when tapped on top. Remove from can; brush top with a little melted butter or margarine. (Top crust will be very brown.) Cool completely on wire rack. (Texture will be coarse.)

Three Sweet Breads

TIME: about 4½ hours—YIELD: 3 loaves

1 cup sugar
1 teaspoon salt
3 packages active dry yeast
8 to 9 cups all-purpose flour
1½ cups milk
½ cup water
1 cup butter or margarine
2 eggs

1. In large bowl, combine sugar, salt, yeast, and 2 cups flour. In 1-quart saucepan over low heat, heat milk, water, and butter or margarine until very warm (120° to 130°F.). (Butter or margarine does not need to melt completely.)

2. With mixer at low speed, gradually beat liquid into dry ingredients. Increase speed to medium; beat 2 minutes, occasionally scraping bowl with rubber spatula. Beat in eggs and 2 cups flour; continue beating 2 minutes, occasionally scraping bowl. With spoon, stir in about 4¼ cups flour to make a soft dough.

3. Turn dough onto lightly floured surface and knead until smooth and elastic, about 10 minutes. Shape dough into ball and place in greased large bowl, turning over so that top of dough is greased. Cover with towel; let rise in warm place (80° to 85°F.), away from draft, until doubled, about 1 hour.

4. Punch down dough. Turn dough onto lightly floured surface; cut into thirds; cover with towel for 15 minutes. Select from variations below.

Golden Sweet Loaf: Grease 9″ by 5″ loaf pan. With lightly floured rolling pin, roll ⅓ of dough into 12″ by 9″ rectangle. Starting from 9-inch end, tightly roll dough jelly-roll fashion; pinch seam to seal. Press ends to seal and tuck under; place, seam-side down, in loaf pan. Cover with towel; let rise in warm place until doubled, about 1½ hours.
  Preheat oven to 350°F. Bake loaf 35 minutes or until loaf sounds hollow when lightly tapped with fingers. Remove from pan immediately. Cool on wire rack. If you like, sprinkle top of loaf generously with *confectioners' sugar*. Makes 1 loaf.

Cinnamon-Nut Bread: In small bowl, combine ¼ *cup packed light brown sugar, ¼ cup chopped pecans,* and *½ teaspoon ground cinnamon.* After rolling dough into rectangle (above), evenly sprinkle sugar mixture on dough; roll up as directed. Makes 1 loaf.

Raisin Bread: After rolling dough into rectangle (above), evenly sprinkle ¾ *cup raisins* on dough; roll up as directed. Makes 1 loaf.

151

Sticky Buns

TIME: about 4 hours or start day ahead—YIELD: 15 buns

⅓ cup sugar
1 teaspoon salt
1 package active dry yeast
about 5½ cups all-purpose flour
1½ cups water
1 cup butter or margarine
1 egg
1 cup packed dark brown sugar
½ cup dark corn syrup
1 cup pecan halves, chopped
½ cup dark seedless raisins or currants
1 teaspoon ground cinnamon

1. In large bowl, combine sugar, salt, yeast, and 2 cups flour. In 1-quart saucepan over low heat, heat water and ½ cup butter or margarine until very warm (120° to 130°F.). (Butter or margarine does not need to melt completely.)

2. With mixer at low speed, gradually beat liquid into dry ingredients just until blended. Increase speed to medium; beat 2 minutes, occasionally scraping bowl with rubber spatula. Beat in egg and 1 cup flour to make a thick batter; continue beating 2 minutes, scraping bowl often. With wooden spoon, stir in 2¼ cups flour to make a soft dough.

3. Turn dough onto well-floured surface and knead until smooth and elastic, about 10 minutes, working in about ¼ cup more flour while kneading. Shape dough into a ball and place in greased large bowl, turning dough over so that top is greased. Cover with towel and let rise in warm place (80° to 85°F.), away from draft, until doubled, about 1 hour. (Dough is doubled when two fingers pressed lightly into dough leave a dent.)

4. Meanwhile, in 1-quart saucepan over medium heat, heat brown sugar, corn syrup, and ½ cup butter or margarine to boiling; reduce heat to low; cook 3 minutes. Measure ½ cup brown-sugar mixture into small bowl; stir in pecans, raisins, and cinnamon; set aside. Evenly spread remaining brown-sugar mixture into 13" by 9" baking pan.

5. Punch down dough. Turn dough onto lightly floured surface; cover with bowl and let rest 15 minutes for easier shaping.

6. On lightly floured surface with floured rolling pin, roll dough into a 15" by 12" rectangle. Sprinkle dough with pecan mixture. Starting with a 15-inch side, tightly roll dough, jelly-roll fashion; pinch seam to seal. Place roll seam-side down; cut crosswise into 15 slices. Place slices, cut-side down, in baking pan. Cover pan with towel and let dough rise in warm place until doubled, about 45 minutes. (Dough is doubled when one finger very lightly pressed against dough leaves a dent.)

7. Preheat oven to 375°F. Bake buns 30 minutes or until lightly browned. Invert pan onto platter. Let pan remain on buns to allow syrup to drip on buns: remove pan. Serve warm or, to serve later, invert buns onto foil; wrap with foil. Just before serving, reheat buns in 375°F. oven 15 to 20 minutes until warm.

Sweet Christmas Wreath Bread

TIME: about 4½ hours or start day ahead—YIELD: 2 loaves

1 cup sugar
1 teaspoon salt
2 packages active dry yeast
about 9 cups all-purpose flour
2 cups milk
1 cup butter or margarine
3 eggs
1 tablespoon grated lemon peel
1 teaspoon almond extract
¼ cup slivered blanched
  almonds

1. In large bowl, combine sugar, salt, yeast, and 2½ cups flour. In 1-quart saucepan over low heat, heat milk and butter or margarine until very warm (120° to 130° F.). (Butter or margarine does not need to melt completely.)

2. With mixer at low speed, gradually beat liquid into dry ingredients just until blended. Increase speed to medium; beat 2 minutes, occasionally scraping bowl with rubber spatula.

3. Reserve 1 egg white for brushing top of loaves. To mixture in large bowl, gradually beat in egg yolk, remaining 2 eggs, lemon peel, almond extract, and 2 cups flour to make a thick batter; continue beating 2 minutes, scraping bowl often. With wooden spoon, stir in 3¾ cups flour to make a soft dough.

4. Turn dough onto well-floured surface and knead until smooth and elastic, about 10 minutes, working in about ¾ cup more flour while kneading. Shape dough into a ball and place in greased large bowl, turning dough over so that top is greased. Cover with towel and let rise in warm place (80° to 85° F.), away from draft, until doubled, about 1 hour. (Dough is doubled when 2 fingers pressed lightly into dough leave a dent.)

5. Punch down dough. Turn dough onto lightly floured surface; cut dough into 6 equal pieces; cover with towel and let rest 15 minutes for easier shaping. Meanwhile, grease 2 large cookie sheets.

6. On floured surface with hands, roll 1 piece of dough into a 24-inch-long rope. Repeat with 2 more pieces of dough. Place 3 ropes side-by-side and loosely braid, beginning in the middle and working toward each end. Place braid on a cookie sheet and shape into a ring; join ends and pinch to seal so ring holds together. Repeat with remaining dough pieces. Cover breads with towels and let dough rise in warm place until doubled, about 1 hour. (Dough is doubled when 1 finger very lightly pressed against dough leaves a dent.)

7. Preheat oven to 350° F. In cup, with fork, beat reserved egg white. With pastry brush, brush loaves with egg white; top with almonds. Place cookie sheets with loaves on 2 oven racks; bake 15 minutes. Switch cookie sheets between upper and lower racks so both loaves brown evenly; bake about 20 to 25 minutes longer until loaves are golden and sound hollow when lightly tapped with fingers. If loaves start to brown too quickly, cover loosely with foil. Remove loaves from cookie sheets and cool on wire racks.

TO FREEZE AND SERVE UP TO 1 MONTH LATER: When loaves are cool, wrap each loaf tightly with foil or freezer wrap; seal, label, and freeze. To thaw, remove wrap; let bread stand at room temperature 2 hours.

Little Braided Herb Breads

TIME: about 4½ hours or start day ahead—YIELD: 6 loaves

½ cup sugar
2 teaspoons salt
3 packages active dry yeast
about 6½ cups all-purpose flour
1 cup milk
½ cup water
6 tablespoons butter or
  margarine
3 eggs
¼ cup grated Parmesan cheese
1½ teaspoons thyme leaves

1. In large bowl combine sugar, salt, yeast, and 2 cups flour. In 2-quart saucepan over low heat, heat milk, water, and butter or margarine until very warm (120° to 130° F.). (Butter or margarine does not need to melt completely.)

2. With mixer at low speed, gradually beat liquid into dry ingredients just until blended. Increase speed to medium; beat 2 minutes, occasionally scraping bowl with rubber spatula. Beat in eggs, Parmesan cheese, thyme, and 1 cup flour to make a thick batter; continue beating 2 minutes, scraping bowl often. With wooden spoon, stir in 3 cups flour to make a soft dough.

3. Turn dough onto lightly floured surface and knead until smooth and elastic, about 10 minutes, working in about ½ cup more flour while kneading. Shape dough into a ball and place in greased large bowl, turning dough over so that top is greased. Cover with towel and let rise in warm place (80° to 85° F.), away from draft, until doubled, about 1 hour. (Dough is doubled when 2 fingers pressed lightly into dough leave a dent.)

4. Grease six 5¾″ by 3¼″ loaf pans. When dough is ready, punch down dough; turn onto lightly floured surface; cover with bowl and let rest 15 minutes for easier shaping.

5. Cut dough into 9 equal pieces. With floured hands, roll 1 dough piece into an 18-inch-long rope. Repeat with 2 more dough pieces. Place 3 ropes side-by-side and loosely braid, beginning in the middle and working toward each end. Braid should be about 12 inches long. Cut braid crosswise in half. Pinch cut ends; tuck ends under to seal to make 2 small braided loaves. Place each loaf, seam-side down, in a prepared pan. Repeat with remaining dough. Cover with towel and let rise in warm place until doubled, about 30 minutes. (Dough is

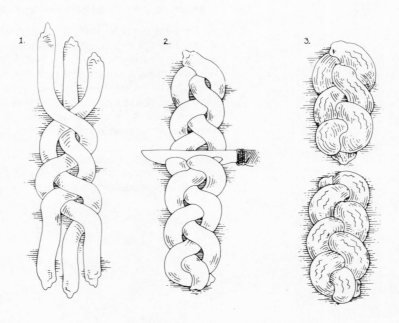

1.　　　　　2.　　　　　3.

doubled when 1 finger very lightly pressed against dough leaves a dent.)

6. Preheat oven to 400° F. Bake 15 minutes or until loaves are golden and sound hollow when lightly tapped with fingers. Remove from pans immediately; cool on wire racks.

Brioche Loaf

TIME: start day ahead—YIELD: 2 loaves

¼ cup sugar
1 teaspoon salt
2 packages active dry yeast
about 4½ cups all-purpose flour
1 cup milk
1 cup butter or margarine
5 eggs
1 teaspoon lemon extract
1 egg yolk
1 teaspoon water

1. In large bowl, combine sugar, salt, yeast, and 1½ cups flour. In 1-quart saucepan over medium heat, heat milk and butter or margarine until very warm (120° to 130°F.). (Butter or margarine does not need to melt completely.)

2. With mixer at low speed, graually beat liquid mixture into dry ingredients until just blended. Increase speed to medium; beat 2 minutes, occasionally scraping bowl with rubber spatula. Gradually beat in eggs, lemon extract, and 1½ cups flour to make a thick batter; continue beating 2 minutes, occasionally scraping bowl. With spoon, stir in 1½ cups flour to make a very soft dough. Continue beating with spoon for 5 minutes.

3. Place dough in greased large bowl. Cover with towel; let rise in warm place (80° to 85°F.), away from draft, until doubled, about 1 hour. Stir dough down; cover bowl tightly with foil or plastic wrap and refrigerate overnight.

4. About 2 hours before serving, punch down dough by pushing down the center of dough with fist, then pushing edges of dough into center. Turn dough onto lightly floured surface; cover with bowl; let dough rest 15 minutes for easier shaping.

5. Meanwhile, grease two 9″ by 5″ loaf pans.

6. Divide dough in half. Cut one eighth of dough from one half; set aside. With lightly floured rolling pin, roll rest of dough-half into a 9″ by 8″ rectangle. Starting with 8-inch side, tightly roll dough, jelly-roll fashion; pinch seam to seal. Press ends to seal and tuck under. Place, seam-side down, in loaf pan.

7. With sharp knife, cut an 8-inch-long and ½-inch-deep slit in center of dough. With fingers, gently pull slit slightly apart. Divide the reserved one-eighth of dough into halves; roll into two 9-inch ropes. Twist the two ropes together and place twist on top of slit, tucking ends under loaf. Repeat with other dough-half. Cover pans with towel; let dough rise in warm place until doubled, about 1 hour.

8. Preheat oven to 375°F. In small bowl, combine egg yolk and water. Brush top of each loaf with egg-yolk mixture. Bake 40 minutes or until bread is browned and loaves sound hollow when tapped with fingers. Remove loaves immediately from pans; cool 30 minutes; cut into thin slices. Serve warm.

Sally Lunn

TIME: about 3½ hours—YIELD: 1 loaf

3 tablespoons sugar
1¼ teaspoons salt
1 package active dry yeast
3¼ cups all-purpose flour
1 cup milk
3 tablespoons butter or
   margarine
2 eggs

1. In large bowl, combine sugar, salt, yeast, and 1¼ cups flour. In small saucepan over low heat, heat milk and butter or margarine until very warm (120° to 130°F.). (Butter or margarine does not need to melt completely.) With mixer at low speed, gradually beat liquid into dry ingredients. Increase speed to medium; beat 2 minutes, occasionally scraping bowl with rubber spatula. Beat in eggs and ¾ cup flour or enough to make a thick batter; continue beating 2 minutes, occasionally scraping bowl. With spoon, stir in remaining 1¼ cups flour.

2. Cover bowl with towel; let dough rise in warm place (80° to 85°F.), away from draft, until doubled, about 1 hour.

3. Grease and flour well 10-inch tube pan. With spoon, stir down dough. Spoon dough into tube pan; with well-floured hands, pat dough evenly in pan. Cover with towel; let rise in warm place (80° to 85°F.), away from draft, until doubled, about 1 hour.

4. Preheat oven to 300°F. Bake 40 minutes or until bread is golden and sounds hollow when lightly tapped with fingers. With spatula, loosen bread from sides and center of pan; remove from pan and cool on wire rack.

Fondue Bread

TIME: about 2 hours—YIELD: 1 loaf

3½ teaspoons sugar
2 teaspoons salt
2 packages active dry yeast
about 4 cups all-purpose flour
½ cup butter or margarine
1 cup milk
2 eggs
2 pounds Muenster cheese,
   shredded
about 2 teaspoons sliced
   blanched almonds for garnish

1. In large bowl, combine sugar, salt, yeast, 1 cup flour. In 1-quart saucepan over low heat, heat butter or margarine and milk until very warm (120° to 130°F.). (Butter or margarine does not need to melt completely.)

2. With mixer at low speed, gradually beat liquid into dry ingredients; beat until just mixed. Increase speed to medium; beat 2 minutes, occasionally scraping bowl with rubber spatula. Beat in 1 cup flour or enough to make a thick batter; continue beating 2 minutes, occasionally scraping bowl with rubber spatula. With spoon, stir in about 2 cups flour to make a soft dough.

3. Turn dough onto lightly floured surface and knead until smooth and elastic, about 10 minutes, adding more flour while kneading, if necessary. Shape dough into ball; cover with bowl and let rest 15 minutes for easier shaping. Meanwhile, reserve one egg white. In large bowl, thoroughly combine remaining eggs with cheese; set aside. Grease 9-inch round cake pan.

4. On lightly floured surface with floured rolling pin, roll dough into a rectangle about 24″ by 6″. Lengthwise along center of dough, evenly shape cheese mixture into cylinder. Fold sides of dough over cheese filling, making about 1- to 1½-inch overlap; pinch seam to seal. Place roll, seam-side down, in pan to make a ring, overlapping ends slightly; pinch ends together to seal. Cover with towel; let rest in warm place 10 minutes.

5. Preheat oven to 375°F. Brush loaf with reserved egg white. Garnish top of bread with almonds. Bake 1 hour or until bread is golden and sounds hollow when lightly tapped with fingers. Remove bread from pan immediately; let stand 15 minutes for easier cutting.

6. To serve, cut bread into wedges. Makes enough for 8 main-dish servings or 16 snack servings.

TO REHEAT: Wrap bread in foil; heat in 350°F. oven for 30 minutes or until bread is warm and cheese is melted.

Cinnamon Butterfly Rolls

TIME: about 4½ hours—YIELD: 18 rolls

½ cup sugar
1 teaspoon salt
1 package active dry yeast
about 4⅓ cups all-purpose flour
1 cup milk
butter or margarine
2 teaspoons vanilla extract
2 eggs
½ cup packed brown sugar
½ cup pecans, chopped
½ cup raisins
1 teaspoon ground cinnamon

1. In bowl, mix sugar, salt, yeast, and 1 cup flour. Heat milk and ½ cup butter until very warm (125° F.). With mixer at low speed, beat liquid into dry ingredients. At medium speed, beat 2 minutes. Beat in vanilla, 1 egg, and 1 cup flour; beat 2 minutes. Stir in 2 cups flour to make a soft dough.

2. On floured surface, knead dough 10 minutes, working in about ⅓ cup flour; shape into ball; place in greased bowl, turning dough over so that top is greased. Cover with towel; let rise in warm place until doubled, 1½ hours.

3. Punch down dough; turn onto floured surface; cover with bowl and let rest 15 minutes for easier shaping. Grease 2 cookie sheets. Mix brown sugar, pecans, raisins, cinnamon. Melt 4 tablespoons butter.

4. Preheat oven to 350° F. Cut dough in half. Roll into 17½" by 12" rectangle. Brush with half of melted butter; top with half of sugar mixture. From 17½-inch edge, roll dough, jelly-roll fashion; pinch to seal. Cut into 9 wedges, 2½ inches at wide side, 1 inch at short side. Turn wedges short-side up; press handle of wooden spoon across each wedge to form butterfly-like wings. Repeat. Place on cookie sheets; let rise until doubled, about 30 minutes.

5. Beat remaining egg; use to brush rolls. Bake 20 minutes until golden.

Babas

TIME: start early in day or up to 3 days ahead—SERVINGS: 12

1 package active dry yeast
2 tablespoons sugar
½ teaspoon salt
2 cups all-purpose flour
½ cup milk
6 tablespoons butter or
   margarine
2 eggs
Rum Sauce or Maple Sauce
   (right)
½ cup apricot preserves
red and green candied cherries
   for garnish

1. In large bowl, combine yeast, sugar, salt, and ½ cup flour. In 1-quart saucepan over low heat, heat milk and butter or margarine until very warm (120° to 130°F.). (Butter or margarine does not need to melt completely.) With mixer at low speed, gradually beat liquid into dry ingredients. Increase speed to medium; beat 2 minutes, occasionally scraping bowl with rubber spatula. Gradually beat in eggs and ½ cup flour to make a thick batter; continue beating 2 minutes, occasionally scraping bowl. With wooden spoon, stir in 1 cup flour to make a soft dough.

2. Cover bowl with towel; let dough rise in warm place (80° to 85°F.), away from draft, until doubled, about 1 hour. (Dough is doubled when it looks bubbly and moist, with an uneven, soft top.)

3. Grease twelve 4-ounce baba molds* or 2½-inch muffin-pan cups. With spoon, stir down dough. Spoon dough into molds to come half way up side of mold. Cover with towel; let rise in warm place until dough is doubled, about 30 minutes. (Dough will rise about ½ inch above top of molds.)

4. Preheat oven to 350°F. Meanwhile, prepare either Rum Sauce or Maple Sauce.

5. Bake 20 to 25 minutes until Babas are golden and tops sound hollow when lightly tapped with fingers. Cool Babas in molds on wire racks 15 minutes.

6. Remove Babas from molds to large baking dish. With toothpick or skewer, prick Babas in many places; spoon sauce mixture over Babas, basting frequently with sauce in dish. When Babas are cool, cover baking dish and refrigerate, turning Babas occasionally to absorb sauce evenly.

7. To serve, in 1-quart saucepan over low heat, melt apricot preserves, stirring occasionally. Place Babas with their sauce in a serving dish; brush with preserves. Garnish tops of Babas with red and green candied cherries, each cut in half.

Rum Sauce: In 2-quart saucepan over medium heat, heat *2 cups water* and *1 cup sugar* to boiling; continue cooking until sugar is completely dissolved, stirring occasionally. Remove saucepan from heat; stir in *1 cup rum*.

Maple Sauce: In 2-quart saucepan over medium heat, heat *2 cups water*, *½ cup maple syrup*, and *½ cup sugar* to boiling; continue cooking until sugar is dissolved, stirring occasionally. Remove saucepan from heat.

*Baba molds can be purchased in housewares departments of department stores, or write for catalog to Kitchen Glamor, 26670 Grand River, Detroit, MI 48240.

Potato Bread

TIME: about 5½ hours or start day ahead—YIELD: 2 loaves

3 medium potatoes (1 pound)
water
2 tablespoons sugar
2 teaspoons salt
2 packages active dry yeast
about 7¾ cups all-purpose flour
milk
4 tablespoons butter or
    margarine
2 eggs

1. In 2-quart saucepan over high heat, heat unpeeled potatoes and enough water to cover to boiling. Reduce heat to medium-low; cover and cook 25 to 30 minutes until potatoes are fork-tender. Drain; cool potatoes until easy to handle, about 30 minutes. Peel potatoes; place in medium bowl. With potato masher or slotted spoon, mash potatoes until smooth; set aside.

2. In large bowl, combine sugar, salt, yeast, and 1½ cups flour. In 2-quart saucepan, mix mashed potatoes, 1½ cups milk, and ½ cup water; add butter or margarine; over low heat, heat until very warm (120° to 130°F.). (Butter or margarine does not need to melt completely.) With mixer at low speed, gradually beat potato mixture into dry ingredients just until blended; beat in eggs. Increase speed to medium; beat 2 minutes, occasionally scraping bowl with rubber spatula. Beat in 1½ cups flour to make a thick batter; continue beating 2 minutes, scraping bowl often. With wooden spoon, stir in 3¼ cups flour to make a soft dough.

3. Turn dough onto well-floured surface and knead until smooth and elastic, about 10 minutes, working in about 1½ cups more flour while kneading. Shape dough into a ball and place in greased large bowl, turning dough over so that top is greased. Cover with towel and let rise in warm place (80° to 85°F.), away from draft, until doubled, about 1 hour. (Dough is doubled when two fingers pressed lightly into dough leave a dent.)

4. Grease two 2-quart round casserole dishes. Punch down dough. Turn dough onto lightly floured surface; cut dough in half. Shape one half of dough into a ball; place in a casserole. Repeat. Cover loaves with towels and let dough rise in warm place until doubled, about 1 hour. (Dough is doubled when one finger very lightly pressed against dough leaves a dent.)

5. Preheat oven to 400°F. With sharp knife, cut 2 parallel slashes on top of each loaf. Brush loaves with some milk. Bake 40 minutes or until loaves are well browned and sound hollow when lightly tapped with fingers. Remove loaves from casseroles immediately; cool on wire racks.

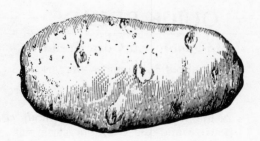

Anadama Bread

TIME: about 5 hours or start early in day—YIELD: 2 loaves

1½ teaspoons salt
1 package active dry yeast
about 5 cups all-purpose flour
2½ cups water
½ cup molasses
4 tablespoons butter or
   margarine
½ cup cornmeal

1. In large bowl, combine salt, yeast, and 2 cups flour. In 2-quart saucepan over medium heat, heat water, molasses, and butter or margarine to boiling. Slowly stir in cornmeal; cook 2 minutes, stirring constantly. Cool mixture to very warm (120° to 130°F.), about 30 minutes.

2. With mixer at low speed, gradually beat cornmeal mixture into dry ingredients just until blended. Increase speed to medium; beat 2 minutes, occasionally scraping bowl. Beat in ½ cup flour or enough to make a thick batter; continue beating 2 minutes, scraping bowl with rubber spatula. With spoon, stir in 2¼ cups flour to make a soft dough.

3. Turn dough onto lightly floured surface and knead until smooth and elastic, about 10 minutes, adding about ¼ cup more flour while kneading. Shape dough into a ball and place in greased large bowl, turning dough over so that top is greased. Cover with towel; let rise in warm place (80° to 85°F.), away from draft, until doubled, about 1 hour. (Dough is doubled when two fingers pressed lightly into dough leave a dent.)

4. Punch down dough. Turn dough onto lightly floured surface; cut in half; cover with towel and let rest 15 minutes for easier shaping.

5. Meanwhile, grease two 9" by 5" loaf pans.

6. With lightly floured rolling pin, roll one dough-half into a 12" by 8" rectangle. Starting at 8-inch end, tightly roll dough, jelly-roll fashion; pinch seam and ends to seal. Place, seam-side down, in loaf pan. Repeat with remaining dough. Cover and let rise in warm place (80° to 85°F.), away from draft, until doubled, about 40 minutes. (Dough is doubled when one finger pressed very lightly against dough leaves a dent.)

7. Preheat oven to 400°F. Bake loaves 50 minutes or until they sound hollow when lightly tapped with fingers. Cool on wire racks.

QUICK BREADS

Old-Fashioned Corn Bread

TIME: about 35 minutes—SERVINGS: 8

1 cup all-purpose flour
¾ cup cornmeal
¼ cup sugar
1 tablespoon double-acting
   baking powder
½ teaspoon salt
⅔ cup milk
⅓ cup salad oil
1 egg

1. Grease 8" by 8" baking pan.

2. Into medium bowl, measure flour, cornmeal, sugar, baking powder, and salt. With fork, stir in milk, salad oil, and egg just until blended.

3. Pour batter into baking pan. Bake 25 minutes or until golden.

Fried Indian Bread (Poori)

TIME: about 1½ hours—YIELD: 20

1 cup all-purpose flour
1 cup whole-wheat flour
½ cup water
1 teaspoon salt
salad oil

1. In medium bowl, stir all-purpose flour, whole-wheat flour, water, salt, and 1½ teaspoons salad oil until blended (mixture will be dry). In bowl, with hand, knead dough until it holds together and is smooth, about 10 minutes. Shape dough into ball and place in greased bowl; cover with plastic wrap; let rest 10 minutes.

2. Meanwhile, in 12-inch skillet over medium heat, heat 1 inch salad oil to 400°F. on deep-fat thermometer. (Or, heat oil in electric skillet set at 400°F.) With hands, shape dough into 20 balls. On lightly floured surface, with floured rolling pin, roll each ball into paper-thin circle, 4 inches in diameter (edges may be ragged). Keep the remaining dough and finished circles covered with plastic wrap to prevent drying out.

3. Drop circles, one at a time, into hot oil. With back of slotted spoon, gently hold circle under surface of oil until it puffs up, about 10 seconds. Fry about 20 seconds longer or until lightly browned, turning once. Drain Poori on paper towels. Serve warm.

TO REHEAT: Preheat oven to 325°F. Wrap Poori in foil in single layer; heat 5 minutes. (Reheated Poori will be flat.)

Cranberry-Raisin Bread

TIME: about 4 hours or start day ahead—YIELD: 2 loaves

3 large oranges
4 cups all-purpose flour
1¾ cups sugar
1 tablespoon double-acting
  baking powder
1½ teaspoons salt
1 teaspoon baking soda
½ cup butter or margarine
2 eggs
2 cups fresh or frozen
  cranberries, coarsely chopped
1 cup dark seedless raisins

1. Preheat oven to 350°F. Grease and flour two 8½" by 4½" loaf pans. From oranges, grate 1 tablespoon peel and squeeze 1½ cups juice; set aside.

2. In large bowl, mix flour and next 4 ingredients. With pastry blender or 2 knives used scissor-fashion, cut in butter or margarine until mixture resembles coarse crumbs.

3. In medium bowl with fork, beat eggs, orange juice, and orange peel until blended; stir into flour mixture just until flour is moistened. Gently fold cranberries and raisins into batter. Spoon batter evenly into loaf pans.

4. Bake 1 hour and 10 minutes or until toothpick inserted into center of bread comes out clean. Cool breads in pans on wire rack 10 minutes; remove from pans. Cool breads completely on rack.

TO FREEZE AND SERVE UP TO 1 MONTH LATER: When loaves are cool, wrap each loaf tightly with foil or freezer wrap; seal, label, and freeze. To thaw, remove wrap; let breads stand at room temperature about 2 hours.

161

Chocolate-Nut Breads

TIME: about 4 hours or start day ahead—YIELD: 4 loaves

1¾ cups all-purpose flour
½ cup sugar
1¼ teaspoons baking soda
¼ teaspoon salt
1 cup water
¼ cup salad oil
1 teaspoon vanilla extract
1 egg
1 cup pecans, chopped
½ cup dark seedless raisins
2 squares semisweet chocolate, melted

1. Preheat oven to 350° F. Grease four 10¾-ounce soup cans or four 4½" by 2½" loaf pans.

2. In large bowl, with fork, mix flour, sugar, baking soda, and salt. In medium bowl, with fork, beat water, salad oil, vanilla, and egg until blended; stir egg mixture into flour mixture just until flour is moistened. Gently fold pecans, raisins, and melted chocolate into batter. Spoon batter evenly into prepared soup cans.

3. Bake 40 minutes or until a toothpick inserted into center of bread comes out clean. Cool breads in soup cans on wire rack 10 minutes; remove from cans. Cool bread completely on wire rack.

TO FREEZE AND SERVE UP TO 1 MONTH LATER: When loaves are cool, wrap each loaf tightly with foil or freezer wrap; seal, label, and freeze. To thaw, remove wrap; let breads stand at room temperature about 1 hour.

Pumpkin Bread

TIME: about 2½ hours or start early in day—YIELD: 2 loaves

3 cups all-purpose flour
1½ cups sugar
1½ teaspoons ground cinnamon
1 teaspoon baking soda
1 teaspoon salt
¾ teaspoon ground nutmeg
¾ teaspoon ground cloves
½ teaspoon double-acting baking powder
3 eggs
1 16-ounce can pumpkin
1 cup salad oil
1 cup golden or dark seedless raisins
½ cup California walnuts, chopped

1. Preheat oven to 350°F. Grease two 8½" by 4½" loaf pans. In large bowl, with fork, mix first 8 ingredients. In medium bowl, with fork, beat eggs, pumpkin, and salad oil until blended. Stir pumpkin mixture into flour mixture just until flour is moistened. Gently stir in raisins and walnuts. Spoon batter evenly into loaf pans.

2. Bake bread 1¼ hours or until toothpick inserted in center comes out clean. Cool bread in pans on wire rack 10 minutes; remove bread from pans; cool on rack.

Spoon Bread

TIME: about 1½ hours—SERVINGS: 8

2 cups cornmeal
2 teaspoons double-acting baking powder
1½ teaspoons salt
½ teaspoon baking soda
water
2 cups milk
2 eggs

1. Preheat oven to 350°F. Grease 2-quart casserole.

2. In medium bowl, mix first 4 ingredients with 1 cup water. In 3-quart saucepan over high heat, heat 1 cup water to boiling; reduce heat to low; stir in cornmeal mixture; cook, stirring constantly, until very thick. Remove saucepan from heat.

3. With hand beater, gradually beat milk, then eggs, into mixture until smooth. Pour into casserole. Bake 1 hour or until set. Serve as an accompaniment.

Christmas Soda Bread

TIME: about 4½ hours or start day ahead—YIELD: 1 loaf

4 cups all-purpose flour
3 tablespoons sugar
1 tablespoon double-acting
  baking powder
1 teaspoon salt
1 teaspoon baking soda
6 tablespoons butter or
  margarine
1 3½-ounce container diced
  mixed candied fruits
1 cup pitted dates, diced
1½ teaspoons grated lemon peel
2 eggs
1½ cups buttermilk

1. Preheat oven to 350° F. Grease well 1½-quart round casserole. In large bowl, with fork, mix first 5 ingredients. With pastry blender or 2 knives used scissor-fashion, cut in butter or margarine until mixture resembles coarse crumbs. Stir in mixed candied fruits, dates, and lemon peel.

2. In cup with fork, beat eggs slightly; remove 1 tablespoon and reserve. Stir buttermilk and remaining egg into flour mixture just until flour mixture is moistened. (Dough will be sticky.) Turn dough onto well-floured surface; with floured hands, knead about 10 strokes to mix thoroughly. Shape dough into a ball; place in casserole. In center of ball, with sharp knife, cut a 4-inch cross about ¼ inch deep. Brush dough with reserved egg.

3. Bake bread 1¼ hours or until toothpick inserted in center of loaf comes out clean. Cover loaf with foil during last 15 minutes of baking. Cool loaf in casserole on wire rack 10 minutes; remove from casserole and cool completely on wire rack.

Banana-Pecan Bread

TIME: about 4 hours or start day ahead—
YIELD: 3 small loaves or 1 large loaf

1¾ cups all-purpose flour
⅔ cup sugar
1 teaspoon double-acting baking
  powder
½ teaspoon salt
¼ teaspoon baking soda
½ cup butter or margarine,
  softened
1 cup mashed bananas (about 2
  ripe large bananas)
½ cup coarsely chopped pecans
1 teaspoon grated lemon peel
2 eggs, slightly beaten

1. Preheat oven to 350° F. Grease three 5¾″ by 3¼″ loaf pans or one 9″ by 5″ loaf pan. In large bowl, with fork, mix first 5 ingredients. With pastry blender or 2 knives used scissor-fashion, cut in butter or margarine until mixture resembles coarse crumbs. With fork, stir bananas, pecans, lemon peel, and eggs into flour mixture just until flour is moistened. Spoon batter evenly into loaf pans.

2. Bake small loaves 40 minutes, large loaf 55 minutes or until toothpick inserted into center of bread comes out clean. Cool breads in pans on wire rack 10 minutes; remove from pans. Cool breads completely on wire rack.

TO FREEZE AND SERVE UP TO 1 MONTH LATER: When loaves are cool, wrap each loaf tightly with foil or freezer wrap; seal, label, and freeze. To thaw, remove wrap; let breads stand at room temperature 2 hours.

Old-Fashioned Buttermilk Biscuits

TIME: about 30 minutes—YIELD: 9 biscuits

3 cups all-purpose flour
2 tablespoons sugar
4 teaspoons double-acting
    baking powder
1½ teaspoons salt
½ cup shortening
1 cup buttermilk

1. Preheat oven to 450°F. In large bowl, with fork, mix flour, sugar, baking powder, and salt. With pastry blender or two knives used scissor-fashion, cut in shortening until mixture resembles coarse crumbs; add buttermilk. With fork, quickly stir just until mixture forms a soft dough and leaves side of bowl.

2. On lightly floured surface, with floured hands, knead dough 10 times. Pat dough into a 7½-inch square; cut into 9 squares.

3. Place squares on cookie sheet, about 1 inch apart. Bake 12 to 15 minutes until golden.

Golden Country Biscuits

TIME: about 30 minutes or start early in day—YIELD: 8 biscuits

2 cups all-purpose flour
1 tablespoon double-acting
    baking powder
1 tablespoon sugar
1 teaspoon salt
⅓ cup butter or margarine
⅔ cup milk
½ cup golden raisins
1 egg, beaten

1. Preheat oven to 450°F. In medium bowl, with fork, mix flour, baking powder, sugar, and salt. With pastry blender or two knives used scissor-fashion, cut in butter or margarine until mixture resembles coarse crumbs.

2. With fork, stir in milk and raisins just until mixture forms soft dough and leaves side of bowl.

3. On lightly floured surface with lightly floured hands, knead dough 10 times. Divide dough into 8 equal pieces; lightly shape each piece into a ball. Place biscuits, about ½ inch apart, on large cookie sheet. Brush biscuits with egg. Bake 10 to 12 minutes until golden.

Holiday Biscuits

TIME: about 45 minutes or day ahead—YIELD: about 5 dozen

6 cups all-purpose flour
½ cup instant nonfat dry-milk
    powder
¼ cup double-acting baking
    powder*
¼ cup sugar
2 teaspoons salt
2 teaspoons cream of tartar
2 cups shortening
water

*Yes, ¼ cup.

1. In large bowl with fork, mix all ingredients except shortening and water. With pastry blender or 2 knives used scissor-fashion, cut shortening into flour mixture until mixture resembles coarse crumbs. Stir in 1½ cups water until mixture is just moistened. (If dough is too dry, add ¼ to ½ cup more water.)

2. Preheat over to 400°F. Turn dough onto well-floured surface. With floured hands, knead dough 8 to 10 times until smooth. With floured rolling pin, roll dough into 13½" by 9" rectangle; cut into 1½-inch squares. With pancake turner, place squares on ungreased large cookie sheet, about ½ inch apart. Bake biscuits 20 to 25 minutes until golden.

TO PREPARE UP TO 3 MONTHS AHEAD: Prepare biscuits as above but do not bake. Place squares on cookie sheets, cover and freeze; place frozen squares in plastic bags and keep frozen. About 40 minutes before serving, preheat oven to 400°F. Remove squares as needed and bake frozen on cookie sheet 30 to 35 minutes until golden.

Bacon-Corn Muffins

TIME: about 1 hour—YIELD: 12 muffins

1 8-ounce package sliced bacon
1 cup all-purpose flour
1 cup yellow cornmeal
2 tablespoons sugar
4 teaspoons double-acting
   baking powder
½ teaspoon salt
1 8½- to 8¾-ounce can cream-
   style golden corn
½ cup milk
1 egg

1. Grease twelve 2½-inch muffin-pan cups.

2. In 12-inch skillet over medium-low heat, cook bacon until browned; remove to paper towels to drain. Crumble bacon; set aside. Reserve ¼ cup bacon drippings.

3. Preheat oven to 425°F. In medium bowl, with fork, mix flour, cornmeal, sugar, baking powder, and salt. In small bowl, with fork, beat corn, milk, egg, and reserved bacon drippings. With spoon, stir corn mixture into flour mixture just until flour is moistened; fold in crumbled bacon.

4. Spoon batter into muffin-pan cups. Bake 15 minutes or until toothpick inserted in center comes out clean. Carefully remove muffins from pan.

Applesauce Muffins

TIME: about 45 minutes or start day ahead—YIELD: 12 muffins

3 cups all-purpose flour
⅓ cup sugar
4 teaspoons double-acting
   baking powder
1 teaspoon ground cinnamon
¾ teaspoon baking soda
½ teaspoon salt
1½ cups applesauce
6 tablespoons butter or
   margarine, melted
½ cup milk
1 egg
¾ cup California walnuts or
   pecans, chopped

1. Grease twelve 3-inch muffin-pan cups;* set aside.

2. Preheat oven to 400°F. In large bowl, with fork, mix first 6 ingredients. In medium bowl, with fork, beat applesauce, melted butter or margarine, milk, and egg until blended; stir into flour mixture just until flour is moistened. (Batter will be lumpy.) With spoon, stir in nuts.

3. Spoon batter into muffin-pan cups. Bake 20 to 25 minutes until toothpick inserted into center of muffin comes out clean. Immediately remove from pans. Serve muffins warm. To serve later, cool muffins on wire rack; wrap muffins in single layer with foil. Just before serving, reheat wrapped muffins in preheated 400°F. oven 10 minutes or until warm.

TO FREEZE AND SERVE UP TO 1 MONTH LATER: When muffins are cool, wrap muffins tightly with foil or freezer wrap; seal, label, and freeze. To thaw, remove wrap; let muffins stand at room temperature 1 hour.

*Or use twenty-four 2½-inch muffin-pan cups; bake 15 minutes. Makes 24 muffins.

Maple-Bran Muffins

TIME: about 1 hour—YIELD: 9 muffins

2½ cups bran flakes, crushed
1¼ cups all-purpose flour
1 teaspoon baking soda
¼ teaspoon salt
1 egg
¾ cup buttermilk*
⅓ cup maple syrup or maple-flavor syrup
¼ cup salad oil

*In place of buttermilk, use ¾ cup milk mixed with 2 teaspoons cider vinegar. Let mixture stand a few minutes to allow vinegar to "sour" milk.

1. Preheat oven to 350°F. Grease nine 2½-inch muffin-pan cups.

2. In large bowl, with fork, mix first 4 ingredients. In small bowl, with fork, beat egg, buttermilk, maple syrup, and salad oil until blended. Stir egg mixture into flour mixture just until flour is moistened.

3. Spoon into muffin-pan cups. Bake 25 minutes or until lightly browned. Immediately remove muffins from pan.

Walnut-Date Loaves

TIME: about 4 hours or start day ahead—YIELD: 2 loaves

4 cups California walnuts
3 cups all-purpose flour
1½ cups packed brown sugar
4 teaspoons double-acting baking powder
1½ teaspoons salt
½ cup butter or margarine, softened
4 eggs
1½ cups milk
2 tablespoons grated orange peel
2 teaspoons vanilla extract
2 10-ounce containers pitted dates, cut into large pieces

1. Preheat oven to 325°F. Grease two 8½" by 4½" loaf pans. Coarsely break 1½ cups walnuts.

2. In large bowl, with fork, mix flour, brown sugar, baking powder, and salt. With pastry blender or 2 knives used scissor-fashion, cut in butter or margarine until mixture resembles coarse crumbs.

3. In medium bowl, with fork, beat eggs, milk, orange peel, and vanilla until blended; stir into flour mixture just until flour is moistened. Gently fold dates and coarsely broken walnuts into batter. Spoon batter evenly into loaf pans. Sprinkle remaining walnuts on top of batter in pans.

4. Bake 1 hour and 20 minutes or until toothpick inserted into center of bread comes out clean. Cool breads in pans on wire rack 10 minutes; remove from pans. Cool breads completely on rack.

TO FREEZE AND SERVE UP TO 1 MONTH LATER: When loaves are cool, wrap each loaf tightly with foil or freezer wrap; seal, label, and freeze. To thaw, remove wrap; let breads stand at room temperature about 2 hours.

Citrus Loaf

TIME: about 2¼ hours—SERVINGS: 12

1 medium lemon
1 medium orange
2¼ cups all-purpose flour
1½ teaspoons double-acting
    baking powder
¾ teaspoon salt
sugar
¾ cup butter or margarine
3 eggs
½ cup milk

1. Preheat oven to 350°F. Grease 9" by 5" loaf pan. From lemon, grate 1 tablespoon peel and squeeze 1 tablespoon juice. From orange, grate 1 tablespoon peel and squeeze 5 tablespoons juice; set aside.

2. In large bowl with fork, mix flour, baking powder, salt, and 1 cup sugar. With pastry blender or 2 knives used scissor-fashion, cut in butter to resemble coarse crumbs. Stir in lemon and orange peels.

3. In small bowl, with fork, beat eggs, milk, and 4 tablespoons orange juice; stir mixture into flour mixture just until flour is moistened. Spoon batter evenly into prepared pan. Bake 1 hour or until knife inserted into center of loaf comes out clean. Cool loaf in pan on wire rack 10 minutes; remove from pan.

4. In small saucepan over medium-high heat, heat lemon juice and remaining 1 tablespoon orange juice with 2 tablespoons sugar to boiling. Cook, stirring often, until slightly thickened, about 3 minutes. Brush mixture evenly over top of loaf.

SPECIAL BREADS

Herbed Toast

TIME: about 20 minutes or start early in day—SERVINGS: 8

16 thin slices white bread
½ cup butter or margarine
½ teaspoon savory
½ teaspoon fennel seeds,
    crushed

1. With knife, cut off crusts from bread slices. (Reserve crusts for making bread crumbs another day.) Arrange bread slices on cookie sheets.

2. Preheat oven to 400°F. In small saucepan over medium heat, heat butter or margarine, savory, and fennel seeds until butter melts. Brush bread slices with butter mixture; bake 15 minutes or until golden on both sides, turning bread slices once.

Herbed Dinner Rolls

TIME: about 30 minutes—YIELD: 16 rolls

3 tablespoons grated Parmesan
    cheese
¼ teaspoon thyme leaves
2 8-ounce packages refrigerated
    crescent dinner rolls
1 egg white, beaten
poppy seeds

1. Preheat oven to 375°F. In small bowl, mix Parmesan cheese and thyme.

2. Separate crescent-roll dough into 8 rectangles. Press perforations together on each rectangle. Brush some egg white over rectangles.

3. Sprinkle cheese mixture over 6 rectangles. Stack 3 cheese-topped rectangles, then top with a plain rectangle. Repeat with remaining 4 rectangles. Cut each rectangle lengthwise in half; then cut each half crosswise in half. Cut each quarter into 2 triangles. Sprinkle rolls with poppy seeds; bake on large cookie sheet 10 to 15 minutes until golden.

Sautéed Italian-Bread Slices

TIME: about 10 minutes—SERVINGS: 4

¼ cup olive oil
⅛ teaspoon turmeric
8 slices Italian bread, cut
 1″ thick

1. In 12-inch skillet over medium-high heat, stir olive oil and turmeric until blended and hot.

2. Add Italian bread; cook until lightly browned on both sides.

Garlic Bread

TIME: about 25 minutes—SERVINGS: 8

¼ cup olive oil
⅛ teaspoon salt
3 to 4 medium garlic cloves,
 crushed
1 16-ounce loaf long Italian
 bread

1. In small saucepan over low heat, cook olive oil, salt, and garlic 5 minutes, stirring occasionally.

2. Meanwhile, preheat oven to 350°F. Slice Italian bread crosswise into 1-inch-thick slices, being careful not to cut slices all the way through. Place bread on large cookie sheet.

3. With pastry brush, brush one side of each slice with oil mixture. Bake bread 15 minutes or until heated through.

Whole-Wheat Garlic Croutons

TIME: about 15 minutes or start early in day—YIELD: 4 cups

12 slices whole-wheat bread
5 tablespoons butter or
 margarine
3 tablespoons olive or salad oil
2 medium garlic cloves, crushed
¼ teaspoon oregano leaves

1. Cut whole-wheat bread into ½-inch pieces. In 12-inch skillet over medium heat, heat butter or margarine, olive oil, garlic, and oregano until butter melts.

2. Add bread and cook, stirring frequently, until bread is lightly browned and crisp.

Condiments and Sauces

PICKLES AND RELISHES

Tangy Corn Relish

YIELD: about 5 pints

12 ears corn, husks and silk removed
3 cups cider vinegar
2 medium green peppers, diced (about 1½ cups)
2 medium red peppers, diced (about 1½ cups)
2 medium tomatoes, diced (about 1½ cups)
2 medium onions, diced (about 1 cup)
1½ cups sugar
4½ teaspoons salt
1 teaspoon celery seeds
1 teaspoon dry mustard
1 teaspoon turmeric
5 1-pint canning jars and caps

1. With sharp knife, cut kernels from corn to make 8 cups kernels.

2. In 5-quart saucepot over high heat, heat corn and remaining relish ingredients to boiling. Reduce heat to low; simmer 20 minutes, stirring occasionally.

3. Meanwhile, prepare jars and caps for processing: Check jars to be sure they have no nicks, cracks, or sharp edges that will prevent an airtight seal or cause breakage. Wash jars, lids, and screw bands (or caps and rubber rings) in hot soapy water; rinse well. Leave jars and lids in hot water until ready to use. Wet rubber rings before using to make them more pliable.

4. Immediately ladle hot corn mixture into hot jars to within ¼ inch from top of jar—keep mixture simmering while filling jars. Close jars as manufacturer directs.

5. Place jars on rack in canner half full with boiling water, far enough apart so water can circulate freely. Add additional boiling water if needed so that water is 1 to 2 inches above tops of jars—do not pour water directly on jars. Over high heat, heat to boiling. Cover canner; reduce heat to medium; boil gently 15 minutes. With jar lifter or tongs, remove jars from canner; set jars several inches apart, on wire racks. Complete seal on jars with glass or zinc caps as manufacturer directs. Do *not* tighten screw bands. Cool at least 12 hours.

6. Now, test seal: Press lid at center; if center is down and stays down, jar is sealed. Turn jars with glass or zinc caps and rubber rings partly over; if no leakage, jars are sealed. Store unsealed jars in refrigerator to use within one month. Store sealed jars in cool, dark, dry place to use within one year.

Green-Tomato Chow Chow

YIELD: about 6 pints

12 medium green tomatoes
    (about 5 pounds)
2 pounds green beans
4 medium red peppers
4 medium onions
4 quarts water
1 cup salt
6 1-pint canning jars and caps
2½ cups white vinegar
1½ cups sugar
1 tablespoon minced, peeled
    ginger root or ¾ teaspoon
    ground ginger
1 tablespoon dry mustard
1 tablespoon mustard seeds
1 teaspoon turmeric

1. Cut and discard stem ends from tomatoes; cut tomatoes into bite-sized chunks. Cut green beans into 2-inch pieces. Cut red peppers into bite-sized chunks. Cut onions into wedges.

2. In 10-quart enamel, stainless steel, or glass container, stir water and salt until salt is dissolved. Add vegetables; cover and let stand in cool place about 6 hours.

3. Prepare jars and caps for processing: Check jars to be sure they have no nicks, cracks, or sharp edges that will prevent an airtight seal or cause breakage. Wash jars, lids, and screw bands (or caps and rubber rings) in hot soapy water; rinse well. Leave jars and lids in hot water until ready to use. Wet rubber rings before using to make them more pliable.

4. Drain vegetables; rinse with running cold water; drain thoroughly. In 8-quart saucepot or Dutch oven over high heat, heat vinegar, sugar, ginger, dry mustard, mustard seeds, and turmeric to boiling, stirring occasionally. Reduce heat to medium; cover and cook 5 minutes. Add vegetables; heat to boiling. Reduce heat to low; cover and simmer 10 minutes longer, stirring occasionally.

5. With slotted spoon, spoon hot vegetables into hot jars to ¼ inch from top of jar. Immediately ladle hot vinegar mixture over vegetables in jars to ¼ inch from top of jar—keep mixture simmering while filling jars. With small spatula, carefully remove any air bubbles between vegetables and jar. Close jars as manufacturer directs.

6. Place jars on rack in canner half full with boiling water, far enough apart so that water can circulate freely. Add additional boiling water if needed so that water level is 1 to 2 inches above tops of jars—do not pour water directly on jars. Over high heat, heat to boiling. Cover canner; reduce heat to medium; boil gently 10 minutes. With jar lifter or tongs, remove jars from canner; set jars several inches apart on wire racks. Complete seal on jars with glass or zinc caps as manufacturer directs. Do *not* tighten screw bands. Cool at least 12 hours.

7. Now, test seal: Press lid at center; if center is down and stays down, jar is sealed. Turn jars with glass or zinc caps and rubber rings partly over; if no leakage, jars are sealed. Store unsealed jars in refrigerator to use within one month. Store sealed jars in cool, dark, dry place to use within one year.

Cauliflower Pickles

YIELD: about 5 pints

2 medium heads cauliflower
  (about 3 pounds)
2 medium carrots
½ cup salt
water
5 1-pint canning jars and caps
2 cups white vinegar
¾ cup sugar
2 teaspoons mustard seeds
1 teaspoon crushed red pepper
1 teaspoon celery seeds
½ teaspoon whole cloves
5 sprigs fresh dill

1. Cut cauliflower into flowerets. Thinly slice carrots.

2. In 6-quart enamel, stainless steel, or glass container, stir salt and 6 cups water until salt is dissolved. Add cauliflower and carrots; cover and let stand in cool place about 6 hours.

3. Prepare jars and caps for processing: Check jars to be sure they have no nicks, cracks, or sharp edges that will prevent an airtight seal or cause breakage. Wash jars, lids, and screw bands (or caps and rubber rings) in hot soapy water; rinse well. Leave jars and lids in hot water until ready to use. Wet rubber rings before using to make them more pliable.

4. Drain vegetables; rinse with running cold water; drain thoroughly. In 8-quart saucepot or Dutch oven over high heat, heat vinegar, sugar, mustard seeds, crushed red pepper, celery seeds, cloves, and 4 cups water to boiling, stirring occasionally. Reduce heat to medium; cover and cook 5 minutes. Add vegetables; heat to boiling. Reduce heat to low; cover and simmer 5 minutes longer, stirring occasionally.

5. In each hot jar, place 1 dill sprig. With slotted spoon, spoon hot vegetables into hot jars to ¼ inch from top of jar. Immediately ladle hot vinegar mixture over vegetables in jar to ¼ inch from top of jar—keep mixture simmering while filling jars. With small spatula, carefully remove any air bubbles between vegetables and jar. Close jars as manufacturer directs.

6. Place jars on rack in canner half full with boiling water, far enough apart so that water can circulate freely. Add additional boiling water if needed so that water level is 1 to 2 inches above tops of jars—do not pour water directly on jars. Over high heat, heat to boiling. Cover canner; reduce heat to medium; boil gently 15 minutes. With jar lifter or tongs, remove jars from canner; set jars, several inches apart, on wire racks. Complete seal on jars with glass or zinc caps as manufacturer directs. Do *not* tighten screw bands. Cool at least 12 hours.

7. Now, test seal: Press lid at center; if center is down and stays down, jar is sealed. Turn jars with glass or zinc caps and rubber rings partly over; if no leakage, jars are sealed. Store unsealed jars in refrigerator to use within one month. Store sealed jars in cool, dark, dry place to use within one year.

Pickled Vegetable Medley

YIELD: about 6 pints

4 medium carrots
4 medium celery stalks
3 large cucumbers
3 medium red peppers
2 medium onions
1 medium head broccoli
4 quarts water
1 cup salt
6 1-pint canning jars and caps
6½ cups white vinegar
2 cups sugar
2 tablespoons mustard seeds
½ teaspoon crushed red pepper

1. Cut carrots and celery into ½-inch-long pieces. If desired, peel cucumbers, leaving a few strips of skin on cucumbers for color; cut cucumbers into ½-inch-thick slices. Cut red peppers into ¼-inch-wide strips. Cut onions into ¼-inch-thick slices. Cut broccoli into bite-sized flowerets.

2. In 10-quart enamel, stainless steel, or glass container, stir water and salt until salt is dissolved. Add vegetables; cover and let stand in cool place about 6 hours.

3. Prepare jars and caps for processing: Check jars to be sure they have no nicks, cracks, or sharp edges that will prevent an airtight seal or cause breakage. Wash jars, lids, and screw bands (or caps and rubber rings) in hot soapy water; rinse well. Leave jars and lids in hot water until ready to use. Wet rubber rings before using to make them more pliable.

4. Drain vegetables; rinse with running cold water; drain thoroughly. In 8-quart saucepot or Dutch oven over high heat, heat vinegar, sugar, mustard seeds, and crushed red pepper to boiling, stirring occasionally. Reduce heat to medium; cover and cook 5 minutes. Add vegetables; heat to boiling. Reduce heat to low; cover and simmer 5 minutes longer, stirring occasionally.

5. With slotted spoon, spoon hot vegetables into hot jars to ¼ inch from top of jar. Immediately ladle hot vinegar mixture over vegetables in jars to ¼ inch from top of jar—keep mixture simmering while filling jars. With small spatula, carefully remove any air bubbles between vegetables and jar. Close jars as manufacturer directs.

6. Place jars on rack in canner half full with boiling water, far enough apart so that water can circulate freely. Add additional boiling water if needed so that water level is 1 to 2 inches above tops of jars—do not pour water directly on jars. Over high heat, heat to boiling. Cover canner; reduce heat to medium; boil gently 15 minutes. With jar lifter or tongs, remove jars from canner; set jars several inches apart, on wire racks. Complete seal on jars with glass or zinc caps as manufacturer directs. Do *not* tighten screw bands. Cool at least 12 hours.

7. Now, test seal: Press lid at center; if center is down and stays down, jar is sealed. Turn jars with glass or zinc caps and rubber rings partly over; if no leakage, jars are sealed. Store unsealed jars in refrigerator to use within one month. Store sealed jars in cool, dark, dry place to use within one year.

Marinated Vegetable Relish Tray

TIME: about 4 hours or start day ahead—SERVINGS: 16

Radish Roses (right)
Tangy Green Beans (right)
Herbed Broccoli Flowerets (right)
Spiced Carrot Slices (right)
Zesty Brussels Sprouts (right)

1. Prepare vegetables from recipes following.

2. Drain Radish Roses; arrange with vegetables in rows on large platter.

Radish Roses: With paring knife, cut 5 or 6 very thin slices from sides of each radish *from one 6-ounce bag radishes.* Place radishes in bowl of iced water. Cover bowl and refrigerate until "petals" open.

Tangy Green Beans: In 12-inch skillet over medium heat, in 1 inch boiling water, heat *1 pound green beans* to boiling. Reduce heat to low; cover and simmer 10 minutes or until beans are tender-crisp; drain. In medium bowl, combine green beans with *3 tablespoons salad or olive oil, 1 tablespoon capers, 1 teaspoon salt, 1/4 teaspoon sugar,* and *1/8 teaspoon oregano leaves.* Cover and refrigerate to blend flavors, stirring occasionally.

Herbed Broccoli Flowerets: In 12-inch skillet over medium heat, in 1 inch boiling water, heat *1 large bunch of broccoli,* cut into 2" by 1" flowerets, to boiling. Reduce heat to low; cover and simmer 10 minutes or until broccoli is tender-crisp; drain. In medium bowl, combine broccoli with *3 tablespoons salad or olive oil, 3 tablespoons red wine vinegar, 1 tablespoon chopped parsley, 1 1/2 teaspoons sugar, 1/2 teaspoon salt,* and *1/2 teaspoon oregano leaves.* Cover and refrigerate to blend flavors, stirring occasionally.

Spiced Carrot Slices: Peel and thinly slice carrots from *one 16-ounce bag carrots.* In 12-inch skillet over medium heat, in 1 inch boiling water, heat carrots to boiling. Reduce heat to low; cover and simmer 5 to 10 minutes until tender-crisp; drain. In medium bowl, combine carrots with *3 tablespoons water, 2 tablespoons salad or olive oil, 4 teaspoons brown sugar, 1 teaspoon salt, 1/4 teaspoon dry mustard, 1/4 teaspoon ground cinnamon,* and *1/8 teaspoon ground ginger.* Cover and refrigerate to blend flavors, stirring occasionally.

Zesty Brussels Sprouts: In 12-inch skillet over medium heat, in 1 inch boiling water, heat *two 10-ounce containers Brussels sprouts* to boiling—cut Brussels sprouts in half if they are large. Reduce heat to low; cover and simmer 15 minutes or until Brussels sprouts are tender-crisp; drain. In medium bowl, combine Brussels sprouts with *1/4 cup cider vinegar, 2 tablespoons sugar, 3/4 teaspoon salt, 1/4 teaspoon dry mustard,* and *1/8 teaspoon pepper.* Cover and refrigerate to blend flavors, stirring occasionally.

Sunchoke Pickles

TIME: about 4 hours or start up to 1 week ahead—YIELD: 4 cups

1 medium onion, thinly sliced
1 cup water
1 cup white vinegar
½ cup sugar
½ teaspoon salt
½ teaspoon mustard seeds
½ teaspoon dry mustard
⅛ teaspoon celery seeds
⅛ teaspoon crushed red pepper
2 pounds sunchokes (Jerusalem artichokes)

1. In 2-quart saucepan, combine first 9 ingredients; set aside. Peel sunchokes; cut into thin slices. Add sliced sunchokes to mixture in saucepan as soon as they are sliced. (Sunchokes will darken upon exposure to air after peeling.)

2. Over high heat, heat sunchoke mixture to boiling. Reduce heat to low; simmer, uncovered, about 15 minutes or until sunchokes are tender-crisp, stirring occasionally.

3. Pour sunchokes and their liquid into medium bowl. Cover and refrigerate until well chilled, about 3 hours. Serve with hamburgers, roast poultry, pork, or beef.

Pickled Celery Stalks

TIME: start day ahead or start up to 1 week ahead—
YIELD: about 5 cups

2¼ cups white vinegar
2¼ cups sugar
1 teaspoon mustard seeds
1 teaspoon ground ginger
¼ teaspoon cracked black pepper
4 3-inch-long cinnamon sticks
3 medium bunches celery

1. In 2-quart saucepan, combine vinegar, sugar, mustard seeds, ginger, pepper, and cinnamon sticks; over high heat, heat to boiling. Reduce heat to low; cover and simmer 5 minutes to blend flavors. Refrigerate liquid until chilled.

2. Meanwhile, cut off root ends and leaves to separate celery stalks. With vegetable peeler, peel tough stringy fiber from celery stalks. Then cut each stalk crosswise in half; if any stalk is too large, you may also want to cut lengthwise in half.

3. Place celery in large bowl; pour vinegar mixture over celery; cover and refrigerate at least 24 hours. Drain celery before serving. Serve as pickles with sandwiches or cold meats.

Mincemeat Relish

TIME: about 15 minutes or start up to 1 week ahead—
YIELD: about 5½ cups

1 28-ounce jar prepared mincemeat
1 15½- to 20-ounce can crushed pineapple in pineapple juice
½ cup California walnuts, chopped
¼ cup orange-flavor liqueur
1 tablespoon grated orange peel

In medium bowl, stir mincemeat, pineapple with its juice, and remaining ingredients until mixed. Cover and refrigerate to use up within 1 week. Serve with roast poultry, baked ham, pork chops, or on top of ice cream.

Cranberry-Ginger Relish

TIME: about 20 minutes or start up to 1 week ahead—YIELD: 3 cups

1 12-ounce package frozen
   cranberries
1½ cups sugar
1 cup dark seedless raisins
¼ cup water
1 tablespoon minced preserved
   ginger
1 teaspoon salt
¼ teaspoon ground allspice

1. In 3-quart saucepan over high heat, heat all ingredients to boiling, stirring occasionally. Reduce heat to low; cover and simmer 10 minutes or until cranberries pop and mixture thickens slightly.

2. Serve relish warm or cold with roast turkey, duckling, chicken, grilled pork chops, baked ham, or hamburgers.

Cranberry-Pineapple Relish

TIME: start early in day or up to 2 weeks ahead—YIELD: 8 cups

2 16-ounce cans pineapple
   chunks in heavy syrup
2 12-ounce packages cranberries
2 cups sugar
2 cups dark seedless raisins
1 tablespoon minced preserved
   ginger
2 teaspoons salt
½ teaspoon ground allspice

1. Drain pineapple, reserving ½ cup syrup. In 4-quart saucepan over high heat, heat cranberries, sugar, raisins, ginger, salt, allspice, and reserved pineapple syrup to boiling, stirring occasionally.

2. Reduce heat to low; cover and simmer 10 minutes or until cranberries pop. Add pineapple chunks; continue cooking 5 minutes or until mixture thickens slightly. Cover and refrigerate to use up within 2 weeks. Serve as an accompaniment to roast turkey, duckling, chicken, grilled pork chops, or baked ham.

Curried Three Fruit Relish

TIME: about 20 minutes—SERVINGS: 6

1 16- to 17-ounce can sliced
   cling peaches, drained
1 16- to 17-ounce can apricot
   halves, drained
1 16-ounce can sliced pears,
   drained
⅓ cup packed brown sugar
¼ cup dark seedless raisins
1 tablespoon curry powder
4 tablespoons butter or
   margarine
½ teaspoon salt

In 3-quart saucepan, combine all ingredients. Over medium heat, heat mixture to boiling, stirring frequently. Reduce heat to low; cover and simmer 10 minutes to blend flavors, stirring occasionally. Serve as accompaniment.

No-Cook Cranberry Relish

TIME: about 20 minutes or start early in day—YIELD: about 5 cups

In medium bowl, stir *two 16-ounce cans whole-berry cranberry sauce* and *1 10-ounce package frozen strawberries in quick-thaw pouch,* thawed, until mixed.

SAUCES AND SALAD DRESSINGS

Hearty Home-Style Meat Sauce

TIME: about 2¼ hours—YIELD: 4 cups

3 tablespoons olive or salad oil
2 tablespoons butter or
  margarine
2 tablespoons chopped parsley
1 medium onion, diced
1 large carrot, coarsely shredded
  (1 cup)
1 pound beef chuck shoulder
  steak, boneless, finely chopped
⅔ cup milk
1 28-ounce can tomatoes
1½ teaspoons salt
¾ teaspoon sugar
½ teaspoon cracked pepper

1. In heavy 4-quart saucepan over medium heat, in hot olive oil and butter or margarine, cook parsley, onion, and carrot until tender, stirring occasionally. Add chopped chuck shoulder steak and cook just until meat loses its pink color.

2. Increase heat to medium-high. Add milk and continue cooking until milk evaporates, stirring frequently. Stir in tomatoes with their liquid and remaining ingredients; over high heat, heat to boiling. Reduce heat to low; simmer, uncovered, 1½ hours or until meat is very tender, stirring occasionally. Skim off fat from sauce, if necessary. Makes enough to serve over *one 16-ounce package spaghetti* as 6 main-dish servings.

Spicy Creole Freezer Sauce

TIME: about 1¾ hours—YIELD: about 8 pints

½ cup salad oil
½ cup all-purpose flour
3 medium onions, diced
3 medium green peppers, diced
3 medium celery stalks, diced
2 garlic cloves, crushed
8 pounds tomatoes, chopped
1 6-ounce can tomato paste
4 teaspoons salt
1 tablespoon sugar
1¼ teaspoons hot pepper sauce

1. In 8-quart Dutch oven over medium-high heat, cook salad oil and flour, stirring constantly, until flour is dark brown. Add onions, green peppers, celery, and garlic; cook until vegetables are tender, stirring occasionally.

2. Add tomatoes and remaining ingredients; over high heat, heat to boiling. Reduce heat to low; cover and simmer 1 hour, stirring occasionally. Use sauce to serve over cooked rice, broiled chicken, pork chops, fish, or meat loaf.

TO FREEZE AND SERVE UP TO 1 YEAR LATER: Ladle sauce into eight 1-pint freezer-safe wide-mouthed containers or freezer-weight plastic bags, leaving at least 1 inch space at top of container. Close containers; label and freeze. Reheat frozen sauce with a little water to avoid scorching.

Dieter's Zesty Tomato Salad Dressing

TIME: about 10 minutes or start up to 1 week ahead—YIELD: about 2¼ cups

1 6-ounce can cocktail vegetable
  juice
1 cup tarragon vinegar
¼ cup salad oil
¼ cup water
1 teaspoon dry mustard
½ teaspoon salt
½ teaspoon pepper
¼ teaspoon onion powder
⅛ teaspoon garlic powder

In small bowl, with wire whisk or fork, mix all ingredients until well blended. Store salad dressing in tightly covered jar or cruet in refrigerator to use up within 1 week. Mix well again just before using. Serve on tossed green salad, cottage cheese, or chef's salad.

Herb Dressing

TIME: about 10 minutes or start early in day—YIELD: 2 cups

1⅓ cups olive or salad oil
½ cup red wine vinegar
1 tablespoon salt
1 teaspoon sugar
1 teaspoon thyme leaves
1 teaspoon basil leaves
¼ teaspoon pepper

In small bowl, with spoon or wire whisk, mix all ingredients until blended. Cover and refrigerate. Stir before using.

Creamy Mustard Dressing

TIME: about 10 minutes or start early in day—YIELD: about 1¾ cups

¾ cup sour cream
½ cup prepared mustard
½ cup milk
1¼ teaspoons sugar
½ teaspoon salt

In small bowl, with spoon or wire whisk, mix all ingredients until blended. Cover and refrigerate. Stir before using.

Lemony Anchovy Dressing

TIME: about 15 minutes or start early in day—YIELD: 2 cups

3 large lemons
1 2-ounce can anchovy fillets, drained
1⅓ cups olive or salad oil
2 tablespoons minced parsley
5 teaspoons sugar
½ teaspoon salt
½ teaspoon cracked pepper

Grate 2 tablespoons lemon peel and squeeze ⅔ cup juice from lemons. In small bowl, with fork, mash anchovies. Add lemon peel, lemon juice, olive oil, and remaining ingredients; mix well. Cover and refrigerate. Stir before using.

No-Salt Herb-and-Spice Mix

TIME: start up to 1 month ahead—YIELD: ¼ cup

3 tablespoons savory
2 teaspoons whole black peppercorns
1 teaspoon fennel seeds
1 teaspoon ground ginger
⅛ teaspoon garlic powder

In small bowl, stir all ingredients until mixed. Spoon into pepper mill. Use to sprinkle on chicken, fish, or pork before cooking or serve at table to sprinkle over vegetables or salad.

Creamy Tarragon Dressing

TIME: about 20 minutes or start up to 1 week ahead—YIELD: 2 cups

1 8-ounce package cream cheese, softened
½ cup mayonnaise
½ cup milk
2 tablespoons tarragon vinegar
1 teaspoon sugar
¾ teaspoon tarragon
¾ teaspoon salt
⅛ teaspoon pepper

In blender at low speed or in food processor with knife blade attached, blend all ingredients until smooth. Refrigerate dressing to use up within 1 week. Serve dressing over tossed green salad, cold cooked potatoes, hard-cooked eggs, or as a dip for raw vegetables.

Calorie-Wise Herb Salad Dressing

TIME: about 10 minutes or start up to 1 week ahead—**YIELD:** about 2¼ cups

1 cup red wine vinegar
⅔ cup water
½ cup salad oil
1 tablespoon basil
1 tablespoon chervil
2 tablespoons honey
1½ teaspoons dry mustard
¾ teaspoon salt
½ teaspoon pepper

In small bowl, with wire whisk or fork, mix all ingredients until well blended. Store salad dressing in tightly covered jar or cruet in refrigerator to use up within 1 week. Mix well again just before using. Serve on tossed green salad, sliced tomatoes, or cooked broccoli.

JELLY, CONSERVES, AND PRESERVES

Spiced Sherry Jelly

YIELD: about four 8-ounce glasses

about 4 8-ounce jelly glasses
    and lids or other 8-ounce heat-
    safe glasses
paraffin
1 3-inch-long cinnamon stick
½ teaspoon whole cloves
½ teaspoon whole allspice
cheesecloth
2½ cups cream sherry
½ cup water
¼ cup lemon juice
1 1¾-ounce package powdered
    fruit pectin
3 cups sugar

1. Prepare glasses and lids: Check glasses to be sure there are no nicks, cracks, or sharp edges. Wash glasses and lids in hot soapy water; rinse well. Invert lids on dish rack or clean towel, away from draft, to drain dry. To sterilize glasses, place glasses in 5-quart saucepot or kettle and cover with water; over high heat, heat to boiling. Reduce heat to medium; boil gently 10 minutes. Leave glasses in hot water until just before putting jelly on to cook, then remove and invert on clean towel to drain.

2. Melt paraffin: Place paraffin in small, clean can; place can in 2-quart saucepan filled with 1 inch water. Over medium heat, heat, uncovered, until paraffin is melted; keep warm.

3. Break cinnamon stick into small pieces. Wrap cinnamon, cloves, and allspice in piece of double-thickness cheesecloth; tie with string.

4. In heavy 3-quart saucepan place spice bag; add sherry, water, lemon juice, and pectin; over high heat, heat sherry mixture to boiling, stirring frequently; immediately stir in sugar. Stirring constantly, heat until mixture comes to a full rolling boil; boil 1 minute; discard spice bag. Remove saucepan from heat; with metal spoon, skim off foam.

5. Immediately, ladle jelly into glasses to within ½ inch from top. Into each, quickly pour 1 tablespoon hot paraffin over mixture to make ⅛-inch-thick layer that covers jelly completely, spreading paraffin with tip of spoon so it touches side of glass all around. Prick any air bubbles in paraffin. When cool, cover glasses with lids. Store opened jelly in refrigerator to use up within 1 month. Store unopened jelly in cool, dark, dry place to use up within 1 year.

6. Serve jelly as an accompaniment to roast poultry, pork, or spread on plain cracker or toast.

178

Plum-Nut Freezer Conserve

YIELD: about eight 8-ounce glasses

8 8-ounce freezer-safe,
   dishwasher-safe jelly glasses
   or containers with tight-fitting
   lids
boiling water
2 pounds fully ripened plums
1 medium orange
⅓ cup California walnuts, finely
   chopped
½ teaspoon salt
5½ cups sugar
1 1¾-ounce package powdered
   fruit pectin
¾ cup water

1. Prepare glasses and lids: Check to be sure they have no nicks, cracks, or sharp edges. Wash glasses and lids in hot soapy water; rinse well. Carefully and slowly pour boiling water inside and out of glasses and lids; invert on dish rack or clean cloth towel, away from draft, to drain dry. Or, wash in dishwasher with very hot rinse cycle (150°F., or higher) and leave in dishwasher until ready to fill.

2. Remove pits from plums (do not peel). Finely chop plums to measure 2¾ cups; place in large bowl. From orange, grate 1 teaspoon peel and squeeze ¼ cup juice. Add orange peel and juice to plums with walnuts and salt. With rubber spatula, stir in sugar until thoroughly mixed; let stand 10 minutes.

3. In 1-quart saucepan over medium heat, heat pectin and water to boiling; boil 1 minute, stirring. Stir pectin mixture into fruit; continue stirring 3 minutes—no less! A few sugar crystals will remain.

4. Ladle plum mixture into glasses to ½ inch from top of glasses; cover with lids. Let stand at room temperature for 24 hours or until set. Freeze conserve to use within one year, or store in refrigerator to use within 3 weeks.

Freezer Peach-Orange Conserve

YIELD: about six 8-ounce glasses

6 8-ounce freezer-safe,
   dishwasher-safe jelly glasses
   or containers with tight-fitting
   lids
boiling water
about 1¼ pounds fully ripened
   peaches
1 medium orange
¼ cup California walnuts, finely
   chopped
3 tablespoons chopped
   Maraschino cherries
2 tablespoons lemon juice
½ teaspoon salt
4¼ cups sugar
1 1¾-ounce package powdered
   fruit pectin
¾ cup water

1. Prepare glasses and lids: Check glasses to be sure they have no nicks, cracks, or sharp edges. Wash glasses and lids in hot soapy water; rinse well. Carefully and slowly pour boiling water inside and out of glasses and lids; invert on dish rack or clean cloth towel, away from draft, to drain dry. Or, wash in dishwasher with very hot rinse cycle (150°F., or higher) and leave in dishwasher until ready to fill.

2. Peel, pit, and slice peaches. In large bowl with potato masher or slotted spoon, thoroughly crush peaches to make 1½ cups. From orange, grate 2 teaspoons peel. Peel and section orange; dice sections to measure ¼ cup. Add orange peel and sections, chopped nuts, cherries, lemon juice, and salt to peaches in bowl. With rubber spatula, stir in sugar until thoroughly mixed; let stand 10 minutes.

3. In 1-quart saucepan over medium heat, heat fruit pectin and water to boiling; boil 1 minute, stirring constantly. Stir pectin mixture into fruit; continue stirring 3 minutes—no less! A few sugar crystals will remain.

4. Ladle peach mixture into glasses to ½ inch from top of glass; cover with lids. Let stand at room temperature for 24 hours or until set. Freeze conserve to use within one year, or store in refrigerator to use within 3 weeks.

Honey-Lemon Preserves

YIELD: 4 half-pints

9 large lemons
water
½ teaspoon baking soda
3 3-inch-long cinnamon sticks
1½ teaspoons whole cloves
1½ teaspoons whole allspice
cheesecloth
2 cups sugar
1 cup honey
⅓ cup orange juice
4 half-pint canning jars and lids

1. With sharp knife, cut each lemon lengthwise in half; place each half cut-side down, then cut cross-wise into thin slices. Discard end pieces and seeds; place lemon slices in 3-quart saucepan with enough water to cover; add baking soda; over high heat, heat to boiling. Reduce heat to low; simmer 10 minutes or until lemon rinds are tender, stirring occasionally. Drain lemon slices, discarding liquid; set lemon slices aside.

2. Break cinnamon sticks into small pieces. Wrap cinnamon, cloves, and allspice in piece of double-thickness cheesecloth; tie with string; set aside.

3. In same 3-quart saucepan, combine, sugar, honey, and orange juice; over high heat, heat to boiling. Reduce heat to medium; cook, stirring constantly, until sugar is completely dissolved. Add spice bag and lemon slices; heat to boiling. Reduce heat to low; simmer 20 minutes, stirring occasionally; discard spice bag.

4. Meanwhile, prepare jars and caps for processing. Check jars to be sure they have no nicks, cracks, or sharp edges that will prevent an airtight seal or cause breakage. Wash jars, lids, and screw bands (or caps and rubber rings) in hot soapy water; rinse well. Leave jars and lids in hot water until ready to use. Wet rubber rings before using to make them more pliable.

5. Immediately, ladle hot lemon-slice mixture into hot jars to within ¼-inch from top. (Keep mixture simmering while filling jars.) Close jars as manufacturer directs.

6. Place jars on rack in canner half full with boiling water, far enough apart so water can circulate freely. Add additional boiling water if needed so that water level is 1 to 2 inches above tops of jars. (Do not pour water directly on jars.) Over high heat, heat to boiling. Cover canner; reduce heat to medium; boil gently 10 minutes. With jar lifter or tongs, remove jars from canner; set jars, several inches apart, on wire racks. Complete seal on jars with glass or zinc caps as manufacturer directs. Do *not* tighten screw bands. Cool at least 12 hours.

7. Now, test seal: Press lid at center; if center is down and stays down, jar is sealed. Turn jars with glass or zinc caps and rubber rings partly over; if no leakage, jars are sealed. Store unsealed jars in refrigerator to use within 1 month. Store sealed jars in cool, dark, dry place to use within 1 year.

8. Use lemon slices to serve as relish with baked ham, roast poultry or lamb, or as topping for ice cream and cakes.

SPREADS

Apple Butter

YIELD: 11 half-pints

6 pounds McIntosh or Rome Beauty apples, each cut into quarters
4 cups apple cider or apple juice
2½ cups sugar
1 teaspoon ground cinnamon
½ teaspoon ground nutmeg
¼ teaspoon ground cloves
¼ teaspoon salt
about 11 ½-pint canning jars and caps

1. In heavy 8-quart saucepot over high heat, heat apples and apple cider to boiling. Reduce heat to medium; cover and cook about 20 minutes or until apples are very tender, stirring occasionally. Remove saucepot from heat. Press apple mixture through food mill or coarse sieve into very large bowl; discard peels and seeds.

2. Return apple mixture to saucepot; add sugar, cinnamon, nutmeg, cloves, and salt; over high heat, heat to boiling. Reduce heat to medium; cook, stirring frequently, 1¼ hours or until mixture is thickened and mounds when dropped from a spoon.

3. Meanwhile, prepare jars and caps for processing. Check jars to be sure they have no nicks, cracks, or sharp edges that will prevent an airtight seal or cause breakage. Wash jars, lids, and screw bands (or caps and rubber rings) in hot, soapy water; rinse well. Leave jars and lids in hot water until ready to use. Wet rubber rings before using to make them more pliable.

4. Ladle hot apple mixture into hot jars to within ¼ inch from top of jar—keep apple mixture simmering while filling jars. Close jars as manufacturer directs.

5. Place jars on rack in canner half full with boiling water, far enough apart so water can circulate freely. Add additional boiling water if needed so that water level is 1 to 2 inches above tops of jars—do not pour water directly on jars. Over high heat, heat to boiling. Cover canner; reduce heat to medium; boil gently 10 minutes. With jar lifter or tongs, remove jars from canner; set jars several inches apart, on wire racks. Complete seal on jars with glass or zinc caps as manufacturer directs. Do *not* tighten screw bands. Cool at least 12 hours.

6. Now, test seal: Press lid at center; if center is down and stays down, jar is sealed. Turn jars with glass or zinc caps and rubber rings partly over; if no leakage, jars are sealed. Store unsealed jars in refrigerator to use within 1 month. Store sealed jars in cool, dark, dry place to use within 1 year.

Avocado Butter

TIME: about 15 minutes or start early in day—YIELD: about 1½ cups

1 medium avocado, peeled and cut into chunks
6 tablespoons butter or margarine, cut into small pieces
1 tablespoon lime juice
2 teaspoons minced preserved ginger
¾ teaspoon salt
½ teaspoon grated onion

1. In blender at medium speed or in food processor with knife blade attached, blend all ingredients until smooth. Spoon mixture into small bowl.

2. Serve immediately for easy spreading. Or, to serve later, cover and refrigerate Avocado Butter. Just before serving, let stand at room temperature 15 minutes to soften slightly for easier spreading.

181

Whipped Honey Butter

TIME: start early in day or day ahead—YIELD: about 1¼ cups

1 cup butter or margarine,
    softened
2 tablespoons honey
⅛ teaspoon cinnamon

1. In small bowl with mixer at medium speed, beat butter or margarine until fluffy; beat in honey and cinnamon until blended.

2. Spoon butter mixture into a small crock or bowl. Cover and refrigerate.

3. About 30 minutes before serving, remove Honey Butter from refrigerator to soften slightly for easier spreading.

Peach Butter

YIELD: about eight half-pints

6 pounds ripe peaches (about 20
    medium peaches)
3 cups sugar
¾ teaspoon salt
¾ teaspoon ground cinnamon
8 ½-pint canning jars and caps

1. Prepare peaches: In 5-quart Dutch oven or saucepot over high heat, heat 3 inches water to boiling; add peaches, a few at a time; cook 15 seconds. With slotted spoon, remove peaches to large bowl of cold water. Remove from water and with knife, peel off skins. Cut peaches in half; discard pits. Cut peaches into bite-sized pieces. Discard water in Dutch oven.

2. In same Dutch oven over medium heat, cook peaches until very soft, about 15 minutes, stirring frequently. Remove Dutch oven from heat. Press peaches through food mill or coarse sieve into large bowl.

3. Return peach pulp to Dutch oven; stir in sugar, salt, and cinnamon; over high heat, heat to boiling. Reduce heat to medium-low; cook 30 minutes or until mixture is thickened and mounds when dropped from a spoon, stirring frequently.

4. Meanwhile, prepare jars and caps for processing: Check jars to be sure they have no nicks, cracks, or sharp edges that will prevent an airtight seal or cause breakage. Wash jars, lids, and screw bands (or caps and rubber rings) in hot soapy water; rinse well. Leave jars and lids in hot water until ready to use. Wet rubber rings before using to make them more pliable.

5. Ladle hot peach mixture into hot jars to within ¼ inch from top of jar—keep peach mixture simmering while filling jars. Close jars as manufacturer directs.

6. Place jars on rack in canner half full with boiling water, far enough apart so water can circulate freely. Add additional boiling water if needed so that water level is 1 to 2 inches above tops of jars—do not pour water directly on jars. Over high heat, heat to boiling. Cover canner; reduce heat to medium; boil gently 10 minutes. With jar lifter or tongs, remove jars from canner; set jars several inches apart, on wire racks. Complete seal on jars with glass or zinc caps as manufacturer directs. Do *not* tighten screw bands. Cool at least 12 hours.

7. Now, test seal: Press lid at center; if center is down and stays down, jar is sealed; remove screw bands. Turn jars with glass or zinc caps and rubber rings partly over; if no leakage, jars are sealed. Store unsealed jars in refrigerator to use within one month. Store sealed jars in cool, dark, dry place to use within one year.

Gingered Orange Mustard

TIME: about 10 minutes or start up to 2 weeks ahead—YIELD: about ¾ cup

½ cup Dijon-style mustard
⅓ cup orange marmalade
½ teaspoon ground ginger
1½ teaspoons Worcestershire

In small bowl, with spoon, mix all ingredients until well blended. Cover and refrigerate mustard to use up within 2 weeks.

Caraway-Horseradish Mustard

TIME: about 10 minutes or start up to 2 weeks ahead—YIELD: about ¾ cup

½ cup Dijon-style mustard
2 teaspoons caraway seeds, crushed
1½ teaspoons prepared white horseradish

In small bowl with spoon, mix all ingredients until well blended. Cover and refrigerate mustard to use up within 2 weeks.

Cocktail Roquefort Spread

TIME: about 20 minutes or start up to 1 week ahead—YIELD: 1½ cups

1 8-ounce package cream cheese, softened
¼ pound Roquefort or blue cheese, softened
2 tablespoons milk
1 tablespoon prepared mustard
1 teaspoon pepper

1. In blender at medium speed or in food processor with knife blade attached, blend all ingredients until smooth. If not serving right away, cover and refrigerate to use up within 1 week.

2. To serve, let cheese mixture stand at room temperature to soften slightly. Serve as a spread on crackers, celery sticks, or cucumber slices.

Cheddar-Bacon Spread

TIME: about 20 minutes or start up to 3 days ahead—YIELD: about 1¾ cups

4 slices bacon
1 10-ounce package extra-sharp Cheddar cheese, shredded (2½ cups)
½ cup milk
¼ cup mayonnaise
1 teaspoon Worcestershire
⅛ teaspoon ground red pepper

1. In 10-inch skillet over medium-low heat, cook bacon until crisp. Remove to paper towels to drain; crumble bacon; set aside.

2. In blender at medium speed or in food processor with knife blade attached, blend Cheddar cheese and remaining ingredients until smooth. Stir in crumbled bacon.

3. If not serving right away, cover and refrigerate. To serve, remove spread to room temperature to soften slightly.

Pork Rillettes

TIME: start early in day or up to 3 days ahead—YIELD: about 2 cups

3 pounds pork shoulder blade
   roast, boneless (fresh pork
   butt)
1 cup water
2 teaspoons salt
1½ teaspoons coarsely ground
   black pepper
1 teaspoon marjoram leaves
½ teaspoon thyme leaves
1 bay leaf
1 garlic clove, crushed
toasted French-bread slices or
   crackers

1. With sharp knife, cut pork into ½-inch cubes. In 5-quart Dutch oven, combine pork cubes with remaining ingredients except toasted French bread; over high heat, heat to boiling. Reduce heat to low; cover and simmer until meat is very tender and falls apart when tested with a fork, about 2½ hours, stirring occasionally.

2. When meat is done, uncover Dutch oven and, over low heat, cook meat until all liquid has evaporated, stirring often. Discard bay leaf.

3. With two forks, pull meat into shreds. Spoon mixture into 2-cup covered crock; pack down well. Refrigerate. Use mixture as spread on toasted French-bread slices or crackers.

Cakes

Zuccotto (Florentine Cream Cake)

TIME: start early in day or day ahead—SERVINGS: 12

1 16- to 17-ounce package
  pound cake mix
¼ cup almond-flavor liqueur
6 squares semisweet chocolate
2 cups heavy or whipping cream
instant espresso coffee powder
1 5⅝-ounce package vanilla-
  flavor instant pudding and pie
  filling
2¼ cups milk
1 teaspoon almond extract
¼ cup slivered almonds
2 tablespoons sugar

1. Prepare cake mix as label directs for one 9-inch loaf pan; cool completely.

2. Line 2½-quart bowl with plastic wrap. Cut pound cake into ½-inch-thick slices; cut each slice diagonally in half to make 2 triangles. Sprinkle almond-flavor liqueur over cake triangles. Line bowl bottom and side with cake triangles, making sure there are no spaces between triangles and bowl is completely covered. Reserve remaining cake triangles.

3. In heavy 1-quart saucepan over low heat, melt 4 squares chocolate; cool slightly. Coarsely grate remaining 2 squares chocolate.

4. In small bowl with mixer at medium speed, beat 1¼ cups heavy or whipping cream and 2 teaspoons instant espresso until soft peaks form. In large bowl, prepare instant pudding as label directs but use only 2¼ cups milk. With wire whisk or rubber spatula, gently fold whipped cream and almond extract into prepared instant pudding. Fold in grated chocolate.

5. Spread two-thirds whipped-cream mixture evenly to cover cake in bowl. Fold melted chocolate into remaining whipped-cream mixture; use to fill center of dessert. Top dessert with remaining cake triangles. Cover with plastic wrap and refrigerate at least 4 hours.

6. To serve, toast almonds: Preheat oven to 375°F. Place almonds in single layer in 8″ by 8″ baking pan. Bake 10 minutes or until almonds are golden, stirring occasionally. Cool almonds; coarsely chop. In small bowl with mixer at medium speed, beat sugar, remaining heavy or whipping cream, and 2 teaspoons instant espresso until soft peaks form.

7. Unmold dessert onto plate; discard plastic wrap. Frost dessert with whipped-cream mixture. Sprinkle almonds on top of dessert.

Torta di Ricotta

TIME: start early in day or day ahead—SERVINGS: 16

1½ cups crushed almond
   macaroons (about 40 cookies)*
3 tablespoons butter or
   margarine, softened
1 large lemon
2 15- to 16-ounce containers
   ricotta cheese (about 4 cups)
6 eggs
1 cup sugar
1 cup heavy or whipping cream
¼ cup all-purpose flour
1 tablespoon almond-flavor
   liqueur
¼ teaspoon salt
¼ cup sliced blanched almonds

*Or, if you desire, substitute 1½
cups graham-cracker crumbs and 2
teaspoons almond extract for almond
macaroons.

1. Preheat oven to 350°F. In 10″ by 3″ springform pan, with hand, mix almond macaroons and butter or margarine; press onto bottom of pan. Bake crust 15 minutes or until golden. Cool on wire rack.

2. From lemon, grate 1 tablespoon peel and squeeze enough juice to make 3 tablespoons; set aside.

3. Into large bowl, press ricotta through fine sieve. With mixer at low speed, beat ricotta until smooth and creamy. Beat in lemon peel and juice, eggs, and remaining ingredients except almonds. Continue beating until mixture is well blended, occasionally scraping bowl with rubber spatula.

4. Pour ricotta mixture over crust in pan; sprinkle with almonds. Bake 1 hour. Turn oven off; let cheesecake remain in oven 1 hour. Remove cheesecake from oven; cool in pan on wire rack. Remove side of pan. Cover; refrigerate at least 4 hours or until chilled.

Cinnamon-Cream Torte

TIME: start up to 3 days ahead—SERVINGS: 16

¾ cup butter or margarine,
   softened
½ cup sugar
1 tablespoon ground cinnamon
1 egg
1½ cups all-purpose flour
2 cups heavy or whipping cream
cocoa

1. Tear 9 sheets of waxed paper, each about 8½ inches long. On one sheet of waxed paper, trace bottom of 8-inch round cake pan. Evenly stack all the waxed paper with the marked sheet on top. With kitchen shears, cut out circles.

2. Into large bowl, measure butter or margarine, sugar, cinnamon, egg, and 1 cup flour. With mixer at low speed, beat ingredients until well mixed, constantly scraping bowl with rubber spatula. Increase speed to medium; beat 3 minutes or until light and fluffy, occasionally scraping bowl. With spoon, stir in remaining ½ cup flour to make a soft dough.

3. Preheat oven to 375°F. With damp cloth, moisten 1 large or 2 small cookie sheets. Place 2 waxed-paper circles on large cookie sheet, or 1 on each small cookie sheet. With metal spatula, spread ¼ cup dough in a very thin layer on each circle. Bake 6 to 8 minutes until lightly browned around the edges.

4. Remove cookie sheet to wire rack; cool 5 minutes. With pancake turner, carefully remove cookie, still on waxed paper, to wire rack to cool completely. Allow cookie sheet to cool before spreading waxed-paper circles with more dough. (The more cookie sheets you have the faster you can bake the cookies.) Repeat until all dough is baked. Makes 9 cookies. Stack cooled cookies carefully on flat plate; cover with plastic wrap and store in cool, dry place.

5. Early in day that torte will be served, in large bowl with mixer at medium speed, beat heavy or whipping cream until soft peaks form. Carefully peel off paper from 1 cookie; place on cake plate; spread

with about ½ cup whipped cream. Repeat layering until all cookies are used, ending with whipped cream on top.

6. With small strainer, lightly sprinkle cocoa on top of whipped cream. If you desire, with dull edge of knife, mark top of cake into 16 servings. Refrigerate at least 4 hours to let cookies soften slightly for easier cutting.

Zuppa Inglese

TIME: about 4 hours or start early in day—SERVINGS: 10

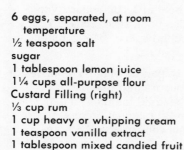

6 eggs, separated, at room
    temperature
½ teaspoon salt
sugar
1 tablespoon lemon juice
1¼ cups all-purpose flour
Custard Filling (right)
⅓ cup rum
1 cup heavy or whipping cream
1 teaspoon vanilla extract
1 tablespoon mixed candied fruit

1. Preheat oven to 350°F. Prepare cake: In large bowl with mixer at high speed, beat egg whites and salt until soft peaks form. Beating at high speed, gradually sprinkle in ¼ cup sugar, beating until sugar is completely dissolved. (Whites should stand in stiff, glossy peaks.)

2. In small bowl with same beaters and with mixer at high speed, beat egg yolks, lemon juice, and ¾ cup sugar until very thick. With wire whisk or rubber spatula, gently fold egg-yolk mixture and flour into beaten egg whites. Spoon batter into 9″ by 3″ springform pan. Bake 35 to 40 minutes until cake is golden and top springs back when lightly touched with finger. Invert cake in pan on wire rack; cool completely.

3. Meanwhile, prepare Custard Filling.

4. Assemble dessert: Gently loosen cake from pan. With serrated knife, slice cake horizontally into 3 layers. Into 3-quart glass bowl (about 9-inch diameter), spoon 2 tablespoons vanilla custard. Place first cake layer on custard (if necessary, cut cake layer to fit bowl); brush with some rum; top with half of remaining vanilla custard. Place second cake layer on custard; brush with rum; top with all of chocolate custard. Place third cake layer on custard; brush with remaining rum; top with remaining vanilla custard. Cover and refrigerate until well chilled, about 2 hours.

5. To serve, in small bowl with mixer at medium speed, beat heavy or whipping cream, vanilla extract, and 2 teaspoons sugar until soft peaks form. Spoon whipped-cream mixture onto dessert; garnish with candied fruit.

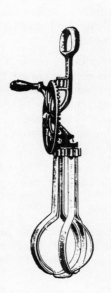

Custard Filling: In heavy 2-quart saucepan with wire whisk, mix 2½ cups milk, ⅓ cup sugar, ¼ cup cornstarch, ½ teaspoon salt, and 4 egg yolks. Over medium-low heat, cook, stirring constantly, until mixture is thickened and coats the back of a spoon. Remove saucepan from heat. Stir in 1 teaspoon vanilla extract; set aside.

In small saucepan over low heat, melt 2 squares semisweet chocolate. Remove saucepan from heat; stir in ½ cup custard; set aside.

Manhattan-Style Cheesecake

TIME: start early in day or day ahead—SERVINGS: 16

⅔ cup butter or margarine, softened
all-purpose flour
sugar
2 egg yolks
grated peel of 1 lemon
3 8-ounce packages cream cheese, softened
2 tablespoons milk
3 eggs
2 large kiwi fruit
½ pint strawberries
2 tablespoons apple jelly

1. In small bowl with mixer at low speed, beat butter or margarine, 1 cup all-purpose flour, 3 tablespoons sugar, 1 egg yolk, and half of grated lemon peel until mixed. Shape dough into ball; wrap and refrigerate 1 hour.

2. Preheat oven to 400°F. Press one-third of dough onto bottom of 10″ by 3″ springform pan; bake 8 minutes; cool. Turn oven control to 475°F.

3. Meanwhile, in large bowl with mixer at medium speed, beat cream cheese just until smooth; slowly beat in 1 cup sugar. With mixer at low speed, beat in 2 tablespoons flour, milk, eggs, 1 egg yolk, and remaining lemon peel. At medium speed, beat 5 minutes, occasionally scraping bowl with rubber spatula.

4. Press remaining dough around side of pan to within 1¾ inches of top; do not bake. Pour cream-cheese mixture into pan; bake 10 minutes. Turn oven control to 300°F.; bake 20 minutes longer. Turn off oven; let cheesecake remain in oven 20 minutes. Remove; cool cake in pan on wire rack; refrigerate until chilled, about 2 hours.

5. To serve, peel and thinly slice kiwi fruit; cut each strawberry in half. Arrange kiwi fruit and strawberries on top of cheesecake to make a pretty design. In small saucepan over low heat, melt apple jelly. With pastry brush, lightly brush fruit with melted jelly.

Light Cottage Cheesecake

TIME: start early in day or day ahead—SERVINGS: 16

½ cup graham-cracker crumbs
2 tablespoons butter or margarine, softened
2 envelopes unflavored gelatin
1 cup water
1 lemon
1 16-ounce container cottage cheese (2 cups)
½ cup sugar
2 eggs, separated, at room temperature
¼ cup sliced blanched almonds, toasted
fresh daisies for garnish (optional)

1. Preheat oven to 350°F. In 9″ by 2″ springform pan, with hand, mix graham-cracker crumbs and butter or margarine; press onto bottom of pan. Bake crust 10 minutes. Cool on wire rack.

2. In 1-quart saucepan, evenly sprinkle gelatin over water. Cook over medium heat until gelatin is completely dissolved, stirring frequently. Remove saucepan from heat; set aside.

3. From lemon, grate 1 tablespoon peel and squeeze enough juice to make 2 tablespoons. Into large bowl, press cottage cheese through fine sieve. With mixer at medium speed, beat cottage cheese, sugar, egg yolks, lemon peel, lemon juice, and gelatin mixture until smooth, occasionally scraping bowl with rubber spatula. Refrigerate until mixture mounds slightly when dropped from a spoon, about 10 minutes.

4. In small bowl with mixer at high speed, beat egg whites until stiff peaks form. With rubber spatula or wire whisk, fold beaten egg whites into cottage-cheese mixture. Spoon mixture over crust in pan; cover and refrigerate until firm, at least 3 hours.

5. To serve, carefully remove side of pan from cheesecake; place cake on chilled plate. Arrange toasted almonds on top of cheesecake around edge to form decorative border. Garnish center of cake with daisies, if desired.

Cranberry Swirl Cheescake

TIME: start early in day or day ahead—SERVINGS: 16

5 eggs
3 envelopes unflavored gelatin
water
1 medium orange
4 8-ounce packages cream
  cheese, softened
1 teaspoon vanilla extract
sugar
1¾ cups cranberries
1½ cups finely crushed vanilla
  wafers (about 40 cookies)
4 tablespoons butter or
  margarine, softened
small holly leaves or other
  nontoxic leaves for garnish

1. Separate eggs, placing egg yolks in large mixing bowl and egg whites in small mixing bowl. Reserve 1 tablespoon egg white in refrigerator for coating cranberries for garnish later.

2. In 1-quart saucepan, evenly sprinkle gelatin over 2 cups water. Cook over medium heat until gelatin is completely dissolved, stirring frequently. Remove saucepan from heat; set aside.

3. From orange, grate 1 tablespoon peel and squeeze 2 tablespoons juice.

4. To large bowl with egg yolks, add cream cheese, vanilla, orange juice, orange peel, and 1 cup sugar; with mixer at low speed, beat until mixture is blended. Gradually beat in 1¾ cups gelatin mixture. Increase speed to medium; beat until cheese mixture is very smooth, scraping bowl often with rubber spatula.

5. With mixer at high speed, beat egg whites in small bowl until stiff peaks form. With rubber spatula or wire whisk, fold egg whites into cream-cheese mixture. Cover and refrigerate until cheese mixture mounds slightly when dropped from a spoon, about 45 minutes.

6. Meanwhile, set aside 6 cranberries for garnish. In 2-quart saucepan over high heat, cook ¾ cup sugar, 2 tablespoons water, and remaining cranberries 5 minutes or until cranberries pop, stirring ocasionally; stir in remaining ¼ cup gelatin mixture. In blender at medium speed, blend cranberry mixture until smooth; pour mixture into small bowl; cover and refrigerate until cranberry mixture mounds slightly when dropped from spoon.

7. In 10″ by 3″ springform pan, with hand, mix crushed vanilla wafers and butter or margarine; press onto bottom of pan.

8. Alternately spoon cream-cheese mixture and cranberry mixture into prepared springform pan. With knife, cut through mixtures to make a pretty swirl design. Cover and refrigerate until set, about 3 hours.

9. While cheesecake sets, prepare cranberry garnish: In pie plate, with fork, beat reserved 1 tablespoon egg white slightly. Onto waxed paper, measure 1 tablespoon sugar. Brush reserved cranberries with egg white; then coat cranberries completely with sugar. Place frosted cranberries on wire rack to dry, about 1 hour. Store frosted cranberries, lightly covered with plastic wrap, in refrigerator until serving time.

10. To serve, carefully remove side of pan from cheesecake. Garnish cheesecake with frosted cranberries and leaves.

Bee Cake

TIME: about 5 hours or start early in day—SERVINGS: 12

3 tablespoons sugar
¼ teaspoon salt
1 package active dry yeast
about 2¼ cups all-purpose flour
½ cup milk
3 tablespoons butter or
   margarine
1 egg
Honey-Almond Topping (right)
Almond-Cream Filling (right)

1. In small bowl, combine sugar, salt, yeast, and ½ cup flour. In 1-quart saucepan over low heat, heat milk and butter or margarine until very warm (120° to 130°F.). (Butter or margarine does not need to melt completely.)

2. With mixer at low speed, gradually beat liquid into dry ingredients just until blended. Increase speed to medium; beat 2 minutes, occasionally scraping bowl with rubber spatula. Gradually beat in egg and ½ cup flour to make a thick batter; continue beating 2 minutes, scraping bowl often. With wooden spoon, stir in 1 cup flour to make a soft dough.

3. Turn dough onto well-floured surface and knead until smooth and elastic, about 5 minutes, working in more flour while kneading, about 2 tablespoons. Shape dough into a ball and place in greased medium bowl, turning dough over so that top is greased. Cover bowl with towel and let rise in warm place (80° to 85°F.), away from draft, until doubled, about 1 hour. (Dough is doubled when 2 fingers pressed lightly into dough leave a dent.)

4. Punch down dough. Turn dough onto lightly floured surface; cover with bowl and let rest 15 minutes for easier shaping. Grease 9″ by 3″ springform pan.

5. With floured hands, pat dough into prepared pan. Cover with towel and let rise in warm place until doubled, about 45 minutes. (Dough is doubled when 1 finger very lightly pressed against dough leaves a dent.)

6. Preheat oven to 325°F. Meanwhile, prepare Honey-Almond Topping; set aside.

7. Gently spoon Honey-Almond Topping onto dough. Bake cake 30 to 35 minutes until golden. Cool cake in pan on wire rack 10 minutes; remove from pan. Cool cake completely on wire rack.

8. To serve, prepare Almond-Cream Filling. With serrated knife, cut cake horizontally in half to form 2 layers. Spread bottom layer with filling; top with almond-topped layer.

Honey-Almond Topping: In 2-quart saucepan over low heat, heat *3 tablespoons butter* or margarine and *3 tablespoons packed light brown sugar* until butter is melted and sugar is dissolved. Add *one 4-ounce can slivered blanched almonds,* chopped, and *¼ cup honey;* over medium heat, heat to boiling, stirring frequently. Remove saucepan from heat; stir in *¼ teaspoon almond extract* and *⅛ teaspoon salt.*

Almond-Cream Filling: In small bowl with mixer at medium speed, beat *½ cup heavy or whipping cream* until soft peaks form; set aside. Prepare *one 3½-to 3¾-ounce package vanilla-flavor instant pudding and pie filling* as label directs, but use only *¾ cup milk.* With rubber spatula, fold whipped cream and *½ teaspoon almond extract* into pudding.

Poppy-Seed Cake with Custard Sauce

TIME: about 1½ hours—SERVINGS: 12

1 18.5- or 18.75-ounce package
   yellow-cake mix with pudding
¼ cup poppy seeds
2 cups milk
¼ cup sugar
⅛ teaspoon salt
3 egg yolks
¼ teaspoon almond extract

1. Grease and flour 10-inch tube pan. Prepare cake-mix batter as label directs, but add poppy seeds before beating. Spoon batter into prepared pan. Bake in preheated 350°F. oven 40 minutes (or the length of time indicated on label for 10-inch tube pan) until toothpick inserted in center of cake comes out clean. Cool cake in pan on wire rack 15 minutes; remove cake from pan; cool on wire rack at least 15 minutes.

2. Meanwhile, prepare custard sauce: In heavy 2-quart saucepan over low heat, or in double boiler over hot, *not boiling,* water, with wire whisk, beat milk, sugar, salt, and egg yolks until blended. Cook, stirring constantly, until mixture thickens and coats spoon, about 20 minutes. Stir in almond extract. Pour custard into small bowl.

3. To serve, cut cake into slices. Serve slices topped with custard sauce. (Refrigerate any remaining custard sauce to serve cold later.)

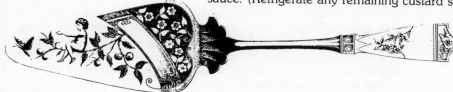

Parisian Mocha-Cream Loaf

TIME: about 2½ hours—SERVINGS: 12

1½ cups cake flour
⅔ cup milk
¼ cup shortening
1¼ teaspoons double-acting
   baking powder
½ teaspoon salt
½ teaspoon almond extract
1 egg
sugar
1½ cups heavy or whipping
   cream
1 tablespoon cocoa
1 tablespoon instant espresso
   coffee powder
¼ cup sliced blanched almonds,
   toasted and chopped
2 tablespoons apricot preserves

1. Preheat oven to 375°F. Grease and flour 13" by 9" baking pan. Into large bowl, measure first 7 ingredients and ¾ cup sugar. With mixer at low speed, beat ingredients until well mixed, constantly scraping bowl with rubber spatula. Increase speed to medium; beat 3 minutes or until batter is light and fluffy, occasionally scraping bowl. Spread batter evenly in baking pan.

2. Bake 20 minutes or until top of cake is golden and toothpick inserted in center of cake comes out clean. Cool cake in pan on wire rack 10 minutes; remove cake from pan; cool cake completely on wire rack.

3. In small bowl with mixer at medium speed, beat ½ cup heavy or whipping cream until soft peaks form. Spoon whipped cream into decorating bag with medium rosette tube; refrigerate. In same bowl with same beaters, beat remaining 1 cup heavy or whipping cream, cocoa, instant espresso, and 1 tablespoon sugar until soft peaks form for mocha cream.

4. With serrated knife, cut cake crosswise into thirds. Place 1 cake layer on serving plate; spread top with ½ cup mocha-cream mixture. Repeat with second cake layer and another ½ cup mocha-cream mixture. Top with remaining cake layer. Frost top and sides of cake with remaining mocha-cream mixture.

5. Pipe whipped cream in decorating bag on top of cake to form 1-inch diamond shapes. Fill every other diamond with toasted almonds; fill remaining diamonds with apricot preserves.

191

Chocolate-Cherry Cake

TIME: about 3 hours or start early in day—SERVINGS: 14

cocoa
sugar
2 cups all-purpose flour
1⅓ cups water
⅔ cup butter or margarine,
    softened
1½ teaspoons baking soda
1¼ teaspoons vanilla extract
½ teaspoon double-acting
    baking powder
½ teaspoon salt
3 eggs
1 21-ounce can cherry-pie filling
1 tablespoon cornstarch
Lemon-Rum Whipped Cream
    (right)

1. Preheat oven to 350°F. Grease two 9-inch round cake pans; dust bottoms and sides of pans with cocoa. Into large bowl, measure ⅔ cup cocoa, 1⅓ cups sugar, and next 8 ingredients; with mixer at low speed, beat ingredients just until blended. Increase speed to high; beat 2 minutes.

2. Pour batter into pans. Bake 25 minutes or until toothpick inserted in center of cake comes out clean. Cool cake in pans on wire racks 10 minutes. Remove from pans; cool completely.

3. Meanwhile, in 1-quart saucepan, combine cherries, cornstarch, and ⅓ cup sugar. Cook over medium heat, stirring constantly, until mixture thickens and boils; boil 1 minute. Refrigerate mixture until cool.

4. Prepare Lemon-Rum Whipped Cream.

5. Place 1 cake layer, rounded-side down, on cake plate; spread with three-fourths of whipped-cream mixture; top with second cake layer, rounded-side up. With decorating bag and large rosette tube, pipe remaining whipped cream around edge on top of cake to make a pretty border. Spoon cherry mixture evenly on center of cake. Refrigerate until serving time.

Lemon-Rum Whipped Cream: In small bowl with mixer at medium speed, beat *1 cup heavy or whipping cream, 2 tablespoons confectioners' sugar, 1 teaspoon lemon peel,* and *½ teaspoon rum extract* until stiff peaks form.

Chocolate-and-Creams

TIME: about 4 hours or start early in day—SERVINGS: 24

1 18.5- to 18.75-ounce package
    devil's food cake mix with
    pudding
½ cup California walnuts,
    chopped
1½ cups heavy or whipping
    cream
1 tablespoon sugar
1 teaspoon vanilla extract
1 square semisweet chocolate,
    finely chopped
thin strips of orange peel for
    garnish (optional)

1. Preheat oven to 350°F. Grease and flour 15½″ by 10½″ jelly-roll pan. Prepare cake mix as label directs; stir in walnuts. Bake cake in prepared jelly-roll pan 20 minutes or until toothpick inserted in center comes out clean. Cool cake in pan on wire rack 15 minutes. Loosen edges of cake with spatula; invert cake onto rack; cool completely.

2. With serrated knife, cut cake lengthwise in half; cut each half crosswise in half. Working with one-fourth of cake at a time, slice cake horizontally into 2 layers.

3. In small bowl with mixer at medium speed, beat heavy cream, sugar, and vanilla until stiff peaks form. Fold chopped chocolate into whipped-cream mixture.

4. Spread whipped-cream mixture on bottom cake layers. Place top cake layers on cream-covered layers. Cut each into 6 pieces. If desired, garnish each sandwich with an orange-peel strip. Refrigerate until serving time.

Dreamy Chocolate Cake

TIME: start early in day—SERVINGS: 16

2 8-ounce packages semisweet-
  chocolate squares
1⅓ cups sugar
2 eggs, separated
butter or margarine, softened
2¼ cups all-purpose flour
1 cup water
½ cup sour cream
1 teaspoon double-acting baking
  powder
1 teaspoon baking soda
½ teaspoon orange extract
¼ teaspoon salt
1½ cups heavy or whipping
  cream
confectioners' sugar

1. Prepare chocolate cake: Grease and flour bottom and side of 10″ by 3″ springform pan. Preheat oven to 350°F. In heavy 1-quart saucepan over low heat, heat 3 squares semisweet chocolate until melted and smooth, stirring occasionally. In large bowl with mixer at medium speed, beat sugar, egg yolks, and ½ cup butter or margarine until light and fluffy, about 5 minutes, scraping bowl occasionally with rubber spatula. With mixer at low speed, beat in melted chocolate, flour, water, sour cream, baking powder, baking soda, orange extract, and salt; increase speed to medium; beat 2 minutes.

2. In small bowl with mixer at high speed, beat egg whites until soft peaks form. With rubber spatula or wire whisk, gently fold beaten egg whites into chocolate mixture. Pour batter into prepared pan. Bake 45 minutes or until cake springs back when lightly touched with finger. Cool cake in pan on wire rack 10 minutes; then carefully remove side of pan. Cool cake completely on wire rack.

3. Meanwhile, prepare chocolate garnish: Cut waxed paper into 15″ by 12″ rectangle; place on large cookie sheet. In heavy 1-quart saucepan over low heat, heat 5 squares semisweet chocolate until melted and smooth, stirring occasionally. Remove saucepan from heat. With metal spatula, spread chocolate to evenly cover waxed-paper rectangle; refrigerate until firm, about 30 minutes. Remove cookie sheet from refrigerator. With pastry wheel or knife, cut chocolate crosswise into ten 1½-inch-wide strips. Carefully peel waxed paper from chocolate; refrigerate until ready to use.

4. Prepare chocolate cream: In 2-quart saucepan over medium heat, heat heavy cream, 8 squares semisweet chocolate, and 4 tablespoons butter or margarine to boiling, stirring constantly, until mixture is smooth. Pour mixture into large bowl; let cool completely at room temperature. With mixer at high speed, beat chocolate mixture until light and fluffy.

5. Remove cake from cake-pan bottom. With serrated knife, cut cake horizontally into 2 layers. Place 1 cake layer on cake platter; spread with one-third of chocolate cream; top with second cake layer. With spatula, spread remaining chocolate cream around side and on top of cake.

6. Remove chocolate strips from refrigerator; let stand about 5 minutes to soften slightly. Arrange chocolate strips in a circular fashion on top of cake. Lightly dust top of cake with confectioners' sugar; refrigerate.

7. To serve, let cake stand at room temperature 20 minutes to allow chocolate to soften slightly for easier cutting.

Ice-Cream-Filled Chocolate Cake Ring

TIME: start early in day—SERVINGS: 16

2 pints coffee ice cream
1 18.5- to 18.75-ounce package
  devil's food cake mix
1 cup California walnuts,
  coarsely chopped
Butterscotch Glaze (right)

1. With medium (number 16) ice-cream scoop, scoop ice cream into balls and arrange on chilled jelly-roll pan or cookie sheet. Freezer-wrap and freeze.

2. Grease and flour 12-cup ring mold. Prepare cake mix as label directs but fold walnuts into batter and bake in ring mold 40 minutes until toothpick inserted in center comes out clean. Cool in mold on wire rack 10 minutes; remove from mold; cool completely on wire rack.

3. Spread Butterscotch Glaze on top of cake and garnish with reserved butterscotch pieces; cover.

4. To serve, arrange ice-cream balls in center of cake. Serve immediately.

Butterscotch Glaze: Set aside 2 tablespoons butterscotch pieces for garnish from *one 6-ounce package butterscotch pieces.* In double boiler over hot, *not boiling* water, melt remaining candy with *2 tablespoons butter* or margarine, *1 tablespoon milk,* and *1 tablespoon light corn syrup* until smooth, stirring occasionally.

Carrot Cake Ring

TIME: about 4 hours or start day ahead—SERVINGS: 16

2 cups all-purpose flour
1¼ cups salad oil
1 cup packed dark brown sugar
¾ cup sugar
2 teaspoons baking soda
2 teaspoons ground cinnamon
1 teaspoon salt
1 teaspoon vanilla extract
¼ teaspoon ground cloves
½ 6-ounce can frozen orange-
  juice concentrate
4 eggs
2 cups shredded carrots (about 3
  medium carrots)
1 cup California walnuts,
  chopped
½ cup dark seedless raisins
confectioners' sugar (optional)

1. Preheat oven to 350°F. Grease and flour 10-inch Bundt pan. Into large bowl, measure first 11 ingredients. With mixer at low speed, beat ingredients just until mixed, constantly scraping bowl with rubber spatula. Increase speed to high; beat 4 minutes, occasionally scraping bowl.

2. With rubber spatula, fold in carrots, walnuts, and raisins. Spoon batter into prepared pan. Bake 55 to 60 minutes until toothpick inserted in center of cake comes out clean. Cool cake in pan on wire rack 10 minutes; remove cake from pan; let cool completely on wire rack. If desired, sprinkle cake with confectioners' sugar.

Tempting Fruit and Nut Ring

TIME: start early in day or up to 1 month ahead—SERVINGS: 40

1 10-ounce container pitted dates
1 4-ounce container candied
    pineapple slices
½ cup dried apricot halves
⅔ cup orange juice
1 cup butter or margarine,
    softened
¾ cup sugar
2¼ cups all-purpose flour
¼ cup honey
½ teaspoon double-acting
    baking powder
½ teaspoon ground cardamom
½ teaspoon ground cinnamon
¼ teaspoon salt
5 eggs
1½ cups California walnuts,
    chopped

1. Dice dates, pineapple, and apricots. In small bowl, mix diced fruit and orange juice; let stand 15 minutes, stirring occasionally.

2. Preheat oven to 300°F. Grease well 12-cup ring mold. In large bowl with mixer at medium speed, beat butter or margarine and sugar until light and fluffy. Add flour and next 6 ingredients. With mixer at low speed, beat ingredients until well mixed, constantly scraping bowl with rubber spatula. Increase speed to high; beat 3 minutes, occasionally scraping bowl.

3. With rubber spatula, fold nuts and fruit mixture with its liquid into batter. Spoon batter evenly into prepared ring mold. Bake 1½ hours or until toothpick inserted into center of cake comes out clean. Cool cake in pan on wire rack 10 minutes; remove from pan; cool completely on wire rack. Wrap fruitcake tightly with foil or plastic wrap. Refrigerate to use up within 1 month. Makes one 3½-pound fruitcake.

Glazed Fruitcake Loaves

TIME: start day ahead or up to 2 months ahead—SERVINGS: 64

FRUITCAKE:
1 cup butter or margarine,
    softened
½ cup packed dark brown sugar
2½ cups all-purpose flour
1 cup dark corn syrup
⅓ cup orange-flavor liqueur or
    orange juice
1 teaspoon double-acting baking
    powder
1 teaspoon ground cinnamon
½ teaspoon salt
½ teaspoon ground nutmeg
½ teaspoon ground cloves
5 eggs
2 16-ounce containers mixed
    candied fruit
1 16-ounce container pitted
    dates, coarsely chopped
    (3 cups)
3 cups California walnuts,
    chopped
2 cups dark seedless raisins

DECORATION:
6 red candied cherries
6 green candied cherries
2½ cups confectioners' sugar
3 tablespoons orange juice

1. Grease two 9" by 5" loaf pans. Line bottoms and sides of pans with foil; press out wrinkles as much as possible so cake surface will come out smooth.

2. In large bowl with mixer at medium speed, beat butter or margarine and brown sugar until light and fluffy. At low speed, beat in flour and next 8 ingredients until well mixed, constantly scraping bowl with rubber spatula. With spoon, stir in mixed candied fruit, dates, walnuts, and raisins. Spoon batter into prepared pans, packing down batter to eliminate air pockets. Bake in 275°F. oven 2 to 2¼ hours until toothpick inserted in center of loaf comes out clean. Cool loaves in pans on wire racks 10 minutes. Remove from pans; carefully peel off foil. Cool loaves completely on wire racks. Wrap each loaf tightly with foil or plastic wrap. Refrigerate to use up within 2 months.

3. To serve, if desired, decorate cake: Cut candied cherries into slivers. In bowl with spoon, mix confectioners' sugar and orange juice; spread glaze over tops of loaves. Quickly arrange cherry slivers on glaze to make pretty flowers. Let cake stand at room temperature 30 minutes to allow glaze to dry. Cut each loaf into 16 slices; then cut each slice in half. Makes two 3½-pound fruitcakes.

Holiday Cherry Fruitcake

TIME: start day ahead or up to 2 months ahead—SERVINGS: 50

2 cups pecan halves
3 7.5- to 8-ounce containers red
  candied cherries (3 cups)
1 7.5- to 8-ounce container green
  candied cherries (1 cup)
1 cup orange-flavor liqueur
1 3.5- to 4-ounce container diced
  candied orange peel (½ cup)
1½ cups California walnuts,
  coarsely broken
1 cup dark seedless raisins
3½ cups all-purpose flour
2 cups butter or margarine,
  softened
1½ cups sugar
6 eggs
1 teaspoon salt
¼ cup light corn syrup

1. Line 10-inch tube pan with foil; press out wrinkles as much as possible so cake surface will come out smooth. Set aside ½ cup pecan halves and 5 red cherries for garnish; cut each of the remaining cherries in half.

2. In large bowl or 6-quart saucepot, combine remaining 1½ cups pecan halves, red and green cherry halves, ¾ cup orange-flavor liqueur, and next 3 ingredients; let stand 10 minutes or until all liqueur is absorbed, stirring occasionally. Stir in 2 cups flour until fruit and nuts are evenly coated.

3. In another bowl with mixer at medium speed, beat butter or margarine and sugar until light and fluffy, constantly scraping bowl with rubber spatula. Add eggs, salt, remaining 1½ cups flour, and ¼ cup orange-flavor liqueur; at low speed, beat until well mixed, frequently scraping bowl with rubber spatula. Stir batter into fruit mixture in bowl until well mixed.

4. Spoon batter into pan, packing down batter evenly to eliminate air pockets. Bake in 300°F. oven 2½ hours or until toothpick inserted in center of cake comes out clean. Cool cake in pan on wire rack; remove cake from pan and carefully peel off foil.

5. In small saucepan over medium heat, heat corn syrup to boiling; boil 1 minute. With pastry brush, quickly brush a dab of syrup on each reserved pecan half and red cherry to attach on top of cake as garnish. Wrap fruitcake tightly with foil or plastic wrap. Refrigerate to use up within 2 months. Makes one 6-pound fruitcake.

Miniature Fruitcakes

TIME: about 2 hours or start up to 2 weeks ahead—YIELD: 4 dozen

1½ cups all-purpose flour
⅓ cup packed light brown sugar
⅓ cup light corn syrup
6 tablespoons butter or
  margarine, softened
1½ teaspoons double-acting
  baking powder
1½ teaspoons vanilla extract
¼ teaspoon salt
3 eggs
3 8-ounce containers mixed
  candied fruit
1 3½- to 4-ounce can slivered
  blanched almonds (1 cup)
1 3-ounce can pecans (1 cup),
  coarsely chopped

1. Place forty-eight 1¾″ by 1″ miniature foil baking cups in jelly-roll pan or on cookie sheet or grease and flour forty-eight 1¾″ by 1″ muffin-pan cups; set aside. Preheat oven to 300°F.

2. In large bowl with mixer at low speed, beat first 8 ingredients until blended; increase speed to medium; beat 3 minutes or until batter is very smooth, scraping bowl often with rubber spatula. Stir in candied fruit and nuts.

3. Spoon about 1 tablespoon batter into each foil baking cup or greased and floured muffin-pan cup. Bake 30 to 35 minutes until toothpick inserted in center of a cake comes out clean. Cool fruit cakes in foil cups on wire racks. If using muffin-pan cups, cool in pans on wire racks 10 minutes; remove from pans; cool on wire racks. Store in tightly covered container to use up within 2 weeks.

Banana Fruitcake

TIME: start early in day or up to 1 month ahead—SERVINGS: 40

3 3½- to 4-ounce containers candied red cherries (about 1½ cups)
1 8-ounce package dried figs, chopped (1 cup)
1 3.5-ounce container diced candied citron (about ½ cup)
1 4-ounce container diced candied orange peel (½ cup)
1 4-ounce container diced candied lemon peel (½ cup)
2 cups golden raisins
1½ cups pecans, chopped
½ cup dark seedless raisins
3¾ cups all-purpose flour
1½ cups sugar
1 cup butter or margarine, softened
¾ cup orange juice
¾ cup mashed bananas (about 2 ripe medium bananas)
2 teaspoons double-acting baking powder
1 teaspoon orange extract
½ teaspoon salt
6 eggs

1. Line 10-inch tube pan with foil; press out wrinkles as much as possible so cake surface will come out smooth. Cut each red cherry in half; reserve about 18 cherry halves for garnish. In large bowl, combine remaining cherry halves, figs, next 6 ingredients, and ¾ cup flour until fruits and nuts are evenly coated with flour.

2. In another large bowl, with mixer at low speed, beat remaining 3 cups flour with remaining ingredients just until blended, constantly scraping bowl with rubber spatula. Increase speed to medium; beat 4 minutes longer, occasionally scraping bowl. Stir batter into fruit mixture until well mixed.

3. Preheat oven to 300°F. Pour batter into prepared pan, packing down batter evenly to eliminate air pockets. Bake 2½ hours until toothpick inserted in center of cake comes out clean. Cool cake in pan on wire rack 30 minutes; remove from pan and carefully peel off foil. Cool cake completely on rack. Arrange reserved cherry halves on top of cake in clusters. Wrap fruitcake tightly with foil or plastic wrap. Refrigerate. Makes one 5½ pound fruitcake.

Heavenly Pineapple Cake

TIME: about 3 hours or start early in day—SERVINGS: 16

1 8-ounce can crushed pineapple in its own juice
water
6 eggs, separated, at room temperature
½ teaspoon cream of tartar
sugar
2 cups cake flour
1 tablespoon double-acting baking powder
½ teaspoon salt
¾ teaspoon almond extract
Almond Glaze (right)

1. Drain pineapple, reserving juice. Add water to pineapple juice to make ¾ cup. Set crushed pineapple and juice mixture aside.

2. In small bowl with mixer at high speed, beat egg whites and cream of tartar until soft peaks form. Beating at high speed, sprinkle in ½ cup sugar, 2 tablespoons at a time, beating well after each addition until sugar is completely dissolved. (Whites should stand in stiff, glossy peaks.)

3. Preheat oven to 350°F. In large bowl with same beaters and with mixer at high speed, beat egg yolks, flour, baking powder, salt, almond extract, pineapple-juice mixture, and ½ cup sugar until light and fluffy, about 3 minutes. With rubber spatula, gently fold egg-white mixture and crushed pineapple into flour mixture just until blended.

4. Pour batter into ungreased 10-inch tube pan. Bake 60 to 65 minutes until top of cake springs back when lightly touched with finger. Invert cake in pan on bottle: cool completely.

5. To serve, with metal spatula, gently loosen cake from pan and remove to plate. Prepare Almond Glaze; spread glaze over cake.

Almond Glaze: In small bowl, mix *1 cup confectioners' sugar, 2 tablespoons milk*, and *¾ teaspoon almond extract* until smooth.

197

Cinnamon-Apple Cake

TIME: about 2 hours or start early in day—SERVINGS: 12

5 medium red cooking apples,
  such as Rome Beauty
1¾ cups sugar
1 cup butter or margarine,
  softened
3 cups all-purpose flour
1 cup milk
2 teaspoons ground cinnamon
1 teaspoon double-acting baking
  powder
1 teaspoon salt
2 teaspoons vanilla extract
3 eggs
¾ cup pecans, chopped
3 tablespoons apple jelly

1. Peel and dice 3 apples. Core and slice remaining apples into rings; cut each ring in half; set aside.

2. Preheat oven to 350°F. Grease and flour 13" by 9" baking dish. In large bowl with mixer at high speed, beat sugar and butter or margarine until light and fluffy. Reduce speed to low; add flour and next 6 ingredients; beat just until blended. Increase speed to medium; beat 3 minutes.

3. With rubber spatula, gently fold pecans and diced apples into batter. Spread batter evenly in prepared baking dish. Arrange apple slices on top of batter.

4. In 1-quart saucepan over medium heat, melt apple jelly. With a pastry brush, brush apple jelly over apple slices. Bake 45 to 50 minutes, until toothpick inserted in center of cake comes out clean. Serve cake warm or cool cake in pan on wire rack to serve later.

Fruit Savarin

TIME: start day ahead—SERVINGS: 16

1 package active dry yeast
2 cups all-purpose flour
sugar
salt
½ cup milk
6 tablespoons butter or
  margarine
2 eggs
2 cups orange juice
2 tablespoons lemon juice
¼ cup orange-flavor liqueur
½ cup apricot preserves
1 large red eating apple
1 large pear
½ pound red or green seedless
  grapes
1 cup heavy or whipping cream

1. In large bowl, combine yeast, ½ cup flour, 2 tablespoons sugar, and ½ teaspoon salt. In 1-quart saucepan over low heat, heat milk and butter or margarine until very warm (120° to 130°F.). (Butter or margarine does not need to melt completely.) With mixer at low speed, gradually beat liquid into dry ingredients. Increase speed to medium; beat 2 minutes, occasionally scraping bowl with rubber spatula. Gradually beat in eggs and ½ cup flour to make a thick batter; continue beating 2 minutes, occasionally scraping bowl. With wooden spoon, stir in 1 cup flour to make a soft dough.

2. Cover bowl with towel; let dough rise in warm place (80° to 85°F.), away from draft, until doubled, about 1 hour. (Dough is doubled when it looks bubbly and moist, with an uneven, soft top.)

3. Grease 8-cup fluted ring mold or 10-inch Bundt pan. With spoon, stir down dough. Spread dough evenly in mold. Cover with towel; let rise in warm place until doubled, about 45 minutes. (Dough is doubled when 1 finger very lightly pressed against dough leaves a dent.)

4. Preheat oven to 350°F. Bake cake 20 to 25 minutes until golden and top sounds hollow when lightly tapped. Cool cake in mold on wire rack 15 minutes.

5. While cake is cooling, prepare orange sauce: In 2-quart saucepan, combine orange juice, lemon juice, ¼ cup sugar, and ½ teaspoon salt; cook over medium heat until sugar is dissolved, about 5 minutes, stirring frequently. Remove from heat; stir in orange-flavor liqueur.

6. With skewer or toothpick, prick cake in many places. Slowly spoon half of orange sauce over cake; let cake remain in mold 15 minutes. Invert cake from mold onto rack in jelly-roll pan; prick holes

in top; slowly spoon remaining orange sauce over cake. Let cake stand 20 minutes, basting with sauce that dripped in jelly-roll pan until all sauce is absorbed. Wrap cake in plastic wrap and refrigerate.

7. To serve, in 1-quart saucepan over low heat, melt apricot preserves, stirring occasionally. Place cake on dessert platter; brush cake with apricot preserves. Cut apple and pear into bite-sized chunks; toss with grapes. Spoon fruit in center of cake. In small bowl with mixer at medium speed, beat heavy or whipping cream until soft peaks form. Spoon whipped cream into small bowl to serve with cake and fruit.

Applesauce Fig Cake

TIME: about 2 hours—SERVINGS: 8

1 8- to 8½-ounce jar or can applesauce
1¼ cups all-purpose flour
⅓ cup sugar
⅓ cup shortening
1 teaspoon baking soda
½ teaspoon ground cinnamon
½ teaspoon salt
¼ teaspoon ground cloves
1 egg
milk
¾ cup dried figs, chopped
½ cup California walnuts, chopped
1 3-ounce package cream cheese, softened
2 tablespoons honey

1. Preheat oven to 350°F. Grease and flour 9" by 9" baking pan. In large bowl, with fork or wire whisk, mix first 9 ingredients and 3 tablespoons milk until well blended. Stir in figs and walnuts.

2. Spoon batter into prepared pan. Bake cake 30 minutes or until toothpick inserted in center comes out clean. Cool cake in pan on wire rack.

3. Meanwhile, in small bowl with mixer at high speed, beat cream cheese, honey, and 1 teaspoon milk until smooth; cover; refrigerate.

4. To serve, cut cake into 8 pieces. Top each piece with a dollop of cream-cheese mixture.

Cinnamon-Spice Ring

TIME: about 3 hours or start early in day—SERVINGS: 16

1½ cups all-purpose flour
1½ cups whole-wheat flour
1 cup butter or margarine, softened
¾ cup packed brown sugar
½ cup molasses
1½ teaspoons baking soda
1 teaspoon ground cinnamon
½ teaspoon salt
¼ teaspoon ground cloves
1 8-ounce container sour cream
2 eggs
1 cup California walnuts, chopped
Lemon Glaze (right)

1. Preheat oven to 325°F. Grease 12-cup ring mold or 9-inch tube pan. Into large bowl, measure all ingredients except walnuts and glaze. With mixer at low speed, beat ingredients until well mixed, constantly scraping bowl with rubber spatula. Increase speed to medium: beat 3 minutes, occasionally scraping bowl.

2. With rubber spatula, fold in walnuts. Pour batter into prepared pan. Bake 50 to 55 minutes until toothpick inserted in center of cake comes out clean. Cool cake in pan on wire rack 10 minutes; remove cake from pan; let cool completely on wire rack.

3. Prepare Lemon Glaze. Spread glaze over cake.

Lemon Glaze: In cup, stir ¾ cup confectioners' sugar and 1 to 2 tablespoons lemon juice until smooth and of easy spreading consistency.

Brittle Cake

TIME: about 40 minutes—SERVINGS: 8

1 10¾- to 12-ounce frozen
  ready-to-serve pound cake
1 cup heavy or whipping cream
1 1.6-ounce bar peanut candy*
  or 1½ ounces peanut brittle,
  ground
2 tablespoons raspberry or
  strawberry preserves

*Or, substitute ⅓ cup whole
blanched almonds, toasted and
ground, for peanut candy.

1. With sharp knife, slice frozen cake horizontally into 3 layers.

2. In small bowl with mixer at medium speed, beat heavy or whipping cream until soft peaks form. Set aside 1 tablespoon ground peanut candy; fold remaining peanut candy into whipped cream.

3. To assemble cake, place one cake layer on serving plate; spread with 1 tablespoon preserves, then with ½ cup whipped-cream mixture. Repeat layering, ending with cake. Cover top and sides of cake with remaining whipped-cream mixture. Sprinkle reserved peanut candy over top. Refrigerate.

Nut-Cracker Cake

TIME: about 3½ hours or start day ahead—SERVINGS: 16

3 squares semisweet chocolate
6 eggs, separated, at room
  temperature
sugar
¼ cup all-purpose flour
2 tablespoons salad oil
1¼ teaspoons double-acting
  baking powder
1 teaspoon ground cinnamon
1½ teaspoons almond extract
¼ teaspoon ground cloves
1 cup California walnuts, finely
  chopped
1 cup graham-cracker crumbs
2 cups heavy or whipping cream

1. Grate 1 square semisweet chocolate; set aside. Grease and flour two 8-inch round cake pans.

2. In large bowl with mixer at high speed, beat egg whites until soft peaks form; gradually beat in ½ cup sugar, 2 tablespoons at a time, beating after each addition until sugar is completely dissolved. (Whites should stand in stiff, glossy peaks.)

3. Preheat oven to 350°F. With same beaters, in small bowl with mixer at low speed, beat flour, next 5 ingredients, egg yolks, and ½ cup sugar until well mixed, constantly scraping bowl with rubber spatula. Increase speed to medium and beat 2 minutes, occasionally scraping bowl.

4. Reserve 2 teaspoons chopped walnuts for garnish. With rubber spatula, gently fold egg-yolk mixture into beaten egg whites; then fold in graham-cracker crumbs, grated chocolate, and remaining chopped walnuts.

5. Pour batter into pans and bake 30 minutes or until toothpick inserted in center of cakes comes out clean. Cool cakes in pans on wire racks 10 minutes; remove from pans and cool completely on racks.

6. Meanwhile, with vegetable peeler, shave curls from remaining chocolate for garnish.

7. When cake is cool, with serrated knife, cut each cake horizontally in half to form 2 layers; set aside.

8. In large bowl with mixer at medium speed, beat heavy or whipping cream until soft peaks form. Reserve ½ cup whipped cream for garnish. Place 1 cake layer on cake platter; spread with one-fourth of remaining whipped cream. Repeat with remaining cake layers and whipped cream. Spoon reserved whipped cream into decorating bag with large star tube; use to decorate top of cake. Garnish cake with reserved chopped walnuts and chocolate curls. Refrigerate until serving time.

Honey-Nut Chiffon Cake

TIME: start early in day or day ahead—SERVINGS: 16

7 eggs, separated, at room
    temperature
½ teaspoon cream of tartar
½ cup sugar
2¼ cups all-purpose flour
¾ cup apple juice
½ cup honey
½ cup salad oil
1 tablespoon double-acting
    baking powder
1 teaspoon vanilla extract
½ teaspoon salt
1 cup California walnuts,
    chopped

1. Preheat oven to 325°F. In large bowl with mixer at high speed, beat egg whites and cream of tartar until soft peaks form. Beating at high speed, gradually beat in sugar, 2 tablespoons at a time, beating after each addition until sugar is completely dissolved. (Whites should stand in stiff, glossy peaks.)

2. In another large bowl with same beaters and with mixer at low speed, beat egg yolks, flour, and remaining ingredients except walnuts until well blended, scraping bowl often with rubber spatula. Stir in walnuts.

3. With rubber spatula or wire whisk, gently fold flour mixture into beaten egg whites just until blended. Pour batter into ungreased 10-inch tube pan. Bake 1¼ hours or until top springs back when lightly touched with finger. Invert cake in pan on funnel or bottle; cool completely in pan.

4. To serve, with metal spatula, carefully loosen cake from pan; place on cake plate.

Orange Chiffon Cake

TIME: about 3½ hours or start early in day—SERVINGS: 16

1 cup egg whites, at room
    temperature (7 or 8 egg
    whites)
½ teaspoon cream of tartar
sugar
2¼ cups cake flour
¾ cup orange juice
½ cup salad oil
1 tablespoon double-acting
    baking powder
3 tablespoons grated orange peel
1 teaspoon salt
5 egg yolks
Fluffy Orange Frosting (right)

1. Preheat oven to 325°F. In large bowl with mixer at high speed, beat egg whites and cream of tartar until soft peaks form; beating at high speed, gradually sprinkle in ½ cup sugar, 2 tablespoons at a time; beat until sugar is completely dissolved. (Whites should stand in stiff, glossy peaks.) Do not scrape sides of bowl during beating. Set aside.

2. In another large bowl, with mixer at low speed, beat 1 cup sugar with remaining ingredients except frosting until blended. With rubber spatula, gently fold mixture into beaten egg whites.

3. Pour batter into ungreased 10-inch tube pan and bake 1 hour and 15 minutes or until top springs back when lightly touched with finger. Invert cake in pan on bottle; cool completely. Frost top and sides with Fluffy Orange Frosting. Keep refrigerated.

Fluffy Orange Frosting: In small saucepan over medium heat, heat *one 12-ounce jar sweet orange marmalade** to boiling, stirring occasionally. In large bowl with mixer at high speed, beat *2 egg whites,* at room temperature, *½ teaspoon vanilla extract, 10 drops yellow food color,* and *dash salt* just until soft peaks form. Slowly pour in hot preserves, continuing to beat for 6 to 8 minutes until frosting is fluffy and forms peaks when beaters are raised.

*If using a bitter marmalade, beat in sugar to taste.

Torta di Mandorla (Almond Torte)

TIME: about 2½ hours or start day ahead—SERVINGS: 10

1½ cups all-purpose flour
1 cup butter or margarine,
  softened
¾ cup sugar
⅓ cup milk
1¼ teaspoons double-acting
  baking powder
1 teaspoon grated orange peel
¼ teaspoon salt
¼ teaspoon almond extract
3 eggs
1 cup whole blanched almonds,
  finely ground
⅓ cup apricot preserves
confectioners' sugar

1. Grease 9″ by 2″ springform pan. Preheat oven to 350°F.

2. In large bowl with mixer at low speed, beat first 9 ingredients just until blended, constantly scraping bowl with rubber spatula. Continue beating 2 minutes, occasionally scraping bowl. Stir in ground almonds. Spoon batter into prepared pan. Bake 40 minutes or until toothpick inserted in center of cake comes out clean. Cool cake in pan on wire rack 10 minutes. Remove cake from pan; cool completely.

3. With serrated knife, cut cake horizontally in half to make 2 layers. Place 1 layer on cake platter; spread with apricot preserves. Top with remaining cake layer. On sheet of waxed paper, trace 9-inch circle. From half of circle, cut 5 equal wedges. Evenly space wedges on top of torte. Sprinkle top of torte with confectioners' sugar. Carefully remove waxed-paper wedges.

Walnut-Maple Torte

TIME: about 3 hours or start early in day—SERVINGS: 12

3¼ cups California walnuts
sugar
3 tablespoons all-purpose flour
1 teaspoon double-acting baking
  powder
¼ teaspoon salt
6 eggs, separated, at room
  temperature
½ teaspoon maple-flavor extract
1 cup heavy or whipping cream

1. In blender at medium speed, blend about ½ cup walnuts and 2 teaspoons sugar until nuts are very finely ground; remove to medium bowl. Repeat until all walnuts are ground, each time using about ½ cup walnuts and 2 teaspoons sugar. (Sugar absorbs some of the moisture in the walnuts and helps to keep them from caking during blending.) Reserve 2 teaspoons ground-walnut mixture for garnish.

2. Preheat oven to 350°F. Grease two 9-inch round cake pans; line bottoms with waxed paper; grease paper. In medium bowl combine flour, baking powder, salt, and remaining ground-walnut mixture.

3. In large bowl with mixer at high speed, beat egg whites until soft peaks form.

4. In small bowl with mixer at high speed, beat egg yolks, maple extract, and ¾ cup sugar until thick. With wire whisk or rubber spatula, gently fold nut mixture, then yolk mixture into beaten egg whites.

5. Pour batter into prepared pans. Bake 25 minutes or until top of cake springs back when touched with finger. Cool cake in pans on wire racks 5 minutes. Remove cake from pans; remove waxed paper and cool cake layers completely on wire racks.

6. In small bowl with mixer at medium speed, beat heavy cream until soft peaks form. Place 1 cake layer on cake plate; spread with about two thirds of whipped cream. Spoon remaining whipped cream into decorating bag with a large rosette tube; use to decorate top of torte. Sprinkle whipped cream on top of torte with reserved ground-walnut mixture. Refrigerate cake until serving time.

Strawberry Shortcake

TIME: about 45 minutes—SERVINGS: 10

2 cups all-purpose flour
2 teaspoons double-acting
  baking powder
1 teaspoon salt
sugar
⅓ cup shortening
⅔ cup milk
2 pints strawberries
3 tablespoons butter or
  margarine, softened
1 cup heavy or whipping cream,
  whipped

1. Preheat oven to 425°F. Grease 8-inch round cake pan. In medium bowl, with fork, mix flour, baking powder, salt, and 2 tablespoons sugar. With pastry blender or 2 knives used scissor-fashion, cut in shortening until mixture resembles coarse crumbs. Add milk; with fork, quickly stir just until mixture forms soft dough and leaves side of bowl.

2. On lightly floured surface with floured hands, knead dough 10 times. Pat dough evenly into prepared pan. Bake 15 minutes or until golden.

3. Meanwhile, wash strawberries. Reserve 4 whole strawberries for garnish; hull and halve or quarter remaining strawberries. In medium bowl, with rubber spatula, toss cut-up strawberries with ½ cup sugar until sugar dissolves. (Do *not* let strawberries stand too long or they will become very liquidy.)

4. Invert shortcake on work surface. With long serrated knife, carefully split hot shortcake horizontally. Spread both cut surfaces of shortcake with butter or margarine.

5. Place bottom half of shortcake, cut-side up, on dessert platter; top with half of strawberry mixture. Arrange top cake half, cut-side down, on strawberry mixture. Spoon remaining strawberry mixture over top of cake. Pile whipped cream on top of strawberries. Garnish cream with reserved whole strawberries.

Blueberry Buckle

TIME: about 1½ hours or start early in day—SERVINGS: 12

1 tablespoon double-acting
  baking powder
1 teaspoon salt
all-purpose flour
sugar
butter or margarine
½ cup milk
1 egg, slightly beaten
1 pint frozen blueberries*
  (3 cups)
1 teaspoon ground cinnamon

*Use only frozen blueberries that are
packed without sugar.

1. Preheat oven to 375°F. In large bowl, with fork, mix baking powder, salt, 2 cups flour, and ¼ cup sugar. With pastry blender or 2 knives used scissor-fashion, cut in ½ cup butter or margarine until mixture resembles coarse crumbs; add milk and egg. With fork, quickly stir just until flour mixture forms a soft dough and leaves side of bowl. Pat mixture into 9″ by 9″ by 2″ baking pan. (If desired, use baking pan with removable bottom so cake can be removed from pan in one piece.) Sprinkle frozen blueberries over mixture in pan.

2. Prepare crumb topping: in same bowl, combine cinnamon, ½ cup flour, ½ cup sugar, and 4 tablespoons butter or margarine. With hands, quickly knead ingredients together until mixture resembles large crumbs. Sprinkle topping over blueberries.

3. Bake dessert 1 hour or until toothpick inserted in center comes out clean and topping is golden brown. Cool dessert in pan on wire rack 15 minutes. Serve warm or cool completely to serve later. Cut into 12 pieces.

Individual Blueberry Crisps

TIME: about 40 minutes—SERVINGS: 6

¼ teaspoon ground cinnamon
1 21-ounce can blueberry-pie
  filling
⅓ cup all-purpose flour
¼ cup sugar
1 tablespoon salad oil
½ teaspoon double-acting
  baking powder
⅛ teaspoon salt
1 egg
½ 8-ounce container sour cream

1. Stir cinnamon into blueberry-pie filling. Spoon blueberry mixture into six 6-ounce custard cups. Set custard cups in 15½" by 10½" jelly-roll pan for easier handling; set aside.

2. Preheat oven to 350°F. In small bowl, with spoon, mix flour and remaining ingredients except sour cream just until blended. Spoon batter on top of blueberry mixture in custard cups. Bake 20 minutes or until top is golden.

3. To serve, garnish top of each serving with a dollop of sour cream.

Blueberry Snacking Cake

TIME: about 2½ hours or start early in day—SERVINGS: 25

2¾ cups all-purpose flour
1 cup milk
¾ cup sugar
⅔ cup butter or margarine,
  softened
2½ teaspoons double-acting
  baking powder
1 teaspoon vanilla extract
½ teaspoon salt
3 eggs
1 pint blueberries (about 2½
  cups)
1 cup California walnuts,
  coarsely chopped

1. Preheat oven to 350°F. Grease 15½" by 10½" jelly-roll pan.

2. In large bowl with mixer at low speed, beat first 8 ingredients until just blended, constantly scraping bowl with rubber spatula. Increase speed to medium; beat 2 minutes, occasionally scraping bowl. With rubber spatula, gently fold in blueberries and walnuts. Spread batter evenly in prepared pan.

3. Bake 45 minutes or until toothpick inserted in center comes out clean. Cool in pan on wire rack. Cut cake crosswise into 5 strips; then cut each strip into 5 pieces.

Blueberry Coffee Cake

TIME: about 2 hours or start early in day—SERVINGS: 16

Pecan Topping (right)
1 cup butter or margarine
1 cup sugar
1¾ cups all-purpose flour
2 teaspoons double-acting
  baking powder
2 teaspoons grated lemon peel
¼ teaspoon salt
4 eggs
1 pint blueberries

1. Prepare Pecan Topping; set aside.

2. Preheat oven to 325°F. Grease and flour 13" by 9" baking dish. In large bowl with mixer at medium speed, beat butter or margarine and sugar until light and fluffy. Reduce speed to low; add flour, baking powder, lemon peel, salt, and eggs; beat just until blended, occasionally scraping bowl with rubber spatula. Increase speed to medium; beat until smooth.

3. Spread batter evenly in baking dish; top with blueberries. Pinch Pecan Topping into small pieces; sprinkle on cake. Bake 45 minutes or until golden and toothpick inserted in center comes out clean. Serve warm, or cool coffee cake completely on wire rack to serve cold later.

Pecan Topping: In small saucepan over medium heat, melt ½ cup *butter* or margarine; remove saucepan from heat. Stir in *1 cup all-purpose flour*, *½ cup pecans*, chopped, *¼ cup sugar*, and *1 tablespoon grated lemon peel* to form a soft dough.

Butter-Rich Coffee Cake

TIME: about 4½ hours or start day ahead—**SERVINGS:** 16

2 teaspoons grated lemon peel
¼ teaspoon salt
1 package active dry yeast
sugar
about 4 cups all-purpose flour
¾ cup milk
1¼ cups butter or margarine
1 egg
¼ cup sliced blanched almonds

1. In large bowl, combine lemon peel, salt, yeast, ½ cup sugar, and 1 cup flour. In 1-quart saucepan over low heat, heat milk and ½ cup butter or margarine until very warm (120° to 130°F.). (Butter or margarine does not need to melt completely.)

2. With mixer at low speed, gradually beat liquid into dry ingredients just until blended. Increase speed to medium; beat 2 minutes, occasionally scraping bowl with rubber spatula. Gradually beat in egg and 1 cup flour to make a thick batter; continue beating 2 minutes longer, scraping bowl often. With wooden spoon, stir in 1¾ cups flour to make a soft dough.

3. Turn dough onto well-floured surface and knead until smooth and elastic, about 10 minutes, working in about ¼ cup more flour while kneading. Shape dough into a ball and place in greased medium bowl, turning dough over so that top is greased. Cover bowl with towel and let rise in warm place (80° to 85°F.), away from draft, until doubled, about 1 hour. (Dough is doubled when two fingers pressed lightly into dough leave a dent.)

4. Punch down dough. Turn dough onto lightly floured surface; cover with bowl and let rest for 15 minutes for easier rolling.

5. With floured rolling pin, roll dough into 15" by 10" rectangle. Cut ½ cup butter or margarine into thin slices. Starting at one of the 10-inch sides, place half of butter slices over two-thirds of rectangle to within ½ inch of edges. Fold unbuttered third of dough over middle third; fold opposite end over to make 5" by 10" rectangle.

6. Again roll dough into 15" by 10" rectangle. Place remaining butter slices on dough and fold as in step 5. Wrap folded dough in plastic wrap; chill 15 minutes for easier rolling.

7. Meanwhile, grease 15½" by 10½" jelly-roll pan. Roll folded dough into 15½" by 10½" rectangle; place in jelly-roll pan. Cover pan with towel and let rise in warm place until doubled, about 1 hour. (Dough is doubled when one finger very lightly pressed against dough leaves a dent.)

8. Preheat oven to 375°F. In 1-quart saucepan over medium-low heat, melt remaining ¼ cup butter or margarine. Remove saucepan from heat; stir in ¼ cup sugar; set aside. With thumb, make deep indentations in dough, about 1 inch apart. With pastry brush, brush butter mixture over top of dough; sprinkle with almonds. Bake 20 minutes or until lightly golden. Cool cake in pan on wire rack 10 minutes. Serve warm or cool cake completely on wire rack to serve later.

Plum-Peach Coffee Cake

TIME: about 2 hours or start early in day—SERVINGS: 16

Crumb Topping (right)
1 30- to 31-ounce can whole
   purple plums, drained
1 cup butter or magarine,
   softened
1 cup sugar
1¾ cups all-purpose flour
2 teaspoons double-acting
   baking powder
2 teaspoons grated lemon peel
¼ teaspoon salt
4 eggs
1 16-ounce can sliced cling
   peaches, drained

1. Prepare Crumb Topping; set aside. Cut each plum in half; discard pit.

2. Preheat oven to 325°F. Grease and flour 13″ by 9″ baking dish. In large bowl with mixer at medium speed, beat butter or margarine and sugar until light and fluffy. Reduce speed to low; add flour and next 4 ingredients; beat just until blended, occasionally scraping bowl with rubber spatula. Increase speed to medium; beat until smooth.

3. Spread batter evenly in baking dish; top with half of plums. Pinch Crumb Topping into small pieces; sprinkle on top of cake. Bake cake 20 minutes. Quickly top cake with peaches and remaining plums; bake 30 to 35 minutes longer until top of cake is golden and toothpick inserted in center comes out clean. Serve warm or cool cake completely on wire rack to serve cold later.

Crumb Topping: In small saucepan over medium heat, melt ½ cup butter or margarine; remove saucepan from heat. Stir in 1 cup all-purpose flour, ¼ cup sugar, and 1 tablespoon grated lemon peel to form soft dough.

Toasted Coconut Pound Cakes

TIME: about 3 hours or start day ahead—
YIELD: 2 large or 6 small loaves

2 16-ounce packages pound-
   cake mix
1 cup toasted coconut flakes*
1 tablespoon lemon juice

*Or, spread 1 cup flaked coconut
evenly in jelly-roll pan; bake in
325°F. oven 10 minutes or until
delicately browned, stirring often.

1. Preheat oven to 325°F. Grease and flour six 5¾″ by 3¼″ loaf pans or two 8½″ by 4½″ loaf pans. In large bowl, prepare both packages of pound-cake mix together as label directs; then stir in coconut flakes and lemon juice.

2. Pour batter into pans; bake small loaves 1 hour and large loaves 1 hour and 35 minutes or until toothpick inserted in center of loaf comes out clean. Cool loaves in pans on wire racks 10 minutes; remove from pans and cool completely on racks.

Golden German Pound Cake

TIME: about 3 hours or start day ahead—SERVINGS: 24

2 cups sugar
1 cup butter or margarine,
   softened
3½ cups cake flour
1 cup milk
1½ teaspoons double-acting
   baking powder
2 teaspoons vanilla extract
⅛ teaspoon salt
6 egg yolks
confectioners' sugar

1. Preheat oven to 350°F. Grease and flour 10-inch Bundt pan* or two 9″ by 5″ loaf pans. Into large bowl, measure sugar and butter or margarine; with mixer at high speed, beat until light and fluffy. Add flour and next 5 ingredients; at low speed, beat until well mixed, constantly scraping bowl with rubber spatula. Beat at high speed 4 minutes, occasionally scraping bowl.

2. Pour batter into pan and bake in Bundt pan 1 hour or in loaf pans 45 to 50 minutes, until toothpick inserted in center comes out clean. Cool cake in pan on wire rack 10 minutes; remove from pan; cool completely on rack. If desired, lightly sprinkle top of cake with confectioners' sugar. Makes 1 ring, or 2 loaves.

*Bundt pan will give best, most attractive results.

Scandinavian Tea Cake

TIME: about 4½ hours or start early in day—SERVINGS: 12

⅓ cup sugar
¼ teaspoon salt
1 package active dry yeast
about 3 cups all-purpose flour
¾ cup milk
butter or margarine
1 egg
½ cup packed light brown sugar
½ cup golden raisins
1½ teaspoons ground cinnamon
Confectioners' Glaze (right)

1. In large bowl, combine sugar, salt, yeast, and ¾ cup flour. In small saucepan over low heat, heat milk and 6 tablespoons butter or margarine until very warm (120° to 130°F.). (Butter or margarine does not need to melt completely.)

2. With mixer at low speed, gradually beat liquid into dry ingredients just until blended. Increase speed to medium; beat 2 minutes, occasionally scraping bowl with rubber spatula. Gradually beat in egg and 1 cup flour to make a thick batter; continue beating 2 minutes, scraping bowl often. With wooden spoon, stir in 1 cup flour to make a soft dough.

3. Turn dough onto well-floured surface and knead until smooth and elastic, about 5 minutes, working in about ¼ cup more flour while kneading. Shape dough into a ball and place in greased large bowl, turning dough over so that top is greased. Cover bowl with towel and let rise in warm place (80° to 85°F.), away from draft, until doubled, about 1 hour. (Dough is doubled when two fingers pressed lightly into dough leave a dent.)

4. Punch down dough. Turn dough onto lightly floured surface; cover with bowl and let rest 15 minutes for easier shaping. Grease large cookie sheet. In small saucepan over low heat, melt 2 tablespoons butter or margarine.

5. With floured rolling pin, roll dough into a 14-inch square. With pastry brush, brush dough with melted butter or margarine; sprinkle with brown sugar, raisins, and cinnamon. Roll dough, jelly-roll fashion; place, seam-side down, on cookie sheet. Shape roll into ring; press ends together to seal and tuck under. With kitchen shears, cut ring, up to but not through inside edge, at 1-inch intervals. Starting at top of ring, and moving cookie sheet clockwise, gently pull and twist each cut piece, arranging pieces slightly overlapping. Cover with towel and let rise in warm place until doubled, about 1 hour. (Dough is doubled when one finger very lightly pressed against dough leaves a dent.)

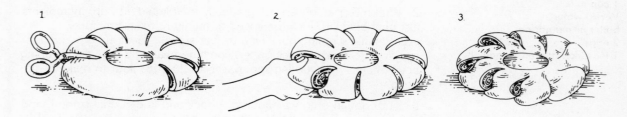

6. Preheat oven to 350°F. Bake 25 minutes or until ring sounds hollow when lightly tapped with fingers. Cool ring on wire rack. Prepare Confectioners' Glaze; spoon glaze over cake.

Confectioners' Glaze: In small saucepan over low heat, melt *1 tablespoon butter* or margarine; remove saucepan from heat. Stir in *1 cup confectioners' sugar, ½ teaspoon vanilla extract,* and *1 to 2 tablespoons milk* until smooth and easy spreading consistency.

207

Jelly Roll

TIME: about 2 hours or start early in day—SERVINGS: 10

¾ cup all-purpose flour
1 teaspoon double-acting baking
  powder
½ teaspoon salt
4 eggs, separated, at room
  temperature
sugar
½ teaspoon vanilla extract
confectioners' sugar
1 10-ounce jar currant jelly or
  other favorite jelly

1. Grease 15½" by 10½" jelly-roll pan; line with waxed paper.

2. Preheat oven to 375°F. In small bowl, with fork, stir flour, baking powder, and salt; set aside. In another small bowl with mixer at high speed, beat egg whites until soft peaks form. Beating at high speed, gradually sprinkle in ⅓ cup sugar, beating until sugar is completely dissolved. (Whites should stand in stiff, glossy peaks.)

3. In large bowl with same beaters and with mixer at high speed, beat egg yolks until thick and lemon-colored; beating at high speed, gradually sprinkle in ½ cup sugar. Beat in vanilla.

4. With rubber spatula, gently fold flour mixture and beaten egg whites into egg-yolk mixture until thoroughly blended. Spread batter evenly in pan and bake 15 minutes or until top springs back when lightly touched with finger.

5. Meanwhile, generously sprinkle clean cloth towel with about ⅓ cup confectioners' sugar. When cake is done, immediately invert cake onto towel; carefully peel waxed paper from cake. Starting at narrow end, roll cake with towel, jelly-roll fashion. Cool completely on rack.

6. When cake is cool, unroll cake; spread top evenly with jelly. Starting at same narrow end, roll cake without towel. Sprinkle roll with confectioners' sugar.

Cinnamon Bubble Ring

TIME: about 4½ hours or start day ahead—YIELD: 1 loaf

1 teaspoon salt
2 packages active dry yeast
sugar
about 6 cups all-purpose flour
1 cup milk
½ cup water
butter or margarine
2 eggs
1 teaspoon ground cinnamon

1. In large bowl, combine salt, yeast, ½ cup sugar, and 2 cups flour. In 1-quart saucepan over low heat, heat milk, water, and 4 tablespoons butter or margarine until very warm (120° to 130°F.). (Butter or margarine does not need to melt completely.)

2. With mixer at low speed, gradually beat liquid into dry ingredients just until blended. Increase speed to medium; beat 2 minutes, occasionally scraping bowl with rubber spatula. Beat in eggs and 1 cup flour to make a thick batter; continue beating 2 minutes, scraping bowl often. With wooden spoon, stir in 2½ cups flour to make a soft dough. ·

3. Turn dough onto well-floured surface and knead until smooth and elastic, about 10 minutes, working in about ½ cup more flour while kneading. Shape dough into a ball and place in greased large bowl, turning dough over so that top is greased. Cover bowl with towel and let rise in warm place (80° to 85°F.), away from draft, until doubled, about 1 hour. (Dough is doubled when two fingers pressed lightly into dough leave a dent.)

4. Punch down dough. Turn dough onto lightly floured surface; cover with bowl and let rest 15 minutes for easier shaping.

5. Meanwhile, in small bowl, combine cinnamon and ½ cup sugar;

set aside. In small saucepan over low heat, melt 2 tablespoons butter or margarine; set aside. Grease 10-inch tube pan.

6. Cut dough in half; cut each half into 16 pieces. Shape each piece into a ball by tucking ends under. Place half of balls in tube pan; brush with one-half of melted butter or margarine; sprinkle with one-half of sugar mixture. Repeat with remaining balls, melted butter, and sugar mixture. Cover pan with towel; let rise in warm place until doubled, about 45 minutes. (Dough is doubled when one finger very lightly pressed against dough leaves a dent.)

7. Preheat oven to 350°F. Bake 30 to 35 minutes until loaf is browned and sounds hollow when lightly tapped with fingers. If top browns too quickly, cover with foil during last 10 minutes of baking time. Cool loaf in pan on wire rack 5 minutes; remove loaf from pan; serve warm or cool loaf completely on wire rack; wrap with foil. Just before serving, warm loaf in 350°F. oven 10 to 15 minutes to heat through. Serve as coffee cake. If desired, let each person pull off his own serving of bread. Makes 32 servings.

Cake Roll with Lemon-Curd Filling

TIME: about 4 hours or start early in day—SERVINGS: 16

2 medium lemons
½ cup butter or margarine
sugar
8 eggs
¾ cup all-purpose flour
⅔ cup cornstarch
½ teaspoon salt
confectioners' sugar
Lemon Glaze (right)
about 1 tablespoon sliced
   blanched almonds, toasted
   (optional)
about 1 teaspoon assorted
   cinnamon decors (optional)

1. Prepare lemon-curd filling: From lemons, grate 1 tablespoon peel and squeeze ¼ cup juice. In double boiler over hot, *not boiling,* water, or in heavy 2-quart saucepan over low heat, stir lemon peel, lemon juice, butter or margarine, and ¾ cup sugar until butter is melted.

2. In small bowl, with fork or wire whisk, beat 2 eggs; add eggs to butter mixture and cook, stirring constantly, until mixture is very thick and coats the back of a spoon well, about 15 minutes. Cover and refrigerate lemon curd 3 hours or until very cold.

3. Meanwhile, prepare cake roll: Preheat oven to 350°F. Grease 15½" by 10½" jelly-roll pan; line with waxed paper. In small bowl with fork, mix well flour, cornstarch, and salt; set aside. In large bowl with mixer at high speed, beat ¾ cup sugar and 6 eggs until very thick, about 10 minutes. Gently fold flour mixture, one third at a time, into egg mixture. Spread batter in jelly-roll pan; bake 20 to 25 minutes until golden and top of cake springs back when lightly touched with finger.

4. Lightly sprinkle clean cloth towel with confectioners' sugar. When cake is done, immediately invert cake onto towel. Carefully peel waxed paper from cake. Starting at a narrow end, roll cake with towel, jelly-roll fashion. Place cake, seam-side down, on wire rack to cool.

5. When ready to fill cake, unroll cake. Spread top of cake evenly with lemon curd. Starting at same narrow end, reroll cake without towel. Place cake, seam-side down, on platter.

6. Prepare Lemon Glaze. Spread glaze over cake roll. If desired, garnish top of cake with sliced almonds and cinnamon decors to make flowers. Refrigerate cake until serving time.

Lemon Glaze: In small bowl, mix *1 cup confectioners' sugar, 5 teaspoons lemon juice,* and *1 teaspoon lemon peel* until smooth.

Colonial Gingerbread

TIME: about 3 hours or start early in day—SERVINGS: 12

2 cups all-purpose flour
1 cup molasses
¾ cup buttermilk
½ cup sugar
½ cup butter or margarine, softened
1 teaspoon baking soda
1 teaspoon ground ginger
1 teaspoon ground cinnamon
½ teaspoon salt
1 egg
confectioners' sugar

1. Preheat oven to 325°F. Grease and flour 9" by 9" by 2" baking pan.

2. Into large bowl, measure all ingredients except confectioners' sugar; with mixer at low speed, beat until blended, constantly scraping bowl with rubber spatula. Increase speed to medium and continue beating 3 minutes, occasionally scraping bowl.

3. Pour batter into pan and bake 1 hour or until toothpick inserted in center comes out clean. Cool gingerbread in pan on wire rack.

4. To serve, sprinkle top of cake with confectioners' sugar.

Peanut-Butter Cupcakes

TIME: about 2 hours or start early in day—YIELD: 24 cupcakes

1¾ cups all-purpose flour
1 cup milk
¾ cup sugar
½ cup chunky or creamy peanut butter
4 tablespoons butter or margarine, softened
1 tablespoon double-acting baking powder
¾ teaspoon vanilla extract
½ teaspoon salt
2 eggs
⅔ cup milk-chocolate pieces

1. Preheat oven to 350°F. Grease twenty-four 2½-inch muffin-pan cups.

2. Into large bowl, measure all ingredients except chocolate pieces. With mixer at low speed, beat ingredients just until blended. Increase speed to high; beat 2 minutes.

3. Spoon batter into muffin-pan cups. Top each cupcake with some milk-chocolate pieces. Bake 18 to 20 minutes until toothpick inserted in center of a cupcake comes out clean. Cool cupcakes in pans on wire racks 10 minutes; remove from pans and cool completely.

Apple-Spice Squares

TIME: about 2 hours or start up to 3 days ahead—YIELD: 24 squares

1 6-ounce can pecan halves
1½ cups whole-wheat flour
1½ cups all-purpose flour
1 cup sugar
1 cup butter or margarine, softened
¾ cup molasses
½ cup packed brown sugar
2 teaspoons baking soda
¾ teaspoon ground cinnamon
½ teaspoon salt
¼ teaspoon ground cloves
1 15-ounce jar applesauce
2 eggs

1. Reserve 24 pecan halves; chop remaining pecans.

2. Preheat oven to 350°F. Grease 15½" by 10½" jelly-roll pan. Into large bowl, measure chopped pecans, flours, and remaining ingredients. With mixer at low speed, beat ingredients until well blended, occasionally scraping bowl with rubber spatula. Increase speed to medium; beat 3 minutes.

3. Spoon mixture into jelly-roll pan. Arrange reserved pecan halves on top of mixture so that when cake is cut after cooking, pecans will be in the center of each of 24 squares. Bake 35 minutes or until toothpick inserted into center of cake comes out clean. Cool cake in pan on wire rack. Cut into about 2½" by 2½" squares.

Chocolate Party Cake

TIME: about 3 hours or start early in day—SERVINGS: 16

1 18½- to 18¾-ounce package
   devil's food cake mix with
   pudding
1 square unsweetened chocolate
1¼ cups light corn syrup
2 egg whites, at room
   temperature
dash salt
1 teaspoon vanilla extract

1. Prepare cake mix as label directs for 13″ by 9″ baking pan. Cool cake in pan as label directs; remove from pan and cool completely.

2. In small saucepan over low heat, melt chocolate. Remove saucepan from heat; let chocolate cool slightly.

3. Meanwhile, in 1-quart saucepan over medium heat, heat corn syrup to boiling; remove saucepan from heat.

4. In large bowl with mixer at high speed, beat egg whites until foamy; add salt and continue beating just until soft peaks form. Slowly pour in hot syrup and continue beating 6 to 8 minutes until frosting is fluffy and forms pointed, stiff peaks when beater is raised. Beat in vanilla.

5. Place cake on cake plate. Spread frosting on top and sides of cake. Spoon melted chocolate into small decorating bag with small writing tube (or use paper cone with tip cut to make ⅛-inch diameter hole). Pipe chocolate in parallel lines crosswise on frosting on cake. Then, draw tip of knife across lines at evenly spaced intervals, first in one direction, and then in the other to make feather design.

Happy Day Rainbow Cake

TIME: start early in day or day ahead—SERVINGS: 16

1 18½-ounce package yellow
   cake mix
2 teaspoons grated orange peel
1 cup heavy or whipping cream
⅓ cup raspberry preserves
⅓ cup apricot preserves
yellow food color
red food color
1 16-ounce package
   confectioners' sugar
¾ teaspoon cream of tartar
¾ teaspoon vanilla extract
3 egg whites
1 tablespoon water

1. Preheat oven to 350°F. Grease and flour three 9-inch square cake pans (or use three 9-inch round cake pans). Prepare cake mix as label directs, but fold in orange peel. Pour batter into cake pans; bake cake layers 20 minutes or until cake is golden and toothpick inserted in center of cake comes out clean. Cool cake as label directs.

2. Meanwhile, in small bowl with mixer at medium speed, beat heavy or whipping cream until soft peaks form. Spoon half of whipped cream into another bowl. Fold raspberry preserves into whipped cream in one bowl; fold apricot preserves into whipped cream in second bowl and stir in enough yellow and red food colors to tint filling a pretty orange color; set aside.

3. In large bowl with mixer at low speed, mix confectioners' sugar, cream of tartar, vanilla extract, and egg whites just until blended. With mixer at high speed, beat icing until soft peaks form. Stir in enough red food color to tint icing a pale pink color. Spoon about ¾ cup icing into another small bowl and stir into it enough red food color to tint icing a deep pink color. With mixer at high speed, beat icing in small bowl until stiff peaks form. Stir water into icing in large bowl until blended. Cover both bowls with plastic wrap to prevent icing from drying out.

4. Assemble cake: Place first cake layer on flat cake plate; spread with raspberry filling. Place second cake layer on raspberry filling; spread with apricot filling; top with remaining cake layer. Spread pale pink icing on sides and top of cake. Spoon deep pink icing into small decorating bag with small rosette tube; use to pipe a pretty design on sides and top of cake. For easier slicing, refrigerate cake 1 hour.

Three-Tiered Wedding Cake

TIME: start day ahead—SERVINGS: 120

14-inch, 10-inch, and 6-inch
   round cake pans
6 18.5- to 18.75-ounce packages
   yellow or white cake mix
6 cups water
3 cups sugar
3 cups cornstarch
3 cups salad oil
24 eggs
6 tablespoons grated orange peel
1 tablespoon orange extract
Orange Filling (page 213)
Boiled Icing (page 213)
Ornamental Icing (page 213)
about 3 dozen fresh roses of your
   favorite color for decoration

1. Each tier is made of 2 cake layers. To make layers: Preheat oven to 325°F. Grease and flour all three cake pans. In large bowl, prepare 2 packages cake mix together but adding 2 cups water, 1 cup sugar, 1 cup cornstarch, 1 cup salad oil, 8 eggs, 2 tablespoons grated orange peel, and 1 teaspoon orange extract; set aside 1¼ cups cake batter. Pour remaining cake batter into 14-inch cake pan. Bake 1 hour until toothpick inserted in center of cake comes out clean. Remove cake to large rack (or use oven or refrigerator rack); cool 10 minutes; remove from pan and cool completely on wire rack.

2. Turn oven control to 350°F. In large bowl, prepare 1 package cake mix but adding 1 cup water, ½ cup sugar, ½ cup cornstarch, ½ cup salad oil, 4 eggs, 1 tablespoon grated orange peel, and ½ teaspoon orange extract. Pour batter into 10-inch cake pan. Pour reserved 1¼ cups batter into 6-inch cake pan. Bake 6-inch cake 25 minutes; bake 10-inch cake 55 minutes or until toothpicks inserted in center of cakes come out clean. Cool cakes in pans on wire racks 10 minutes. Remove cakes from pans to cool completely.

3. Repeat steps 1 and 2 to make 6 cake layers in all.

4. Prepare Orange Filling.

5. Assemble cake: For bottom tier, place one 14-inch layer on large platter or large foil-covered cutting board. To make icing the cake easier, set cake platter on turntable or lazy Susan. With knife, cut 1 inch from top edge all around cake and ½ inch deep. Scoop out ½-inch-deep layer evenly from cake center to make depression for filling so cake filling will not squeeze out from cake center when cake is assembled. Fill depression on top of cake with 3½ cups Orange Filling. Place second 14-inch cake layer on top of filled cake layer. Insert 6 wooden skewers, about 5 inches long or the same height as bottom cake tier, all the way into cake to form a 9-inch circle in center of cake for support for the next tier.

6. For next tier, place 10-inch cake layer over a 10-inch round foil-covered cardboard. With knife, cut ¾ inch from top edge all around cake and ½ inch deep. Scoop out ½-inch-deep layer of cake center. Fill depression on 10-inch cake layer with 2 cups Orange Filling. Place second 10-inch cake layer on filled 10-inch cake layer. Carefully arrange 10-inch cake tier including foil-covered cardboard on center of bottom tier. Insert 6 wooden skewers, the same height as second cake tier, all the way into cake to form a 5-inch circle in center of cake for support for top tier.

7. For top tier, place 6-inch cake layer over a 6-inch round foil-covered cardboard. With knife, cut ½ inch from top edge all around and ½ inch deep. Scoop out ½-inch-deep layer of cake center. Fill depression on 6-inch cake layer with 1 cup Orange Filling. Place second 6-inch cake layer on filled 6-inch cake layer. Place 6-inch cake tier including foil-covered cardboard on center of second tier.

8. Now, tuck several strips of waxed paper around edge of bottom cake layer and cake platter to protect it from icing spills and drips.

9. Prepare Boiled Icing. When icing is ready, immediately spoon

about half of icing over top of cake, allowing icing to flow down to second tier. Quickly, using metal spatula, spread icing around side of top tier. Adding more icing as needed, spread icing on second tier. Spoon remaining icing on bottom tier; let icing flow down on side of cake; quickly and gently, with spatula, spread icing smoothly over entire bottom tier. Allow icing to set before decorating. Remove waxed-paper strips.

10. Decorate cake: Prepare Ornamental Icing; spoon into large decorating bag with medium rosette or star tube; use to decorate around sides of cake tiers.

11. Refrigerate cake or keep the cake in cool, safe place until needed. Decorate with fresh roses just before guests arrive. To serve wedding cake, see diagram (page 214).

Orange Filling: In 4-quart saucepan, combine *2¼ cups sugar, ⅔ cup cornstarch,* and *½ teaspoon salt.* Gradually stir in *3¼ cups water* until smooth; stir in *8 egg yolks,* slightly beaten. Over medium-low heat, heat to boiling; boil 1 minute, stirring constantly. Remove saucepan from heat. Stir in *1 cup orange juice, ¼ cup butter* or margarine, and *3 tablespoons grated orange peel* until butter is melted. Cover and refrigerate at least 2 hours or until mixture is chilled.

Boiled Icing: In 1-cup measure, over *¾ cup water* sprinkle *1 teaspoon unflavored gelatin;* let stand 3 minutes. Into large bowl, measure *6 cups confectioners' sugar,* and *6 egg whites.* In heavy 3-quart saucepan, combine *2½ cups sugar, 1½ cups light corn syrup,* and gelatin mixture; set candy thermometer in place. Over medium heat, heat mixture to boiling, stirring constantly, until temperature reaches 220°F., about 15 minutes.

Now, with mixer at high speed, start beating egg-white mixture in bowl until stiff and glossy. Meanwhile, continue cooking corn-syrup mixture until thermometer reaches 230°F. or until syrup spins a 2-inch thread when dropped from a spoon, stirring occasionally. Remove from heat. (If desired, pour hot mixture into heat-safe 2-cup measure for easier pouring.) Reduce speed to medium; very slowly, pour corn-syrup mixture into egg-white mixture and continue beating until mixture is thick and glossy and swirl marks of beaters hold their shape when mixer is stopped. (Use icing immediately, or icing will become very stiff.)

Ornamental Icing: In large bowl with mixer at low speed, beat *two 16-ounce packages confectioners' sugar, 6 egg whites,* at room temperature, *1 teaspoon cream of tartar,* and *1½ teaspoons orange extract* until mixed; increase speed to high and beat until mixture is very stiff and knife drawn through mixture leaves a clean-cut path. Keep bowl covered with plastic wrap until ready to use to prevent icing from drying out.

Guide to Cutting Our Wedding Cake

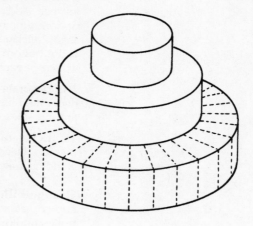

STEP 1: With cake knife held close to base of second tier, cut down to base of bottom tier and around to make a complete circle. Now cut bottom tier into about 40 slices, cutting just to circle. Remove slices.

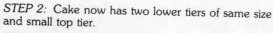
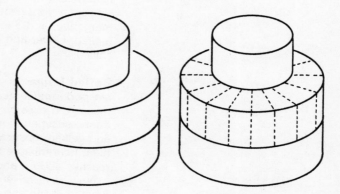

STEP 2: Cake now has two lower tiers of same size and small top tier.

STEP 3: Repeating procedure in step 1, cut second tier by making circular cut around base of smaller top tier. Cut off about 24 slices from second tier, cutting just to circle. Remove slices. Now remove top tier on its foil-covered cardboard. Cut into 12 slices; serve.

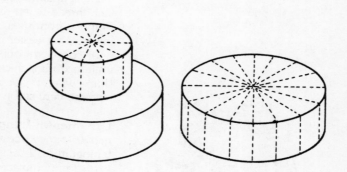

STEP 4: Cut remaining center of second tier into 12 slices and remove.

STEP 5: Remove foil-covered cardboard on which second tier had rested and cut remaining center of bottom tier into about 32 slices.

Cookies

Old-Fashioned Oatmeal Jumbos

TIME: about 2 hours or start up to 2 weeks ahead—
YIELD: about 2½ dozen

1 cup all-purpose flour
1 cup shortening
¾ cup granulated brown sugar
  or packed light brown sugar
½ cup sugar
3 tablespoons water
¾ teaspoon salt
½ teaspoon baking soda
¾ teaspoon vanilla extract
1 egg
3½ cups quick-cooking oats,
  uncooked

1. Preheat oven to 375°F. Grease large cookie sheet. Into large bowl, measure all ingredients except oats. With mixer at low speed, beat ingredients until well blended, occasionally scraping bowl with rubber spatula. With wooden spoon, stir in oats until well mixed.

2. Drop half of dough by heaping tablespoonfuls, about 2 inches apart, onto cookie sheet. Bake 10 to 12 minutes until golden. With metal spatula, carefully remove cookies to wire racks to cool. Repeat until all dough is used, greasing cookie sheet each time. Store in tightly covered container to use up within 2 weeks.

Maple Meltaways

TIME: about 1¼ hours or start up to 2 weeks ahead—
YIELD: about 4 dozen

2 cups all-purpose flour
1 cup butter or margarine,
  softened
¾ cup sugar
1½ teaspoons maple-flavor
  extract
¼ teaspoon salt
about ⅔ cup pecan halves

1. Into large bowl, measure all ingredients except pecan halves. With mixer at low speed, beat ingredients until blended, occasionally scraping bowl with rubber spatula. Increase speed to medium; beat until light and fluffy.

2. Preheat oven to 350°F. Drop dough by rounded teaspoonfuls, about 1 inch apart, onto ungreased cookie sheet. Gently press a pecan half into top of each cookie. Bake 12 minutes or until lightly browned. Cool cookies slightly on cookie sheet, then with pancake turner, carefully loosen cookies and remove to wire rack to cool completely. Repeat with remaining dough and pecans. Store cookies in tightly covered container to use up within 2 weeks.

Cinnamon Spiced Ginger Crisps

TIME: about 3 hours or start up to 2 weeks ahead—YIELD: 6 dozen

2 cups all-purpose flour
sugar
¾ cup butter or margarine, softened
½ cup dark molasses
1½ teaspoons ground ginger
1½ teaspoons ground cinnamon
1 teaspoon baking soda
½ teaspoon salt
½ teaspoon ground nutmeg
1 egg

1. Into large bowl, measure flour, ¾ cup sugar and remaining ingredients. With mixer at low speed, beat ingredients until just mixed. Increase speed to medium and beat 2 minutes, occasionally scraping bowl with rubber spatula. Wrap dough in waxed paper; refrigerate 1 hour or until slightly firm so dough will be easier to handle (or dough may be placed in freezer for 20 minutes).

2. Preheat oven to 375°F. On lightly floured surface, divide dough into about 72 equal pieces. With hands, roll dough into balls; coat each ball lightly with sugar. Place balls about 2 inches apart on greased cookie sheets. With the bottom of a glass, flatten each ball to a ⅛-inch-thick circle. If desired, sprinkle cookies lightly with sugar.

3. Bake 8 to 10 minutes until lightly browned around the edges. Cool cookies 2 minutes on cookie sheets; then, with pancake turner, carefully remove to wire racks to cool completely. Store cookies in tightly covered container to use up within 2 weeks.

Butterfly Cookies

TIME: about 2 hours or start up to 1 week ahead—YIELD: 20 cookies

1¾ cups all-purpose flour
½ teaspoon double-acting baking powder
sugar
¾ cup butter or margarine
⅓ cup iced water
1 egg, slightly beaten

1. In large bowl with fork, combine flour, baking powder, and ¼ cup sugar. With pastry blender or 2 knives used scissor-fashion, cut in butter or margarine until mixture resembles coarse crumbs.

2. With fork, stir in iced water just until mixture forms a soft dough and leaves side of bowl, adding about 1 tablespoon more iced water if needed. On lightly floured surface with floured hands, pat dough into 6″ by 6″ square. Wrap dough in plastic wrap and chill in freezer for 30 minutes for easier handling.

3. On lightly floured surface, roll chilled dough into 18″ by 8″ rectangle. Starting from one 8-inch end, fold one-third of dough over middle one-third; fold opposite one-third over both to make 8″ by 6″ rectangle.

4. Repeat step 3. Wrap dough in plastic wrap; freeze 30 minutes again.

5. Remove dough from freezer. On lighly floured surface, roll dough into 10″ by 8″ rectangle. Cut dough crosswise into twenty 8″ by ½″ strips.

6. Preheat oven to 375°F. Place one strip on its cut side, on ungreased large cookie sheet, curling ends inward until ends touch center of strip to resemble a butterfly. Repeat with remaining strips, placing 2 inches apart on cookie sheet. Brush tops lightly with egg; sprinkle with some sugar. Bake 20 minutes or until golden. With pancake turner, remove cookies to wire rack to cool. Store in tightly covered container to use up within 1 week.

Fudge-Nut Brownies

TIME: about 2½ hours or start early in day—YIELD: 2½ dozen

6 squares unsweetened chocolate
¾ cup butter or margarine
6 eggs
2½ cups sugar
1½ teaspoons vanilla extract
½ teaspoon salt
1½ cups all-purpose flour
1 8-ounce can California
  walnuts, chopped

1. In heavy 1-quart saucepan over low heat, melt chocolate and butter or margarine, stirring frequently.

2. Preheat oven to 325°F. Grease and flour 15½″ by 10½″ jelly-roll pan. In large bowl with mixer at low speed, beat eggs, sugar, vanilla, and salt until well mixed, constantly scraping bowl with rubber spatula. Add chocolate mixture; increase speed to medium and beat 5 minutes, occasionally scraping bowl. With spoon, stir in flour and nuts until blended.

3. Pour batter into jelly-roll pan. Bake 45 minutes. Cool brownies in pan on wire rack. Cut into 30 pieces.

Peanut-Topped Brownies

TIME: about 2½ hours or start up to 3 days head—YIELD: 20

1½ cups packed brown sugar
1 cup all-purpose flour
¾ cup cocoa
¾ cup butter or margarine,
  softened
½ teaspoon baking soda
½ teaspoon vanilla extract
¼ teaspoon salt
3 eggs
¾ cup unsalted peanuts,
  chopped
1¼ cups peanut-butter flavor
  chips
½ cup flaked coconut, toasted

1. Preheat oven to 350°F. Grease 13″ by 9″ baking pan. In large bowl with mixer at low speed, beat first 8 ingredients until well mixed, constantly scraping bowl with rubber spatula. Increase speed to high and beat 3 minutes, occasionally scraping bowl.

2. With spoon, stir in ½ cup chopped peanuts. Spread batter evenly into prepared baking pan. Bake 30 minutes or until brownie pulls away from sides of pan.

3. Remove baking pan to wire rack. Immediately sprinkle peanut-butter flavor chips over hot brownies; let stand 5 minutes. With metal spatula, evenly spread melted chips over brownies; sprinkle with coconut and remaining ¼ cup nuts, patting down gently. Cut into 20 pieces. Cool in pan on wire rack. Cover pan with foil; use up brownies within 3 days.

Soft Banana-Spice Cookies

TIME: about 1½ hours or start up to week ahead—
YIELD: about 2 dozen

2 ripe large bananas
2¼ cups all-purpose flour
½ cup butter or margarine,
  softened
2 teaspoons double-acting
  baking powder
1 teaspoon vanilla extract
½ teaspoon salt
¼ teaspoon baking soda
¼ teaspoon ground nutmeg
2 eggs
sugar
ground cinnamon
2 tablespoons minced
  crystallized ginger

1. Into large bowl, cut bananas into large chunks; with potato masher or slotted spoon, mash banana chunks until smooth. Add flour, butter or margarine, baking powder, vanilla extract, salt, baking soda, nutmeg, eggs, 1 cup sugar, and ¼ teaspoon cinnamon. With mixer at low speed, beat ingredients until blended, occasionally scraping bowl with rubber spatula. Increase speed to medium; beat 1 minute.

2. Preheat oven to 350°F. In cup, combine minced ginger, 2 tablespoons sugar, and ½ teaspoon cinnamon; set aside. Using about 2 tablespoons batter for each cookie, spoon batter, 2 inches apart, on ungreased cookie sheets. Sprinkle cookies with ginger mixture. Bake 18 to 20 minutes until golden. With pancake turner, remove cookies to wire racks to cool. Store cookies in tightly covered container to use up within 1 week.

217

Jam-Filled Spice Cookies

TIME: about 2½ hours or start up to week ahead—
YIELD: about 2½ dozen

1 cup butter or margarine
½ cup sugar
3 cups all-purpose flour
½ cup dark corn syrup
1 teaspoon ground cinnamon
1 teaspoon ground ginger
½ teaspoon ground cloves
1 egg
apricot and/or raspberry
  preserves

1. In large bowl with mixer at medium speed, beat butter or margarine and sugar until light and fluffy. At low speed, beat in flour and remaining ingredients except preserves; beat until well mixed, constantly scraping bowl with rubber spatula. With hands, shape dough into a ball; wrap with plastic wrap; refrigerate until easy to handle, about 1 hour.

2. Preheat oven to 350°F. On lightly floured surface with floured rolling pin, roll half of dough ¼ inch thick, keeping remaining dough refrigerated. With floured 2½-inch round cookie cutter, cut dough into rounds. With floured ¾-inch round cookie cutter, cut out centers from half of rounds.

3. With pancake turner, place rounds, ½ inch apart, on ungreased cookie sheets. Bake 10 to 12 minutes until lightly browned. With pancake turner, remove cookies to wire racks to cool. Repeat with remaining dough and trimmings.

4. To assemble cookies, spoon about ¾ teaspoon apricot or raspberry preserves in center of each cookie without cut-out center; top each with a cookie with cut-out center, gently pressing cookies together. Store in tightly covered container to use up within 1 week.

Brown-Edged Wafers

TIME: about 1½ hours or start up to week ahead—
YIELD: about 3½ dozen cookies

1¼ cups all-purpose flour
¾ cup butter or margarine,
  softened
½ cup sugar
1 teaspoon vanilla extract
¼ teaspoon salt
2 eggs

1. Preheat oven to 350° F. Grease large cookie sheets.

2. In small bowl with mixer at low speed, beat all ingredients until blended, occasionally scraping bowl with rubber spatula.

3. Drop dough by heaping teaspoonfuls, 2 inches apart, onto cookie sheets. Bake about 12 minutes or until edges of cookies are browned. With pancake turner, remove cookies to wire racks to cool. Store in tightly covered container to use up within 1 week.

Bourbon Balls

TIME: about 30 minutes or start up to 2 weeks ahead—
YIELD: about 3½ dozen

confectioners' sugar
2½ cups finely crushed vanilla
  wafers (about 60 wafers)
1 cup California walnuts, finely
  chopped
¼ cup bourbon
2 tablespoons cocoa
3 tablespoons corn syrup

1. In large bowl with fork, mix 1 cup confectioners' sugar and remaining ingredients.

2. Sprinkle some confectioners' sugar onto waxed paper. With hands, shape wafer mixture into 1-inch balls. Roll each ball in confectioners' sugar.

3. For best storing, wrap each ball in plastic wrap. Store in tightly covered container to use up within 2 weeks.

Clockwise from center: Tangy Corn Relish, page 169; Pickled Vegetable Medley, page 172; Cauliflower Pickles, page 171; Green-Tomato Chow Chow, page 170; Plum-Nut Freezer Conserve, page 179; Peach Butter, page 182, and Freezer Peach-Orange Conserve, page 179

Clockwise from top left: Chocolate-Cherry Cake, page 192; Dreamy Chocolate Cake, page 193; Chocolate-and-Creams, page 192, and Carrot Cake Ring, page 194

Clockwise from top left:
Pasta Salad, page 16;
Cheddar and Swiss cheese
wedges with pumpernickel
and rye breads;
Creamy Mustard, Herb, and
Lemony Anchovy salad
dressings, page 177;
Whole-Wheat Garlic
Croutons, page 168;
Blueberry Coffee Cake,
page 204; red onions;
salad-green bowl;
platter of salad go-alongs:
cherry tomatoes;
frozen artichoke hearts;
Marinated Green Beans,
page 32;
avocado slices; salami;
Zesty Lima-Bean Salad,
page 16;
Tuna-Stuffed Eggs,
page 140;
bottled cocktail corn,
and sardines in oil.

Six Golden Hens, page 97

Spumoni Elegante, page 233

Broiled Cod Steaks Montauk, page 108,
and Skillet Potatoes, page 24

Sugar Pretzels

TIME: about 1½ hours or start up to 2 weeks ahead—
YIELD: about 1½ dozen

3 cups all-purpose flour
1 cup butter or margarine, softened
½ cup sugar
1 teaspoon grated lemon peel
1 teaspoon lemon extract
¼ teaspoon salt
2 eggs
¼ cup rainbow sugar crystals

1. Into large bowl, measure first 6 ingredients, 1 egg, and 1 egg yolk; reserve remaining egg white to brush on cookies later. With mixer at low speed, beat ingredients until well blended, occasionally scraping bowl with rubber spatula.

2. Preheat oven to 400°F. With hands, roll 2 tablespoonfuls mixture into a 12-inch-long rope. Shape rope into a loop-shaped pretzel. Repeat with remaining dough. Place pretzels, 1 inch apart, on ungreased cookie sheets. Brush pretzels with egg white; sprinkle with sugar crystals. Bake 10 to 12 minutes until golden. Carefully remove pretzel cookies to racks to cool. Store cookies in tightly covered container to use up within 2 weeks.

Buttery Almond Cookies

TIME: about 2 hours or start up to 2 weeks ahead—YIELD: 2 dozen cookies

2 cups all-purpose flour
1 cup butter or margarine, softened
¾ cup confectioners' sugar
¾ teaspoon almond extract
½ teaspoon double-acting baking powder
1 egg white
⅓ cup sliced blanched almonds

1. Into large bowl, measure flour, butter or margarine, confectioners' sugar, almond extract, and baking powder. With hand, knead ingredients until well blended and mixture holds together.

2. Preheat oven to 350° F. Pat dough evenly into 13″ by 9″ baking pan. With dull edge of knife, mark dough into twenty-four pieces (do not cut through dough). With pastry brush, brush dough with egg white; then sprinkle with almonds.

3. Bake 30 to 35 minutes until lightly browned. While cookies are still warm, with knife, cut dough through markings. Cool cookies in pan on wire rack. Remove cookies from pan. Store cookies in tightly covered container to use up within 2 weeks.

Almond Refrigerator Cookies

TIME: about 4½ hours or start up to 2 weeks ahead—
YIELD: about 6 dozen

2¼ cups all-purpose flour
1 cup sugar
1 cup butter or margarine, softened
1½ teaspoons double-acting baking powder
1 teaspoon almond extract
½ teaspoon salt
1 egg
1 4-ounce can blanched slivered almonds, finely chopped

1. Into large bowl, measure all ingredients except almonds. With mixer at low speed, beat ingredients until well blended, occasionally scraping bowl with rubber spatula. Stir in almonds. With hands, roll dough into three 6-inch-long rolls. Wrap each roll with plastic wrap. Refrigerate rolls 3 hours or until firm enough to slice.*

2. To bake, preheat oven to 350°F. Slice 1 roll of dough crosswise into ¼-inch-thick slices. Place slices, 1 inch apart, on ungreased large cookie sheet. Bake 15 minutes or until lightly browned. With pancake turner, remove cookies to wire rack to cool. Repeat with remaining dough. Store cookies in tightly covered container to use up within 2 weeks.

*Dough can be refrigerated up to 1 week before baking.

219

Delicate Almond-Rich Tuiles

TIME: about 1½ hours or start up to 2 days ahead—
YIELD: about 2½ dozen

1 3½-ounce can sliced natural or blanched almonds
2 egg whites
⅓ cup sugar
2 tablespoons cornstarch
2 tablespoons all-purpose flour
3 tablespoons butter or margarine, melted
¼ teaspoon vanilla extract

1. Preheat oven to 425°F. Grease well large cookie sheet.

2. Spread ⅓ cup sliced almonds in 13" by 9" baking pan. Toast almonds in oven about 5 minutes or until lightly browned, stirring occasionally. Cool almonds in pan on wire rack. When cool, blend almonds in blender at medium speed until very finely ground.

3. In medium bowl with wire whisk or fork, beat egg whites until foamy. Beat in ground almonds, sugar, cornstarch, and flour. Stir in melted butter or margarine and vanilla. Spoon 1 level teaspoon batter onto cookie sheet; spread with back of spoon into paper-thin oval, about 4" by 3". Repeat to make 4 ovals, 2 inches apart. Sprinkle ovals with some of remaining sliced almonds.

4. Bake 3 to 4 minutes until edges are golden. Remove cookie sheet from oven and with pancake turner, quickly remove cookies, one by one, and drape lengthwise across rolling pin or bottles to cool. Allow cookie sheet to cool completely. Repeat with remaining batter and almonds, greasing cookie sheet well each time. (The more cookie sheets you have, the faster you can bake the cookies.) Store in tightly covered container to use up within 2 days.

Almond Chocolate-Chip Meringues

TIME: about 2 hours or start up to 3 days ahead—
YIELD: about 3 dozen

⅓ cup light corn syrup
¼ cup sugar
2 egg whites
¼ teaspoon salt
½ teaspoon almond extract
½ cup slivered blanched almonds, toasted
½ cup semisweet-chocolate pieces

1. Line 2 large cookie sheets with foil. Preheat oven to 300°F. In 1-quart saucepan over medium heat, heat corn syrup and sugar to boiling, stirring constantly; boil 1 minute. Remove saucepan from heat.

2. In large bowl with mixer at high speed, beat egg whites and salt until stiff peaks form; beat in almond extract. Beating constantly, slowly pour hot syrup into egg whites in a thin, steady stream. Continue beating until mixture stands in stiff, glossy peaks. Fold in almonds and chocolate pieces. Drop mixture by tablespoonfuls onto prepared cookie sheets.

3. Bake meringues 25 minutes. Turn oven off; leave meringues in oven 30 minutes to dry. With small spatula, carefully loosen and remove meringues from foil; cool completely on wire racks. Store meringues in tightly covered container to use up within 3 days.

Dark-Chocolate Walnut Drops

TIME: about 2 hours or start up to 2 weeks ahead—YIELD: 1½ dozen

1½ squares unsweetened
   chocolate, melted
½ cup all-purpose flour
½ cup sugar
¼ cup butter or margarine,
   softened
½ teaspoon salt
1½ teaspoons vanilla extract
¼ teaspoon double-acting
   baking powder
1 egg
2 cups California walnuts,
   coarsely broken

1. Preheat oven to 350°F. Grease cookie sheets. Into large bowl, measure all ingredients except walnuts. With mixer at low speed, beat ingredients until blended. Increase speed to high; beat 1 minute, occasionally scraping bowl with rubber spatula. With rubber spatula, stir in walnuts.

2. Drop mixture by rounded tablespoonfuls, 1 inch apart, onto cookie sheets. Bake 15 minutes. With pancake turner, remove cookies to wire racks; cool. Store cookies in tightly covered container to use up within 2 weeks.

Oatmeal-Chocolate Triangles

TIME: about 2 hours or start up to 3 days ahead—YIELD: 2 dozen

butter or margarine
¾ cup quick-cooking oats
¾ cup California walnuts, finely
   chopped
½ cup packed brown sugar
all purpose-flour
baking soda
salt
1 square semisweet chocolate
½ cup sugar
1½ teaspoons vanilla extract
1 egg

1. Preheat oven to 350°F. Grease 12″ by 8″ baking pan. In small saucepan over low heat, melt ⅓ cup butter or margarine; remove saucepan from heat. Into small bowl, measure oats, walnuts, brown sugar, ¼ cup flour, ¼ teaspoon baking soda, and ⅛ teaspoon salt; stir in melted butter or margarine. With mixer at low speed, beat ingredients until well mixed, occasionally scraping bowl with rubber spatula. Pat mixture into prepared pan; bake 10 minutes.

2. Meanwhile, in 2-quart saucepan over low heat, melt chocolate and ½ cup butter or margarine, stirring frequently. Remove saucepan from heat, stir in sugar, vanilla, egg, ¾ cup flour, ¼ teaspoon baking soda, and ¼ teaspoon salt until smooth. Pour batter over baked layer; bake 20 minutes longer or until toothpick inserted in center comes out clean. Cool in pan on wire rack. When cool, cut into 24 triangle cookies. Store in tightly covered container to use up within 3 days.

Chocolate Chip Walnut Cookies

TIME: about 2 hours or start up to 2 weeks ahead—
YIELD: about 2½ dozen

1 cup all-purpose flour
1 cup sugar
½ cup butter or margarine,
   softened
1 teaspoon vanilla extract
⅛ teaspoon salt
2 eggs
2 squares unsweetened
   chocolate, melted
1 6-ounce package semisweet-
   chocolate pieces (1 cup)
1¾ cups California walnuts,
   coarsely broken

1. Preheat oven to 350°F. Into large bowl, measure first 7 ingredients. With mixer at low speed, beat ingredients until blended, occasionally scraping bowl with rubber spatula. With spoon, stir in chocolate pieces and ¾ cup walnuts.

2. Drop chocolate mixture by heaping tablespoonfuls, about 2 inches apart, onto cookie sheet. With back of spoon, spread each cookie into a 2-inch round; top with some remaining walnuts.

3. Bake cookies 12 minutes. With pancake turner, remove cookies to wire rack to cool. Repeat until all dough and walnuts are used. Store cookies in tightly covered container to use up within 2 weeks.

Oatmeal Drop Cookies

TIME: about 1 hour—YIELD: about 2 dozen

¾ cup California walnuts
¾ cup all-purpose flour
½ cup packed light brown sugar
½ cup butter or margarine, softened
½ teaspoon maple extract
¼ teaspoon double-acting baking powder
¼ teaspoon salt
1 egg
1 cup quick-cooking oats, uncooked

1. Reserve about 24 large walnut pieces; chop remaining walnuts.

2. Into large bowl, measure flour and next 6 ingredients. With mixer at low speed, beat ingredients until well blended, occasionally scraping bowl with rubber spatula. With spoon, stir in chopped walnuts and oats.

3. Preheat oven to 375°F. Grease large cookie sheet. Drop mixture by rounded tablespoonfuls, about 2 inches apart, on cookie sheet. Press a reserved walnut piece into top of each cookie to flatten cookie slightly. Bake 10 minutes or until well browned around edges (centers will be lighter). With pancake turner, remove cookies to wire racks to cool. Repeat with remaining dough and walnuts. Store any leftover cookies in tightly covered container.

Crispy Nut Bars

TIME: about 1 hour or start early in day—YIELD: 36 bars

butter or margarine
1 10-ounce package regular marshmallows
7 cups oven-toasted rice cereal
1 cup salted peanuts, chopped
3 squares semisweet chocolate

1. Grease cookie sheet. In 3-quart saucepan over low heat, melt 4 tablespoons butter or margarine. Add marshmallows and cook, stirring frequently, until smooth. Remove saucepan from heat; stir in oven-toasted rice cereal and peanuts until well coated.

2. Spoon cereal mixture onto cookie sheet and let cool a few minutes. With hands, press mixture firmly into 12" by 9" rectangle; cool until firm.

3. In small saucepan over low heat, heat chocolate and 2 tablespoons butter or margarine until melted and smooth, stirring constantly. Remove saucepan from heat. With spoon, drizzle chocolate mixture over cereal mixture; cool until chocolate is set. Cut into 36 bars. Use within 2 days.

Molasses-Peanut Jumbles

TIME: about 1¼ hours or start up to 3 days ahead—
YIELD: about 2½ dozen

2 cups all-purpose flour
1 cup packed brown sugar
½ cup butter or margarine, softened
¼ cup molasses
½ teaspoon baking soda
1 3-ounce package cream cheese, softened
1 egg
1 cup salted peanuts, chopped

1. Into large bowl, measure all ingredients except peanuts. With mixer at low speed, beat ingredients just until combined. Increase speed to medium; beat until well blended, occasionally scraping bowl with rubber spatula. With spoon, stir in peanuts.

2. Preheat oven to 375°F. Drop dough by rounded tablespoonfuls, about 2 inches, apart on ungreased cookie sheets. Bake 15 minutes until firm. Cool cookies slightly on cookie sheets; then with pancake turner, carefully loosen cookies and remove to wire racks to cool completely. Store cookies in tightly covered container to use up within 3 days.

Chocolate Thumbprints

TIME: about 2 hours or start up to week ahead—
YIELD: about 2½ dozen

1 6-ounce package semisweet-
  chocolate pieces (1 cup)
1¼ cups all-purpose flour
½ cup butter or margarine,
  softened
¼ cup sugar
½ teaspoon vanilla extract
¼ teaspoon salt
1 egg, separated
1 cup California walnuts,
  chopped

1. In small saucepan over low heat, melt ¼ cup semisweet-chocolate pieces. Remove saucepan from heat. Reserve remaining chocolate pieces for cookie filling.

2. Into small bowl, measure flour, butter or margarine, sugar, vanilla, salt, egg yolk, and melted chocolate. With mixer at low speed, beat ingredients until blended, constantly scraping bowl with rubber spatula. Increase speed to medium; beat 1 minute. With hands, shape dough into ¾-inch balls.

3. Preheat oven to 350°F. In cup with fork, beat egg white until foamy. Place chopped walnuts on sheet of waxed paper. Dip balls into egg white, then into nuts. Place balls, 1 inch apart, on large ungreased cookie sheet. Press thumb into center of each ball to make a ½-inch-deep indentation.

4. Bake cookies about 15 minutes or until set. Remove cookie sheet from oven. Quickly fill indentations of warm cookies with reserved chocolate pieces, smoothing chocolate as it melts with tip of spoon. With metal spatula, remove cookies to wire racks to cool. Store cookies in single layer in tightly covered container to use up within 1 week.

Chocolate-Dipped Crescents

TIME: about 2 hours or start up to week ahead—
YIELD: about 4 dozen

1 cup California walnuts, finely
  chopped
1¾ cups all-purpose flour
¾ cup butter or margarine,
  softened
½ cup confectioners' sugar
1½ teaspoons vanilla extract
¼ teaspoon salt
Chocolate Glaze (right)

1. In large bowl, with hand, knead ¾ cup chopped walnuts with remaining ingredients except Chocolate Glaze until well blended and mixture holds together.

2. Preheat oven to 350°F. With hands, shape 1 rounded teaspoonful cookie dough at a time into 1¾-inch crescent. Place crescents, 1 inch apart, on ungreased cookie sheets. Bake 15 minutes or until lightly browned. Remove cookies to wire racks to cool.

3. Prepare Chocolate Glaze. Dip one end of a cookie into chocolate mixture to cover half of cookie. Gently scrape off excess chocolate across rim of saucepan. Sprinkle chocolate-dipped end of cookie with some reserved chopped walnuts. Place cookie on waxed paper; let chocolate dry. Repeat with remaining cookies, chocolate, and walnuts. Store cookies in tightly covered container to use up within 1 week.

Chocolate Glaze: In heavy 1-quart saucepan over low heat, melt *3 squares semisweet chocolate* and *1 tablespoon butter* or margarine. Remove saucepan from heat. Stir in *1 tablespoon milk* and *1 tablespoon light corn syrup* until blended.

223

Pecan Crisps

TIME: about 2 hours or start up to week ahead—YIELD: 5½ dozen

1 6-ounce can pecan halves
2½ cups all-purpose flour
1 cup butter or margarine,
   softened
¾ cup packed light brown sugar
1 teaspoon vanilla extract
½ teaspoon double-acting
   baking powder

1. Finely chop ½ cup pecans; set aside. Reserve remaining pecan halves for garnish.

2. Into large bowl, measure chopped pecans, flour, and remaining ingredients. With hand, knead ingredients until well blended and dough holds together.

3. Preheat oven to 350°F. Between 2 sheets of waxed paper, roll half of dough ¼ inch thick. With 2-inch flower-shaped cookie cutter, cut dough into cookies.

4. Gently remove cookies with metal spatula to ungreased cookie sheet, 1 inch apart; press a reserved pecan half into top of each. Bake 10 minutes or until lightly browned. Cool cookies slightly on cookie sheet, then with pancake turner, carefully remove to wire rack to cool completely. Repeat with remaining dough and pecans, rerolling trimmings. Store cookies, tightly covered, to use up within 1 week.

Chewy Pecan Pie Bars

TIME: about 3 hours or start up to week ahead—YIELD: 35 bars

1 teaspoon double-acting baking
   powder
all-purpose flour
dark brown sugar
½ cup butter or margarine
4 eggs
1½ cups dark corn syrup
2 teaspoons vanilla extract
2½ cups pecans, chopped

1. Grease 15½" by 10½" jelly-roll pan. Preheat oven to 350°F. In medium bowl with fork, mix baking powder, 1½ cups flour, and ⅔ cup packed brown sugar. With pastry blender or 2 knives used scissor-fashion, cut butter or margarine into flour mixture until mixture resembles very fine crumbs. Pat mixture firmly and evenly into prepared pan. Bake 15 minutes.

2. In large bowl with mixer at medium speed, beat eggs until foamy. Beat in corn syrup, vanilla, ½ cup packed brown sugar, and ½ cup flour until well blended. Pour egg mixture over partially baked layer; sprinkle with pecans. Bake 55 minutes longer or until set. Cool in pan on wire rack. Cut lengthwise into 7 strips; then cut each strip crosswise into 5 pieces. Store in covered container in refrigerator to use up within 1 week.

Hazelnut Mounds

TIME: about 1½ hours or start up to week ahead—
YIELD: about 2½ dozen

¾ cup hazelnuts (also called
   filberts)
1 cup all-purpose flour
½ cup butter or margarine,
   softened
⅓ cup sugar
¾ teaspoon vanilla extract

1. In blender at medium speed or in food processor with knife blade attached, blend hazelnuts until very finely ground.

2. Into medium bowl, measure flour, butter or margarine, sugar, vanilla, and ½ cup ground hazelnuts. With hand, knead ingredients until well blended and mixture holds together.

3. Preheat oven to 350°F. Shape dough into 1-inch balls; roll each ball in remaining hazelnuts. Place balls, 1 inch apart, on ungreased cookie sheet. Bake 20 minutes or until lightly browned. With pancake turner, remove cookies to wire rack to cool. Store cookies in tightly covered container to use up within 1 week.

Christmas Flower Cookies

TIME: about 2 hours or start up to 2 weeks ahead—
YIELD: about 4 dozen

3 cups all-purpose flour
2 cups confectioners' sugar
1 cup butter or margarine, softened
1 teaspoon vanilla extract
½ teaspoon salt
½ teaspoon orange extract
2 eggs
1 cup flaked coconut
1 3½-ounce container red candied cherries
1 3½-ounce container green candied cherries

1. Into large bowl, measure first 7 ingredients. With mixer at low speed, beat ingredients until well blended. With spoon, stir in flaked coconut; set aside.

2. Cut each red and green candied cherry in half; cut each half into 4 slivers; set aside.

3. Preheat oven to 375°F. With floured hands, shape mixture into 1-inch balls. Place balls, 2½ inches apart, on ungreased cookie sheets. Dip bottom of glass into flour; flatten mounds into 3-inch rounds. Arrange some cherry slices on each cookie to resemble flower, alternating colors. Bake 12 to 15 minutes until cookies are lightly browned. With pancake turner, remove cookies to wire racks to cool. Store cookies in tightly covered container to use up within 2 weeks.

Butter Cookie Wreaths

TIME: about 2½ hours or start up to 2 weeks ahead—
YIELD: 20 cookies

1 medium lemon
3 cups cake flour
¾ cup sugar
½ teaspoon salt
1 cup butter or margarine, softened
1 tablespoon rum extract
¼ cup blanched slivered almonds

1. From lemon, grate 1 teaspoon peel and squeeze 1 teaspoon juice.

2. In large bowl, mix lemon peel, flour, sugar, and salt. Using pastry blender or two knives used scissor-fashion, cut butter or margarine into flour mixture until mixture resembles coarse crumbs. Add lemon juice and rum extract; with hand, knead mixture until well blended.

3. Preheat oven to 400°F. Divide half of dough into 20 equal pieces. With hands, roll each dough piece into 9-inch-long rope. On work surface, pinch 2 ropes together at one end. Gently twist ropes together; bring ends together to form a ring, overlapping ends slightly; pinch ends to seal.

4. With pancake turner, place rings, 1 inch apart, on ungreased cookie sheet. Decorate each cookie as desired with some slivered almonds. Bake 10 to 12 minutes until lightly browned. Cool cookies on cookie sheet 5 minutes, then with pancake turner, remove cookies to wire racks to cool completely. Repeat with remaining dough and almonds. Store cookies in tightly covered container to use up within 2 weeks.

Santa Cookies

TIME: about 3½ hours or start up to 3 weeks ahead—
YIELD: about 3 dozen

1 12-ounce package peanut-
    butter-flavor chips
butter or margarine
2 cups all-purpose flour
½ cup sugar
¼ cup honey
2 teaspoons vanilla extract
1½ teaspoons baking soda
½ teaspoon ground cinnamon
1 egg
2½ cups confectioners' sugar
¼ teaspoon cream of tartar
2 egg whites
red food color
about ¼ cup semisweet-
    chocolate pieces or ¼ cup
    dark seedless raisins

1. In heavy 1-quart saucepan over low heat, stir peanut-butter flavor chips and 2 tablespoons butter or margarine until melted, stirring occasionally. Remove saucepan from heat.

2. Into large bowl, measure flour, sugar, honey, vanilla, baking soda, cinnamon, egg, and ½ cup softened butter or margarine. With mixer at low speed, beat ingredients until blended, occasionally scraping bowl with rubber spatula. Add melted peanut-butter-flavor chips. Increase speed to medium; beat until well blended. (Mixture may be crumbly.) Shape dough into a ball; wrap with plastic wrap. Refrigerate dough 30 minutes or until easy to handle. (If dough is refrigerated too long it will become very dry and difficult to roll.)

3. Preheat oven to 375°F. On lightly floured surface with floured rolling pin, roll half of dough to ¼-inch thickness. With floured round cookie cutter (about 3 inches in diameter), cut dough into as many cookies as possible.

4. Place cookies on ungreased cookie sheet, 1½ inches apart. Bake 6 to 8 minutes until cookies are lightly browned. Cool cookies slightly on cookie sheet. With pancake turner, remove cookies to wire racks to cool completely. Repeat with remaining dough, rerolling trimmings.

5. Prepare frosting: In large bowl with mixer at low speed, beat confectioners' sugar, cream of tartar, and egg whites until just mixed. Increase speed to high and beat mixture until very stiff and knife drawn through mixture leaves a clean-cut path. (Keep bowl covered with plastic wrap to prevent mixture from drying out.)

6. Decorate cookies: Spoon two-thirds of frosting into decorating bag with small writing tube. Tint remaining frosting with red food color; spoon red frosting into another decorating bag with small writing tube. With white frosting, attach 2 semisweet-chocolate pieces or 2 raisins on each cookie for eyes. Decorate cookies with red and white frostings to make "Santa faces." Let frosting dry until firm, about 1 hour. Store in tightly covered container to use up within 3 weeks.

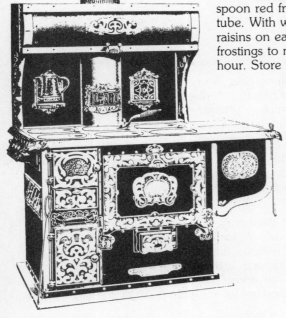

Sugar Christmas Trees

TIME: about 4 hours or start up to week ahead—
YIELD: about 4 dozen

2¼ cups all-purpose flour
¾ cup butter or margarine,
  softened
1 tablespoon milk
2 teaspoons grated lemon peel
1½ teaspoons double-acting
  baking powder
¼ teaspoon salt
1 egg
sugar
¾ cup confectioners' sugar
1 tablespoon water
green food color
red food color
silver decors

1. Into large bowl, measure first 7 ingredients and ¾ cup sugar. With mixer at low speed, beat ingredients until well blended, occasionally scraping bowl with rubber spatula. Shape dough into a ball; wrap with plastic wrap. Refrigerate dough 2 hours or until easy to handle.

2. Preheat oven to 350°F. Grease large cookie sheets. On lightly floured surface with floured rolling pin, roll half of dough ⅛ inch thick, keeping remaining dough refrigerated. With floured 3½-inch Christmas-tree-shaped cookie cutter, cut dough into trees (or cut 3½-inch Christmas-tree pattern from cardboard; use pattern and knife to cut out cookies). With edge of small metal spatula or tip of knife, make several lines in each tree (do not cut through dough) to resemble branches. With floured small star-shaped canapé cutter, cut enough stars from dough trimmings for each Christmas tree; place on trees. Arrange trees, ½ inch apart, on cookie sheets.

3. Sprinkle cookies lightly with sugar. Bake cookies 12 minutes or until golden. With pancake turner, remove cookies to wire racks to cool. Repeat with remaining dough and trimmings.

4. Prepare frosting: In small bowl, stir confectioners' sugar and water until smooth. Spoon half of frosting into another small bowl; stir in enough green food color to tint a bright green; cover with plastic wrap. Into frosting remaining in bowl, stir in enough red food color to tint a bright red color; cover with plastic wrap.

5. Decorate trees: With artist's paint brush, paint green or red frosting on stars on trees; decorate stars with silver decors. Let frosting dry, about 30 minutes. Store cookies in tightly covered container to use up within 1 week.

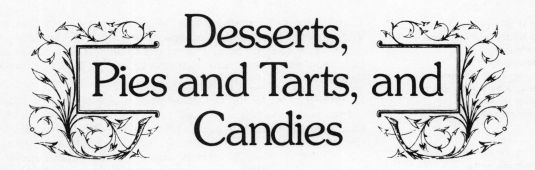

Desserts, Pies and Tarts, and Candies

DESSERT SAUCES AND TOPPINGS

Nutty Sundae Topping

TIME: about 1½ hours or start up to 2 weeks ahead—
YIELD: about 2 cups

¾ cup water
⅔ cup dark corn syrup
½ cup sugar
1 6-ounce can pecans, chopped
¾ teaspoon vanilla extract

1. In 2-quart saucepan over medium heat, heat water, corn syrup, and sugar to boiling. Reduce heat to low; stir in pecans; simmer 15 minutes, stirring occasionally. Remove saucepan from heat; stir in vanilla extract.

2. Cover and refrigerate until chilled to use up within 2 weeks. Stir before using. Use to serve over ice cream, pound cake, poached fruit, waffles, or pudding.

Easy Chocolate Garnishes

Chocolate Leaves: In double boiler over hot, *not boiling,* water or in heavy 1-quart saucepan over low heat, heat *half of 6-ounce package semisweet-chocolate pieces* and *2 teaspoons shortening* until the chocolate is melted and smooth, about 5 minutes, stirring occasionally. With pastry brush or small metal spatula, spread a layer of melted chocolate mixture on *5 medium-sized lemon leaves* (available at florist), using *underside* of leaf for a more distinct leaf design. Refrigerate until chocolate is firm, about 30 minutes. Carefully peel leaf from chocolate. Use to garnish Bavarian cream pie, ice-cream pie, cheesecake, frosted layer cake, or torte.

Chocolate Wedges: Melt chocolate as above. On *10-inch-long sheet of waxed paper* with toothpick, trace circle using bottom of 9-inch round cake pan; cut out circle. Place cake pan, bottom-side up, on work surface; moisten with water. Place waxed-paper circle on pan; the water will prevent paper from sliding. With large metal spatula, evenly spread melted chocolate mixture on waxed paper. Refrigerate until chocolate is firm, about 30 minutes. Heat blade of long knife in hot water; wipe dry. Quickly, but gently, cut chocolate into wedges. Use to garnish as with leaves.

Chocolate Curls: With heat of hand, slightly soften *semisweet-chocolate square*. With vegetable peeler, draw blade along smooth surface to make wide chocolate curls. Use as with leaves, wedges. For individual desserts such as ice cream, parfait, or mousse, make short curls on side of square.

FROZEN DESSERTS

Ice-Cream Grasshoppers

TIME: about 40 minutes—SERVINGS: 4

8 chocolate wafers
1 pint vanilla ice cream, slightly softened
1 tablespoon green crème de menthe

1. In blender at medium speed or in food processor with knife blade attached, blend chocolate wafers to fine crumbs.

2. In small bowl with mixer at low speed, beat ice cream and green crème de menthe until blended. Into 4 freezer-safe parfait or dessert glasses, layer ice-cream mixture and chocolate-wafer crumbs. Freeze until ready to serve.

Ice-Cream Pie with Peanut-Butter Crust

TIME: start early in day or up to 2 weeks ahead—SERVINGS: 12

2 pints vanilla ice cream
½ cup peanut butter
½ cup light corn syrup
2¼ cups oven-toasted rice cereal

FUDGE SAUCE:
¾ cup sugar
½ cup cocoa
½ cup heavy or whipping cream
4 tablespoons butter or margarine
1 teaspoon vanilla extract

1. Place 1 pint vanilla ice cream in refrigerator to soften slightly, about 30 minutes.

2. Meanwhile, in large bowl, stir peanut butter and corn syrup until blended. Add oven-toasted rice cereal, stirring until well coated. Press cereal mixture evenly onto bottom and up side of 9-inch pie plate and form stand-up edge.

3. Evenly spread softened ice cream on crust; freeze until firm, about 1 hour.

4. Meanwhile, prepare Fudge Sauce: In 2-quart saucepan over medium heat, cook sugar, cocoa, heavy or whipping cream, and butter or margarine until mixture is smooth and boils, stirring constantly. Remove saucepan from heat; stir in vanilla. Cool fudge sauce slightly.

5. Pour 1¼ cups fudge sauce over ice cream; return pie to freezer; freeze until fudge sauce hardens, about 20 minutes.

6. Remove second pint ice cream from container to medium bowl; let stand at room temperature, stirring occasionally, until of smooth spreading consistency but not melted. Spread ice cream over fudge sauce. Drizzle remaining fudge sauce over ice cream to make a pretty design. Return pie to freezer; freeze until firm, at least 3 hours. If pie is not used same day, when firm, wrap pie with plastic wrap or foil.

7. To serve, let pie stand at room temperature without plastic wrap 15 minutes for easier slicing.

Party Ice-Cream Roll With Chocolate Sauce

TIME: about 4½ hours or start up to 2 days ahead—SERVINGS: 16

½ cup cake flour
1 teaspoon double-acting baking powder
¼ teaspoon salt
cocoa
4 eggs, separated, at room temperature
sugar
½ cup raspberry jam
2 pints vanilla ice cream, softened
Chocolate Sauce (right)

1. Grease 15½" by 10½" jelly-roll pan; line pan with waxed paper. In small bowl, stir flour, baking powder, salt, and ⅓ cup cocoa.

2. Preheat oven to 375°F. In another small bowl with mixer at high speed, beat egg whites until soft peaks form. Beating at high speed, gradually sprinkle in ¼ cup sugar, beating until sugar is completely dissolved. (Whites should stand in stiff, glossy peaks.)

3. In large bowl with same beaters and with mixer at high speed, beat egg yolks and ½ cup sugar until very thick. With wire whisk or rubber spatula, gently fold flour mixture and beaten egg whites into egg-yolk mixture. Spread batter evenly in pan. Bake until cake springs back when lightly touched with finger, about 15 minutes.

4. Sprinkle clean cloth towel with some cocoa. When cake is done, immediately invert cake onto towel. Carefully peel waxed paper from cake. Starting at narrow end, roll cake with towel, jelly-roll fashion. Place cake, seam-side down, on wire rack; cool completely, about 30 minutes.

5. Unroll cooled cake; spread top evenly with raspberry jam, then with ice cream. Starting at same narrow end, roll cake without towel. Wrap cake tightly with foil; freeze until firm, about 3 hours.

6. To serve, place roll on platter; let stand at room temperature 10 minutes for easier slicing. Meanwhile, prepare Chocolate Sauce. Serve warm sauce in small bowl to spoon over each serving.

Chocolate Sauce: In 2-quart saucepan over medium heat, cook *1 cup heavy or whipping cream, ¾ cup sugar, ½ cup cocoa, 4 tablespoons butter* or margarine, and *¼ teaspoon salt* until mixture is smooth and comes to a boil. Remove saucepan from heat; stir in *1 teaspoon vanilla extract.*

Butter-Pecan Parfaits

TIME: about 3 hours or start early in day—SERVINGS: 4

1 pint butter pecan ice cream
1¼ cups pecans
1 tablespoon butter or margarine
3 tablespoons brown sugar
½ cup heavy or whipping cream

1. Place ice cream in refrigerator to soften slightly, about 30 minutes. Meanwhile, coarsely chop 2 tablespoons pecans; finely chop remaining pecans; set aside.

2. In small saucepan over medium-low heat, melt butter or margarine. Remove saucepan from heat; stir in brown sugar and finely chopped pecans until well mixed.

3. In small bowl with mixer at medium speed, beat heavy or whipping cream until soft peaks form. Spoon half of ice cream into four 6-ounce freezer-safe parfait or wine glasses; top with pecan mixture, then remaining ice cream. Garnish each parfait with a dollop of whipped cream and coarsely chopped pecans. Freeze until firm, about 2 hours.

4. To serve, let parfaits stand at room temperature 10 minutes to soften slightly.

Banana-Split Cake

TIME: start early in day or day ahead—SERVINGS: 16

1 pint vanilla ice cream
¾ cup California walnuts
½ cup graham-cracker crumbs
butter or margarine
sugar
½ cup cocoa
1 cup heavy or whipping cream
1 teaspoon vanilla extract
4 ripe medium bananas
1 pint chocolate ice cream
1 pint strawberry ice cream
6 maraschino cherries for
garnish

1. Place vanilla ice cream in refrigerator to soften slightly, about 40 minutes. Meanwhile, finely chop ½ cup walnuts. Reserve remaining ¼ cup nuts for garnish later. In 9" by 3" springform pan, combine chopped walnuts, graham-cracker crumbs, 3 tablespoons butter or margarine, and 2 tablespoons sugar. With fingers, press mixture to bottom of pan. Evenly spread vanilla ice cream on top of crust; freeze until firm, about 45 minutes.

2. While waiting for vanilla ice cream to harden, in 2-quart saucepan over medium heat, cook cocoa, ½ cup heavy or whipping cream, ¾ cup sugar, and 4 tablespoons butter or margarine until mixture is smooth and boils, stirring constantly. Remove saucepan from heat; stir in vanilla. Cool fudge sauce to room temperature.

3. Split 3 bananas lengthwise in half. Remove pan from freezer. Pour fudge sauce over vanilla ice cream; top with split bananas. Return cake to freezer; freeze 1 hour or until fudge sauce is firm. Place chocolate ice cream in refrigerator to soften slightly.

4. Spread chocolate ice cream over fudge and bananas. Return cake to freezer; freeze about 20 minutes to harden slightly. Remove strawberry ice cream from container to medium bowl; let stand at room temperature, stirring occasionally until of smooth, spreading consistency, but not melted. Spread strawberry ice cream over chocolate ice cream. Return to freezer; cover and freeze until firm, about 3 hours.

5. To serve, with fingers, break reserved ¼ cup walnuts into small pieces. In small bowl with mixer at medium speed, beat remaining ½ cup heavy or whipping cream until soft peaks form. Cut remaining banana diagonally into slices. Run knife or metal spatula, dipped in hot water, around edge of springform pan to loosen ice cream. Remove side of pan. Spread top of cake with whipped cream. Arrange banana slices, cherries, and broken walnuts on whipped cream.

Cassis Sorbet

TIME: start early in day or up to 1 month ahead—YIELD: 3½ cups

2¼ cups water
½ cup sugar
1 10-ounce package frozen
raspberries in quick-thaw
pouch, thawed
⅓ cup black-currant- or black-
raspberry-flavor liqueur
3 tablespoons lemon juice
¼ teaspoon salt

1. In 2-quart saucepan over medium heat, heat water and sugar to boiling; boil 5 minutes, stirring occasionally. Refrigerate sugar syrup until chilled, about 2 hours.

2. In blender at medium speed, blend raspberries, liqueur, lemon juice, and salt until smooth. Press raspberry mixture through sieve to remove seeds.

3. Stir raspberry mixture into cooled sugar syrup until mixed; pour mixture into 8" by 8" baking pan. Cover pan with foil or plastic wrap and freeze until firm, about 3½ hours, stirring occasionally.

4. To serve, let sorbet stand at room temperature 10 minutes to soften slightly. Spoon sorbet into small glasses.

Feather-Light Raspberry Sherbet Roll

TIME: about 4½ hours or start up to 2 weeks ahead—SERVINGS: 16

¾ cup cake flour
1 teaspoon double-acting baking
    powder
½ teaspoon salt
4 eggs, separated, at room
    temperature
sugar
¾ teaspoon vanilla extract
confectioners' sugar
2 pints raspberry sherbet

1. Grease 15½" by 10½" jelly-roll pan; line pan with waxed paper. In small bowl, mix flour, baking powder, and salt; set aside.

2. Preheat oven to 375°F. In another small bowl with mixer at high speed, beat egg whites until soft peaks form. Beating at high speed, gradually sprinkle in ¼ cup sugar, beating until sugar is completely dissolved. (Whites should stand in stiff, glossy peaks.)

3. In large bowl with same beaters and with mixer at high speed, beat egg yolks, vanilla, and ½ cup sugar until thick. With wire whisk or rubber spatula, gently fold flour mixture and beaten egg whites into egg-yolk mixture. Spread batter evenly in jelly-roll pan; bake 15 minutes or until cake is golden and top of cake springs back when lightly touched with finger.

4. Meanwhile, lightly sprinkle clean cloth towel with some confectioners' sugar. When cake is done, immediately invert cake onto towel. Carefully peel waxed paper from cake. Starting at a narrow end, roll cake with towel, jelly-roll fashion. Place cake, seam-side down, on wire rack; cool completely, about 30 minutes. Meanwhile, soften sherbet slightly in refrigerator.

5. Unroll cooled cake. Spread top of cake evenly with sherbet. Starting at same narrow end, reroll cake without towel. Wrap cake tightly with foil; freeze until firm, about 3 hours.

6. To serve, place cake, seam-side down, on chilled platter. If desired, sprinkle cake with some confectioners' sugar.

Strawberry-Orange Ice

TIME: start early in day or up to 1 month ahead—SERVINGS: 20

1¾ cups orange juice*
½ cup lemon juice
3 pints strawberries, hulled
1¾ cups sugar
⅛ teaspoon salt

*If desired, substitute ¼ cup orange-flavor liqueur for ¼ cup of the orange juice.

1. In covered blender at high speed, blend all ingredients until smooth, blending about half at a time. (Or, press strawberries through food mill into large bowl; stir in remaining ingredients.) Pour strawberry mixture into a 13" by 9" baking pan and mix well.

2. Cover pan with foil or plastic wrap and freeze until partially frozen (frozen firm to one inch from the edge of pan), about 4 hours, stirring occasionally.

3. Spoon strawberry mixture into chilled bowl, and, with mixer at medium speed, beat until smooth but still frozen. Return strawberry mixture to baking pan. Cover with foil or plastic wrap and freeze mixture until firm, about 3 hours.

4. To serve, remove mixture from freezer and let stand at room temperature 10 minutes for easier scooping. Makes about 10 cups.

Lemon Granita (Water Ices)

TIME: early in day or start up to 1 month ahead—
YIELD: about 3 cups

2 cups water
1 cup sugar
4 large lemons

1. In 2-quart saucepan over high heat, heat water and sugar to boiling. Reduce heat to medium; cook 5 minutes.

2. Meanwhile, from lemons, grate 2 teaspoons peel and squeeze enough juice to make ¾ cup. Stir lemon peel and juice into sugar mixture; pour into 8" by 8" baking pan. Freeze until firm, about 5 hours, stirring occasionally so mixture freezes evenly.

3. To serve, let granita stand at room temperature 10 minutes to soften slightly. Then with spoon, scrape across surface of granita to create a "pebbly" texture; spoon into dessert dishes. Makes six ½-cup servings.

Orange Granita: Prepare sugar mixture as above. Meanwhile, from *3 large oranges,* grate 2 teaspoons peel and squeeze enough juice to make 1 orange peel, juice, and *2 tablespoons lemon juice* into sugar mixture. Freeze and serve as above.

Strawberry Granita: Prepare sugar mixture as above, but use only *1 cup water* and *½ cup sugar.* Stir *2 pints strawberries,* pureed, and *1 tablespoon lemon juice* into sugar mixture. Freeze and serve as above.

Coffee Granita: Prepare sugar mixture as above, but use *3 cups water, ⅓ cup sugar,* and *¼ cup instant espresso coffee powder.* Freeze and serve as above.

Spumoni Elegante

TIME: start day ahead or up to 2 weeks ahead—SERVINGS: 12

2 cups milk
3 eggs
¼ teaspoon salt
sugar
½ teaspoon orange extract
1 large lime
1 cup heavy or whipping cream
⅓ cup diced mixed candied fruit
1 large strawberry for garnish

1. In heavy 2-quart saucepan, with wire whisk or fork, beat milk, eggs, salt, and ¾ cup sugar until blended. Cook over medium-low heat until mixture thickens and coats a spoon, about 30 minutes, stirring frequently. (Do not boil or mixture will curdle.) Remove saucepan from heat; stir in orange extract. Pour custard mixture into medium bowl; cover and freeze about 3 hours or until almost firm.

2. With back of large spoon, spread frozen mixture evenly to line inside of 8½" by 4½" loaf pan. Cover; freeze about 1 hour.

3. Grate 1 teaspoon peel from half of lime; set aside. Wrap remaining lime with plastic wrap; refrigerate to use for garnish later. In small bowl with mixer at medium speed, beat heavy or whipping cream and ¼ cup sugar until soft peaks form. Fold in candied fruit and grated lime peel. Remove pan from freezer; spoon whipped-cream mixture into center of frozen custard; cover and freeze overnight or until firm.

4. To serve, invert spumoni onto chilled platter. For flower garnish, cut remaining peel from reserved lime for stem and leaves; cut strawberry for petals. Garnish dessert with lime peel and strawberry slices.

233

Almond-Cordial Parfaits

TIME: about 30 minutes—SERVINGS: 4

1 pint coffee ice cream
¼ cup almond-flavor liqueur
¼ cup crushed almond
  macaroons (about 6 cookies)
½ cup heavy or whipping cream,
  whipped

1. Let ice cream stand at room temperature to soften, about 15 minutes.

2. Into four 6-ounce freezer-safe parfait glasses, spoon one-third of ice cream; top with half of almond-flavor liqueur, then another third of ice cream. Sprinkle with half of macarons; top with remaining ice cream and almond-flavor liqueur. Spoon all of the whipped cream on top; sprinkle with remaining macaroons. Serve immediately or place in freezer to serve later.

FRUIT DESSERTS

Gingered Fruit Compote

TIME: about 1 hour—SERVINGS: 6

1 29-ounce jar fruit for salad
1 17-ounce jar figs
2 tablespoons butter or
  margarine
3 tablespoons brown sugar
1½ teaspoons ground ginger

1. Preheat oven to 300°F.

2. Drain fruit well. In 1-quart casserole, combine all ingredients. Bake in oven 40 minutes or until hot and bubbly and fruit is heated through; stir fruit mixture after 15 minutes of baking to mix butter and brown sugar with fruit.

Summer Fruit Bowl

TIME: start early in day—SERVINGS: 16

2 cups water
1½ cups sugar
3 tablespoons lime juice
¾ cup loosely packed mint
  leaves, minced, or 1
  tablespoon dried mint
1 20-pound watermelon
1 small cantaloupe
6 large plums
4 large nectarines
1 pound seedless green grapes

1. In 2-quart saucepan over medium heat, cook water, sugar, and lime juice 15 minutes or until mixture becomes a light syrup. Stir in mint leaves; cover and refrigerate until well chilled.

2. Cut watermelon into bite-sized pieces; discard seeds. Cut cantaloupe into bite-sized pieces; cut plums and nectarines into wedges. Combine cut-up fruits with grapes and arrange in very large bowl. Pour chilled syrup through strainer over fruit. Cover and refrigerate to blend flavors, stirring mixture occasionally.

Springtime Rhubarb Refresher

TIME: about 20 minutes—SERVINGS: 4

1 pound rhubarb, cut into 1-inch
  pieces (about 2½ cups) or 1
  16-ounce package frozen
  rhubarb
¼ cup sugar
¼ cup strawberry jelly
¼ teaspoon ground cinnamon
⅛ teaspoon salt

1. In 2-quart saucepan over medium heat, heat all ingredients to boiling. Reduce heat to low; cover and simmer 10 minutes or until rhubarb is tender, stirring occasionally.

2. Spoon rhubarb mixture into 4 dessert dishes. Serve warm or refrigerate to serve cold later.

Sacramento Fruit Bowl

TIME: start early in day or day ahead—SERVINGS: 12

2 cups water
1½ cups sugar
3 tablespoons lemon juice
2 tablespoons anise seeds
½ teaspoon salt
1 small pineapple
1 small honeydew melon
1 small cantaloupe
2 oranges
2 large nectarines
2 large purple plums
½ pound green grapes
2 kiwi fruit

1. In 2-quart saucepan over medium heat, cook water, sugar, lemon juice, anise seeds, and salt 15 minutes or until mixture becomes a light syrup. Refrigerate until syrup is cool.

2. Meanwhile, remove peel from pineapple, honeydew melon, and cantaloupe. Cut pulp from pineapple and melons into bite-sized chunks. Peel and section oranges. Slice nectarines and plums into wedges—do not peel. Slice grapes in half; remove any seeds.

3. In large bowl, combine cut-up fruit. Pour chilled syrup through strainer over fruit. Cover and refrigerate until well chilled, stirring occasionally.

4. To serve, peel and slice kiwi fruit. Gently stir kiwi-fruit slices into fruit mixture. Serve as first course, salad, or dessert.

Pineapple Upside-Down Cups

TIME: about 30 minutes—SERVINGS: 4

4 teaspoons butter or margarine
¼ cup packed brown sugar
1 8-ounce can pineapple slices in pineapple juice
4 maraschino cherries
1 4½-ounce package refrigerated buttermilk biscuits
heavy cream (optional)

1. Place 1 teaspoon butter or margarine and 1 tablespoon brown sugar in each of four 10-ounce custard cups. Arrange a slice of pineapple and a cherry in each cup.

2. Preheat oven to 450°F. Shape 1½ biscuits into 3-inch round circle; place on top of pineapple in cup. Repeat with remaining biscuits. Place cups in jelly-roll pan for easier handling. Bake 10 to 15 minutes until biscuits are cooked through and golden. If biscuits brown too quickly, cover with sheet of foil during last minutes of baking.

3. To serve, invert each custard cup onto dessert plate. Serve with heavy cream, if desired.

Grape Salad-Dessert Mold

TIME: about 6 hours or start early in day—SERVINGS: 12

3 3-ounce packages lemon-flavor gelatin
boiling water
½ pound red seedless grapes
½ pound green seedless grapes
1 16-ounce container cottage cheese

1. In medium bowl, stir 2 packages lemon-flavor gelatin with 2½ cups boiling water until gelatin is completely dissolved. Refrigerate until mixture mounds slightly when dropped from a spoon, about 1 hour.

2. Cut red and green grapes into halves. Fold grapes into thickened gelatin mixture; pour into 6-cup ring mold. Cover and refrigerate until almost set, about 30 minutes.

3. In small bowl, stir remaining package of lemon-flavor gelatin with ½ cup boiling water until dissolved. In covered blender at high speed, blend gelatin mixture and cottage cheese until smooth. Pour cottage-cheese mixture over gelatin layer in mold. Cover and refrigerate until set, at least 3 hours.

4. To serve, carefully unmold gelatin onto chilled platter.

Poached Peaches with Fresh Raspberry Sauce

TIME: about 2½ hours or start day ahead—SERVINGS: 8

1 tablespoon vanilla extract
water
sugar
8 medium peaches, peeled
1 pint raspberries
8 small nontoxic leaves for
  garnish (optional)

1. In 5-quart Dutch oven over high heat, heat vanilla extract, 6 cups water, and 1¼ cups sugar until sugar dissolves, stirring occasionally. Add peaches; heat to boiling. Reduce heat to low; cover and simmer 8 minutes, occasionally basting peaches with syrup in pan.

2. With slotted spoon, remove peaches to 12" by 8" baking dish; cover and refrigerate until chilled, about 2 hours.

3. Meanwhile, prepare raspberry sauce: In blender at high speed or in food processor with knife blade attached, blend raspberries and ½ teaspoon sugar until smooth, adding water if needed to thin to desired consistency. If desired, press sauce through fine sieve to remove seeds.

4. To serve, into each of 8 stemmed glasses or dessert dishes, spoon some raspberry sauce, then place a peach on sauce. If desired, garnish each peach with a leaf.

Melon Cordial Cups

TIME: about 30 minutes—SERVINGS: 6

1 small honeydew melon
1 small cantaloupe
6 egg yolks
¼ cup sugar
¼ cup almond-flavor liqueur

1. Cut honeydew and cantaloupe into bite-sized chunks. Place fruit in six 12-ounce wine goblets or dessert dishes; set aside.

2. In double boiler over hot, *not boiling,* water, with portable mixer at high speed or hand beater, beat egg yolks and sugar until thick, about 5 minutes. Add almond-flavor liqueur and continue beating until mixture is fluffy and mounds slightly when dropped from a spoon. Spoon mixture over melon. Serve immediately.

Banana Betty

TIME: about 45 minutes—SERVINGS: 8

4 tablespoons butter or
  margarine
6 slices raisin bread with
  cinnamon, diced
1 medium lemon
3 tablespoons sugar
½ teaspoon ground cinnamon
6 medium bananas, cut into
  ½-inch slices
½ cup water
milk

1. Preheat oven to 350°F. Grease 1½-quart casserole. In 1-quart saucepan over medium-low heat, melt butter or margarine. Remove saucepan from heat; stir in raisin bread; set aside.

2. Grate 1 tablespoon peel and squeeze 2 tablespoons juice from lemon. In medium bowl, mix lemon peel, sugar, and cinnamon. Add sliced bananas and lemon juice. With rubber spatula, toss gently to mix well.

3. Place one-third of bread mixture in even layer in casserole; top with one-half of banana mixture. Repeat layering once. Top with remaining bread mixture. Pour water over mixture. Cover casserole and bake 30 minutes or until heated through. Serve with milk.

Pear Dumplings à La Crème

TIME: about 1½ hours or start early in day—SERVINGS: 6

3 ripe medium Bartlett pears
1½ cups all-purpose flour
½ cup butter or margarine, softened
1 3-ounce package cream cheese, softened
¼ teaspoon ground cinnamon
sugar
1 egg, separated
2 cups half-and-half
4 teaspoons cornstarch
¼ teaspoon salt
¼ teaspoon almond extract
6 whole cloves

1. Peel pears. Cut each pear lengthwise in half; remove cores; set aside.

2. Into medium bowl, measure flour, butter or margarine, and cream cheese. With hand, knead mixture until well blended. On lightly floured surface with floured rolling pin, roll half of pastry to ⅛-inch thickness. Using 7-inch round plate as guide, cut 3 circles from pastry. Reserve pastry trimmings.

3. In cup, combine cinnamon and 1 tablespoon sugar. Sprinkle pastry circles with half of sugar mixture. Place a pear half, cut-side up, on each pastry circle. Fold pastry over pears; pinch edges to seal. Place pastry-covered pears, seam-side down, on large cookie sheet. Repeat with remaining pastry and pear halves to make 6 in all.

4. Preheat oven to 375°F. Reroll pastry trimmings; cut to make leaves. Brush pastry-covered pears with egg white; decorate with pastry leaves; brush leaves with egg white. Bake pear dumplings 35 minutes or until pastry is golden. Remove dumplings to wire rack. Cool slightly.

5. Meanwhile, in 2-quart saucepan, combine half-and-half, cornstarch, salt, egg yolk, and 3 tablespoons sugar. Over medium heat, cook, stirring constantly, until custard coats the back of spoon, about 15 minutes. Remove from heat; stir in almond extract. Cool slightly.

6. To serve, in each of 6 dessert dishes, spoon some custard; place a pear dumpling in custard. Insert a whole clove in tip of each dumpling to resemble a stem or refrigerate pears and custard separately to serve chilled later.

Caramel Pears

TIME: about 1½ hours—SERVINGS: 8

6 tablespoons butter or margarine
¼ cup water
3 tablespoons brown sugar
8 medium pears
8 small nontoxic leaves for garnish

1. In shallow casserole or 12″ by 8″ baking dish (the dish should be large enough to hold all the pears in single layer), in 425° oven, heat butter or margarine, water, and brown sugar until mixture is melted and smooth. Remove the casserole from oven.

2. Meanwhile, peel pears. With apple corer, remove cores from bottoms of pears, but do not remove stems. Arrange pears in syrup in casserole. Cover casserole with foil and bake 30 to 40 minutes until pears are tender, occasionally basting pears with syrup in casserole.

3. Garnish each pear with a leaf. Serve pears warm with syrup.

Apple Dessert Pancake

TIME: about 40 minutes—SERVINGS: 8

1 large Golden Delicious apple
4 tablespoons butter
1 teaspoon ground cinnamon
sugar
⅓ cup all-purpose flour
⅓ cup milk
½ teaspoon double-acting
  baking powder
⅛ teaspoon salt
4 eggs, separated

1. Peel, core, and cut apple into ¼-inch slices; set aside.

2. In 10-inch skillet with oven-safe handle (or cover skillet handle with heavy-duty foil), over medium-low heat, melt butter. (Do *not* use margarine because it separates from sugar during cooking.) Stir in cinnamon and ¼ cup sugar; remove skillet from heat. Arrange apple slices in butter mixture, overlapping slices slightly. Return skillet to heat; cook over low heat 10 minutes or until apples are tender-crisp.

3. Meanwhile, preheat oven to 400°F. In medium bowl, with fork, beat flour, milk, baking powder, salt, and egg yolks until blended; set aside. In small bowl with mixer at high speed, beat egg whites and ⅓ cup sugar until soft peaks form. Fold egg-white mixture into egg-yolk mixture.

4. Spread egg mixture evenly over apple slices in skillet. Bake 10 minutes or until pancake is golden brown. Remove skillet from oven. With metal spatula, loosen edge of pancake from skillet. Carefully invert pancake onto warm platter; serve immediately.

Apple Pandowdy

TIME: about 1½ hours—SERVINGS: 9

5 large cooking apples (about 3
  pounds)
⅓ cup sugar
1 teaspoon ground cinnamon
salt
3 tablespoons butter or
  margarine
⅓ cup light molasses
¼ cup water
1 cup all-purpose flour
2 teaspoons double-acting
  baking powder
3 tablespoons shortening
¾ cup milk
heavy or whipping cream
  (optional)

1. Peel, core, and thinly slice apples to make 8 cups. In large bowl with rubber spatula, lightly toss apples, sugar, cinnamon, and ¼ teaspoon salt; spoon apple mixture into 8″ by 8″ by 2″ baking dish.

2. In small saucepan over low heat, melt butter or margarine; remove saucepan from heat. Stir in molasses and water; pour over apple mixture in baking dish; set aside.

3. Preheat oven to 375°F. Prepare biscuit crust: In medium bowl, with fork, mix flour, baking powder, and ¾ teaspoon salt. With pastry blender or two knives used scissor-fashion, cut in shortening until mixture resembles coarse crumbs. With fork, stir milk into dry ingredients just until flour is moistened.

4. With spoon, drop dough by heaping tablespoons into 9 mounds on apple mixture. Bake 45 minutes or until crust is golden and apples are tender.

5. To serve, with spoon, break up crust and stir into apple mixture; serve warm in dessert bowls. If desired, pour some heavy or whipping cream over each serving.

Skillet Apple Dessert

TIME: about 15 minutes—SERVINGS: 6

3 large red cooking apples
4 tablespoons butter or
   margarine
3 tablespoons light brown sugar
2 teaspoons lemon juice
¾ teaspoon ground cinnamon
¼ teaspoon salt
heavy or whipping cream
   (optional)

1. Core apples; cut into ½-inch-thick wedges.

2. In 12-inch skillet over medium heat, in hot butter or margarine, cook apples, sugar, lemon juice, cinnamon, and salt until apples are tender, about 5 minutes, stirring frequently.

3. Spoon apples and their syrup into 6 dessert bowls. If desired, serve with heavy or whipping cream.

Cranberry Baked Apples

TIME: about 45 minutes—SERVINGS: 6

3 medium red cooking apples
1 8-ounce can whole berry
   cranberry sauce
1 tablespoon lemon juice
⅛ teaspoon ground ginger
3 tablespoons butter or
   margarine, cut up

1. Cut each apple lengthwise in half; remove core. Arrange apple halves, cut-side up, in 12″ by 8″ baking dish.

2. Preheat oven to 350°F. In small bowl, mix cranberry sauce, lemon juice, and ginger. Spoon cranberry mixture over apples; dot with butter or margarine.

3. Bake apples 30 minutes or until fork-tender.

CREAMS, MOUSSES, AND SOUFFLÉS

Orange Cream

TIME: about 15 minutes—SERVINGS: 8

2 pints orange sherbet, softened
1 pint vanilla ice cream, softened
¼ cup orange-flavor liqueur
1 tablespoon lime juice

In large bowl with mixer at low speed, blend sherbet, ice cream, orange-flavor liqueur, and lime juice until smooth but not melted—texture is milk-shake consistency. Pour mixture into eight 5-ounce wine glasses.

Orange-Cream Parfaits

TIME: about 1 hour or start early in day—SERVINGS: 10

1 cup water
1 3-ounce package orange-flavor
   gelatin
2 cups ice cubes
1 pint vanilla ice cream, cut into
   chunks
1 11-ounce can mandarin-orange
   sections, drained

1. In 2-quart saucepan over high heat, heat water to boiling. Remove saucepan from heat; add gelatin, stirring until gelatin is completely dissolved. Add ice cubes, stirring constantly until gelatin begins to thicken slightly, about 10 minutes. Discard any undissolved ice.

2. In blender at medium speed, blend gelatin mixture with ice cream about 30 seconds until just mixed. Spoon half of orange-cream mixture into ten 4-ounce dessert glasses. Top with half of mandarin oranges; spoon remaining orange-cream mixture into glasses. Refrigerate parfaits at least 30 minutes or until set. Garnish parfaits with remaining mandarin-orange sections.

Strawberry-Peach Cream

TIME: about 4½ hours or start early in day—SERVINGS: 12

1½ cups milk
½ teaspoon salt
6 eggs, separated, at room
   temperature
sugar
2 envelopes unflavored gelatin
1½ pounds peaches (about 6
   medium peaches)
2 teaspoons lemon juice
1 pint strawberries
½ cup heavy or whipping cream

1. In heavy 2-quart saucepan, with wire whisk or fork, beat milk, salt, egg yolks, and ½ cup sugar until blended. Evenly sprinkle gelatin over mixture. Cook over medium-low heat, stirring constantly, until gelatin is completely dissolved and mixture thickens and coats a spoon, about 20 minutes. (Do not let mixture boil or it will curdle). Remove saucepan from heat. Pour two-thirds of egg-yolk mixture into medium bowl; set both mixtures aside.

2. Peel peaches; discard pits; cut into chunks. In food processor with knife blade attached or in blender at medium speed, blend chopped peaches and lemon juice until smooth to make about 2 cups puree. Stir peach puree into egg-yolk mixture in bowl. Cover and refrigerate until mixture mounds slightly when dropped from a spoon, about 40 minutes, stirring occasionally.

3. Meanwhile, hull strawberries. In food processor or blender, blend strawberries until smooth to make about 1 cup puree. Stir strawberry puree into egg-yolk mixture in saucepan. Cover and refrigerate until mixture mounds slightly when dropped from a spoon, about 30 minutes, stirring occasionally.

4. In large bowl with mixer at high speed, beat egg whites until soft peaks form. Beating at high speed, gradually beat in ¼ cup sugar, beating until sugar is completely dissolved. (Whites should stand in stiff, glossy peaks.)

5. In small bowl with mixer at medium speed, beat heavy or whipping cream until soft peaks form. With wire whisk or rubber spatula, gently fold whipped cream and peach puree into beaten egg whites. Alternately spoon peach and strawberry mixtures into 1½-quart glass bowl. With spoon, cut and twist through mixtures to obtain a marbled effect. Cover and refrigerate until set, about 3 hours.

Pots de Crème au Chocolat

TIME: about 5 hours or start early in day—SERVINGS: 4

1 cup half-and-half
2 squares semisweet chocolate
3 egg yolks
2 tablespoons sugar
¼ teaspoon salt
1 teaspoon vanilla extract
⅓ cup heavy or whipping cream
2 teaspoons grated orange peel
   for garnish

1. In 1-quart saucepan over medium heat, heat half-and-half until hot (do not boil); set aside.

2. Meanwhile, in double boiler over hot, *not boiling* water, melt chocolate squares, stirring occasionally. Remove double-boiler top from heat. With wire whisk or fork, beat egg yolks into melted chocolate until smooth; stir in sugar and salt. Gradually stir in half-and-half until well blended.

3. Place double-boiler top over simmering water; cook until mixture thickens and coats a spoon, about 15 minutes, stirring constantly. Stir in vanilla extract. Pour mixture into four 3-ounce demitasse or pots de crème cups. Refrigerate at least 4 hours or until mixture is set.

4. To serve, in small bowl with mixer at medium speed, beat heavy or whipping cream until stiff peaks form. Spoon whipped cream into small decorating bag with large rosette tube. Top each pot de crème with a large whipped-cream rosette. Garnish with grated orange peel.

Crème Caramel

TIME: about 2½ hours or start early in day—SERVINGS: 6

sugar
4 eggs
2 cups milk
1 teaspoon vanilla extract
¼ teaspoon salt
6 lemon-peel twists for garnish
6 small nontoxic leaves for
   garnish

1. Preheat oven to 325°F. Grease six 6-ounce custard cups. In small saucepan over medium heat, heat ¼ cup sugar until melted and a light caramel color, stirring constantly. Immediately pour into prepared custard cups.

2. In large bowl, with wire whisk or fork, beat eggs and ¼ cup sugar until well blended. Beat in milk, vanilla, and salt until well mixed; pour mixture into custard cups.

3. Place custard cups in 13″ by 9″ baking pan; fill pan with hot water to come halfway up sides of custard cups. Bake 50 to 55 minutes until knife inserted in center of custard comes out clean. Remove cups from water in baking pan; cover and refrigerate until chilled, about 1½ hours.

4. To serve, unmold each custard onto a chilled dessert plate, allowing caramel topping to drip from cup onto custard. Garnish each custard with a lemon-peel twist and a leaf.

Marbled Chocolate Mousse

TIME: start early in day or day ahead—SERVINGS: 12

3 eggs, separated, at room
   temperature
2 cups milk
¾ cup sugar
2 envelopes unflavored gelatin
1½ teaspoons vanilla extract
¼ cup cocoa
2 cups heavy or whipping cream

1. Prepare collar for 1-quart soufflé dish: From roll of waxed paper, tear off a 20-inch strip; fold lengthwise in half. Wrap waxed-paper strip around outside of dish so collar stands 2 inches above rim. Secure with cellophane tape.

2. In 2-quart saucepan, with wire whisk, beat egg yolks, milk, and sugar until well mixed; sprinkle gelatin evenly over mixture. Over medium-low heat, cook, stirring constantly, until gelatin is completely dissolved and mixture coats a spoon, about 10 minutes. Stir in vanilla.

3. Pour half of yolk mixture into medium bowl; stir in cocoa until smooth. Cover and refrigerate both mixtures until they mound slightly when dropped from a spoon, about 30 minutes.

4. In small bowl with mixer at high speed, beat egg whites until stiff peaks form. In large bowl with mixer at medium speed, beat heavy or whipping cream until soft peaks form. With rubber spatula, fold half of beaten egg whites and half of beaten cream into the chocolate mixture; fold remaining egg whites and cream into the vanilla mixture.

5. Alternately spoon chocolate and vanilla mixtures into prepared soufflé dish. With knife, cut through mixtures to make a pretty swirled design. Cover and refrigerate mousse until set, about 3 hours. Carefully remove collar before serving.

241

Mocha-Meringue Heart

TIME: start early in day—SERVINGS: 14

MERINGUE:
5 egg whites, at room
   temperature
¼ teaspoon cream of tartar
⅛ teaspoon salt
¾ cup sugar
1 teaspoon almond extract

MOCHA BUTTER CREAM:
1½ cups butter or margarine
1¾ cups confectioners' sugar
5 egg yolks
1 square unsweetened chocolate,
   melted and cooled
1 tablespoon instant espresso
   coffee powder
1 tablespoon water

DECORATION:
½ square unsweetened
   chocolate, grated
½ cup sliced blanched almonds,
   toasted

1. Prepare Meringue: Line 2 large cookie sheets with foil. Gently, with toothpick, mark two 8-inch hearts on foil on first cookie sheet and one 8-inch heart on foil on second cookie sheet. (Or using 8-inch round plate as guide, mark 3 circles on foil.) Set aside.

2. In large bowl with mixer at high speed, beat egg whites, cream of tartar, and salt until soft peaks form. Beating at high speed, gradually beat in sugar, 2 tablespoons at a time, beating well after each addition until sugar is completely dissolved. Add almond extract and continue beating until meringue stands in stiff, glossy peaks.

3. Preheat oven to 275°F. Spoon one-third of meringue inside each heart outline on cookie sheets. With metal spatula, evenly spread meringue within hearts. Bake 1 hour or until meringues are golden. Cool meringues on cookie sheets 10 minutes. With metal spatula, carefully loosen and remove meringues to wire racks to cool completely.

4. Meanwhile, prepare Mocha Butter Cream: Cut butter into ¼-inch-thick slices. In large bowl with mixer at high speed, beat butter or margarine and confectioners' sugar until smooth. Add egg yolks and continue beating until mixture is slightly thickened and creamy; stir in melted chocolate until blended. In cup, dissolve instant espresso coffee powder in water; stir into butter cream.

5. Assemble dessert: Place first meringue layer on cake plate; spread with one-fourth of butter cream. Place second meringue layer on butter cream; spread with another one-fourth of butter cream; top with remaining meringue layer. Spread remaining butter cream on side and top of dessert.

6. Decorations: Sprinkle top of dessert with grated chocolate and 2 tablespoons toasted almonds to make a pretty design. With hand, press remaining almonds into butter cream on side of dessert.

7. Refrigerate dessert at least 4 hours to soften meringue layers slightly for easier cutting.

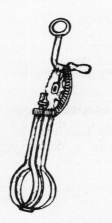

Zabaglione on Fresh Berries

TIME: about 20 minutes—SERVINGS: 4

1½ pints strawberries or 1 pint
   raspberries
3 egg yolks
3 tablespoons sugar
¼ cup dry or sweet Marsala
   wine

1. Arrange strawberries in 4 wine goblets or dessert dishes; set aside.

2. In double boiler over hot, *not boiling,* water, with portable mixer at high speed, or hand beater, beat egg yolks and sugar until very thick, about 5 minutes. Add Marsala and continue beating until mixture is fluffy and mounds slightly when dropped from a spoon. Spoon mixture over strawberries. Serve immediately.

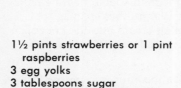

Hot Chocolate Soufflé

TIME: about 2 hours—SERVINGS: 8

½ cup all-purpose flour
sugar
1½ cups milk
3 squares unsweetened
   chocolate, coarsely chopped or
   grated
6 eggs, separated
butter or margarine
¼ teaspoon salt
2 teaspoons vanilla extract
confectioners' sugar

1. Into 2-quart saucepan, measure flour and ¼ cup sugar; with wire whisk or spoon, slowly stir in milk until smooth. Cook over medium heat, stirring constantly, until mixture thickens and boils; continue to cook 1 minute; remove saucepan from heat.

2. Stir chocolate into mixture until melted. Rapidly beat in egg yolks, all at once until well mixed; refrigerate to cool to lukewarm, stirring occasionally.

3. Preheat oven to 375°F. Grease 2½-quart soufflé dish or round casserole with butter or margarine and lightly sprinkle with sugar. In large bowl with mixer at high speed, beat egg whites and salt until soft peaks form; beating at high speed, gradually sprinkle in ¼ cup sugar; beat until sugar is completely dissolved. Whites should stand in stiff peaks. With rubber spatula, gently fold chocolate mixture, one-third at a time, and vanilla into egg whites until blended.

4. Pour mixture into soufflé dish; with back of spoon, about 1 inch from edge of dish, make 1-inch indentation all around (this will produce a "top-hat" effect when soufflé is done). Bake 35 to 40 minues until knife inserted under "top hat" comes out clean.

5. When soufflé is done, sprinkle with confectioners' sugar. Serve immediately.

CUSTARDS AND PUDDINGS

Strawberry-Custard Layered Dessert

TIME: about 2 hours or start early in day—SERVINGS: 6

1 pint strawberries
¼ cup orange-flavor liqueur
½ 10¾- to 12-ounce frozen
   ready-to-serve pound cake,
   thawed
½ cup heavy or whipping cream
1 3½- to 3¾-ounce package
   vanilla-flavor instant pudding
   and pie filling
2 cups milk

1. Wash and hull strawberries, reserving 5 strawberries for garnish. Thinly slice remaining strawberries; place in medium bowl with orange-flavor liqueur; let stand 30 minutes, stirring occasionally.

2. Meanwhile, cut pound cake into ⅛-inch-thick slices; set aside.

3. In small bowl with mixer at medium speed, beat heavy or whipping cream until soft peaks form; set aside. In medium bowl, prepare instant pudding as label directs, using 2 cups milk. With wire whisk or rubber spatula, fold whipped cream into prepared pudding.

4. Arrange half of pound cake slices in single layer in 1½-quart glass bowl, cutting slices to fit if necessary. Top with half of strawberry mixture, then half of pudding mixture. Repeat layering. Cover and refrigerate until well chilled, about 1 hour.

5. To serve, cut each reserved strawberry in half; garnish dessert with strawberries.

Cherry-Cheese Custard

TIME: about 1¼ hours—SERVINGS: 6

1 21-ounce can cherry-pie filling
1 16-ounce container creamed
   cottage cheese
1 8-ounce container sour cream
½ cup sugar
2 teaspoons grated orange peel
1 teaspoon vanilla extract
2 eggs

1. Preheat oven to 325°F. Spoon cherry-pie filling into 8″ by 8″ baking dish; set aside.

2. In blender at medium speed, blend cottage cheese and remaining ingredients until smooth. Carefully pour cheese mixture over cherry filling in baking dish, being careful to cover cherry filling completely. Bake 1 hour or until custard is set.

Steamed Orange-Date Pudding

TIME: about 4 hours or start up to 3 days ahead—SERVINGS: 12

1 large orange
1 8-ounce package pitted dates
¾ cup sugar
½ cup butter or margarine,
   softened
4 eggs
2 cups all-purpose flour
2 teaspoons double-acting
   baking powder
Custard Sauce (right)

1. Heavily grease a 2½-quart bowl. Cut foil 1 inch larger than top of bowl to use as cover. Grease one side of foil very well; set aside.

2. From orange, grate 1 tablespoon peel and squeeze ½ cup juice; set orange peel aside. In blender at medium speed or in food processor with knife blade attached, blend orange juice with dates until well blended; set aside.

3. In large bowl with mixer at medium speed, beat sugar and butter or margarine until light and fluffy. Add eggs, flour, baking powder, orange peel, and date mixture; beat at low speed until blended. Increase speed to medium; beat 1 minute, occasionally scraping bowl with rubber spatula. Spoon pudding mixture into prepared bowl. Cover bowl with foil, greased-side down, tying tightly with string.

4. Set bowl on trivet in 12-quart saucepot. Pour in enough water to come half-way up side of bowl; over high heat, heat to boiling. Reduce heat to low; cover and simmer 2½ to 3 hours until toothpick inserted into center comes out clean.

5. About 30 minutes before pudding is done, prepare Custard Sauce; keep warm.

6. When pudding is done, cool in bowl on wire rack 5 minutes; loosen pudding with metal spatula and invert onto platter. Serve pudding warm with warm Custard Sauce.

Custard Sauce: In heavy 2-quart saucepan with wire whisk, mix *1½ cups milk, 2 tablespoons sugar, ¼ teaspoon salt,* and *4 egg yolks.* Over medium-low heat, cook, stirring constantly, until mixture is slightly thickened and coats back of spoon (do not boil or mixture will curdle). Remove saucepan from heat; stir in *½ teaspoon vanilla extract.*

TO DO AHEAD: Up to 3 days ahead, prepare pudding and sauce as above. Refrigerate sauce in covered small bowl. When pudding is done, remove from bowl and refrigerate until cool; then wrap pudding with foil or plastic wrap; return to refrigerator. To serve, resteam pudding in lightly greased bowl, covered, as directed above for 1½ hours. Reheat sauce in heavy 2-quart saucepan over low heat, stirring constantly, until heated through (do not boil). Serve as above.

Grandma's Best Bread Pudding

TIME: 1¼ hours—SERVINGS: 4

1½ cups milk
¼ cup sugar
1 teaspoon vanilla extract
¼ teaspoon salt
2 eggs
about ½ loaf Italian bread, cut
    into 1-inch chunks (4 cups)
¼ cup dark seedless raisins
1 tablespoon butter or margarine,
    cut up
ground cinnamon
half-and-half (optional)

1. Preheat oven to 350°F. Grease 1-quart casserole; set aside.

2. In medium bowl, with wire whisk or fork, beat milk, sugar, vanilla, salt, and eggs until well mixed; add Italian bread, raisins, and butter; toss until bread is well coated. Sprinkle mixture lightly with cinnamon; spoon into casserole.

3. Bake 55 to 60 minutes until knife inserted in center of pudding comes out clean. If desired, serve with half-and-half.

Bread-and-Butter Pudding

TIME: about 1¼ hours or start early in day—SERVINGS: 8

4 tablespoons butter or
    margarine, softened
12 slices firm white bread
¾ teaspoon ground cinnamon
3 cups milk
⅓ cup sugar
1½ teaspoons vanilla extract
¼ teaspoon salt
4 eggs

1. Preheat oven to 325°F. Grease 8″ by 8″ baking dish. Spread butter or margarine on bread slices. Arrange 4 slices of bread in dish in one layer, overlapping slightly if necessary; sprinkle lightly with ¼ teaspoon cinnamon. Repeat, making two more layers.

2. In medium bowl with wire whisk or fork, beat milk, sugar, vanilla, salt, and eggs until well mixed. Pour egg mixture over bread slices.

3. Bake 55 to 60 minutes until knife inserted in center of pudding comes out clean. Serve pudding warm or refrigerate to serve cold later.

Rice Pudding

TIME: about 3½ hours or start day ahead—SERVINGS: 6

4 cups milk
½ cup regular long-grain rice
¼ cup sugar
¼ teaspoon salt
2 eggs
1 teaspoon vanilla extract
6 maraschino cherries (optional)

1. In 4-quart saucepan over high heat, heat milk, rice, sugar, and salt to boiling. Reduce heat to low; cover and simmer 45 minutes to 1 hour until rice is very tender, stirring occasionally.

2. In small bowl, with fork, beat eggs slightly; stir in small amount of hot-rice mixture. Slowly pour egg mixture back into the rice mixture, stirring rapidly to prevent lumping. Cook, stirring constantly, until rice mixture is thickened, about 5 minutes. (Do not boil or mixture will curdle.) Remove saucepan from heat; stir in vanilla extract.

3. Spoon rice mixture into six 8-ounce goblets or dessert bowls. Cover and refrigerate until well chilled, about 2 hours.

4. To serve, top each dessert with a maraschino cherry if desired.

245

Old-Fashioned Pearl Tapioca Pudding

TIME: start early in day or day ahead—SERVINGS: 8

1 cup large pearl tapioca
2 cups water
5 cups milk
½ teaspoon salt
2 eggs
¾ cup sugar
2 tablespoons butter or margarine
1¼ teaspoons vanilla extract

1. In medium bowl, combine tapioca and water; cover and let stand at room temperature 6 to 12 hours. (If tapioca is soaked too long, it will lose its chewy texture.)

2. About 1¼ hours before serving or early in day, drain tapioca. In 3-quart saucepan over medium heat, heat tapioca, milk, and salt to boiling, stirring constantly with rubber spatula. Reduce heat to low; simmer, uncovered, 45 minutes, stirring frequently.

3. In small bowl, beat eggs with sugar; stir in small amount of hot tapioca mixture. Slowly pour egg mixture back into tapioca mixture, stirring rapidly to prevent lumping. Continue cooking over medium heat until mixture thickens, about 5 minutes, stirring constantly. (Do not boil, or mixture may curdle.) Remove saucepan from heat; stir in butter or margarine and vanilla.

4. Spoon tapioca pudding into eight 6-ounce parfait glasses or dessert dishes. Serve warm or cover and refrigerate to serve cold later.

Quick Tapioca Pudding: About 45 minutes before serving or early in day, in 3-quart saucepan, combine *2¾ cups milk, ⅓ cup sugar, 3 tablespoons quick-cooking tapioca, ¼ teaspoon salt,* and *1 egg* slightly beaten; let stand about 5 minutes. Cook tapioca mixture over medium heat, stirring constantly, until mixture boils. Remove saucepan from heat; stir in *2 tablespoons butter* or margarine and *1 teaspoon vanilla extract.* Serve as above. Makes 6 servings.

PASTRIES

Almond Cream-Puff Ring

TIME: about 3 hours—SERVINGS: 10

1 cup water
½ cup butter or margarine
¼ teaspoon salt
1 cup all-purpose flour
4 eggs
Almond-Cream Filling (page 247)
Chocolate Glaze (page 247)

1. In 2-quart saucepan over medium heat, heat water, butter or margarine, and salt until butter melts and mixture boils. Remove saucepan from heat. With wooden spoon, vigorously stir in flour all at once until mixture forms a ball and leaves side of saucepan.

2. Add eggs to flour mixture, 1 at a time, beating after each addition, until mixture is smooth and satiny. Cool mixture slightly.

3. Preheat oven to 400°F. Lightly grease and flour large cookie sheet. Using 7-inch plate as guide, trace a circle in flour on cookie sheet. Drop batter by heaping tablespoons into 10 mounds, inside circle, to form a ring.

4. Bake ring 40 minutes or until golden. Turn off oven; let ring remain in oven 15 minutes. Remove ring from oven; cool on wire rack.

5. When ring is cool, with long serrated knife, slice horizontally in

half. Prepare Almond-Cream Filling; spoon into bottom of ring. Replace top of ring. Refrigerate.

6. Prepare Chocolate Glaze. Spoon glaze over top of ring.

Almond-Cream Filling: Prepare *one 3½- to 3¾-ounce package vanilla-flavor instant pudding and pie filling* as label directs but use only *1¼ cups milk*. Fold in *1 cup heavy or whipping cream, whipped*, and *1 teaspoon almond extract*.

Chocolate Glaze: In double boiler over hot, *not boiling* water (or in heavy 1-quart saucepan over low heat), heat *½ cup semisweet-chocolate pieces* with *1 tablespoon butter* or margarine, *1½ teaspoons milk*, and *1½ teaspoons light corn syrup* until smooth, stirring occasionally.

Cheese-and-Pear Danish

TIME: about 1½ hours—SERVINGS: 8

1 3-ounce package cream
  cheese, softened
½ cup cottage cheese
⅓ cup confectioners' sugar
1 teaspoon grated lemon peel
1 egg, separated
1 8-ounce package refrigerated
  crescent dinner rolls
1 small pear, peeled and diced

1. In small bowl with mixer at medium speed, beat first 4 ingredients and egg yolk until smooth.

2. Unroll crescent-roll dough into two 10" by 3½" rectangles; overlap long sides to form 10" by 6½" rectangle; press perforations together. Roll into 13" by 8" rectangle; place on cookie sheet.

3. Preheat oven to 375°F. Spoon 2-inch-wide strip cheese mixture lengthwise down center of dough; top with pear. Cut dough on both sides of filling crosswise into ¾-inch strips. Place strips, at angle across filling, alternating sides. Brush with egg white. Bake 20 minutes. Cool on rack.

Prune Crumb Wedges

TIME: about 1¼ hours—SERVINGS: 8

1 12-ounce package pitted
  prunes
¾ cup water
1 3½- to 4-ounce can blanched
  whole almonds, ground
1¾ cups all-purpose flour
¾ cup butter or margarine,
  softened
¼ teaspoon salt
1 egg
sugar
1 tablespoon grated lemon peel

1. In 1-quart saucepan over high heat, heat prunes and water to boiling. Remove saucepan from heat; let stand 15 minutes or until prunes are plump, stirring occasionally.

2. Meanwhile, into large bowl, measure ground almonds, flour, butter or margarine, salt, egg, 1 cup sugar, and 1 teaspoon grated lemon peel. With mixer at low speed, beat ingredients until well mixed, occasionally scraping bowl with rubber spatula. (Mixture will be crumbly.)

3. In blender at high speed or in food processor with knife blade attached, blend prunes with their liquid, 2 tablespoons sugar, and remaining 2 teaspoons grated lemon peel until well mixed.

4. Preheat oven to 425°F. Grease 9-inch round cake pan. Reserve 1 cup crumb mixture. With hands, press remaining crumb mixture onto bottom and halfway up side of pan. Spread prune mixture evenly over crumb mixture; sprinkle with reserved crumb mixture. Cover and bake 30 minutes.

5. Uncover and bake 15 minutes longer or until crumbs are golden. Cool in pan on wire rack.

Golden Fried Rosettes

TIME: start early in day or day ahead—YIELD: about 5 dozen

salad oil
1 cup all-purpose flour
1 cup milk
1 tablespoon vanilla extract
2 teaspoons sugar
¼ teaspoon salt
2 eggs
confectioners' sugar (optional)

1. In 10-inch skillet over medium heat, heat about ¾ inch salad oil to 370°F. on deep-fat thermometer (or heat oil in electric skillet or deep-fat fryer set at 370°F.).

2. In medium bowl, with wire whisk or hand beater, beat flour, milk, vanilla, sugar, salt, and eggs until smooth (or blend in blender). Pour batter into pie plate or deep dish for easier dipping.

3. Heat rosette-timbale iron* in hot oil for 2 minutes; drain excess oil on paper towel; dip hot iron into batter to cover about ¾ of rosette form; quickly return to hot oil, being careful not to touch bottom of pan.

4. Fry until rosette comes off iron; continue frying rosette until golden. If rosette does not come off iron, gently ease it off with a fork. With slotted spoon, remove rosette to paper towels to drain, leaving iron in oil to keep hot. Repeat draining iron, dipping, and frying until all batter is used.

5. When rosettes are cool, store in tightly covered container. If desired, just before serving, sprinkle rosettes with confectioners' sugar.

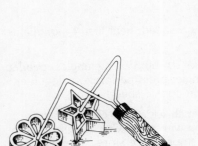

*Rosette-timbale iron (left) can be purchased in housewares departments of department stores, or you can write for a catalog to Maid of Scandinavia, 3244 Raleigh Ave., Minneapolis, MN 55416.

Cenci Rosettes

TIME: about 2 hours or start up to 1 week ahead—YIELD: about 2½ dozen

1¼ cups all-purpose flour
⅛ teaspoon salt
2 eggs
confectioners' sugar
salad oil

1. In medium bowl, with fork, stir flour, salt, eggs, and 1 tablespoon confectioners' sugar until well blended. With floured hand, knead dough in bowl until it holds together and is smooth. Shape dough into a ball and wrap with plastic wrap; let dough rest 30 minutes for easier rolling.

2. On lightly floured surface with floured rolling pin, roll one-fourth of dough at a time, until paper-thin. With pastry wheel or knife, cut dough into 12″ by 1″ strips. Shape each strip loosely into a coil; pinch edges together in a few places so coil will keep its shape. Reroll trimmings until all dough is used.

3. In 12-inch skillet over medium heat, heat 1 inch salad oil to 400° F. on deep-fat thermometer. (Or heat oil in electric skillet set at 400°F.) Drop several dough rosettes at a time into hot oil and fry about 30 seconds or until golden, turning once. Drain pastry on paper towels; cool. Store Cenci Rosettes in tightly covered container. Just before serving, sprinkle lightly with confectioners' sugar.

PIES AND TARTS

Sugar-Frosted Apple Pie

TIME: about 2 hours or start early in day—SERVINGS: 10

8 medium Golden Delicious
    apples, peeled, cored, and
    thinly sliced (about 8 cups)
2 tablespoons all-purpose flour
2 teaspoons lemon juice
1/4 teaspoon salt
sugar
ground cinnamon
Flaky Pastry (right)
1 tablespoon butter or margarine,
    cut into small pieces
milk
5 slices American cheese

1. In large bowl, with rubber spatula, lightly toss apples, flour, lemon juice, salt, 1/2 cup sugar, and 3/4 teaspoon cinnamon; set aside.

2. Prepare Flaky Pastry. On lightly floured surface with floured rolling pin, roll larger pastry ball into a circle about 2 inches larger than 9-inch pie plate. Line pie plate with pastry; with kitchen shears, trim pastry edge, leaving 1-inch overhang. Spoon apple mixture into pie plate; dot with butter or margarine; set aside.

3. Preheat oven to 425°F. Roll smaller pastry ball as for bottom crust; place over filling. Trim pastry edge, leaving 1-inch overhang. Fold overhang under, then bring up over pie-plate rim; pinch to form fluted edge.

4. Reroll trimmings. With floured leaf-shaped cookie cutter or knife, cut 5 leaves, rerolling dough if necessary. Arrange leaves on top of pie. Lightly brush top of pie with milk. With tip of knife, cut a few slashes in top crust to allow steam to escape during baking. In small bowl, mix 1 tablespoon sugar with 1/8 teaspoon cinnamon. Evenly sprinkle sugar mixture over pie.

5. Bake 45 minutes or until crust is golden and apples are tender. Remove pie to wire rack. Cut each cheese slice into a leaf. Gently tuck cheese leaves under pastry leaves on pie. Serve warm or cool pie to serve later.

Flaky Pastry: In medium bowl, stir *2 cups all-purpose flour* and *1 teaspoon salt*. With pastry blender or 2 knives used scissor-fashion, cut *3/4 cup shortening* into flour to resemble coarse crumbs. Sprinkle *5 to 6 tablespoons cold water*, a tablespoon at a time, into mixture, mixing lightly after each addition, until pastry is just moist enough to hold together. Shape pastry into 2 balls, one slightly larger.

Pumpkin Pie

TIME: about 3 hours or start day ahead—SERVINGS: 10

piecrust mix for one 9-inch
    piecrust
1 16-ounce can pumpkin
1 14-ounce can sweetened
    condensed milk
1 1/2 teaspoons ground cinnamon
1/2 teaspoon ground ginger
1/2 teaspoon ground nutmeg
1/2 teaspoon ground cloves
1/2 teaspoon salt
2 eggs

1. Preheat oven to 400°F. Prepare piecrust mix as label directs. On lightly floured surface with floured rolling pin, roll pastry into a circle, about 2 inches larger all around than 9-inch pie plate. Line pie plate with pastry; trim pastry edge, leaving 1-inch overhang. Fold overhang under; pinch to make a high fluted edge; set aside.

2. In large bowl, with wooden spoon, beat pumpkin with remaining ingredients until well mixed. Place pastry-lined pie plate on oven rack; pour in pumpkin mixture. Bake pie 50 minutes until filling is set and knife inserted 1 inch from edge comes out clean. Cool pie on wire rack.

249

Pumpkin Chiffon Pie with Nutty Cookie Crust

TIME: start early in day or day ahead—SERVINGS: 10

1 envelope unflavored gelatin
½ cup milk
1 16-ounce can pumpkin
½ cup sugar
¾ teaspoon ground cinnamon
½ teaspoon salt
⅛ teaspoon ground ginger
3 eggs, separated
¾ cup California walnuts
1 cup gingersnap crumbs (about
   20 gingersnaps)
6 tablespoons butter or
   margarine, softened

1. Prepare pumpkin filling: In heavy 3-quart saucepan, evenly sprinkle gelatin over milk. Cook over medium heat until gelatin is completely dissolved, stirring frequently. Stir in pumpkin, sugar, cinnamon, salt, ginger, and egg yolks. Cook over medium-low heat until mixture is very thick (do not boil) about 15 minutes, stirring constantly. Refrigerate until cool but not set, about 45 minutes.

2. Meanwhile, preheat oven to 375°F. Finely chop ½ cup walnuts; coarsely chop ¼ cup walnuts. In 9-inch pie plate, with hand, mix finely chopped walnuts, gingersnap crumbs, and butter; firmly press mixture to bottom and up side of pie plate. Bake 8 minutes; cool completely on wire rack.

3. In small bowl with mixer at high speed, beat egg whites until stiff peaks form. With wire whisk, gently fold egg whites into pumpkin mixture; evenly spoon mixture into piecrust. Sprinkle with reserved coarsely chopped walnuts. Refrigerate until mixture is set, about 2 hours.

Strawberry Sweetheart Pie

TIME: about 5 hours or start early in day—SERVINGS: 12

piecrust mix for one 9-inch
   piecrust
1½ pints strawberries
1 tablespoon lemon juice
½ cup water
¼ teaspoon salt
sugar
2 envelopes unflavored gelatin
red food color
4 egg whites, at room
   temperature
2 cups heavy or whipping cream

1. Preheat oven to 425°F. Prepare piecrust mix as label directs. On lightly floured surface with floured rolling pin, roll pastry into a circle about 2 inches larger all around than 9-inch pie plate. Line pie plate with pastry; trim pastry edge, leaving 1-inch overhang. Fold overhang under; pinch to make a stand-up edge.

2. With fork, prick bottom and side of piecrust in many places to prevent puffing during baking. Roll pastry trimmings ⅛-inch thick. With floured small heart-shaped cookie cutter, cut out as many pastry hearts as possible. Place pastry hearts on small cookie sheet. Bake piecrust 15 minutes and pastry hearts 10 minutes or until golden. Cool on wire racks.

3. Reserve 1 strawberry for garnish. In blender at medium speed, blend lemon juice and remaining berries until smooth to make about 2½ cups puree; set aside.

4. In heavy 2-quart saucepan, mix water, salt, and ½ cup sugar; sprinkle gelatin evenly over mixture. Cook over medium-low heat until gelatin is completely dissolved, stirring constantly. Remove saucepan from heat; stir in strawberry puree and enough red food color to tint a pretty pink color. Color will become lighter when beaten egg whites and whipped cream are folded in. Refrigerate until mixture mounds when dropped from a spoon, about 45 minutes, stirring occasionally.

5. In large bowl with mixer at high speed, beat egg whites until soft peaks form. Beating at high speed, gradually sprinkle in ⅓ cup sugar, 2 tablespoons at a time, beating well after each addition until sugar is completely dissolved.

6. In small bowl with mixer at medium speed, beat 1½ cups heavy or whipping cream until stiff peaks form. Refrigerate remaining ½ cup cream for garnish. With wire whisk or rubber spatula, gently fold whipped cream and strawberry puree into beaten egg whites. Spoon mixture into baked piecrust. Refrigerate until set, about 3 hours.

7. To serve, gently press baked pastry hearts onto strawberry mixture just above edge of piecrust. Beat remaining heavy or whipping cream until soft peaks form. Garnish pie with whipped cream and reserved strawberry.

Citrus Angel Pie

TIME: start early in day—SERVINGS: 12

4 eggs, separated, at room
   temperature
¼ teaspoon cream of tartar
sugar
4 medium oranges
2 medium lemons
⅛ teaspoon salt
1 envelope unflavored gelatin
1½ cups heavy or whipping
   cream
small nontoxic leaves for garnish

1. Line large cookie sheet with foil. Using 9-inch round plate as guide, outline circle on foil; set aside.

2. Preheat oven to 200°F. In small bowl with mixer at high speed, beat egg whites and cream of tartar until soft peaks form. Beating at high speed, gradually beat in ¾ cup sugar, 2 tablespoons at a time, beating well after each addition until sugar is completely dissolved. (Whites should stand in stiff, glossy peaks.)

3. Spoon about one-third of meringue onto circle; with metal spatula, spread evenly to form a base. Spoon remaining meringue into decorating bag with large rosette tube; pipe meringue along top edge of base to form a pie shell. Bake 2 hours; turn oven control off; let stand in oven 15 minutes or until meringue is crisp but not brown. Cool meringue shell completely on cookie sheet on wire rack.

4. When meringue shell is cool, with metal spatula, carefully loosen and remove from foil onto dessert platter.

5. From 3½ oranges, grate 1 tablespoon peel and squeeze 1½ cups juice. From 1½ lemons, grate 1 tablespoon peel and squeeze 1 tablespoon juice. Reserve orange and lemon halves for garnish. In heavy 2-quart saucepan, with wire whisk or fork, mix egg yolks, orange juice, lemon juice, salt, and ½ cup sugar; sprinkle gelatin evenly over mixture. Cook over low heat, stirring constantly, until gelatin is completely dissolved and mixture is thickened and coats a spoon, about 15 minutes. (Do not boil, or mixture will curdle.) Remove saucepan from heat; stir in orange and lemon peels. Refrigerate until mixture mounds when dropped from a spoon, about 45 minutes, stirring occasionally.

6. In large bowl with mixer at medium speed, beat heavy or whipping cream until soft peaks form. With wire whisk or rubber spatula, gently fold orange mixture into whipped cream. Spoon mixture into meringue shell. Refrigerate until set, about 3 hours.

7. To serve, cut reserved orange and lemon halves into very thin slices; cut slices into half circles. Arrange orange and lemon slices on top of pie; tuck leaves here and there among fruit slices.

Jeweled Citrus Pie

TIME: start early in day—SERVINGS: 10

¾ cup graham-cracker crumbs
4 tablespoons butter or
  margarine, softened
2 tablespoons California walnuts,
  ground
4 teaspoons brown sugar
¼ cup sugar
⅛ teaspoon salt
1 envelope unflavored gelatin
½ cup milk
2 eggs, separated
8 oranges
1 8-ounce package cream
  cheese, softened
water
1 3-ounce package lemon-flavor
  gelatin

1. In 10″ by 2½″ springform pan, with hand, mix graham-cracker crumbs, butter or margarine, walnuts, and brown sugar; press mixture onto bottom of pan; set aside.

2. In 1-quart saucepan, combine sugar, salt, and unflavored gelatin. In cup, with fork, mix milk with egg yolks; stir into gelatin mixture. Cook over low heat, stirring constantly, until mixture is thickened and coats spoon. Remove saucepan from heat; set aside.

3. From 1 orange, grate 2 tablespoons peel; set peel aside; reserve orange. In large bowl with mixer at high speed, beat egg whites until soft peaks form. In small bowl with mixer at medium speed, beat cream cheese with orange peel until well mixed. Reduce speed to low; gradually beat in gelatin mixture until well blended.

4. With rubber spatula, gently fold cheese mixture into egg whites. Carefully pour cheese mixture over crust; refrigerate 30 minutes or until set.

5. In 2-quart saucepan, heat ½ cup water to boiling; stir in lemon-flavor gelatin until dissolved. Stir in ½ cup cold water; refrigerate until slightly thickened but not set.

6. Meanwhile, remove peel and white membrane from all 8 oranges; cut oranges into ½-inch pieces. When lemon-flavor gelatin is ready, stir in orange pieces. Pour gelatin mixture evenly over cheese mixture. Refrigerate until set, about 2 hours.

7. To serve, dip metal spatula in hot water to gently loosen edge of dessert from pan; carefully remove side of springform pan.

Lemon Meringue Pie

TIME: about 4 hours or start early in day—SERVINGS: 10

piecrust mix for one 9-inch
  piecrust
2 to 3 medium lemons
⅓ cup cornstarch
⅛ teaspoon salt
1¼ cups sugar
1½ cups water
4 eggs, separated
1 tablespoon butter or margarine
¼ teaspoon cream of tartar

1. Preheat oven to 425°F. Prepare piecrust mix as label directs. On lightly floured surface with floured rolling pin, roll pastry into a circle about 2 inches larger all around than 9-inch pie plate. Line pie plate with pastry; trim pastry edge, leaving 1-inch overhang. Fold overhang under; pinch to make a high stand-up edge. With fork, prick bottom and side of piecrust in many places to prevent puffing during baking. Bake piecrust 15 minutes; cool on wire rack, about 45 minutes.

2. Grate peel from 1 lemon to make 1 tablespoon; squeeze juice from all lemons to make ½ cup; set peel and juice aside.

3. In 2-quart saucepan, stir cornstarch, salt, and ¾ cup sugar. Stir in water; cook over medium heat, stirring constantly, until mixture is thickened and boils; boil 1 minute. Remove saucepan from heat.

4. In small bowl, with wire whisk or fork, beat yolks; stir in small amount of hot cornstarch mixture; slowly pour yolk mixture back into hot cornstarch mixture in saucepan, stirring rapidly to prevent lumping. Return saucepan to heat; cook, stirring constantly, until filling is thickened. (Do *not* boil, or mixture will curdle.) Gradually stir in lemon juice, lemon peel, and butter; pour into piecrust; cool 10 minutes.

5. Preheat oven to 400°F. In small bowl with mixer at high speed, beat egg whites and cream of tartar until soft peaks form. Beating at high speed, gradually sprinkle in ½ cup sugar, 2 tablespoons at a time, beating after each addition until sugar is completely dissolved. (Whites should stand in stiff, glossy peaks.)

6. With spatula, spread meringue over filling to edge of crust. Swirl meringue with back of spoon to make attractive top. Bake 10 minutes or until golden. Cool on wire rack away from draft. Refrigerate any leftover pie.

Two-Crust Lemon Pie

TIME: start day ahead—SERVINGS: 10

2 medium lemons
1½ cups sugar
piecrust mix for two 9-inch
   piecrusts
4 eggs

1. Cut lemons into paper-thin slices; discard seeds. In medium bowl with rubber spatula, gently stir lemon slices and sugar; cover and let stand at room temperature overnight.

2. About 2 hours before serving, prepare piecrust mix as label directs; shape pastry into 2 balls, one slightly larger. On lightly floured surface with floured rolling pin, roll larger ball into a circle about 2 inches larger than 9-inch pie plate. Line pie plate with pastry; trim edge, leaving 1-inch overhang.

3. In small bowl, with fork or wire whisk, beat eggs. With rubber spatula, gently fold beaten eggs into lemon-slice mixture. Spoon mixture into pastry-lined pie plate.

4. Preheat oven to 450°F. Roll smaller pastry ball as for bottom crust; place over filling. Trim pastry edge, leaving 1-inch overhang. Fold overhang under; with fork, press pastry onto rim of pie plate. With tip of knife, cut a few short slits in top of crust to allow steam to escape during baking. If desired, cut out pastry trimmings to make a pretty design for top of pie.

5. Bake pie 15 minutes; turn oven control to 350°F.; bake 30 minutes longer or until crust is golden and knife inserted in center of pie comes out clean. Serve pie warm or cool completely to serve later.

Pecan-Walnut Pie

TIME: about 3 hours or start day ahead—SERVINGS: 10

piecrust mix for one 9-inch
   piecrust
3 eggs
¾ cup dark corn syrup
¼ cup sugar
¼ cup honey
4 tablespoons butter or
   margarine, melted
1 teaspoon vanilla extract
¼ teaspoon salt
1½ cups pecan halves
1 cup California walnuts

1. Prepare piecrust mix as label directs. On lightly floured surface with floured rolling pin, roll pastry into a circle about 2 inches larger all around than 9-inch pie plate. Line pie plate with pastry; trim pastry edge, leaving 1-inch overhang. Fold overhang under; pinch to make a high fluted edge; set aside.

2. Preheat oven to 350°F. In medium bowl with wire whisk or fork, beat eggs, corn syrup, sugar, honey, butter or margarine, vanilla extract, and salt until well blended. Arrange pecan halves and walnuts on bottom of piecrust; carefully pour egg mixture over them. Bake pie 1 hour or until knife inserted 1 inch from edge comes out clean. Cool pie on wire rack.

253

Chocolate-Brownie Pie

TIME: about 50 minutes—**SERVINGS:** 8

piecrust mix for one 9-inch
   piecrust
4 tablespoons butter or
   margarine
2 squares unsweetened chocolate
½ cup sugar
½ cup milk
¼ cup all-purpose flour
2 tablespoons corn syrup
1 teaspoon vanilla extract
½ teaspoon salt
3 eggs
1 cup California walnuts,
   chopped
1 pint vanilla ice cream
   (optional)

1. Preheat oven to 350°F. Prepare piecrust mix as label directs; use to line 9-inch pie plate.

2. In heavy 2-quart saucepan over low heat, melt butter or margarine and chocolate, stirring occasionally. Remove saucepan from heat. With wire whisk, beat in sugar, milk, flour, corn syrup, vanilla, salt, and eggs until mixed. Stir in walnuts.

3. Pour chocolate mixture into piecrust. Bake pie 30 minutes or until filling is set and puffed. If desired, serve pie with ice cream.

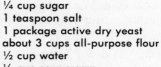

Come-for-Coffee Cherry Pie

TIME: about 4 hours or start early in day—**SERVINGS:** 12

¼ cup sugar
1 teaspoon salt
1 package active dry yeast
about 3 cups all-purpose flour
½ cup water
½ cup sour cream
2 tablespoons butter or
   margarine
1 egg
1 small lemon
2 21-ounce cans cherry-pie
   filling

1. In large bowl, combine sugar, salt, yeast, and 1 cup flour. In 1-quart saucepan over low heat, heat water, sour cream, and butter or margarine until very warm (120° to 130°F.). (Butter or margarine does not need to melt completely.) With mixer at low speed, gradually beat liquid into dry ingredients just until blended. Increase speed to medium; beat 2 minutes, occasionally scraping bowl with rubber spatula. Gradually beat in egg and ½ cup flour to make a thick batter; continue beating 2 minutes, scraping bowl often. With spoon, stir in 1¼ cups flour to make a soft dough.

2. Turn dough onto well-floured surface and knead until smooth and elastic, about 10 minutes, working in about ¼ cup more flour while kneading. Shape dough into a ball and place in greased large bowl, turning dough over so that top is greased. Cover and let rise in warm place (80° to 85°F.), away from draft, until doubled, about 1½ hours. (Dough is doubled when two fingers pressed lightly into dough leave a dent.)

3. Punch down dough. Turn dough onto lightly floured surface; cover with bowl and let rest 15 minutes for easier shaping.

4. Meanwhile, from lemon, grate 1 tablespoon peel and squeeze 1 tablespoon juice. In medium bowl, mix lemon peel, lemon juice, and cherry-pie filling; set aside. Preheat oven to 350°F. Grease 3-quart shallow oval baking dish or 13″ by 9″ baking dish.

5. Reserve one-third of dough for top of pie. Pat remaining dough into bottom and up sides of baking dish. Spoon cherry-pie-filling mixture into dough crust. On lightly floured surface with floured rolling pin, roll out reserved dough into 12″ by 5″ rectangle. With knife, cut dough lengthwise into 9 or 10 strips. Place strips on top of pie to make a lattice design, twisting each strip before attaching to rim; pinch all around to seal. Bake pie 25 to 30 minutes until crust is lightly browned. Serve pie warm or refrigerate to serve cold later.

Black-Bottom Cherry Pie

TIME: about 2½ hours or start early in day—SERVINGS: 10

2 cups California walnuts, finely chopped
3 tablespoons butter or margarine, softened
2 tablespoons brown sugar
1 16½- to 17-ounce jar or can pitted dark sweet cherries
1½ cups heavy or whipping cream
1 3½- to 3¾-ounce package vanilla-flavor instant pudding and pie filling
1 cup milk
¼ teaspoon vanilla extract
2 squares semisweet chocolate, melted

1. Preheat oven to 400°F. In 9-inch pie plate, with hand, mix walnuts, butter or margarine, and brown sugar; press mixture onto bottom and up side of pie plate. Bake crust 8 minutes or until golden. Cool crust on wire rack.

2. Drain cherries; pat dry with paper towels. Reserve 10 whole cherries for garnish; cut each of the remaining cherries in half; set aside.

3. In small bowl with mixer at medium speed, beat 1 cup heavy or whipping cream until stiff peaks form. In large bowl, prepare instant pudding as label directs, but use *only* 1 cup milk. With wire whisk or rubber spatula, gently fold whipped cream and vanilla into pudding mixture.

4. Set aside 1½ cups pudding mixture. With wire whisk, fold melted chocolate into remaining pudding mixture. Spoon chocolate-pudding mixture into crust; top with halved cherries. Evenly spread vanilla-pudding mixture over cherries. Refrigerate pie until set, at least 1 hour.

5. To serve, in small bowl with mixer at medium speed, beat remaining ½ cup heavy or whipping cream until stiff peaks form. Garnish top of pie with dollops of whipped cream and reserved whole cherries.

Apricot-Prune Pie

TIME: about 3½ hours or start early in day—SERVINGS: 10

piecrust mix for two 9-inch piecrusts
3 17-ounce cans apricot halves
2 16- to 17-ounce jars prunes
1 tablespoon all-purpose flour
1 tablespoon minced preserved ginger or ¼ teaspoon ground ginger
1 tablespoon lemon juice
⅛ teaspoon salt
1 egg

1. Prepare piecrust mix as label directs; shape pastry into 2 balls. On lightly floured surface with floured rolling pin, roll 1 pastry ball into a circle about 1½ inches larger all around than 9-inch pie plate. Line pie plate with pastry; with kitchen shears, trim pastry edge, leaving 1-inch overhang. Fold overhang under; with fork, press pastry onto rim of pie plate. Roll remaining pastry ball into 12″ by 10½″ rectangle; cut into twenty-one 12″ by ½″ strips; cover with plastic wrap.

2. Drain apricot halves. Drain prunes; cut each prune in half; discard seeds. In pastry-lined pie plate, carefully combine apricot halves, prune halves, flour, ginger, lemon juice, and salt.

3. Preheat oven to 425°F. Place 6 pastry strips about 1 inch apart across pie filling. (Do not seal ends.) Fold every other strip back halfway from center. Place center cross-strip on pie and replace folded part of strips. Fold back alternate strips and place second cross-strip in place. Repeat with 4 more cross-strips to weave lattice. Trim strips; seal ends.

4. Braid remaining pastry strips into 3 braids, using 3 pastry strips for each braid. In cup beat egg with fork. Brush pastry edge and lattice with egg. Arrange pastry braids around rim of pie plate on pastry; press gently; tuck ends of braids under. Brush pastry braids with egg. Bake pie 40 minutes or until fruit is heated through and crust is golden. Cool pie on wire rack.

Freezer Peach-Pie Filling

TIME: start up to 6 months ahead—YIELD: filling for two 9-inch pies

4 pounds peaches (about 16
    medium peaches)
water
1 cup sugar
⅓ cup quick-cooking tapioca
4 teaspoons ascorbic acid
    mixture for fruit
½ teaspoon salt
½ teaspoon ground cinnamon
heavy-duty foil
2 tablespoons butter or
    margarine

1. Peel peaches: In 5-quart Dutch oven or saucepot over high heat, heat 3 inches water to boiling; add peaches, a few at a time; cook 15 seconds. With slotted spoon, remove peaches to large bowl of cold water. Remove from water and with knife, peel off skins. Cut peaches in half; discard pits. Cut peaches into ¼-inch-thick slices. Discard water in Dutch oven.

2. In same Dutch oven, mix sugar, tapioca, ascorbic acid, salt, and cinnamon. Add peaches; with rubber spatula, toss gently to mix well.

3. Line two 9-inch pie plates with heavy-duty foil, extending it 6 inches beyond rims. Spoon half of peach mixture into each pie plate; dot each with 1 tablespoon butter or margarine. Fold foil loosely over filling. Place pie plates in freezer; freeze until firm, about 4 hours. Seal foil tightly; remove foil-wrapped fillings from pie plates; label and return filling packages to freezer. See recipe for Lattice-Topped Peach Pie, following.

Lattice-Topped Peach Pie: Prepare *piecrust mix for two 9-inch piecrusts* as label directs; shape pastry into 2 balls, one slightly larger. On lightly floured surface with floured rolling pin, roll larger pastry ball into a circle about 2 inches larger all around than 9-inch pie plate. Line pie plate with pastry; with kitchen shears, trim pastry edge, leaving 1-inch overhang. Unwrap one package of Freezer Peach-Pie Filling; place frozen peach mixture in pastry-lined pie plate.

   Preheat oven to 425°F. Roll remaining pastry ball into 12-inch circle; cut into ½-inch-wide strips. Place some strips about 1 inch apart across pie filling; do not seal ends. Fold every other strip back halfway from center. Place center cross-strip on pie and replace folded part of strips. Fold back alternate strips and place second cross-strip in place. Repeat to weave lattice. Trim strips; moisten and seal ends; make a fluted edge.

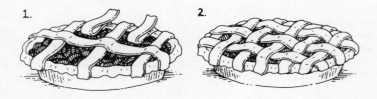

   Bake pie 1¼ hours or until crust is golden and peach mixture begins to bubble. If piecrust begins to brown too much during baking, cover with foil to prevent burning. Cool pie on wire rack. Makes 1 pie or 10 servings.

Freezer Blueberry-Pie Filling

TIME: start up to 6 months ahead—YIELD: filling for two 9-inch pies

1⅓ cups sugar
⅓ cup quick-cooking tapioca
½ teaspoon salt
8 cups blueberries (about 2½ pints)
2 tablespoons lemon juice
heavy-duty foil
2 tablespoons butter or margarine

1. In large bowl, mix sugar, tapioca, and salt. Add blueberries and lemon juice; with rubber spatula, toss gently to mix well.

2. Line two 9-inch pie plates with heavy-duty foil, extending it 6 inches beyond rims. Spoon half of blueberry mixture into each pie plate; dot each with 1 tablespoon butter or margarine. Fold foil loosely over filling.

3. Place pie plates in freezer; freeze until firm, about 4 hours. Seal foil tightly; remove foil-wrapped fillings from pie plates; label and return the packages of filling to freezer. (See recipe for Blueberry Pie, following.)

Blueberry Pie: About 4 hours before serving, prepare *piecrust mix for two 9-inch piecrusts* as label directs; shape pastry into 2 balls, one slightly larger. On lightly floured surface with floured rolling pin, roll larger pastry ball into a circle about 1½ inches larger all around than 9-inch pie plate. Line pie plate with pastry; with kitchen shears, trim pastry edge, leaving ½-inch overhang. Unwrap one package of Freezer Blueberry-Pie Filling; place frozen pie filling in pastry-lined pie plate.
  Preheat oven to 425°F. Roll remaining pastry ball as for bottom crust; with cookie cutter or knife, cut out 2½-inch circle from center of pastry. Place pastry over filling; trim pastry edge, leaving ½-inch overhang. Fold overhang under; with back of floured 4-tined fork, press pastry firmly to rim of pie plate. If you desire, reroll trimmings to decorate top of pie.
  Bake pie 1¼ hours or until crust is golden and blueberry mixture begins to bubble. If piecrust begins to brown too much, cover with foil to prevent burning. Cool pie on wire rack. Makes 1 pie or 10 servings.

Peppermint-Cheese Pie

TIME: start early in day or day ahead—SERVINGS: 10

1 cup California walnuts, finely chopped
1 tablespoon brown sugar
1 tablespoon butter or margarine, softened
2 8-ounce packages cream cheese, softened
½ cup sugar
1 teaspoon vanilla extract
2 eggs
½ cup sour cream
1½ ounces hard peppermint candies, coarsely crushed
miniature candy canes for garnish

1. Preheat oven to 350°F. In 8-inch pie plate, with hand, mix walnuts, brown sugar, and butter or margarine; press mixture onto bottom and side of pie plate. Bake crust 8 minutes.

2. Meanwhile, in small bowl with mixer at low speed, beat cream cheese, sugar, vanilla, and eggs until blended. Increase speed to medium; beat cream-cheese mixture until smooth. Pour cheese mixture into crust. Bake pie 30 minutes. Remove pie from oven; let stand at room temperature 10 minutes to set slightly.

3. In blender at high speed or in food processor with knife blade attached, blend sour cream and crushed hard peppermint candies until candy is completely dissolved. Spoon sour-cream mixture over baked cheese layer. Bake pie 5 minutes longer. Refrigerate pie until well chilled, about 3 hours.

4. To serve, garnish pie with candy canes, if desired.

Banana-Cream Pie

TIME: start early in day—SERVINGS: 10

½ cup sugar
⅓ cup cornstarch
½ teaspoon salt
3 cups milk
2 egg yolks
1½ teaspoons vanilla extract
butter or margarine
1 cup graham-cracker crumbs
½ cup heavy or whipping cream
2 ripe medium bananas
¼ cup apple jelly

1. In 2-quart saucepan, mix sugar, cornstarch, and salt; stir in milk. Cook over medium heat, stirring constantly, until mixture thickens and boils; cook 1 minute. Remove saucepan from heat.

2. In small bowl, beat egg yolks; into egg yolks, stir small amount of hot cornstarch mixture. Slowly pour yolk mixture back into hot cornstarch mixture, stirring rapidly to prevent lumping. Return saucepan to heat; cook, stirring constantly, until mixture thickens and boils. Cook 1 minute. Stir in vanilla and 1 tablespoon butter or margarine. Cover and refrigerate custard until cool but not set, about 1 hour.

3. Meanwhile, preheat oven to 375°F. In 9-inch pie plate, combine graham-cracker crumbs and 4 tablespoons softened butter or margarine. Press onto bottom and side of pie plate. Bake 10 minutes. Cool.

4. When custard is cool, in small bowl with mixer at medium speed, beat heavy or whipping cream until soft peaks form. With wire whisk or rubber spatula, fold whipped cream into custard.

5. Thinly slice bananas. Line piecrust with half of banana slices; top with custard and then remaining banana slices.

6. In 1-quart saucepan over low heat, melt apple jelly. Brush top of pie with melted jelly. Refrigerate until pie is set, about 2 hours.

Boston Cream Pie

TIME: about 2½ hours or start early in day—SERVINGS: 10

1 cup cake flour
¾ cup sugar
⅓ cup milk
6 tablespoons butter or margarine, softened
1½ teaspoons double-acting baking powder
1½ teaspoons vanilla extract
¼ teaspoon salt
¼ teaspoon baking soda
2 eggs
Creamy Custard Filling (right)
Chocolate Icing (page 259)

1. Preheat oven to 375°F. Grease one 9-inch round cake pan. Into large bowl, measure first 9 ingredients. With mixer at low speed, beat ingredients just until mixed, constantly scraping bowl with rubber spatula. Increase speed to high; beat 2 minutes, occasionally scraping bowl.

2. Pour batter into pan. Bake 25 minutes or until toothpick inserted in center of cake comes out clean. Cool cake in pan on wire rack 10 minutes. Remove from pan; cool completely.

3. Prepare Creamy Custard Filling. Cover and refrigerate filling until cool but not set, about 30 minutes.

4. Prepare Chocolate Icing. With serrated knife, cut cake horizontally in half to form 2 layers. Place 1 cake layer on cake platter; spread evenly with cooled custard. Top with second layer, pressing down gently but firmly. Frost top of cake with Chocolate Icing. Refrigerate until serving time.

Creamy Custard Filling: In heavy 2-quart saucepan, stir *2 cups milk, ¼ cup sugar, 3 tablespoons cornstarch, ¼ teaspoon salt,* and *2 egg yolks* until well blended. Cook over medium-low heat, until mixture thickens and boils, about 20 minutes; boil 1 minute. Remove saucepan from heat; stir in *1 teaspoon vanilla extract.*

Chocolate Icing: In heavy 1-quart saucepan over low heat, melt *2 squares semisweet chocolate* and *1 tablespoon butter* or margarine; remove saucepan from heat. With wire whisk or fork, beat in *½ cup confectioners' sugar* and *2 to 3 tablespoons milk* until smooth and of easy spreading consistency.

Marbled Mousse Pie

TIME: about 4½ hours or start early in day—SERVINGS: 12

½ 8½-ounce package chocolate wafers
1 cup California walnuts
4 tablespoons butter or margarine
1½ cups milk
6 eggs, separated
¼ teaspoon salt
sugar
1 envelope unflavored gelatin
1 teaspoon vanilla extract
¼ cup cocoa

1. Preheat oven to 375°F. In blender or in food processor with knife blade attached, blend chocolate wafers to fine crumbs. Add walnuts; blend until nuts are finely chopped. In small saucepan over low heat, melt butter or margarine. In 9-inch pie plate, with fork, mix nut mixture with melted butter or margarine. With hands, press mixture onto bottom and up side of pie plate. Bake crust 10 minutes. Cool crust on wire rack.

2. In heavy 2-quart saucepan, with wire whisk or fork, beat milk, egg yolks, salt, and ½ cup sugar until blended; evenly sprinkle gelatin over mixture. Over medium-low heat, cook, stirring constantly, until gelatin is completely dissolved and mixture thickens and coats a spoon. (Do *not* boil, or mixture will curdle.) Remove saucepan from heat; stir in vanilla.

3. Pour half of egg-yolk mixture into medium bowl; stir in cocoa until blended. Cover and refrigerate both mixtures until mixtures mound slightly when dropped from a spoon, about 30 minutes.

4. In small bowl with mixer at high speed, beat egg whites until soft peaks form. Beating at high speed, beat in ⅓ cup sugar, 2 tablespoons at a time, beating well after each addition until sugar is completely dissolved. (Whites should stand in stiff, glossy peaks.)

5. With wire whisk or rubber spatula, fold half of the beaten egg whites into the cocoa mixture; fold remaining egg whites into the vanilla mixture. Alternately spoon cocoa and vanilla mixtures into cooled piecrust, gently swirling both mixtures to create a marbled effect. Refrigerate pie until set, about 3 hours.

Pecan-Custard Pie

TIME: start early in day—SERVINGS: 10

piecrust mix for one 9-inch
   piecrust
3 eggs
1 cup dark corn syrup
4 tablespoons butter or
   margarine, melted
sugar
vanilla extract
1¼ cups pecan halves
2 cups half-and-half
2 tablespoons cornstarch
⅛ teaspoon salt
1 egg yolk
¼ cup heavy or whipping cream
   (optional)

1. Preheat oven to 350°F. Prepare piecrust mix as label directs. On lightly floured surface with floured rolling pin, roll pastry into a circle about 2 inches larger all around than 9-inch pie plate. Line pie plate with pastry; trim pastry edge, leaving 1-inch overhang. Fold overhang under; pinch to make a high fluted edge; set aside.

2. In medium bowl, with wire whisk or fork, beat eggs, corn syrup, butter or margarine, ¼ cup sugar, and 1 teaspoon vanilla extract until well blended. Reserve 2 tablespoons pecan halves for garnish; arrange remaining pecans in bottom of piecrust; carefully pour egg mixture over them. Bake pie 1 hour or until knife inserted 1 inch in from edge comes out clean. Cool pie on wire rack.

3. In heavy 2-quart saucepan, mix half-and-half, cornstarch, salt, egg yolk, and 3 tablespoons sugar; cook over medium heat, stirring constantly, until mixture thickens and boils, about 20 minutes. Boil mixture 1 minute. Remove saucepan from heat; stir in 1 teaspoon vanilla extract. Pour custard mixture over cooled pie. Refrigerate pie until custard is completely set, about 3 hours.

4. To serve, in small bowl with mixer at medium speed, beat heavy or whipping cream, if desired, until stiff peaks form. Spoon whipped cream into decorating bag with small rosette tube. Decorate top of pie with whipped-cream rosettes and reserved pecan halves.

French Apple Tart

TIME: about 1½ hours—SERVINGS: 12

1 10-ounce package frozen
   ready-to-bake puff pastry
   shells
10 medium Golden Delicious
   apples (about 3½ pounds)
1 cup sugar
½ cup butter
¼ teaspoon almond extract
heavy or whipping cream

1. Let frozen puff pastry shells stand at room temperature to thaw slightly.

2. Meanwhile, peel and core apples. (Golden Delicious apples with greener skin retain shape the best; do *not* use other apples.) Cut each apple lengthwise in half. In heavy 10-inch skillet with oven-safe handle (or cover skillet handle with heavy-duty foil), over medium heat, heat sugar, butter, and almond extract until butter is melted (do *not* use margarine because it separates from sugar during cooking), stirring occasionally. (Sugar will not be completely dissolved.) Remove skillet from heat. Arrange apple halves on their sides around side and in the center of skillet, fitting apples very tightly together. Over medium heat, heat apple mixture to boiling; boil 20 to 40 minutes, depending on juiciness of the apples, until sugar mixture becomes caramel color. Remove skillet from heat.

3. Preheat oven to 450°F. On floured surface, stack puff pastry shells, one on top of the other, pressing shells firmly together. With floured rolling pin, roll pastry into 12-inch circle. Arrange pastry circle on apples; with fork, press pastry onto edge of skillet. With tip of knife, cut slits in pastry. Bake 20 to 25 minutes until pastry is golden and puffed.

4. Remove skillet from oven; let cool on wire rack 10 minutes. Carefully invert tart onto dessert platter. If desired, serve with heavy or whipping cream.

Almond Cordial Pie

TIME: start early in day—SERVINGS: 10

1¼ cups crushed almond
   macaroons (about 30 cookies)*
6 tablespoons butter or
   margarine, softened
3 eggs, separated
½ cup water
¼ cup sugar
¼ teaspoon salt
1 envelope unflavored gelatin
¼ cup almond-flavor liqueur
¼ cup brown crème de cacao
1 cup heavy or whipping cream
2 tablespoons sliced almonds,
   toasted

*Or, if preferred, substitute 1¼ cups
graham-cracker crumbs and 2
teaspoons almond extract for almond
macaroons.

1. Preheat oven to 350°F. In 9-inch pie plate, with hand, mix almond macaroons and butter or margarine; press mixture firmly onto bottom and up side of pie plate. Bake crust 10 minutes or until golden brown. Cool crust on wire rack.

2. In heavy 1-quart saucepan with wire whisk, beat egg yolks, water, sugar, and salt until well mixed. Sprinkle gelatin evenly over egg mixture. Cook over medium-low heat, stirring constantly, until gelatin is completely dissolved and mixture thickens and coats the back of a spoon, about 20 minutes. (Do *not* boil, or mixture will curdle.) Remove saucepan from heat. Stir in almond-flavor liqueur and crème de cacao. Refrigerate until custard mounds slightly when dropped from a spoon, about 15 minutes, stirring occasionally.

3. In large bowl with mixer at high speed, beat egg whites until stiff peaks form; set aside. In small bowl, using same beaters, with mixer at medium speed, beat heavy or whipping cream until stiff peaks form.

4. With rubber spatula or wire whisk, fold custard and whipped cream into beaten egg whites. Spoon filling into cooled crust. Refrigerate pie until completely set, about 3 hours.

5. To serve, garnish pie with toasted almonds.

Party Fruit Tarts

TIME: about 2 hours or start early in day—YIELD: 2 dozen

1½ cups all-purpose flour
½ cup butter or margarine,
   softened
⅓ cup sugar
2 tablespoons water
1 3½- to 3¾-ounce package
   vanilla-flavor instant pudding
   and pie filling
1 cup milk
1 cup heavy or whipping cream
½ teaspoon almond extract
5 medium kiwi fruits, peeled and
   thinly sliced
1 pint strawberries, sliced
½ pound seedless red grapes
½ pound seedless green grapes
⅓ cup apple jelly

1. Prepare tart shells: Into medium bowl, measure flour, butter or margarine, sugar, and water. With hand, knead mixture to form a soft dough.

2. Preheat oven to 375°F. With hands, shape dough into twenty-four 1-inch balls. Gently press a ball of dough onto bottom and up side of each of 24 tiny (2½″ by 1″) fluted tart molds.* With fork, prick dough in several places to prevent puffing during baking. Set tart molds in jellyroll pan. Bake until golden, about 10 minutes. When done, cool in molds on wire racks 10 minutes. Carefully remove tart shells from molds; cool completely on wire racks.

3. When tart shells are cool, prepare instant pudding as label directs but use only 1 cup milk. In small bowl with mixer at medium speed, beat heavy or whipping cream until soft peaks form. With rubber spatula, fold whipped cream and almond extract into pudding. Spoon cream filling into tart shells. Garnish tarts with kiwi-fruit slices, strawberry slices, and grapes.

4. In small saucepan over medium-low heat, heat apple jelly until melted and smooth; brush over fruit. Cover tarts; refrigerate until ready to serve.

*Tart molds may be purchased in housewares departments of department stores, or write for catalog to: Maid of Scandinavia Co., 3244 Raleigh Ave., Minneapolis, MN 55416.

Buttery Plum Tart

TIME: about 4 hours or start early in day—SERVINGS: 10

½ cup butter or margarine,
    softened
all-purpose flour
sugar
ground cinnamon
1½ pounds purple plums, sliced
¼ teaspoon almond extract
¼ cup slivered almonds
½ cup heavy or whipping cream
    (optional)

1. Prepare pastry: Into medium bowl, measure butter or margarine, 1½ cups flour, ⅓ cup sugar, and ¼ teaspoon ground cinnamon. With hand, knead mixture until blended. Pat pastry onto bottom and up side of 9-inch tart pan with removable bottom* or bottom and 1 inch up side of 9-inch springform pan.

2. Preheat oven to 375°F. In large bowl, toss plums, almond extract, ½ cup sugar, 2 tablespoons flour, and ½ teaspoon ground cinnamon. Arrange plum slices, closely overlapping, to form concentric circles on pastry in pan. Sprinkle top with almonds. Bake 45 minutes or until pastry is golden and plums are tender. Cool in pan on wire rack.

3. To serve, carefully remove side of pan from tart. Cut tart into wedges. If desired, serve with heavy or whipping cream to pour over tart.

*Tart pan may be purchased in housewares departments of department stores, or write for catalog to Paprikas Weiss, 1546 Second Avenue, New York, N.Y. 10028.

Berry Angel Tarts

TIME: start early in day—SERVINGS: 8

¼ cup California walnuts, finely
    chopped
1 tablespoon cornstarch
3 egg whites, at room
    temperature
⅛ teaspoon cream of tartar
⅛ teaspoon salt
¾ cup sugar
1 teaspoon vanilla extract
Creamy Custard (following)
about ½ pint blueberries (about
    1¼ cups)
8 strawberries

1. Prepare meringue: In 1-quart saucepan over medium heat, toast chopped walnuts until lightly browned, shaking saucepan frequently. Remove saucepan from heat; stir in cornstarch; set mixture aside.

2. Line large cookie sheet with foil. Preheat oven to 200°F.

3. In small bowl with mixer at high speed, beat egg whites, cream of tartar, and salt until soft peaks form. Beating at high speed, gradually beat in sugar, 2 tablespoons at a time, beating well after each addition until sugar is completely dissolved. (Whites should stand in stiff, glossy peaks.) Beat in vanilla and nut mixture just until blended.

4. Spoon meringue into 8 mounds on foil-lined cookie sheet. With spoon, spread each mound into a 3-inch circle, gently pushing meringue up at edge of circles to form a small rim. Bake 1 hour; turn oven control to off; leave meringues in oven 1½ hours longer to dry completely. With metal spatula, carefully loosen and remove meringues to wire rack to cool, about 1 hour.

5. Meanwhile, prepare Creamy Custard.

6. To serve, spoon custard into meringue shells. Top each with some blueberries and a strawberry.

Creamy Custard: In heavy 2-quart saucepan, stir *1½ cups milk, ¼ cup sugar, 2 tablespoons cornstarch, ¼ teaspoon salt,* and *2 egg yolks* until blended. Cook over medium-low heat until mixture thickens and boils, about 15 minutes. Boil 1 minute. Remove saucepan from heat; stir in *1½ teaspoons vanilla extract.* Cover and refrigerate until mixture is cold, about 1 hour.

In small bowl with mixer at medium speed, beat *¾ cup heavy or whipping cream* until soft peaks form. With rubber spatula or wire whisk, fold whipped cream into custard.

CANDIES

Peanut Brittle

TIME: about 1 hour or start up to week ahead—
YIELD: about 1 pound

1 cup sugar
½ cup light corn syrup
¼ cup water
¼ teaspoon salt
1 cup shelled raw peanuts*
2 tablespoons butter or
  margarine, softened
1 teaspoon baking soda

*Or, use *1 cup salted peanuts* and omit the salt.

1. Grease large cookie sheet. In heavy 2-quart saucepan over medium heat, heat sugar, corn syrup, water, and salt to boiling, stirring frequently until sugar is dissolved. Stir in peanuts. Carefully set candy thermometer in place and continue cooking, stirring frequently, until temperature reaches 300°F. or hard-crack stage (when a small amount of mixture dropped into a bowl of very cold water separates into hard and brittle threads), about 20 minutes.

2. Remove saucepan from heat; immediately stir in butter or margarine and baking soda; pour at once onto cookie sheet. With 2 forks, lift and pull peanut mixture into a rectangle about 14″ by 12″; cool completely.

3. With hands, snap candy into small pieces. Store in tightly covered container to use up within 1 week.

Chocolate-Peanut Clusters

TIME: about 2 hours or start up to 2 weeks ahead—
YIELD: about 2 dozen

2 4-ounce packages sweet
  cooking chocolate
1 tablespoon butter or margarine
1 8- to 8¼-ounce jar unsalted
  peanuts

1. Line 2 cookie sheets with waxed paper; set aside. Coarsely grate chocolate.* Place chocolate and butter or margarine in double-boiler top (not over water); set candy thermometer in place; set double-boiler top aside. Heat water to boiling in double-boiler bottom; remove from heat. Place double-boiler top over hot water; melt chocolate, stirring constantly with rubber spatula, until chocolate temperature reaches 130°F.

2. Immediately discard hot water from double-boiler bottom and refill with cold water to come one-third way up side of double boiler. Set top in place and cool chocolate, stirring constantly but gently, until chocolate temperature reaches 83°F. on special 40° to 120°F. candy and yeast thermometer.†

3. Working quickly, stir peanuts into chocolate mixture. Drop mixture by tablespoonfuls onto waxed-paper-lined cookie sheets; let stand 30 minutes or until chocolate is firm before removing from cookie sheets. Store in tightly covered container in cool place to use up within 2 weeks.

*When working with chocolate, be sure to avoid contact with water; even a few drops of water will cause chocolate to harden and become unmanageable.
†Special 40° to 120°F. candy and yeast thermometer may be purchased in specialty stores or write for catalog to Kitchen Glamor, 26770 Grand River, Detroit, MI 48240.

Butterscotch Candy Squares

TIME: about 1¾ hours or start up to 2 weeks ahead—
YIELD: about 1½ pounds

1 cup sugar
1 cup packed brown sugar
½ cup light corn syrup
½ cup butter or margarine
¼ cup water
2 tablespoons cider vinegar
1 teaspoon vanilla extract
½ teaspoon salt

1. Grease 13" by 9" baking pan. In heavy 3-quart saucepan over medium heat, heat all ingredients to boiling, stirring frequently, until sugar is dissolved. Carefully set candy thermometer in place and continue cooking, without stirring, until temperature reaches 300°F. or hard-crack stage (when a small amount of mixture dropped into a bowl of very cold water separates into hard and brittle threads), about 25 minutes.

2. Pour butterscotch mixture at once into prepared pan; cool in pan on wire rack 10 minutes. While candy is still warm, with knife, cut candy almost through into ½-inch squares; then let candy cool completely.

3. When candy is cool, with hands, break candy into marked squares. Store in tightly covered container to use up within 2 weeks.

Caramels

TIME: about 1¾ hours or start up to 2 weeks ahead—
YIELD: about 1 pound

1 cup sugar
1 cup heavy or whipping cream
3 tablespoons light corn syrup
2 tablespoons butter or margarine
1 teaspoon vanilla extract

1. Grease 8" by 8" baking pan. In heavy 2-quart saucepan over medium heat, heat all ingredients to boiling and until sugar is completely dissolved, stirring frequently. Carefully set candy thermometer in place and continue cooking, stirring frequently, until temperature reaches 245°F. or firm-ball stage (when a small amount of mixture dropped into a bowl of very cold water forms a firm ball which does not flatten on removal from water), about 30 minutes.

2. Pour caramel mixture into prepared pan. Cool in pan on wire rack 30 minutes. With knife, cut candy into thirty-two 4" by ½" pieces; cool completely, about 45 minutes longer. Wrap each caramel in plastic wrap. Store in tightly covered container to use up within 2 weeks.

Meltaway Meltaway Mocha Truffles

TIME: about 2 hours or start up to 2 weeks ahead—
YIELD: about 50 candies

1 12-ounce package semisweet-chocolate or milk-chocolate pieces
¾ cup sweetened condensed milk
1 tablespoon instant espresso coffee powder
2 tablespoons coffee-flavor liqueur
⅛ teaspoon salt
cocoa

1. In double boiler over hot, *not boiling*, water (or in heavy 2-quart saucepan over low heat), melt chocolate pieces, stirring occasionally. Stir in sweetened condensed milk, espresso coffee powder, coffee-flavor liqueur, and salt until well mixed. Refrigerate mixture about 30 minutes or until easy to shape.

2. With hands dusted with cocoa, shape a rounded teaspoon chocolate mixture into a ball. Roll ball immediately in more cocoa. Repeat with remaining mixture. Store in tightly covered container to use up within 2 weeks.

264

Sweet Pralines

TIME: about 2 hours or start up to 2 weeks ahead—
YIELD: about 1 dozen

2 cups sugar
¾ cup evaporated milk
3 tablespoons light corn syrup
dash baking soda
2 tablespoons orange juice
1½ cups pecan halves

1. Line a large cookie sheet with waxed paper; set aside.

2. In heavy 3-quart saucepan over medium heat, heat sugar, evaporated milk, corn syrup, and baking soda to boiling, stirring constantly, until mixture boils and sugar is dissolved. Set candy thermometer in place. Reduce heat to low and continue cooking, stirring frequently, until temperature reaches 234°F. or soft-ball stage (when small amount of mixture dropped into very cold water forms a soft ball that flattens on removal from water).

3. Quickly stir in orange juice and pecans; cook 5 minutes longer, stirring frequently. Remove saucepan from heat; beat 2 to 3 minutes until mixture just begins to lose its gloss.

4. Working quickly, drop mixture by heaping tablespoonfuls, 2 inches apart, onto waxed-paper-lined cookie sheet. (Mixture will spread into 3-inch circles.) Let Pralines stand 30 minutes or until cool before removing from waxed paper. Store in tightly covered container to use up within 2 weeks.

Candied Grapefruit Peels

TIME: start day ahead or up to 2 weeks ahead—
YIELD: about 1½ pounds

4 large grapefruits
water
½ cup light corn syrup
sugar
1 3-ounce package lemon-flavor
   gelatin

1. With sharp knife, score peel of each grapefruit into quarters; pull from fruit. (Reserve fruit to use in salad.) Trim off as much white membrane from peel as possible; cut peel into long, thin strips. You should have about 4 cups firmly packed peel.

2. In 4-quart saucepan over high heat, heat peels and 8 cups water to boiling; boil 15 minutes; drain; rinse. With 8 more cups water, boil peels 15 minutes again; drain.

3. In same saucepan over high heat, heat corn syrup, 1¾ cups sugar, and 1½ cups water until boiling and sugar is dissolved, stirring frequently. Gently stir in peels. Reduce heat to medium-low; cook until most of the syrup has been absorbed, about 40 minutes, stirring occasionally.

4. Remove saucepan from heat; gently stir in gelatin until dissolved; cool 10 minutes. (Mixture will be thin and sticky.) On waxed paper, place 1 cup sugar. Lightly roll peels, a few at a time, in sugar; place in single layer on wire racks. Let peels dry overnight or about 12 hours. Store in tightly covered containers.

Candied Orange Peels: Prepare as above but substitute *10 large oranges* for grapefruit.

Orange-Chocolate Toffee

TIME: about 1½ hours or start up to 2 weeks ahead—
YIELD: about 1 pound

1 cup sugar
1 cup butter
3 tablespoons water
1 teaspoon vanilla extract
1 6-ounce package semisweet-
    chocolate pieces
½ cup slivered blanched
    almonds, toasted and coarsely
    chopped
2 tablespoons grated orange peel

1. Grease large cookie sheet. In heavy 2-quart saucepan over medium heat, heat first 4 ingredients to boiling and until sugar is completely dissolved, stirring frequently. Carefully set candy thermometer in place and continue cooking, stirring frequently, until temperature reaches 310°F. or hard-crack stage (when a small amount of mixture dropped into a bowl of very cold water separates into hard and brittle threads), about 30 minutes. Pour candy mixture at once onto prepared cookie sheet.

2. In heavy 1-quart saucepan over low heat, melt chocolate pieces. Spread chocolate over toffee; sprinkle with chopped almonds and grated orange peel. Place cookie sheet on wire rack; cool candy completely, about 1 hour.

3. When candy is cool, with hands, gently snap candy into small serving-size pieces. Store in tightly covered container to use up within 2 weeks.

Strufoli

TIME: about 5 hours or start day ahead—SERVINGS: 12

1 tablespoon sugar
1 teaspoon grated lemon peel
1 teaspoon vanilla extract
½ teaspoon salt
4 eggs
2½ cups all-purpose flour
salad oil
1½ cups honey
red and green candied cherries
    for garnish

1. In large bowl, mix sugar, lemon peel, vanilla, salt, eggs, and 2 cups flour. With hands, knead in remaining ½ cup flour. Turn dough onto lightly floured surface. With floured knife, cut dough into 20 equal portions. With palms of hands, roll each portion into 9-inch-long pencil-like stick. Cut sticks into ½-inch pieces.

2. In 3-quart saucepan over medium heat, heat about 1½ inches salad oil to 375°F. on deep-fat thermometer or heat oil in deep-fat fryer set at 375°F.

3. Fry dough pieces in hot oil, a handful at a time, until golden, about 5 minutes. With slotted spoon, remove dough pieces to paper towels to drain. Place fried dough in large bowl.

4. In 2-quart saucepan over medium heat, heat honey to boiling. Pour honey over fried dough and mix well. Cover and refrigerate at least 3 hours.

5. To serve, let Strufoli stand at room temperature 1 hour to soften; mix well and spoon onto large plate to form cone shape. If desired, garnish with candied cherries. Let guests pull off pieces of dessert with fingers; provide napkins.

Meringue Mushrooms

TIME: about 4½ hours or start up to week ahead—
YIELD: 30 candies

4 egg whites, at room
    temperature
¼ teaspoon cream of tartar
¾ cup sugar
½ teaspoon almond extract
2 squares semisweet chocolate
cocoa

1. Lightly grease and flour a large cookie sheet.

2. In large bowl with mixer at high speed, beat egg whites and cream of tartar until soft peaks form. Beating at high speed, sprinkle in sugar, 2 tablespoons at a time, beating well after each addition until sugar is completely dissolved; beat in almond extract. (Whites should stand in stiff, glossy peaks.)

3. Spoon meringue into large decorating bag with large writing tube. Pipe meringue onto cookie sheet into 30 mounds, each about 1½ inches in diameter for mushroom caps. Pipe remaining meringue onto cookie sheet into thirty 1¼″ by ½″ lengths for mushroom stems. Bake in 200°F. oven 1¾ hours. Cool completely on cookie sheet on wire rack, about 30 minutes.

4. Assemble and decorate mushrooms: In small saucepan over low heat, melt chocolate. With tip of small knife, cut a small hole into center of underside of mushroom cap; place small amount of melted chocolate in hole. Attach stem to mushroom cap by inserting one end of stem into hole in underside of mushroom cap; repeat with remaining caps and stems. Let chocolate dry completely, about 1 hour. Store mushrooms in tightly covered container. Just before serving, sprinkle tops of mushrooms lightly with cocoa.

Marzipan Vegetables

TIME: about 2 hours or start up to week ahead—
YIELD: about 36 candies

2 cups blanched whole almonds
2 cups confectioners' sugar
1 tablespoon water
1¾ teaspoons almond extract
½ teaspoon salt
1 egg white
green food color
red food color
yellow food color

1. In blender at medium speed, blend almonds, ½ cup at a time, until very finely ground.* In medium bowl, with fork, mix ground almonds, confectioners' sugar, water, almond extract, salt, and egg white until blended.

2. Divide almond paste into thirds. Into first third, knead enough green food color to tint a pretty pea-green color. Into second third, knead enough red and yellow food colors to tint a pretty carrot color. Into remaining third, knead enough yellow food color to tint a pretty yellow-squash color.

3. Reserve about 1 tablespoon of green marzipan for carrot and squash stems. Shape remaining green marzipan into twelve 2½-inch-long open pea pods with peas inside. Shape orange marzipan into twelve 2½-inch-long carrots. Shape half of reserved green marzipan into twelve stems for carrots; press a stem on each carrot. Shape yellow marzipan into twelve 2½-inch-long yellow straight-neck squash. Shape remaining green marzipan into 12 stems for squash. Let "vegetables" dry on wire rack, about 30 minutes. Store in tightly covered container to use up within 1 week.

*If using food processor, blend almonds until very finely ground. Add confectioners' sugar, egg white, water, almond extract, and salt; process to make a stiff paste. Divide almond paste into thirds and add food colors as above.

267

Holiday Apricot Logs

TIME: start early in day or up to 2 weeks ahead—**YIELD:** 2 logs

1 6- to 6½-ounce package dried
    apricots
2 tablespoons water
honey
1 teaspoon grated orange peel
1¾ cups California walnuts,
    finely chopped
1 cup confectioners' sugar

1. In 1-quart saucepan over low heat, cook apricots, water, and 2 tablespoons honey until liquid is absorbed by apricots, stirring occasionally; remove saucepan from heat.

2. In blender at medium speed or in food processor with knife blade attached, blend apricots until pureed. In small bowl, combine pureed apricots with orange peel, 1½ cups chopped walnuts, and ¾ cup confectioners' sugar. With hand, knead mixture until well blended.

3. Divide apricot mixture in half. Shape each half into a 5″ by 1″ log. Brush each log with some honey. Roll logs in remaining walnuts and sprinkle with 2 tablespoons confectioners' sugar. Let logs dry on wire rack about 2 hours; then sprinkle with 2 more tablespoons confectioners' sugar. Wrap each log with plastic wrap; store in tightly covered container to use up within 2 weeks.

4. To serve, cut apricot logs into ¼-inch-thick slices.

Beverages

The Best Iced Tea

TIME: about 20 minutes—SERVINGS: 8

water
3 tablespoons loose tea or 8 tea
   bags
ice cubes
sugar
mint sprigs

1. In 2-quart saucepan over high heat, heat 4 cups water to boiling. Stir in loose tea or tea bags; remove from heat. Cover; steep 5 minutes.

2. Strain (or remove tea bags) into pitcher holding 4 cups cold water. Cover until serving. Pour tea over ice cubes in 12-ounce glasses. Serve with sugar and mint sprigs.

TO PREPARE BY COLD WATER METHOD: About 4½ hours before serving, tie *8 tea bags* together; add to *4 cups cold water* in pitcher. Cover; refrigerate at least 4 hours. Serve with *sugar* and *mint sprigs*. Makes 4 servings.

The Best Lemonade

TIME: 1 hour or start up to 1 week ahead—SERVINGS: 16

8 to 10 lemons
1½ cups sugar
water
ice cubes

1. From one lemon, grate 1 teaspoon peel. With hand, roll each lemon on work surface to soften slightly. Squeeze lemons to make 1½ cups juice.

2. Prepare syrup: in 1-quart pitcher, stir sugar; 1½ cups very hot water, and grated lemon peel until sugar is dissolved. Add lemon juice. Refrigerate.

3. To make each serving, into measuring cup, measure ¼ cup lemon syrup; pour over ice cubes in 12-ounce glass. Stir in ¾ cup cold water.

Sangria Cooler

TIME: start early in day—SERVINGS: 8

1 small orange
1 small lemon
¼ pint strawberries
1 750-ml bottle dry red wine
  (about 3¼ cups)
3 cups orange juice
¼ cup brandy
¼ cup sugar
1 16-ounce bottle club soda
1 tray of ice cubes

1. Thinly slice orange; cut slices into quarters. Thinly slice lemon; cut slices into halves. Hull strawberries; cut each in half; set aside.

2. In large pitcher, stir red wine, orange juice, brandy, and sugar until sugar is dissolved; stir in fruit. Cover and refrigerate.

3. Just before serving, stir club soda into sangria. Pour sangria into glasses over ice cubes, making sure to put some fruit into each glass. Makes about 8 cups.

Café con Leche (Coffee with Milk)

TIME: about 15 minutes—SERVINGS: 10

5 cups water
5 cups milk
8 to 10 tablespoons instant
  coffee granules
8 to 10 tablespoons sugar

In 4-quart saucepan over medium-high heat, heat water and milk until very hot (do not boil). Stir in coffee and sugar until dissolved. Makes 10 cups.

Appendix

How to Follow Our Recipes

Read the recipe before you begin. Be sure you understand all cooking terms used. Check how much time it will take to prepare the recipe, and allow yourself a few extra minutes in case you are interrupted.

Check the ingredient list. Make sure you have everything you need, in the amount called for. Assemble the ingredients.

Don't substitute key ingredients, unless the recipe suggests an alternate. That goes for product forms and package sizes, too. To take one example, some packaged pudding mixes come in both regular-size and family-size packages, and in both regular and instant forms. Using either the wrong size or the wrong kind of pudding in a recipe might result in a disaster!

Seasonings and spices *can* safely be varied. But it's a good idea to follow the recipe exactly the first time, to discover the family's tastes before making changes.

Check the utensils you'll need. Assemble items for measuring, mixing, cooking, and serving. Be sure pans are the right size (see "How to measure pans," below).

Do as much advance preparation as possible. Chop, cut, grate, melt, or otherwise prepare ingredients and have them ready before you start to mix. Grease and flour pans; turn the

oven on at least 10 minutes before putting food in to bake, to allow it to preheat to the proper temperature.

Measure accurately. Our recipes are based on standard, consistent measurements. Use the proper measuring equipment and methods (see "Measuring Ingredients," below).

Mix carefully. Ingredients are combined in different ways (by folding, beating, stirring, etc.) to achieve different results. Be sure to take note of any specific mixing times of cautions given in the recipe.

Clean up as you work. Put empty bowls, used measuring equipment in the sink; throw away paper; sponge up spills. The less cluttered the work surface, the less chance of your making a mistake.

Cook or bake as directed. For best results, use the temperature specified in the recipe. Follow the time suggested too, but to be on the safe side, start checking for doneness before the end, since ovens and heating units vary.

Be careful about doubling or halving a recipe. Though some recipes can be increased or decreased successfully, many more cannot. For best results, make the recipe as given, and repeat it until the desired amount is obtained.

Measuring Ingredients

Using the correct measuring equipment. Accurate measurements are essential if you want the same good results each time you make a recipe. For dry ingredients, use a set of four graduated measuring cups, consisting of ¼-, ⅓-, ½-, and 1-cup measures. For liquids, use a 1-cup liquid measuring cup that is also marked for smaller measurements. Two-cup and 4-cup liquid measuring cups are helpful for measuring larger amounts. A standard set of ¼-, ½-, 1-teaspoon, and 1-tablespoon measuring spoons is used for both dry and liquid ingredients.

Measuring liquids. Always read the line on a measuring cup at eye level when checking the volume of liquid in a cup. With the liquid measure on a level surface, slowly pour the liquid into the cup until it reaches the desired line. If using measuring spoons, pour liquid just to the top of the spoon without letting it spill over.

Measuring sugar. Lightly spoon sugar into a graduated measuring cup, and level off with the straight edge of a knife or spatula.

For brown sugar, pack the sugar lightly into the cup with the back of a spoon, then level off; it will hold its shape when inverted from the cup.

Measuring flour. In the recipes in this book, all the flours are measured and used straight from the flour package or canister. Lightly spoon the flour into a graduated measuring cup or

spoon; never pack flour down or shake or tap the side of the measuring cup. Then, quickly level off the surplus flour in the measuring cup with the straight edge of a small kitchen knife.

Measuring shortening. Liquid shortening, such as salad oil and melted butter or margarine, can be measured in the same way as liquids.

Measure shortening such as lard, vegetable shortening, even peanut butter, as follows: Pack in the shortening firmly, right to the top of the measuring spoon or graduated cup. Level off the shortening with the straight edge, not the flat side, of a knife or spatula.

Measuring butter or margarine. Each ¼-pound stick of butter or margarine measures ½ cup; the wrapping is usually marked off in tablespoons for measuring smaller amounts. With a sharp knife, just cut off the number of tablespoons needed, following the guidelines on the wrapper. For butter or margarine not wrapped in this way, measure and level off as for solid shortening.

How to measure pans. Be sure your pans are the kind and size specified in the recipe. The size of some cookware is expressed in liquid measurement at its level full capacity. Measure top inside of bakeware for length, width, or diameter; measure perpendicular inside for depth. Sizes for skillets or frypans and griddles are stated as the top outside dimensions, exclusive of handles.

Equivalent Amounts

How many cups make a quart? Are three bananas enough to make one cup of mashed? For two tablespoons of grated orange peel, will you need more than one orange? How many cups are there in a pound of flour? These questions are answered below.

Equivalent measures

Dash	2 to 3 drops, or less than 1/8 teaspoon	**1/2 cup**	8 tablespoons	**1 quart**	4 cups
		2/3 cup	10 tablespoons plus 2 teaspoons	**1 gallon**	4 quarts
1 tablespoon	3 teaspoons			**1 peck**	8 quarts
1/4 cup	4 tablespoons	**1 cup**	16 tablespoons	**1 bushel**	4 pecks
1/3 cup	5 tablespoons plus 1 teaspoon	**1 pint**	2 cups	**1 pound**	16 ounces

Food equivalents

Apples	1 pound	3 medium (3 cups sliced)
dried	1 pound	4 1/3 cups (8 cups cooked)
Applesauce		
canned	16-ounce can	1 3/4 cups
Apricots	1 pound	8 to 12 medium
canned	16-ounce can	8 to 12 whole; 12 to 20 halves
dried	1 pound	3 cups (5 cups cooked)
Bananas	1 pound	3 medium (1 1/3 cups mashed)
Beans		
dry	1 pound	2 cups (5 to 7 cups cooked)
green or wax	1 pound	3 cups (2 1/2 cups cooked)
Berries	1 pint	1 3/4 cups
Bread	1-pound loaf	14 to 20 slices
fresh	1 slice with crust	1/2 cup crumbs
dried	1 slice grated	1/4 cup fine crumbs
Broth, chicken or beef	1 cup	1 bouillon cube; 1 envelope bouillon; 1 teaspoon instant bouillon dissolved in 1 cup boiling water
Butter or margarine		
stick	1/4 pound	8 tablespoons (1/2 cup)
whipped	1 pound	3 cups
Cabbage	1 pound	4 1/2 cups shredded
Carrots	1 pound without tops	3 cups shredded; 2 1/2 cups diced

Cheese		
blue	1/4 pound	1 cup crumbled
Cheddar, Swiss	1/4 pound	1 cup shredded
cottage	8 ounces	1 cup
cream	3 ounces	6 tablespoons
spread	5-ounce jar	1/2 cup
Chocolate		
unsweetened	1 ounce	1 square
semisweet pieces	6-ounce package	1 cup
Coconut		
flaked	3 1/2-ounce can	1 1/3 cups
shredded	4-ounce can	1 1/3 cups
Cornmeal	1 pound	3 to 3 1/2 cups
	1 cup uncooked	4 to 4 1/2 cups cooked
Corn syrup	16 ounces	2 cups
Cranberries	1 pound	4 cups
Cranberry sauce	16-ounce can	1 2/3 cups
Cream, heavy or whipping	1 cup	2 cups whipped cream
Cream, sour	8 ounces	1 cup
Currants, dried		
	1 pound	3 1/4 cups
Dates	1 pound	2 1/2 cups pitted
Egg whites, large	1 cup	8 to 10 whites

Food equivalents (continued)

Egg yolks, large	1 cup	12 to 14 yolks
Figs, dried	1 pound	2²/₃ cups chopped
Flour	1 pound	
all-purpose		about 3¹/₂ cups
cake		about 4 cups
Gelatin		
unflavored	1 envelope	1 tablespoon
Graham crackers	14 squares	1 cup fine crumbs
Honey	1 pound	1¹/₃ cups
Lard	1 pound	2 cups
Lemon	1 medium	3 tablespoons juice, about 1 tablespoon grated peel
Lentils	1 pound	2¹/₄ cups (5 cups cooked)
Lime	1 medium	about 2 tablespoons juice
Macaroni		
elbow	4 ounces	1 to 1¹/₄ cups (2 to 2¹/₄ cups cooked)
Maple syrup	12 ounces	1¹/₂ cups
Milk		
evaporated	5¹/₃- or 6-ounce can	²/₃ cup
	13- or 14¹/₂-ounce can	1²/₃ cups
sweetened condensed	14-ounce can	1¹/₄ cups
Molasses	12 ounces	1¹/₂ cups
Mushrooms	1 pound	2 to 3 cups sliced
Noodles	1 pound	6 to 8 cups, uncooked
Nuts	1 pound	
ALMONDS		
in shell		1 to 1¹/₄ cups nutmeats
shelled		3 cups
BRAZIL NUTS		
in shell		1¹/₂ cups nutmeats
shelled		3¹/₄ cups
FILBERTS		
in shell		1¹/₂ cups nutmeats
shelled		3¹/₂ cups
PEANUTS		
in shell		2 to 2¹/₂ cups nutmeats
shelled		3 cups
PECANS		
in shell		2¹/₄ cups nutmeats
shelled		4 cups
WALNUTS		
in shell		2 cups nutmeats
shelled		4 cups
Oats		
uncooked	1 cup	1³/₄ cups cooked
Onion	1 large	³/₄ to 1 cup chopped
Orange	1 medium	¹/₃ to ¹/₂ cup juice 2 tablespoons grated peel
Peaches	1 pound	4 medium (2 cups sliced)
canned	16 ounces	6 to 10 halves 2 cups sliced
Pears	1 pound	4 medium (2 cups sliced)
canned	16 ounces	6 to 10 halves
Peas,		
split, dried	1 pound	2¹/₄ cups (5 cups cooked)
Pepper, green	1 large	1 cup diced
Pineapple	1 medium	2 cups cubed
canned	20 ounces	2¹/₂ cups crushed pineapple with liquid
		10 medium slices
		2¹/₂ cups chunks with liquid
Potatoes	1 pound	
white		3 medium (2¹/₄ cups diced, 1³/₄ cups mashed)
sweet		3 medium
Prunes, dried	1 pound	2¹/₄ cups pitted (4 to 4¹/₂ cups cooked)
Raisins	1 pound	3 cups, loosely packed
Rice	1 cup	
brown		3 to 4 cups cooked
parboiled		3 to 4 cups cooked
precooked		1 to 2 cups cooked
regular long-grain white		3 or more cups cooked
Salad oil	16 ounces	2 cups
Saltines	28 crackers	1 cup fine crumbs
Shortening, vegetable	1 pound	2¹/₃ cups
Spaghetti	1 pound	about 6¹/₂ cups cooked
Sugar	1 pound	
brown		2¹/₄ cups packed
confectioners'		4 to 4¹/₂ cups
granulated white		2¹/₄ to 2¹/₂ cups
Tomatoes	1 pound	3 medium (1¹/₂ cups cooked)
Vanilla wafers	22 wafers	1 cup fine crumbs
Yogurt	¹/₂ pint	1 cup

1982 Recipes, Month by Month

Recipes marked with an asterisk (*) appeared in the column, "Susan, Our Beginning Cook." Those marked with a dagger (†) appeared in "30-Minute Entrées and Desserts." Those marked with a double dagger (‡) appeared in "Favorites from Our Dining Room."

JANUARY
Stir-Fried Chicken and Mushrooms*
Open-Faced Salmon Sandwiches†
Crème Caramel‡

Money-Saving Oven Meals
Fish and Noodles
Chocolate-Brownie Pie
Roast Chicken Paprika
Grandma's Best Bread Pudding
Caramel Pears
Family-Style Pizza
Salmon Quiche
Gingered Fruit Compote
Spicy Oven Pork Chops
Old-Fashioned Corn Bread
Macaroni and Franks Casserole
Cranberry Baked Apples
Citrus Loaf
Turkey Loaf with Zucchini Sauce
Meatless Lasagna
Oatmeal Drop Cookies
Cherry-Cheese Custard
Oven Ham and Beans
Chuck Roast in Wine Sauce
Baked Onions
Prune Crumb Wedges
Country Chicken
Barley-Mushroom Casserole
Saucy Steak and Peppers
Applesauce Fig Cake
Rice and Bean Bake
Deviled Beef Stew
Poppy-Seed Cake with Custard Sauce
Ground Beef and Zucchini Custard
Individual Blueberry Crisps
Barbecued Ribs
Banana Betty
Baked Tuna Squares
Maple-Bran Muffins

FEBRUARY
Skillet Macaroni and Cheese*
Zesty Beef Turnovers†
Veal Forestier‡

Big Pie Cookbook
No-Crust Cheesy Salmon Pie
Greek Pie
"Burrito" Pie
New England Clam Pie
French Apple Tart
Breakfast Tartlets
Sugar-Frosted Apple Pie
Cheese-and-Pepper Country Pie
Pecan-Custard Pie
Pork-Cabbage Pie
Turkey Pot Pie
Apricot-Prune Pie
Citrus Angel Pie
Ice-Cream Pie with Peanut-Butter Crust
Strawberry Sweetheart Pie
Come-for-Coffee Cherry Pie
First-Course Spinach Pie

Marbled Mousse Pie
Tuna Fish Pies
Beef Empanadas
Banana-Cream Pie
Italian Cheese-and-Escarole Pie
Almond Cordial Pie
Black-Bottom Cherry Pie
King-Sized Pork-and-Polenta Pie
Sausage Quiche
Jeweled Citrus Pie
Corn-Bread-Topped Pork Pie
Beefsteak Pie with Whole-Wheat Crust
Beef-and-Potato Pie

MARCH
Apple Dessert Pancake*
Sherried Steak Dinner†
Almond Cream-Puff Ring‡

American Classics Cookbook
Beef-Vegetable Soup
Fudge-Nut Brownies
Succotash
Poached Salmon with Egg Sauce
Apple-Glazed Duckling
New England Boiled Dinner
Cranberry-Ginger Relish
Barbecued Spareribs, Oven-Style
Yankee Pot Roast
Apple Pandowdy
Mother's Oatmeal Bread
Boston Cream Pie
Creamed Cabbage
Saratoga Chips
Pumpkin Bread
Parker House Rolls
Strawberry Shortcake
Bacon-Corn Muffins
Apple Butter
Two-Crust Lemon Pie
Spoon Bread
Vermont Pork and Beans
Plump Roast Chicken with Dressing
Sticky Buns
Potato Bread
Nut-Cracker Cake
Lemon Meringue Pie
Anadama Bread
Old-Fashioned Pearl Tapioca Pudding
New England Clam Chowder
Jelly Roll
Brunswick Stew
Peanut Brittle
Pork Chops with Creamy Gravy
Blueberry Buckle
Black-Bean Soup
Corn Chowder
Candied Sweet-Potato Slices
Rice Pudding
Colonial Gingerbread
Sunchoke Pickles
Fried Chicken
Bread-and-Butter Pudding
Grandma's Tomato Pudding

Old-Fashioned Buttermilk Biscuits
Currant-Glazed Ham Steak
Custard Corn Pudding
Chicken Fricassee with Dumplings
Bourbon Balls
Harvard Beets

APRIL
Chocolate Party Cake*
Linguine with Ham-and-Cheese Sauce†
Party Chicken and Shrimp‡

40-Minute Cookbook
Spring Beef Salad
Pork Scallops alla Francese
New Potatoes with Mock Caviar
Skillet Potatoes
Broiled Cod Steaks Montauk
Danish Meatballs
Ice-Cream Grasshoppers
Chicken-Bacon Nuggets
California Open-Faced Sandwiches
Rice Pilaf
Lamb Kabobs
Tomato Slices with Lemon Dressing
Scallops and Asparagus in Cream
Mushrooms and Green Onions in Lettuce
   Cups
Steaks with Mustard Butter
Brittle Cake
Lamb Chops Teriyaki
Szechwan Chicken
Saucy Chicken Livers
Boston Lettuce Wedges with Pimento
   Dressing
No-Crust Artichoke Quiche
Skillet Apple Dessert
Almond-Cordial Parfaits
Hamburgers Roquefort Style
Shrimp Salad in Avocado Halves
Springtime Rhubarb Refresher
Veal Roman Style
Broiled Rock Cornish Hens à l'Orange
Braised Celery Bites
Creamy Chicken and Fettuccine
Salisbury Steaks with Onions and Peppers
Country Frank Sandwiches
Mussels in Wine
Sautéed Italian-Bread Slices
Chunky Fish Soup au Gratin
Vermicelli with Cheese Sauce and
   Mushrooms
Mexican Beef Pie
Veal Chops in Creamy Anchovy Sauce
Salmon Bisque
Kielbasa with Sauerkraut
Salmon-Avocado Open-Faced Sandwiches
Ziti with Mexican-Style Meat Sauce
Pork Chops with Caper Sauce

Bake a Classic Yeast Bread
White Bread
Whole-Grain Bread
Sally Lunn

"Coffee Can" Batter Bread
Fondue Bread
Swedish Limpa
Italian Bread
Three Sweet Breads
Brioche Loaf

MAY
Strawberry-Orange Ice*
Glazed Lamb Chops with Skillet
    Potatoes†
Fried Indian Bread (Poori)‡

Burgers, Meatballs, Meat Loaves, and More
Pepper Burgers
Filled Meat-Loaf Roll
Beef Patties en Croûte
Almond-Crumb Turkey Cakes
Picadillo "Salad"
Pâté Maison
Beef-Filled Artichokes with Lemon Butter
Pork-Stuffed Cabbage Leaves
Spring Lamb and Vegetable Potpourri
Family-Style Turkey Loaf
Deluxe Open-faced Cheeseburgers
Quick Beef-and-Vegetable Soup
Springtime Burgers in Lettuce Cups
Hamburgers Holstein
Beef-Broccoli Strudel
Mock Tournedos with Herbed Hollandaise
Beef Patties à la Dijonnaise
Middle Eastern Pork-and-Eggplant Dip
Meat-and-Macaroni Casserole with Italian
    Vegetables
Meatballs Stroganoff
Herb-and-Spice Meatballs with Waffles
Milan-Style Meatballs
Meat-and-Potato Loaf
Sausage-Stuffed Turkey Loaf
Meat Patties Italiano
Pork Loaf
Pork Pâté
Beef-Zucchini Pie
Turkey and Broccoli Quiche
Skillet Pork with Dumplings
Beef-Noodle Paprikash
Hot-and-Spicy Chili
Easy Pork Pasties
Cocktail Meatballs
Pasta and Asparagus with Meatballs
Turkey Meatballs with Caper Sauce
Beef-and-Vegetable Pizza

JUNE
Barbecued Beef and Vegetable Kabobs*
Big Chicken Burger†
Sacramento Fruit Bowl‡

Real Italian Cookbook
Roast Leg of Lamb with Herb Seasoning
Garlic Bread
Zucchini with Mozzarella
Zuccotto (Florentine Cream Cake)
Braised Peppers and Potatoes
Zuppa di Pesce (Fish Soup)
Gnocchi al Forno
Risotto
Granita
Chicken in Anchovy Sauce
Veal Scallops with Prosciutto and Sage
Minestrone
Insalata di Calamari (Squid Salad)
Homemade Pasta Dough

Fettuccine
Fettuccine Alfredo
Fettuccine with White Clam Sauce
Fettuccine Primavera
Fettuccine with Pesto Sauce
Tortellini in Escarole Soup
Ravioli
Hearty Home-Style Meat Sauce
Antipasto
Zabaglione on Fresh Berries
Cenci Rosettes
Zuppa Inglese
Caponata
Stuffed Beef Rolls
Torta di Mandorla (Almond Torte)
Flounder Florentine
Pork Chops in Wine
Pasta-Asparagus Salad
Tuscany White-Bean and Tuna Salad
Lasagna, Northern Style
Polenta
Torta di Ricotta

JULY
The Best Iced Tea and Lemonade*
Skillet Cheese Toast†
Beef Scallops with Fresh Tomato Sauce‡

Great Summer Get-Togethers
Blueberry Coffeecake
Marinated Green Beans
Zesty Lima-Bean Salad
Lemony Anchovy Dressing
Creamy Mustard Dressing
Herb Dressing
Tuna-Stuffed Eggs
Pasta Salad
Whole-Wheat Garlic Croutons
Crudités with Creamy Tarragon Dip
Barbecued Steak with Sweet-Pepper
    Sauce
Onion-and-Pepper Sauté
Rice-and-Bean Salad
Summer Fruit Bowl
Pecan Crisps
Party Tacos with Two Fillings
Sangria Cooler
Orange-Cream Parfaits
Fiesta Salad
Café con Leche
Marbled Chocolate Mousse
Orange Cream
Spareribs with Peach Sauce
Light Cottage Cheesecake
Party Fruit Tarts
Summer-Squash and Pepper Slaw
Garden-Vegetable Salad
Party Ice-Cream Roll with Chocolate
    Sauce
Chilled Watercress Soup
Avocado Butter
New-Potato Salad Vinaigrette
Vegetable Borscht
Plantain Chips
Backyard Clambake
Sliced Tomatoes Provençale
Honey-Nut Chiffon Cake
"Hot" Stir-Fried Beef
Noodle Salad with Peanut Sauce
Oriental Summer Salad
Melon with Gingered Cream Cheese

AUGUST
Sunday Chicken Salad*

Flounder in Lemony Dill Sauce†
Spumoni Elegante‡

Summer's Bounty Cookbook
Easy Country Vegetables
Fresh Tomato Sauce with Spaghetti
Deluxe Layered Chef's Salad
Zucchini-Tomato Skillet
Summer Dinner Salad
Harvest-Time Stuffed Vegetables
Zucchini Strips Rémoulade
Grape Salad-Dessert Mold
Dinner Salad for a Crowd
Spicy Creole Freezer Sauce
Pickled Vegetable Medley
Peach Butter
Melon Cordial Cups
Poached Peaches with Fresh Raspberry
    Sauce
Berry Angel Tarts
Blueberry Snacking Cake
Buttery Plum Tart
Cauliflower Pickles
Lettuce with Hot Bacon Dressing
Pear Dumplings à la Crème
Tangy Corn Relish
Green-Tomato Chow Chow
Freezer Peach-Orange Conserve
Plum-Nut Freezer Conserve
Fancy Coleslaw Vinaigrette
Strawberry-Peach Cream
Layered Beef and Cabbage Casserole
Freezer Blueberry Pie Filling
Do-Ahead Company Green Salad
Cheesy Vegetable Pie
Freezer Peach-Pie Filling
Jeweled Beet Salad
Sautéed Beet Greens
Skillet Sausage and Squash Supper
Summer Vegetable Mélange
Vegetables and Pork Tenderloin Stir-Fry
Pepper-and-Tomato Sauté
Spiced Nectarine Slices

SEPTEMBER
Easy Chocolate Garnishes*
Pineapple Upside-Down Cups†
Pickled Shrimp Appetizer‡

The Stretch-the-Meat Cookbook
Cheesy Rice-Chicken Soufflé
Braised Steak, Ranch Style
Sausage Ratatouille
Chuck Steak Paisano
Fried Knackwurst and Potatoes
Chicken Stroganoff
Curried Meatballs with Pasta
Chunky Beef-and-Bean Soup
Spinach-Stuffed Fish Fillets with Parsley
    Rice
Family Short-Ribs-and-Beans Supper
Chicken with Bulgar Pilaf
Bacon-Potato Frittata
Scalloped Beef and Potatoes
Mexican Beef Skillet Melt
Spicy Pork and Tofu
Meat-and-Kasha-Filled Red Cabbage
    Leaves
Golden Buck
Celery-Ham Brunch
Chicken, Tofu, and Rice
Deluxe Whole-Wheat Pizzas
Tuna-Bulgur Salad
Hearty Italian-Style Meatballs

Hungarian Pork and Beans
Thai-Style Pork-Noodle Toss
Four-Bean and Barley Salad
Saucy Broccoli-Liver Bake
Basque Lamb Stew
Baked Eggs and Vegetables Niçoise
Braised Chicken and Vegetables with
  Brown Rice
Spicy Mexican Roll-Ups
Beef-Macaroni Pita Pockets
French-Quarter Fish Creole
Pasta-and-Steak Salad
Cheese-Vegetable Strata

OCTOBER
Baked Acorn Squash—Two Ways*
Chicken Milano†
Orange-Glazed Pork with Potatoes‡

Cake Lover's Cookbook
Dreamy Chocolate Cake
Carrot Cake Ring
Butter-Rich Coffee Cake
Cinnamon-Cream Torte
Manhattan-Style Cheesecake
Heavenly Pineapple Cake
Orange Chiffon Cake
Three-Tiered Wedding Cake
Banana-Split Cake
Bee Cake
Plum-Peach Coffee Cake
Peanut-Butter Cupcakes
Chocolate-Cherry Cake
Parisian Mocha-Cream Loaf
Lemon-Orange Loaf
Chocolate-and-Creams
Scandinavian Tea Cake
Cinnamon-Apple Cake
Feather-Light Raspberry Sherbert Roll
Happy Day Rainbow Cake
Walnut-Maple Torte
Cake Roll with Lemon-Curd Filling
Mocha-Meringue Heart
Cinnamon-Spice Ring
Ice-Cream-Filled Chocolate Cake Ring

**Take a Package of Refrigerated
Crescent Rolls**
Corned Beef and Cabbage Buns
Cheese-and-Pear Danish
Herbed Dinner Rolls
Salami-and-Eggplant Pie

NOVEMBER
Hot Mushroom Turnovers*
Honeyed Ham Steak with Peach Halves†
Swedish Meatballs‡

**Chicken, Turkey, Goose, Duckling
(and More!) Cookbook**
Marinated Vegetable Relish Tray
Creamy Sweet Potatoes
Cracked-Wheat Rolls
Pumpkin Chiffon Pie with Nutty Cookie
  Crust
No-Cook Cranberry Relish
Roast Turkey with Pecan Stuffing, Giblet
  Gravy
Strawberry-Custard Layered Dessert
Festive White and Wild Rice
Curried Three-Fruit Relish
Party Chicken in Herbed Pastry Tray
Sweet-and-Sour Tomato and Cucumber
  Slices

Rock Cornish Hens with Sausage Stuffing
Mashed Potatoes with Cabbage
Golden Country Biscuits
Butter-Pecan Parfaits
Braised Capon with Mushrooms,
  Potatoes, Leeks
Vegetable Mélange
Fruit Savarin
Lettuce and Endive Salad with Avocado
  Dressing
Oysters on Half Shell with
  Green-Peppercorn Sauce
Cassis Sorbet
Roast Duckling with Port-Wine Sauce
Crumb-Coated Potatoes
Braised Hearts of Celery
Herbed Toast
Roast Goose with Chestnut Stuffing,
  Sausage, and Apples
Cauliflower Polonaise
Whipped Honey Butter
Cranberry Swirl Cheesecake

Gifts from the Kitchen
Holiday Cherry Fruitcake
Toasted Coconut Pound Cake
Tempting Fruit and Nut Ring
Golden German Pound Cake
Glazed Fruitcake Loaves
Miniature Fruitcakes
Cinnamon-Spiced Ginger Crisps
Golden Fried Rosettes
Old-Fashioned Oatmeal Jumbos
Delicate Almond-Rich Tuiles
Jam-Filled Spice Cookies
Dark-Chocolate Walnut Drops
Almond Chocolate-Chip Meringues
Chewy Pecan Pie Bars
Crisp Chinese Fried Walnuts
Candied Grapefruit Peels
Meltaway Mocha Truffles
Sweet Pralines
Curried Almonds

Take a Can of Tuna
Tuna Quiche
Tuna and Cabbage Salad
Tuna Loaf Special
Tuna Logs

DECEMBER
Cinnamon Butterfly Rolls*
Quick Eggs and Peppers†
Hot Chocolate Soufflé‡

Christmas Gift Cookbook
Holiday Apricot Logs
Chocolate-Peanut Clusters
Marzipan Vegetables
Meringue Mushrooms
Peppermint-Cheese Pie
Pumpkin Pie
Pecan-Walnut Pie
Peppery Cheese Crackers
Christmas Soda Bread
Orange-Chocolate Toffee
Butterscotch Candy Squares
Caramels
Chocolate-Nut Breads
Banana-Pecan Bread
Cranberry-Raisin Bread
Walnut-Date Loaves
Applesauce Muffins
Little Braided Herb Breads

Cinnamon Bubble Ring
Sweet Christmas Wreath Bread
Pannetone (Italian Sweet Bread)
Onion Flatbread
Cocktail Roquefort Spread
Cheddar-Bacon Spread
Mincemeat Relish
Cranberry-Pineapple Relish
No-Salt Herb-and-Spice Mix
Crème Fraîche
Pâté de Campagne
Pickled Celery Stalks
Calorie-Wise Herb Salad Dressing
Dieter's Zesty Tomato Salad Dressing
Creamy Tarragon Dressing
Caraway-Horseradish Mustard
Gingered Orange Mustard
Steamed Orange-Date Pudding
Pots de Crème au Chocolat
Applesauce-Spice Squares
Strufoli
Banana Fruitcake
Babas
Spiced Sherry Jelly
Honey-Lemon Preserves
Nutty Sundae Topping
Sugar Christmas Trees
Soft Banana-Spice Cookies
Oatmeal-Chocolate Triangles
Butterfly Cookies
Christmas Flower Cookies
Santa Cookies
Chocolate Chip Walnut Cookies
Chocolate Thumbprints
Chocolate-Dipped Crescents
Maple Meltaways
Almond Refrigerator Cookies
Molasses-Peanut Jumbles
Hazelnut Mounds
Buttery Cookie Wreaths
Sugar Pretzels
Buttery Almond Cookies
Brown-Edged Wafers
Peanut-Topped Brownies
Crispy Nut Bars
Holiday Biscuits
Pork Rillettes

Festive Main Dishes
Spinach-Filled Jumbo Shrimp
Fish-and-Shrimp Mousse with Paprika
  Mayonnaise
Fruit-Stuffed Lamb Noisettes
Six Golden Hens
Paella
Veal and Chestnut Braisés
Filet Mignons with Mushroom-Caper Sauce
Baked Ham with Candied Orange-Peel
  Glaze
Beef Tenderloin with Flavored Butters
Stuffed Pork Chops Deluxe
Veal Chops Paprika with Herbed
  Spaetzle
Pork Tenderloin with Hearts of Palm
Roast Capon with Potato-Sausage Stuffing
Holiday Scallops with Julienne Vegetables
Rib Roast with Yorkshire Pudding
Herb Marinated Leg of Lamb
Herbed Duckling with Strawberry Sauce
Roast Goose with Mushroom Gravy
Buffet Salmon with Three Sauces
Pork Roast Blanquette

Index